The Practical Guide to ONTARIO ESTATE ADMINISTRATION
2002

Karen M. Gibbs
Angelique L. Hamilton
Archie J. Rabinowitz
Katja Kim
Risa Awerbuck
Lisa R. Simone
Michelle T. Cass

CARSWELL
A THOMSON COMPANY

© 2001 Thomson Canada Limited

All rights reserved. No part of this publication may be reproduced, stored in a retrieval system, or transmitted, in any form or by any means, electronic, mechanical, photocopying, recording, or otherwise, without the prior written permission of the publisher.

This publication is designed to provide accurate and authoritative information. It is sold with the understanding that the publisher is not engaged in rendering legal, accounting or other professional advice. If legal advice or other expert assistance is required, the services of a competent professional should be sought. The analysis contained herein should in no way be construed as being either official or unofficial policy of any governmental body.

Canadian Cataloguing in Publication Data
The National Library of Canada has catalogued this publication as follows:

Main entry under title:
   The practical guide to Ontario estate administration

Annual.
[No. 1]-
ISSN 1486-7109
ISBN 0-459-26147-9 (4th edition)

1. Executors and administrators – Ontario.   2. Estates (Law) – Ontario.
I. Carswell Company

KE0293.P73   346.71305'6⁻   C99-302005-4

A THOMSON COMPANY

One Corporate Plaza, 2075 Kennedy Road, Toronto, Ontario M1T 3V4
Customer Relations:
Toronto 1-416-609-3800
Elsewhere in Canada/U.S. 1-800-387-5164
Fax 1-416-298-5094

PREFACE

A legal practice which includes Estate Administration can be an interesting and fulfilling challenge. As this text will show, the estate administration practitioner must possess a general knowledge of all fields of law, as well as the ability to keep up with the constantly changing world of estate administration law.

Common sense dictates that since clients are generally dealt with shortly after a death, compassion is a required attribute. Moreover, since it is necessary to delve into the financial affairs of the deceased, which are often intermingled with those of the deceased's spouse and family, a certain type of relationship must be allowed to develop.

"Personal representative", a term often used in this text, refers to an executor, administrator or administrator with Will annexed. This term and others are included in the Glossary at the front of the book. While readers may be relatively new to this field of practice, they may deal with both newer and older files. Accordingly, the Glossary provides a cross-reference to older terms, where relevant.

With the continuing changes in the practice of estate administration. I hope this manual will be of assistance to those responsible for the day-to-day maintenance of estate administration files.

I wish to take this opportunity to thank all the solicitors, law clerks and students, both past and present who gave their time to review various sections of this text. Special thanks to my fellow law clerk, Nancy Galloro, and secretaries Gabriella Giordano and David Todd and to the firm of Goodman and Carr LLP for providing the encouragement and support necessary to complete this text.

Karen M. Gibbs

September 2001

ABOUT THE AUTHORS

Karen M. Gibbs has been a Senior Law Clerk with the law firm of Goodman and Carr LLP for the past thirteen years in the Estates and Trust area with an emphasis on Passing of Accounts. She is a former director of the Institute of Law Clerks of Ontario and continues to take an active role in the further education of law clerks.

Angelique L. Hamilton received her Bachelor of Civil Law in 1983 and her Bachelor of Law in 1984, both from McGill University. She was called to the Ontario Bar in 1986 and joined the Toronto law firm of Goodman and Carr LLP that same year. She became a partner at Goodman and Carr LLP in 1994. In July of 1997, Ms. Hamilton left Goodman and Carr LLP to establish her own practice.

Ms. Hamilton's practice consists of personal tax and estate planning and tax planning for corporations and non-arm's length corporate reorganizations.

She has lectured and written extensively on tax planning to minimize U.S. estate tax for Canadians.

She is a member of The Joint Committee on Taxation of The Canadian Bar Association and The Canadian Institute of Chartered Accountants. She is also a member of the Estate Planning Council of Toronto.

Archie J. Rabinowitz, B.A., LL.B., is a Partner at Goodman and Carr LLP specializing in Estate Litigation. He is a member of the Canadian Bar Association — Ontario, Trusts and Estates Section Executive, and a former lecturer at the Bar Admissions Course.

Katja Kim received her LL.B. from Queens University in 1998 and was called to the Bar in 2000 and is a member of Goodman and Carr LLP's Personal Planning and Tax Groups. Katja's practice focuses on estate planning, succession planning, preparation of wills and trusts, powers of attorney and related areas of tax laws.

Risa Awerbuck received her LL.B. from Osgoode Hall Law School in 1986 and was called to the Bar in 1988. She is a member of Goodman and Carr LLP's Personal Planning and Tax Groups and concentrates her practice on the preparation of wills, powers of attorney for personal care and property, estate planning and administration. Risa has advised clients and spoken on estate planning issues including the provisions of the *Family Law Act*, methods of effectively reducing probate fees, the imposition of income and capital gains tax on death, transferring and gifting of assets and the consequences which may arise therefrom and the various uses of trusts.

Michelle T. Cass received her LL.B. from Osgoode Hall Law School in 1992 and was called to the Ontario Bar in 1994 and to the Bar of the State of New York in 1995. She joined Goodman and Carr in January 1998 as an Associate and practiced with the Personal Planning and Tax Groups until 2000 when she decided to continue her practice in New York.

Lisa R. Simone received her LL.B. from Osgoode Hall Law School in 1991 and was called to the Ontario Bar in 1993. She was an associate with the firm of Goodman and Carr in the Personal Planning Services Group until 1998. She continues her practice in estate planning and administration at the firm of Fasken Martineau DuMoulin LLP. Lisa has spoken on estate planning and various related tax issues. She is a member of the Canadian Bar Association and the Law Society of Upper Canada.

TABLE OF CONTENTS

Preface ....*iii*
About the Authors...*v*
Statutes and Rules Frequently Referred To ....*xxi*
Glossary ....*xxiii*

Chapter 1: **Last Will and Testament** 1

1. What is a Will 2
2. Why Have a Will?..3
     (a) Rules of Intestacy 3
     (b) Effective Immediately 4
     (c) Ability to Choose Executors 4
     (d) Ability to Choose Beneficiaries..4
     (e) Ability to Appoint Guardians 5
     (f) Property Provision for Minor Beneficiaries 5
     (g) Tax and Probate Fee Planning 6
     (h) *Family Law Act* Protection for Beneficiaries 6
3. Formal Requirement for Executing a Valid Will in Ontario............................6
     (a) Formal or Attested Wills 6
     (b) Holograph Wills..7
     (c) Wills by Members of the Forces on Active Service 8
     (d) Foreign Wills and International Wills 8
     (e) International Wills 8
     (f) Multiple Wills 9
4. Who May Make a Will 9
     (a) Age Requirement..9
     (b) Testamentary Capacity 10
5. Grounds for Invalidating a Will 10

- (a) Lack of Testamentary Capacity ... 10
- (b) Improper Execution ... 11
- (c) Undue Influence ... 11
- (d) Suspicious Circumstances ... 11
- (e) Fraud or Forgery ... 11

6. Revocation of a Will ... 12
    - (a) Subsequent Will ... 12
    - (b) Marriage ... 12
    - (c) Written Declaration ... 12
    - (d) Destruction ... 12
    - (e) Effect of Divorce ... 13
7. Alterations to Wills and Codicils ... 13
8. Revival of a Will ... 14
9. Will Drafting ... 14
    - (a) Gathering Information ... 14
        - (i) Personal Information ... 14
            - Citizenship ... 14
            - Marital Status ... 15
            - Children ... 15
            - Assets and Liabilities ... 16
            - Type of Ownership ... 16
            - Location of Assets ... 17
            - Plans, Policies and Insurance ... 17
    - (b) Taking Instructions ... 17
        - (i) Executors and Trustees ... 17
        - (ii) Organ Donation and Funeral Arrangements ... 20
        - (iii) Policies and Plans ... 20
        - (iv) Legacies ... 20
            - Ademption ... 21
            - Abatement ... 21
            - Lapse ... 21
            - Memoranda ... 22
                - A Legal Memorandum ... 22
                - A Precatory Memorandum ... 22
            - Gifts to Charities ... 23
            - Gifts to Individuals ... 23
        - (iv) Residue ... 23
            - Outright, or in Trust ... 23
            - Dispositions to a Spouse or a "Spousal Trust" ... 25
            - Survivorship Clause ... 25
            - Common Accident ... 26
    - (c) Limitations on Freedom to Dispose of Property ... 26
        - (i) Jointly-Owned Property with Right of Survivorship ... 27
        - (ii) The *Family Law Act* ... 27

| (iii) Dependants' Relief 28
| (iv) Contractual Obligations.. 29
| (v) Other Restrictions on Alienation 30
10. Conclusion 30
       Figure 1-1: Example of Last Will and Testament 31

Chapter 2: **Prior to the Grant** 39

1. Differing Roles of the Personal Representative and Solicitor 39
       (a) Personal Representative's Responsibilities 40
       (b) Solicitor's Responsibilities 41
2. Location of Will 42
3. Locating Assets 43
4. Locating Liabilities 43
5. To Obtain a Court Grant or Not 44
       (a) Real Estate 44
           (i) Real Estate Registered under the Registry System 44
           (ii) Real Estate Registered under the Land Titles System 45
       (b) Shareholdings 45
           (i) Private Corporations 46
           (ii) Public Corporations 46
       (c) Money on Deposit 46
       (d) Safety Deposit Box 46
       (e) Canada Savings Bonds 47
       (f) Other Assets 47
6. Valuing the Estate 47
7. Intestacy 47
       (a) Distribution on an Intestacy 48
       (b) Who is Entitled to Apply as Estate Trustee Without a Will 49
       (c) Posting Security 49
8. Forms
       Figure 2-1: Letter to Solicitor re: Location of Deceased's Will and
                          Authorization of Personal Representative 51
       Figure 2-2: General Letter to a Bank 52
       Figure 2-3: Letter to the Bank of Canada re: Search 53
       Figure 2-4: Letter to the Bank where Deceased Held Assets 54
       Figure 2-5: Letter to Transfer Agent Requesting Waiver of Requirement
                          of the Court Certificate 55
       Figure 2-6: Notarial Certificate 56
       Figure 2-7: Sample of Information Required for Statement of Assets 57

Chapter 3: **Letters Testamentary** 59

1. Jurisdiction to File Grant 61

2. Calculating Court Fees on Applications for Estate Trustee 61
3. Role of the Court as a Will Depository 62
4. Notice of Applications 63
5. Application for Certificate of Appointment of Estate Trustee With a Will 64
   (a) Generally 64
   (b) Documents to be Filed with Court 65
   (c) Other Documents that may be Required 66
6. Application for Certificate of Appointment of Estate Trustee With a Will Limited to Assets Referred to in the Will 67
   (a) Generally 67
   (b) Documents to be Filed with Court 67
   (c) Other Documents that may be Required 67
7. Application for Certificate of Appointment of Estate Trustee Without a Will 67
   (a) Generally 67
   (b) Documents to be Filed with Court 69
   (c) Other Documents that may be Required 69
8. Application for Certificate of Appointment as Succeeding Estate Trustee With a Will 70
   (a) Generally 70
   (b) Documents to be Filed with Court 70
   (c) Other Documents that may be Required 70
9. Application for Certificate of Appointment as Succeeding Trustee Without a Will 71
   (a) Generally 71
   (b) Documents to be Filed with Court 71
   (c) Other Documents that may be Required 72
10. Confirmation By Resealing of Appointment of Estate Trustee With or Without a Will 72
    (a) Generally 72
    (b) Documents to be Filed with Court 73
    (c) Other Documents that may be Required 73
11. Certificate of Ancillary Appointment of Estate Trustee With a Will 73
    (a) Generally 73
    (b) Documents to be Filed with Court 74
    (c) Other Documents that may be Required 74
12. Certificate of Foreign Estate Trustee's Nominee as Estate Trustee Without a Will 74
    (a) Generally 74
    (b) Documents to be Filed with Court 75
13. Certificate of Estate Trustee During Litigation 75
    (a) Generally 75
    (b) Documents to be Filed with Court 76
    (c) Other Documents that may be Required 76
14. Forms

Figure 3-1:	Letter to Court Enclosing Application for Certificate of Appointment of Estate Trustee With a Will	77
Figure 3-2:	Letter to Court Enclosing Application for Certificate of Appointment of Estate Trustee Without a Will	78
Figure 3-3:	Letter to Court Enclosing Application for Certificate of Appointment of Succeeding Estate Trustee With a Will	79
Figure 3-4:	Letter to Court Enclosing Application for Certificate of Appointment of Succeeding Estate Trustee Without a Will	80
Figure 3-5:	Letter to Court Enclosing Application for Confirmation by Resealing of Appointment of Estate Trustee (With or Without a Will)	81
Figure 3-6:	Letter to Court Enclosing Application for Certificate of Ancillary Appointment of Estate Trustee With a Will	82
Figure 3-7:	Letter to Court Enclosing Application for Certificate of Appointment of Estate Trustee During Litigation	83
Figure 3-8:	Notice of Deposit to Estate Registrar (Form 74.1)	84
Figure 3-9:	Notice of the Withdrawal to Estate Registrar (Form 74.2)	85
Figure 3-10:	Application for Certificate of Appointment of Estate Trustee With a Will (Individual Applicant) (Form 74.4)	86
Figure 3-11:	Application for Certificate of Appointment of Estate Trustee With a Will (Individual Applicant) Limited to Assets Referred to in the Will (Form 74.4.1)	88
Figure 3-12:	Application for Certificate of Appointment of Estate Trustee With a Will (Corporate Applicant) (Form 74.5)	90
Figure 3-13:	Application for Certificate of Appointment of Estate Trustee With a Will (Corporation Applicant) Limited to Assets Referred to in the Will (Form 74.5.1)	92
Figure 3-14:	Affidavit of Service of Notice (With a Will) (Form 74.6)	94
Figure 3-15:	Notice of an Application for a Certificate of Appointment of Estate Trustee With a Will (Form 74.7)	96
Figure 3-16:	Affidavit of Execution of Will or Codicil (Form 74.8)	99
Figure 3-17:	Affidavit Attesting to the Handwriting and Signature of a Holograph Will or Codicil (Form 74.9)	100
Figure 3-18:	Affidavit of Condition of Will or Codicil (Form 74.10)	101
Figure 3-19:	Renunciation of Right to a Certificate of Appointment of Estate Trustee (or Succeeding Estate Trustee) With a Will (Form 74.11)	102
Figure 3-20:	Consent to Applicant's Appointment as Estate Trustee With a Will (Form 74.12)	103
Figure 3-21:	Certificate of Appointment of Estate Trustee With a Will (Form 74.13)	104
Figure 3-22:	Certificate of Appointment of Estate Trustee With a Will Limited to the Assets Referred to in the Will (Form 74.13.1)	106
Figure 3-23:	Application for Certificate of Appointment of Estate Trustee Without a Will (Individual Applicant) (Form 74.14)	108

xii TABLE OF CONTENTS

Figure 3-24: Application for Certificate of Appointment of Estate Trustee Without a Will (Corporate Applicant) (Form 74.15) 110
Figure 3-25: Affidavit of Service of Notice (Without a Will) (Form 74.16) 112
Figure 3-26: Notice of an Application for Certificate of Appointment of Estate Trustee Without a Will (Form 74.17) 113
Figure 3-27: Renunciation of Prior Right to a Certificate of Appointment of Estate Trustee Without a Will (Form 74.18) 115
Figure 3-28: Consent to Applicant's Appointment as Estate Trustee Without a Will (Form 74.19) 116
Figure 3-29: Certificate of Appointment of Estate Trustee Without a Will (Form 74.20) 117
Figure 3-30: Application for Certificate of Appointment of a Foreign Estate Trustee's Nominee as Estate Trustee Without a Will (Form 74.20.1) 119
Figure 3-31: Nomination of Applicant by a Foreign Estate Trustee (Form 74.20.2) 121
Figure 3-32: Certificate of Appointment of Foreign Estate Trustee's Nominee as Estate Trustee Without a Will (Form 74.20.3) 122
Figure 3-33: Application for Certificate of Appointment as Succeeding Estate Trustee With a Will (Form 74.21) 123
Figure 3-34: Consent to Applicant's Appointment as Succeeding Estate Trustee With a Will (Form 74.22) 125
Figure 3-35: Certificate of Appointment of Succeeding Estate Trustee With a Will (Form 74.23) 126
Figure 3-36: Application for Certificate of Appointment as Succeeding Estate Trustee Without a Will (Form 74.24) 128
Figure 3-37: Consent to Applicant's Appointment as Succeeding Estate Trustee Without a Will (Form 74.25) 130
Figure 3-38: Certificate of Appointment of Succeeding Estate Trustee Without a Will (Form 74.26) 131
Figure 3-39: Application for Confirmation by Resealing of Appointment or Certificate of Ancillary Appointment of Estate Trustee (Form 74.27) 133
Figure 3-40: Application for Confirmation by Resealing of Appointment or Certificate of Ancillary Appointment of Estate Trustee (Form 74.27) 135
Figure 3-41: Confirmation by Resealing of Appointment of Estate Trustee (Form 74.28) 137
Figure 3-42: Certificate of Ancillary Appointment of Estate Trustee With a Will (Form 74.29) 138
Figure 3-43: Application for Certificate of Appointment of Estate Trustee During Litigation (Form 74.30) 140
Figure 3-44: Certificate of Appointment of Estate Trustee During Litigation (Form 74.31) 142

Figure 3-45: Bond — Insurance or Guarantee Company (Form 74.32) 144
Figure 3-46: Bond — Personal Sureties (Form 74.33) 146
Figure 3-47: Registrar's Notice of Application With a Will (Form 74.34) 150
Figure 3-48: Registrar's Notice of Application Without a Will (Form 74.35) ..151
Figure 3-49: Affidavit in Support of Request for an Order that the
Requirement of Posting a Bond be Dispensed With 152
Figure 3-50: Order to Dispense With Bond 153
Figure 3-51: Affidavit as to Evidence of Signature 155
Figure 3-52: Undertaking 156
Figure 3-53: Affidavit re Multiple Wills 157
Figure 3-54: Order 159
List of Addresses of Offices of Superior Court of Justice 161

Chapter 4: **Administering an Estate** 167

1. Locating and Dealing With Assets 169
    (a) Proof of Death 170
    (b) Opening the Estate Bank Account 170
    (c) Dealing with the Safety Deposit Box 170
    (d) Dealing with Money on Deposit 171
    (e) Without a Court Certificate 171
    (f) With the Court Certificate 171
    (g) Dealing with Term Deposits and Guaranteed Investment
        Certificates..172
    (h) Dealing with Real Estate 172
        (i) Under the *Registry Act*, R.S.O. 1990, c. R.20 172
            Joint Property..172
            Without a Court Certificate 173
            With a Court Certificate 173
        (ii) Under the *Land Titles Act*, R.S.O. 1990, c. L.5 173
            Joint Property..173
            Without a Court Certificate 173
            With a Court Certificate 173
        (iii) Possible Difficulties Dealing with Real Estate............................173
    (i) Dealing with Canada Savings Bonds and other Government of
        Canada Securities 174
        (i) Without a Court Certificate 174
        (ii) With a Court Certificate 174
    (j) Dealing with other Bonds and Shares 175
        (i) Valuing Public Shares..175
        (ii) Valuing Bonds 175
        (iii) Without a Certificate 175
        (iv) With a Certificate 176
    (k) Dealing with Life Insurance 176

            (i) Where there is a Named Beneficiary 176
            (ii) Estate as Beneficiary 177
        (l) Dealing with Registered Retirement Savings Plans 177
            (i) Dealing with Registered Retirement Savings Plans and
                Spouses 177
                    Named Beneficiary 177
                    Estate is Beneficiary, or No Beneficiary Named 178
        (m) Dealing with Pension Plans 178
        (n) Dealing with Canada Pension Plan Benefits 178
            (i) Death Benefit 178
            (ii) Survivor's Benefit 179
            (iii) Orphan's Benefit 179
        (o) Dealing with Motor Vehicles 180
        (p) Dealing with Other Assets 180
    2. Locating and Dealing with Liabilities 180
        (a) *Family Law Act* Election 180
        (b) Payment of Debts 182
        (c) Advertisement for Creditors 182
        (d) Insolvent Estates 182
    3. Finalizing the Estate 183
        (a) Finalizing the Value of the Estate with the Court 183
        (b) Documents to be Filed 183
        (c) Arranging Return of Security from Court 184
        (d) Distributions 184
        (e) Ongoing Estates 185
        (f) Payment of Money into Court 185
        (g) Keeping a Tickler System 186
        (h) Obtaining Status Certificates 187
        (i) Succession Duty 187
    4. Forms
        Figure 4-1: Letter to Registrar General Requesting Birth, Marriage and
                    Death Certificates 188
        Figure 4-2: Letter to Insurance Company Requesting Particulars on a
                    Claim 189
        Figure 4-3: Letter to Insurance Company Proving Claim for Named
                    Beneficiary 190
        Figure 4-4: Letter to Broker Requesting Information on Securities and
                    What Commission Costs Will be to Sell Securities 191
        Figure 4-5: Letter to Transfer Agent Requesting Transfer of Shares 192
        Figure 4-6: Letter to Newspaper with Notice to Creditors 193
        Figure 4-7: Letter to Revenue Canada Requesting Final Clearance
                    Certificate (Terminal, Partial and Final) 194
        Figure 4-8: Letter to Canada Pension Plan Applying for Death Benefit,
                    Survivors' Benefits, Orphan's Benefit 195

Figure 4-9: Letter to Canada Pension Plan to Cancel Pension Cheques 196
Figure 4-10: Letter to Old Age Security to Cancel Cheques 197
Figure 4-11: Letter Instructing Bank to Issue Cheque for Probate Fees 198
Figure 4-12: Letter to Bank Without a Certificate 199
Figure 4-13: Letter to Bank With a Certificate 200
Figure 4-14: Letter to Bank of Canada to Transfer Bonds to Beneficiary
 (or Cash Bonds) 201
Figure 4-15: Letter to Beneficiaries re: FLA Clause 202
Figure 4-16: Letter to Court, Toronto Region, re: Filing of FLA Election 203
Figure 4-17: Letter to Court re: Probate Fees Owing 204
Figure 4-18: Letter to Court re: Refund of Probate Fees 205
Figure 4-19: Letter to Court re: No Additional Probate Fees Owing 206
Figure 4-20: Authorization re: Safety Deposit Box 207
Figure 4-21: Power of Attorney to Transfer Bonds - Shares 208
Figure 4-22: Declaration of Transmission (re: Shares) 209
Figure 4-23: Declaration of Transmission (re: Bonds and Debentures) 210
Figure 4-24: Election under the *Family Law Act, 1986* 211
Figure 4-25: Consent 212
Figure 4-26: Affidavit re: Increase in Probate Value 213
Figure 4-27: Affidavit re: Decrease in Probate Value 214

Chapter 5: **Court Disputes** 215
1. Request for Notice of Commencement of Proceeding — Rule 74.03 216
2. Orders for Assistance 216
    (a) Order to Accept or Refuse Appointment — Rule 74.15(1)(a) and (b) ..217
    (b) Order to Consent or Object to Proposed Appointment —
        Rule 74.15(1)(c) 217
    (c) Order to File Statement of Assets of the Estate — Rule 74.15(1)(d) 217
    (d) Order for Further Details — Rule 74.15(1)(e) 218
    (e) Order to Beneficiary Witness — Rule 74.15(1)(f) 218
    (f) Order to Former Spouse — Rule 74.15(1)(g) 218
    (g) Order to Pass Accounts — Rule 74.15(1)(h) 218
    (h) Order for Other Matters — Rule 74.15(1)(i) 219
3. Contentious Proceedings 219
        (i) Notice to the Profession — Toronto Region — Estates List 219
        (ii) Mandatory Mediation — Estates, Trusts and Substitute
             Decisions 220
        (iii) *Courts Improvement Act, 1996* 224
        (iv) Case Management in Estates and Related Matters 224
        (v) Rule 75 — Contentious Proceedings in Estate Matters 224
    (a) Objection to Issuing a Certificate of Appointment — Rule 75.03 224
    (b) Revocation of Certificate of Appointment 225
    (c) Return of Certificate — Rule 75.05(1) 225

xvi TABLE OF CONTENTS

  (d) Application or Motion for Directions 226
  (e) Statement of Submission of Rights 226
4. Additional Prescribed Forms 227
5. Claims Against Estate 227
6. Dependant's Relief Claims 227
7. *Family Law Act* Claims 228
8. Forms
  Figure 5-1: Request for Notice of Commencement of Proceeding (Form 74.3) 230
  Figure 5-2: Order to Accept or Refuse Appointment as Estate Trustee With a Will (Form 74.36) 231
  Figure 5-3: Order to Accept or Refuse Appointment as Estate Trustee Without a Will (Form 74.37) 233
  Figure 5-4: Order to Consent or Object to a Proposed Appointment of an Estate Trustee With or Without a Will (Form 74.38) 235
  Figure 5-5: Order to File a Statement of Assets of the Estate (Form 74.39) 237
  Figure 5-6: Order to Beneficiary Witness (Form 74.40) 239
  Figure 5-7: Order to Former Spouse (Form 74.41) 241
  Figure 5-8: Order to Pass Accounts (Form 74.42) 243
  Figure 5-9: Notice of Objection (to Issuing a Certificate of Appointment) (Form 75.1) 245
  Figure 5-10: Request for Assignment of Mediator (Form 75.1A) 247
  Figure 5-11: Notice by Mediator (Form 75.1B) 249
  Figure 5-12: Statement of Issues (Form 75.1C) 251
  Figure 5-13: Certificate of Non-Compliance (Form 75.1D) 253
  Figure 5-14: Notice that Objection Has Been Filed (Form 75.2) 255
  Figure 5-15: Notice to Objector (Form 75.3) 257
  Figure 5-16: Notice of Appearance (Form 75.4) 259
  Figure 5-17: Notice of Application for Directions (Form 75.5) 261
  Figure 5-18: Notice of Motion for Directions (Form 75.6) 264
  Figure 5-19: Statement of Claim Pursuant to Order Giving Directions (Form 75.7) 266
  Figure 5-20: Order Giving Directions (Form 75.8) — Whether by Application or Motion 269
  Figure 5-21: Order Giving Directions (Trial of Issue-Motion) (Form 75.9) 272
  Figure 5-22: Statement of Submission of Rights to the Court (Form 75.10) 275
  Figure 5-23: Notice of Settlement (Form 75.11) 277
  Figure 5-24: Rejection of Settlement (Form 75.12) 279
  Figure 5-25: Notice of Contestation (Form 75.13) 281
  Figure 5-26: Claim Against Estate (Form 75.14) 283
  Figure 5-27: Election under the *Family Law Act, 1986* (Form 210) 285

Chapter 6: **Passing of Accounts** 287

1. Introduction..288
2. Documents to be Filed with the Court 288
3. Uncontested Passings 289
4. Contested Passings 290
5. Notice of Objection to Accounts..290
6. Form of Accounts 291
7. Executor's Compensation and Powers of Investment 292
   - (i) Executor's Compensation..292
   - (ii) Powers of Investment 293
8. Special Fee 294
9. Specific Problems which Often Occur in the Preparation of Accounts 294
   - (a) Ex-dividends 294
   - (b) Mortgage Payments 294
   - (c) Accrued Interest to the Date of Death 295
   - (d) Distinguishing Between Capital and Revenue Expenses 295
10. Costs 295
11. Unprobated Wills — Jurisdiction of Court to Pass Accounts of Estate Trustees...296
12. Forms
    - Figure 6-1: Order to Pass Accounts (Form 74.42)............................297
    - Figure 6-2: Affidavit Verifying Estate Accounts (Form 74.43).......299
    - Figure 6-3: Notice of Application to Pass Accounts (Form 74.44) ...300
    - Figure 6-4: Notice of Objection to Accounts (Form 74.45)..............303
    - Figure 6-5: Notice of No Objection to Accounts (Form 74.46).......305
    - Figure 6-6: Notice of Non-Participation in Passing of Accounts (Form 74.46.1) 306
    - Figure 6-7: Affidavit in Support of Unopposed Judgment on Passing of Accounts (Form 74.47) 307
    - Figure 6-8: Notice of Withdrawal of Objection (Form 74.48).........308
    - Figure 6-9: Request for Costs (Form 74.49) 309
    - Figure 6-10: Request for Costs (Form 74.49.1)..................................310
    - Figure 6-11: Request for Increased Costs (Form 74.49.2)................312
    - Figure 6-12: Request for Increased Costs (Form 74.49.3)................314
    - Figure 6-13: Judgment on Passing of Accounts (Unopposed) (Form 74.50) 316
    - Figure 6-14: Judgment on Passing of Accounts (Opposed) (Form 74.51) 320
    - Figure 6-15: Sample Accounts (Form 74.51) 324

Chapter 7: **Taxation on Death** 341

1. Preparation of Tax Returns for the Terminal Year 342
2. Calculating Income in the Terminal Year 343
   - (a) General Principles 343
     - (i) Residence 343
     - (ii) Sourcing of Income 344

            (iii) Cash versus Accrual Basis of Accounting 344
      (b) Sources of Income in the Terminal Year 345
            (i)   Income Received Prior to Death 345
            (ii)   Periodic Payments 345
            (iii) Rights or Things 345
            (iv)   Proprietorship or Partnership Income 347
                   Death Terminates the Partnership 347
                   Death does not Terminate the Partnership 347
            (v)   Income from a Testamentary Trust 347
            (vi)   Capital Property 348
                   Non-Depreciable Capital Property 348
                   Depreciable Capital Property 348
                   Capital Gains Exemption 349
                   Principal Residence Exemption 349
            (vii) Eligible Capital Property 350
            (viii) Resource Properties and Land Inventories 350
            (ix)   Registered Retirement Savings Plan Income 351
                   Unmatured Registered Retirement Savings Plan 351
                   Matured RRSP 352
                   RRSP Contribution in the Terminal Year 352
            (x)   RRIF Income 353
            (xi)   Registered Pension Plan Income 353
            (xii) Deferred Profit Sharing Plan Income 354
            (xiii) Life Insurance Proceeds 355
            (xiv) Reserves 355
            (xv)   Employee Stock Options 356
3. Miscellaneous Special Rules Regarding Death 356
      (a) Tax Credits in the Year of Death 356
            (i)   Medical Expenses 356
            (ii)   Charitable Donations 357
            (iii) Foreign Tax Credits 357
      (b) Capital Losses 357
      (c) Death Benefits 358
      (d) Forgiveness of Debt 358
      (e) Alternative Minimum Tax 358
      (f) Tax Instalments 358
      (g) Avoiding Double Tax on Shares of a Private Corporation 359
4. Interpretation Bulletins Dealing with Taxation on Death 359
5. Schedule A 361
      (a) Tax Treatment of Partnership Income 361
6. Glossary of Terms 362

Chapter 8: **Rollovers and Estate Taxation** 367

1. Rollovers 368
    (a) Property Left to Spouse, Common-Law Partner or Trust 368
    (b) Property Left to Children 370
        (i) Farm Property 370
        (ii) RRSP and RRIF Proceeds 371
2. Estate Taxation 371
    (a) Introduction 371
        (i) Residence of Estate 371
        (ii) Testamentary versus *Inter-vivos* Trusts 371
        (iii) Filing Requirements 372
        (iv) Multiple Trusts 372
    (b) Estate Income and Distribution 372
        (i) Income Paid or Payable to a Beneficiary 372
        (ii) Benefits to Beneficiaries 373
        (iii) Preferred Beneficiary Elections 374
        (iv) Flow-Through (or Sourcing) of Trust Income 374
        (v) Non-Resident Beneficiaries 375
        (vi) Cashing Out an Income Interest 375
    (c) Distributions of Estate Capital 376
        (i) Distributions 376
        (ii) Clearance Certificates 376
        (iii) 21-Year Deemed Disposition Rule 377
        (iv) Land Transfer Tax 377
    (d) Notice of Objection 378
    (e) Goods and Services Tax 378
        (i) Application of Part IX of the *ETA* 379
        (ii) Supply (Distribution) of Business Assets 379
        (iii) Supply (Distribution) of Other Assets 379
        (iv) Clearance Certificate 379
        (v) Executor's Fees 380
    (f) U.S. Estate Tax 380
        (i) U.S. Situs Assets 380
        (ii) Taxable Estate 380
        (iii) U.S. Estate Tax Rates 381
        (iv) Exemptions and Credits in Calculating U.S. Estate Tax 381
        (v) Foreign Tax Credit 382
        (vi) Filing Requirements 382
3. Schedule A 382
    (a) U.S. Estate Tax Rates in U.S. Dollars 382
Index 383

STATUTES AND RULES FREQUENTLY REFERRED TO

Absentees Act, R.S.O. 1990, c. A.3
Accumulations Act, R.S.O. 1990, c. A.5
Age of Majority and Accountability Act, R.S.O. 1990, c. A.7
Apportionment Act, R.S.O. 1990, c. A.23
Charities Accounting Act, R.S.O. 1990, c. C.10
Child and Family Services Act, R.S.O. 1990, c. C.11
Children's Law Reform Act, R.S.O. 1990, c. C.12
Courts Improvement Act, 1996, S.O. 1996, c. 25
Crown Administration of Estates Act, R.S.O. 1990, c. C.47
Estate Administration Tax Act, S.O. 1998, c. 34
Estates Act, R.S.O. 1990, c. E.21
Estates Administration Act, R.S.O. 1990, c. E.22
Family Law Act, R.S.O. 1990, c. F.3
Income Tax Act, R.S.C. 1985, c. 1 (5th Supp.)
Insurance Act, R.S.O. 1990, c. I.8
Land Titles Act, R.S.O. 1990, c. L.5
Perpetuities Act, R.S.O. 1990, c. P.9
Registry Act, R.S.O. 1990, c. R.20
Rules 74 and 75 of the Rules of Civil Procedure, R.R.O. 1990, Reg. 194
Settled Estates Act, R.S.O. 1990, c. S.7
Substitute Decisions Act, 1992, S.O. 1992, c. 30
Succession Law Reform Act, R.S.O. 1990, c. S.26
Trillium Gift of Life Network Act, R.S.O. 1990, C. H.20
Trustee Act, R.S.O. 1990, c. T.23
Variation of Trusts Act, R.S.O. 1990, c. V.1

GLOSSARY

NOTE TO READER: The term "Personal Representative" is used throughout this text to include Executor With or Without a Will, Administrator or the new term Estate Trustee.

NEW TERMS FROM RULE 74.01 OF THE RULES OF CIVIL PROCEDURE

Certificate of Appointment of Estate Trustee: letters probate, letters of administration or letters of administration with the will annexed.

Estate Trustee: An executor, administrator or administrator with the will annexed.

Estate Trustee During Litigation: An administrator appointed pending an action.

Estate Trustee With a Will: An executor or an administrator with the will annexed.

Estate Trustee Without a Will: An administrator.

Objection to Issuing of Certificate of Appointment (Notice of Objection): A caveat.

GENERAL TERMS*

Administration Bond: Except where otherwise provided by law, every person to whom a grant of administration, including administration with the will annexed, is committed shall give a bond to the judge of the court by which the grant is made, to enure for the benefit of the Accountant of the Ontario Court, with a surety or sureties as may be required by the judge, conditioned for the due collecting, getting in, administering and accounting for the property of the deceased, and the bond shall be in the form prescribed by the rules of the court, and in cases not provided for by the rules, the bond shall be in such form as the judge by special order may direct.[1]

---

* As found in Dukelow and Nuse, *The Dictionary of Canadian Law*, 2nd ed. (Toronto: Carswell, 1995), unless otherwise annotated.

1 *Estates Act*, R.S.O., 1990, c. E.21, s. 35.

Administrator: The person to whom the property of a person dying intestate is committed for administration and whose duties with respect thereto correspond with those of an executor. Now often referred to as estate trustee without a will.

Administratrix: A woman appointed to administer the estate of a person who died without appointing an executor in a will or without leaving a will.

Ancillary Letters Probate or Letters of Administration With Will Annexed: Where a foreign court of competent jurisdiction has granted probate of administration with the will annexed of an estate that includes property in Ontario, and application for ancillary probate or administration with the will annexed is made and it is shown that the executor or administrator is by the law of the domicile of the deceased entitled to receive the property, and the inventory required by section 32 of the *Estates Act* is filed, ancillary letters shall be issued. Now referred to as certificate of ancillary appointment of estate trustee with a will.[2]

Beneficiary: 1. A person designated or appointed as one to whom or for whose benefit insurance money is to be payable. 2. A person entitled to benefit from a trust or will.

Bequest: Personal property given by will. *See also* Specific Bequest.

Caveat: [L. let one take heed] In the context of estates, a formal notice or caution given by a person interested, to a Court, Judge, or public officer, against the performance of certain judicial or ministerial acts. A caution, or caveat, while in force, may stop probate or administration from being granted without notice to or knowledge of the person who enters it. Now referred to as objection to issuing of certificate of appointment.

Certificate of Ancillary Appointment of Estate Trustee With a Will: *See* Ancillary Letters Probate or Letters of Administration With Will Annexed.

Certificate of Appointment of Estate Trustee With a Will: *See* Letters Probate, Letters Double Probate and Letters of Administration With Will Annexed.

Certificate of Appointment of Estate Trustee Without a Will: *See* Letters of Administration.

Certificate of Appointment of Succeeding Estate Trustee With a Will: *See* Letters Double Probate or Letters of Administration de Bonis Non Administratis With Will Annexed.

Certificate of Appointment of Succeeding Estate Trustee Without a Will: *See* Letters of Administration de Bonis Non Administratis.

Cestui Que Trust: A beneficiary; beneficial owner of trust property.

Children's Lawyer (Office of the): (formerly the Office of the Official Guardian) The law of Ontario calls upon the Children's Lawyer to assist the courts and others in au-

---

2 Rules of the Superior Court of Justice in Estates Proceedings, R.R.O. 1990, Reg. 197, r. 30.

thority, such as executors and trustees, to deal with the property rights interests of children. The purpose of the law is to make sure that the investments of children are safe and secure.[3]

Citation: In probate matters, notice of proceedings given to anyone whose interests are or may be affected. Under the new Rules,[4] citation orders are now called orders for assistance.

Codicil: An addition or change made to a will by a testator.

Committee: A person appointed by the court to look after a person or the affairs of a person or a mentally incompetent person.

Confirmation by Resealing of Appointment of Estate Trustee With or Without a Will: *See* Resealing Letters Probate or Letters of Administration.

Deed: A document signed, sealed and delivered through which an interest, property or right passes.

Devise: A disposition or gift by will.

Dower: A life interest in one-third of any freehold estate of inheritance of which the husband died solely seised in possession either through a tenant or by himself and which he either brought with him into the marriage or acquired afterwards. The concept of dower right is now obsolete.

Estate: All the property of which a testator or an intestate had power to dispose by will, otherwise than by virtue of a special power of appointment, less the amount of funeral, testamentary and administration expenses, debts and liabilities, and succession duties payable out of the estate on death. Includes both real and personal property.

Execute: To carry into effect, to complete.

Executor: A person appointed in a testator's will to carry out directions and requests set out there and to distribute property according to the will's provisions. Now often referred to as estate trustee with a will.

Executrix: A woman appointed by a testator to carry out the instructions in the will.

Guardian: In respect of a child, any person, other than a parent of the child, who is under a legal duty to provide for the child or who has, in law or in fact, the custody or control of the child.

Holograph Will: A will written entirely in the testator's own hand.

Intangible Property: A right of ownership over any personal property that is not a chattel or a mortgage, and includes, without limiting the generality of the foregoing, (a) money, a cheque, a bank draft, a deposit, interest, a dividend and income, (b) a credit

---

3   Brian A. Schnurr, *Estate Litigation*, 2nd ed. (Toronto: Carswell, 1994) (looseleaf) at section 6.1.
4   Rules of Civil Procedure, R.R.O. 1990, Reg. 194.

balance, a customer overpayment, a gift certificate, a security deposit, a refund, a credit memo, an unpaid wage and an unused airline ticket, (c) a share or any other intangible ownership interest in a business organization, (d) money deposited to redeem a share, a bond, a coupon or other security, or to make a distribution, (e) an amount due and payable by the insurer under the terms of an insurance policy, and (f) an amount distributable from a trust or custodial fund established under a plan to provide education, health, welfare, vacation, severance, retirement, death, share purchase, profit sharing, employee savings, supplemental unemployment insurance or similar benefits.

Inter Vivos Gift: A gift made while the donor is living.

Inter Vivos Trust: Created by writing, a deed or oral declaration, a trust which is to take effect during the lifetime of the trust's creator.

Intestacy: The condition or state of dying without a valid will.

Issue: Descendants, including a descendant conceived before and born alive after the person's death. (*See Succession Law Reform Act*, R.S.O. 1990, c. S.26, s. l(l)).

Joint Tenancy: 1. Describes ownership when the four unities of possession, time, interest and title are present and there are no words of severance. 2. Created where the same interest in real or personal property is passed by the same conveyance to two or more persons in the same right or by construction or operation of law jointly, with a right of survivorship, *i.e.*, the right of the survivor or survivors to the whole property.

Jus Accrescendi: The right of survivorship which is essential to joint tenancy.

Lapse: To fail, said of a bequest or devise of property which goes into residue as if the gift had not been made when the person to whom the property was bequeathed or devised dies before the testator.

Legacy: 1. The means by which personal property is disposed of by will. 2. A personal gift as opposed to a "bequest" to charity.

Letters of Administration: An instrument, granted by a ... Court, giving authority to an administrator to manage and distribute the estate of a person who died without making a will. Now referred to as certificate of estate trustee without a will.

Letters of Administration de Bonis Non Administratis: Upon the death of the administrator of an estate leaving part of the assets unadministered, an application may be made for a grant of letters of administration *de bonis non administratis* to complete the administration of the estate. Now referred to as certificate of succeeding estate trustee without a will.[5]

Letters of Administration de Bonis Non Administratis With Will Annexed: Where the executor of an estate has died intestate and there are no other executors to carry on the administration of the estate or where the administrator with will annexed of an estate has died leaving part of the estate unadministered, the beneficiaries under the will

---

5   Rules of the Superior Court of Justice in Estates Proceedings, R.R.O. 1990, Reg. 197, r. 24

may nominate any person to make application for a grant of administration *de bonis non administratis* with the will annexed to complete the administration of the estate. Now referred to as certificate of succeeding estate trustee with a will.[6]

Letters of Administration Pendente Lite: An administrator appointed pending an action. Now referred to as estate trustee during litigation. "Pending an action touching the validity of the will of a deceased person, or for obtaining, recalling or revoking any probate or grant of administration, the Superior Court of Justice has jurisdiction to grant administration in the case of intestacy and may appoint an administrator of the property of the deceased person, and the administrator so appointed has all the rights and powers of a general administrator, other than the right of distributing the residue of the property, and every such administrator is subject to the immediate control and direction of the court ."[7]

Letters of Administration With Will Annexed: Special letters of administration used when the executor named in the will is unwilling or unable to serve, or when no executor was named in the will. Now referred to as certificate of estate trustee with a will.

Letters Double Probate: Where all of the executors named in a will have not made application for probate and the right has been reserved to one or more of them to make application for probate at some future time, or if an alternative executor is called upon to complete the administration, and, in either case, if it is desired to have the appointment of such executor or executors confirmed by the court, the grant for which the application is made shall be termed "double probate". Now referred to as certificate of succeeding estate trustee with a will.[8]

Letters Probate: An instrument, granted by a ... court, giving authority to an executor to carry out the provisions of a person's will. Now referred to as certificate of estate trustee with a will.

Next-of-Kin: 1. The mother, father, children, brothers, sisters, spouse and common law spouse of a deceased person, or any of them. 2. (a) The spouse and children of the deceased person; or (b) if there is no spouse or children, ... the persons who are entitled to share under the *Intestate Succession Act* in the estate of the deceased person.

Per Capita: [L. by heads] In equal shares, one a person.

Per Stirpes: "By roots" or "by stocks". When used in the context of a gift to issue, it indicates that the gift will be divided among a certain number of "stirpes" on the date that the gift vests, and will be distributed within each stirpe according to generation. Children never take concurrently with their parents in a stirpital distribution. Instead, all generations of descendants represent their ancestors and take the share to which those ancestors would have been entitled had they survived until the distribution date.

Personal Representative: 1. An executor, an administrator, and an administrator with

---

6 Rules of the Superior Court of Justice in Estates Proceedings, R.R.O. 1990, Reg. 197, r. 27.
7 *Estates Act*, R.S.O. 1990, c. E.21, s. 28.
8 Rules of the Superior Court of Justice in Estates Proceedings, R.R.O. 1990, Reg. 197, r. 15.

the will annexed. 2. Where used with reference to holding shares in that capacity, means an executor, administrator, guardian, tutor, trustee, receiver or liquidator or the committee of or curator to a mentally incompetent person.

Public Guardian and Trustee (Office of the): (formerly the Office of the Public Trustee) The Public Trustee represents a variety of interests in estate litigation including the estates of deceased persons, incapable persons and absentees. Furthermore, the Public Trustee has an independent role, in addition to, not in substitution for or as representative of, any charitable beneficiaries in proceedings affecting charitable interests or charitable property.[9]

Resealing Letters Probate or Letters of Administration: Where a Certificate of Appointment of Estate Trustee, Letters Probate or Letters of Administration have been issued out of a British court of competent jurisdiction, the original grant may be resealed by the Superior Court of Justice and an ancillary certificate is not required. This procedure includes any grant issued in the United Kingdom, a province or territory of Canada, or a country in British Commonwealth.[10]

Solemn Form: Now referred to as formal proof of a testamentary instrument under rr.75.01 and 75.06.[11] Rule 19 of the Rules of the Superior Court of Justice in Estates Proceeding, allowed "[w]here probate or letters of administration with the will annexed are sought of a Will that is lost or destroyed, the proof shall be made in solemn form".[12]

Specific Bequest: The gift of a certain item of personal estate in a will.

Sui Juris: Of one's own right, without disability.

Tangible Personal Property: Personal property that can be seen, weighed, measured, felt or touched or that is in any way perceptible to the senses.

Tangible Property: Property having a physical existence.

Tenancy in Common: A condition created when there are words of severance or one of the four unities is lacking; unequal sharing may be created; each tenant may dispose of their share by will.

Testate: Having executed a will.

Testator: 1. The person making a will, whether the person be male or female. 2. A person who has died leaving a will.

Testatrix: A woman who has made a will.

Title: A vested right or title, something to which the right is already acquired, though the enjoyment may be postponed.

---

9 Brian A. Schnurr, *Estate Litigation*, 2nd ed. (Toronto: Carswell, 1994) (looseleaf) at section 7-1.
10 Anne E.P. Armstrong, *Estate Administration: A Solicitor's Reference Manual*, vol.1 (Toronto, Carswell, 1994) at section 2.12.3.
11 Rules of Civil Procedure, R.R.O. 1990, Reg. 194.
12 R.R.O. 1990, Reg. 197, r. 19.

Trust: A trust arises ... whenever a person is compelled in equity to hold property over which he has control for the benefit of others (the beneficiaries) in such a way that the benefit of the property accrues not to the trustee, but to the beneficiaries."

Trustee: Someone who holds property in trust.

Will: 1. The written statement by which a person instructs how her or his estate should be distributed after death. 2. Includes a testament, a codicil, an appointment by will or by writing in the nature of a will in exercise of a power and any other testamentary disposition. 3. Includes testament, codicil, and every other testamentary instrument of which probate may be granted.

Under the new Rules,[13] "will" includes any testamentary instrument of which probate or administration may be granted.

---

13 Rules of Civil Procedure, R.R.O. 1990, Reg. 194, r. 74.01.

1
LAST WILL AND TESTAMENT*

Lisa R. Simone
(Revised by Michelle T. Cass and further revised by Risa Awerbuck and Katja Kim)†

1. What is a Will?
2. Why Have a Will?
   (a) Rules of Intestacy
   (b) Effective Immediately
   (c) Ability to Choose Executors
   (d) Ability to Choose Beneficiaries
   (e) Ability to Appoint Guardians
   (f) Property Provision for Minor Beneficiaries
   (g) Tax and Probate Fee Planning
   (h) *Family Law Act* Protection for Beneficiaries
3. Formal Requirement for Executing a Valid Will in Ontario
   (a) Formal or Attested Wills
   (b) Holograph Wills
   (c) Wills by Members of the Forces on Active Service
   (d) Foreign Wills and International Wills
   (e) International Wills
   (f) Multiple Wills
4. Who May Make a Will
   (a) Age Requirement
   (a) Testamentary Capacity
5. Grounds for Invalidating a Will
   (a) Lack of Testamentary Capacity
   (b) Improper Execution
   (c) Undue Influence
   (d) Suspicious Circumstances
   (e) Fraud or Forgery
6. Revocation of a Will
   (a) Subsequent Will

---

* See example of a Last Will and Testament at end of this chapter.
† The authors wish to acknowledge their reliance upon the following works in their preparation of this chapter: B.A. Schnurr, *The 2001 Annotated Ontario Estates Statutes* (Toronto: Carswell, 2000); 41st Bar Admission Course, Phase 3, Fall 1999, Estate Planning and Administration, Student Notes; 42nd Bar Admission Course, Phase 3, November 2000, Reference Materials; R. Hull, Q.C. & M.C. Cullity, Q.C., *Macdonell, Sheard and Hull on Probate Practice*, 3d ed. (Toronto: Carswell, 1981).

- (b) Marriage
- (c) Written Declaration
- (d) Destruction
- (e) Effect of Divorce
7. Alterations to Wills and Codicils
8. Revival of a Will
9. Will Drafting
    - (a) Gathering Information
        - (i) Personal Information
            - Citizenship
            - Marital Status
            - Children
            - Assets and Liabilities
            - Type of Ownership
            - Location of Assets
            - Plans, Policies and Insurance
    - (b) Taking Instructions
        - (i) Executors and Trustees
        - (ii) Organ Donation and Funeral Arrangements
        - (iii) Policies and Plans
        - (iv) Legacies
            - Ademption
            - Abatement
            - Lapse
            - Memoranda
                - A Legal Memorandum
                - A Precatory Memorandum
            - Gifts to Charities
            - Gifts to Individuals
        - (v) Residue
            - Outright, or in Trust
            - Dispositions to a Spouse or a "Spousal Trust"
            - Survivorship Clause
            - Common Accident
    - (c) Limitations on Freedom to Dispose of Property
        - (i) Jointly-Owned Property with Right of Survivorship
        - (ii) The *Family Law Act*
        - (iii) Dependants' Relief
        - (iv) Contractual Obligations
        - (v) Other Restrictions on Alienation
10. Conclusion

    Figure 1-1: Example of Last Will and Testament

1. WHAT IS A WILL?

A Will is a legally enforceable document by which a person, known as a testator or testatrix, sets out how his or her estate is to be distributed after his or her death, and who is to be appointed as the executor and trustee of his or her Will. The executor and trustee, also referred to in Ontario as the "Estate Trustee" (referred to as the "Trustees" in this chapter), under the *Rules of Civil Procedure*, is the person or persons who has or have the responsibility to administer the testator's estate in accordance with the provisions of the Will.

Generally, unless specifically restricted, a person's Will deals with all of his or her worldwide property, both real and personal, owned at the time of his or her death or in which the person has a right or beneficial interest at the time of his or her death.

A person's Will only takes effect upon his or her death; it has no effect during the person's lifetime. A person may revoke or change his or her Will at any time provided he or she has testamentary capacity.

In Ontario, Part I of the *Succession Law Reform Act*, R.S.O. 1990, c. S.26 (the "*SLRA*") sets out the various ways that a valid Will may be made and the formal requirements which must be met.

2. WHY HAVE A WILL?

A Will is an essential part of a person's estate plan. In addition to allowing a person to decide among whom and by whom his or her estate will be distributed, it helps to ensure that the person's dependants will be properly provided for and that his or her estate will be administered in an orderly, timely and efficient manner.

(a) Rules of Intestacy

If a person dies without a valid Will, he or she is said to have died intestate. As there is no Will appointing Trustees, no one has authority to deal with the deceased's estate. An application for a Certificate of Appointment of Estate Trustee Without a Will (formerly known as Letters of Administration) must be submitted to the Superior Court of Justice (Ontario Division) in accordance with r. 74.05 of the *Rules of Civil Procedure* in order for the court to appoint an administrator to administer the deceased's estate. In these circumstances, the administrator derives his or her authority to deal with the assets from the Certificate of Appointment. Pursuant to s. 29 of the *Estates Act*, R.S.O 1990, c. E.21, as amended (the "*Estates Act*") in making such appointment, the court will prefer the surviving spouse, children, grandchildren, great-grandchildren, father, mother, or siblings, in that order.

If a person dies intestate, his or her estate does not automatically become the property of the Crown. The deceased's estate will be distributed in accordance with provisions of Part II of the *SLRA* and only if no next of kin of the deceased can be located does the deceased's estate become the property of the Crown, and the *Escheats Act*, R.S.C. 1985, c. E-13 applies.

How and among whom a deceased's estate is distributed depends on whom the deceased is survived by. If the deceased is survived only by a spouse and no children, his or her spouse will receive the entire estate. It is important to note that the definition of "spouse" set out in s. 1(1) of the *SLRA* is restricted to either of a man and woman who are married to each other. Accordingly, a common-law spouse and a same-sex partner are not included in the definition of spouse, however the definition does include a spouse from whom the deceased is separated but not divorced.

If the deceased is survived by a spouse and one or more children, the spouse is entitled to receive a preferential share, the amount of which is prescribed by regulation, and is presently $200,000, and the balance of the estate is divided between or among the spouse and the surviving child or children. If the deceased is survived by a spouse and one child, the balance of the estate will be divided equally between the spouse and child. If the deceased is survived by a spouse and more than one child, one-third of the balance of the estate is paid to the spouse and two-thirds is divided equally among the children. If the deceased is only survived by children, the estate is divided equally among the children. If any of the deceased's children are minors, that is, under the age of 18 years, their shares of the estate must be converted into cash and paid into court to be administered by the office of the Children's Lawyer. If any money is needed for a child's benefit prior to the age of 18 years, an application to the office of the Children's Lawyer for funds must be made by the child's guardian. The child's share of the estate, or the remainder thereof, will be paid out to the child upon him or her attaining the age of 18 years.

It should be noted that under the *Family Law Act*, R.S.O. 1990, c. F.3. (the "*FLA*") there is an exception to the above rules. The *FLA* provides that if the deceased is survived by a spouse, his or her spouse has the right to choose to receive the entitlement under Part II of the *SLRA* or to receive the entitlement under s. 5 of the *FLA*.

If a deceased leaves no surviving spouse or children, his or her estate will be paid to the deceased's parents, siblings, nephews and nieces or next of kin, in that order.

The benefits of having a Will are discussed below.

(b) Effective Immediately

A Will takes effect from the date of the testator's death. The Trustees appointed in the Will derive their authority from the Will and not from the Certificate of Appointment of Estate Trustee With a Will (formerly known as Letters Probate), which confirms the Trustees' appointment. Accordingly, the Trustees have the ability to deal with the testator's estate immediately upon his or her death. Whether a Certificate of Appointment of Estate Trustee With a Will will have to be obtained will depend upon the type and value of the assets held in the testator's estate.

(c) Ability to Choose Executors

As stated, one of the benefits of having a Will is that a testator can choose the person or persons he or she thinks is or are most capable to act as Trustee(s). The administrator appointed by the court may not be the person whom the testator would have selected.

A person can appoint one or more persons to act as Trustees, or he or she can appoint a trust company carrying on business in Ontario either alone or together with any other person or persons he or she chooses.

A person's choice of Trustee will depend on his or her personal or family circumstances and the complexity of his or her estate. Notwithstanding the foregoing, the Trustee will always have numerous responsibilities and liabilities and therefore the person chosen should have proper judgment and business sense, as well as the ability to relate well with the testator's beneficiaries. The testator should obtain the consent of any person he or she wishes to act as Trustee before making the appointment in his or her Will.

(d) Ability of Choose Beneficiaries

Generally the testator is free to decide how and to whom his or her estate is to be distributed. The testator can provide that all of his or her estate is to be paid outright to his or her spouse, or alternatively, the testator can distribute his or her estate among family, friends and charities, in whatever proportions he or she decides. Further, the testator may decide to have his or her estate distributed outright or held in trust, or a combination thereof.

However, the testator should be advised that there may be legal restrictions on his or her freedom to dispose of his or her estate as he or she chooses. The testator may be restricted by the *FLA*, the *SLRA*, or other restrictions which may arise by agreement, such as marriage contracts, separation agreements, or shareholder agreements. These matters are discussed in further detail in this chapter.

(e) Ability to Appoint Guardians

If the testator has children under the age of 18 years, the Will should include a provision appointing a guardian of such children in the event the child's other parent predeceases the testator or dies at the same time. If the testator's spouse survives him or her, he or she automatically has custody of their minor children (unless they are separated or divorced and sole custody of the children has been awarded to the testator). As with the appointment of the Trustees, the testator should obtain the consent of any person the testator wishes to act as guardian of his or her children before making such appointment in his or her Will.

Pursuant to s. 61 of the *Children's Law Reform Act*, R.S.O. 1990, c. C.12 a provision in a Will naming a guardian is only effective for 90 days. The guardian named in the Will must make an application to the court within the 90-day period following the testator's death to have his or her appointment confirmed. Notwithstanding that the appointment in the Will is not binding for more than 90 days, if there is any dispute as to who should be appointed as the child's guardian, the appointment in the Will is evidence of the testator's wishes and generally the court will allow the application for custody unless the contesting party can persuade the court that it is not in the child's best interests to appoint the guardian named in the Will.

(f) Property Provision for Minor Beneficiaries

A Will is particularly important if there are any gifts to children who are minors. As stated, if a person dies without a Will, the law provides that any part of a deceased's estate to which a minor is entitled must be liquidated and the proceeds paid into court and held for such minor until he or she attains the age of 18 years. Under a Will the testator may establish a trust for any child who is a minor at the time of the testator's death and postpone the distribution of such child's share of the estate beyond the age of 18 years. For example, the terms of the trust may provide for the child's share to be held in trust until the child attains the age of 25 years. Until such time, the Trustees may be authorized to make such payments of income and/or capital to or for the benefit of the child as they consider advisable. In addition, the trust provisions can provide that one-half of the capital of the trust be paid when the child attains the age of 21 years and the balance paid when the child attains the age of 25 years. This is extremely beneficial as it helps to ensure that the child will not receive his or her share of the testator's estate until he or she is financially responsible to manage it on his or her own and it avoids the child receiving a windfall early in life.

(g) Tax and Probate Fee Planning

Another important benefit that a Will provides is that it is often used for estate planning purposes in order to minimize both income tax consequences triggered on death and the Estate Administration Tax (formerly known as and referred to as "probate fees" in this chapter), which may be payable on death if a Certificate of Appointment of Estate Trustee With a Will has to be issued for the administration of the estate. As discussed, when there is an intestacy, if assets are not held jointly, it is likely that a Certificate of Appointment of Estate Trustee Without a Will will have to be issued and probate fees will be payable at the time the application is submitted to the court.

(h) *Family Law Act* Protection for Beneficiaries

Pursuant to s. 4(2) of the *FLA*, income from property inherited by a married beneficiary can be protected from the claim of the beneficiary's spouse on separation or death if the Will expressly states that such income is to be protected. Generally the Will provides that any income, including any increase in the value of the inheritance (*i.e.*, capital gains), will be excluded from the spouse's net family property. If no specific provision is included in the Will, or if a person dies without a Will, only the capital amount inherited by the beneficiary will be protected.

3. FORMAL REQUIREMENT FOR EXECUTING A VALID WILL IN ONTARIO

Part I of the *SLRA*, Testate Succession, sets out the formalities that must be met to make a valid Will. Section 3 of the *SLRA* provides that a Will must be in writing to be valid, accordingly an oral statement, tape recording or unsigned Will will not be valid. The following is a discussion of the various forms a valid Will may take pursuant to the *SLRA*.

(a) Formal or Attested Wills

Section 4 of the *SLRA* provides that except with respect to holograph Wills and Wills of members of the armed forces, a Will must be signed at its end by the testator, or by some other person in the testator's presence and by the testator's direction. The testator should sign the Will using his or her customary signature notwithstanding that his or her full name may be set out in the Will. A saving provision is provided for in s. 7 of the *SLRA* in the event the Will is not signed at the end of the document, however any dispositions or directions underneath the signature will be of no force and effect.

The testator must sign or acknowledge the signature in the presence of two or more witnesses who must be present at the same time and the witnesses must then sign the Will in the presence of the testator. A witness to a Will should not be a beneficiary under the Will or a spouse of a beneficiary. If a beneficiary or his or her spouse witnesses the Will, s. 12 of the *SLRA* provides that any gift so made will be void so far as it concerns the witness, his or her spouse, or a person claiming under either of them. However the court, on application, can allow the gift if it is satisfied that the witness did not exercise any improper or undue influence upon the testator. Pursuant to ss. 14 and 13 of the *SLRA*, respectively, a Trustee named in the Will can act as a witness, and a creditor of the testator may also act as a witness without jeopardizing his or her position as a creditor.

If the testator is blind or illiterate, the Will, prior to it being signed, must be read over to the testator in the presence of the witnesses. It should be noted that there is no provision in the *SLRA* which sets out this requirement, however, the Affidavit of Execution of Will or Codicil, Form 74.8 in the *Rules of Civil Procedure*, includes a note that a paragraph confirming that the Will was read over to the testator, and that the testator appeared to understand the contents of the Will, must be included in the affidavit.

Further, it is a common practice in Ontario for the testator and each of the witnesses to initial the bottom right hand corner of each page of the Will, except for the last page, which is signed. There is no legal requirement that each page be initialled, rather it indicates that the testator has seen each page and that no pages have been replaced.

Generally the testator only signs one original copy of the Will. Several "true" or conformed copies are then prepared. Only one original copy of the Will is signed as the presumption of revocation may apply if all signed copies of the Will cannot be located at the testator's death.

It is good practice to have the Affidavit of Execution of Will completed by one of the witnesses immediately after the Will has been fully executed. If a Certificate of Appointment of Estate Trustee With a Will is required, the affidavit must be submitted to the court with the original Will when the application is made. Completion of the affidavit after execution of the Will avoids having to subsequently locate the witness or the possibility of witnesses having passed away.

Often the original Will will be held by the law firm that prepared the document. However, if the testator wishes to keep the original Will he or she should be advised that it should be kept in a safe, fire-proof location. The testator should advise the Trustees where the original Will is kept.

(b) Holograph Wills

A holograph Will is a Will wholly in the testator's handwriting and signed by him or her, without the requirement that the testator's signature be witnessed. Section 6 of the *SLRA* provides that a Will prepared in such manner is valid.

It is important to note that a Will prepared on a stationer's form is not a valid holograph Will as it contains portions that are preprinted. A Will prepared on one of these forms must be executed in accordance with the requirements discussed above.

Notwithstanding the foregoing, if the Will is not properly executed but the handwritten portions express the testator's wishes, the handwritten portions of the Will may be able to be submitted for probate.

(c) Wills by Members of the Forces on Active Service

Section 5 of the *SLRA* sets out the requirements to be met for Wills made by persons who are members of the forces on active service. This includes a person who is a member of the Canadian Forces placed on active service under the *National Defence Act*, a member of any other naval, land or air force while on active service, or a sailor when at sea or in the course of a voyage. If an individual falls within any one these three categories, he or she may make a valid Will if it is signed by him or her or by some other person in his or her presence and by his or her direction without any further formality or any requirement that it be signed in the presence of any witnesses.

(d) Foreign Wills and International Wills

If a testator has property, real or personal, in more than one jurisdiction, a Will may be prepared in each jurisdiction in which the testator's property is located.

Section 37 of the *SLRA* provides that a Will is valid and admissible to probate if at the time it was made it complied with the internal law of the place where:

- the Will was made;
- the testator was then domiciled;
- the testator then had his or her habitual residence; or
- the testator then was a national if there was in that place one body of law governing the Wills of nationals.

If a testator has a foreign Will or intends to execute one, it is imperative that each Will clearly sets out which property it applies to, that the Wills are to operate simultaneously and the later Will should include a provision that it does not revoke the earlier Will dealing with the property in another jurisdiction.

After the testator's death, each Will is probated, if required, in the court of the jurisdiction in which the property is located and to which the Will applies. This avoids the necessity of having to apply for a foreign grant or having the Will translated into a foreign language for the court.

(e) International Wills

If a testator has property in more than more jurisdiction, another possible alternative is for the testator to have a Will prepared in international form to deal with all of his or her worldwide property. Section 42 of the *SLRA* sets out the "Convention Providing a Uniform Law on the Form of an International Will" and the formalities required for a valid international Will. However, before an international Will is prepared, you must confirm whether the country where the property is situated is a signatory to the Convention.

(f) Multiple Wills

As probate fees levied in Ontario are significant (0.5% on the first $50,000 and 1.5% on the excess over $50,000), ways to minimize this tax are an integral part of estate planning.

In addition to holding assets as joint tenants, and designating beneficiaries on RRSPs and RRIFs and insurance policies, the use of multiple Wills, in certain situations, is becoming an increasingly popular method to minimize probate fees. As mentioned, a Certificate of Appointment of Estate Trustee With a Will is not always required to transfer an asset, however, if it is required to deal with certain assets governed by the Will, probate fees must be paid on the total value of all assets governed by the Will. Generally probate is not required to deal with shares held in a private corporation, such as a family business or holding company. Accordingly, if the testator holds shares in a private corporation or corporations which form a significant portion of his or her estate and have substantial value, consideration should be given to preparing multiple Wills.

When multiple Wills are used, two Wills, primary and secondary Wills, or non-corporate and corporate Wills, are prepared. One Will deals with all assets requiring probate and the other deals with all assets that do not require probate. On the testator's death, only the Will dealing with the assets requiring probate is submitted to the court and probate fees will only be paid on the assets governed by the Will submitted. This position was upheld in *Granovsky Estate v. Ontario* (1998), 21 E.T.R. (2d) 25, 156 D.L.R. (4th) 557, 1998 CarswellOnt 518 (Ont. Gen. Div.), wherein Madame Justice Greer held that the secondary Will would not require probate and accordingly no probate fees were payable on the assets governed by the secondary Will. The *Granovsky* decision was initially appealed but the appeal was subsequently abandoned on April 12, 1999. Chapter 3 discusses the applicable *Rules of Civil Procedure* forms regarding multiple Wills.

Precautionary measures similar to those discussed with respect to the preparation of foreign Wills should be taken when drafting multiple Wills. The assets passing under each Will must be clearly identified, it should be clear that both Wills are to exist simultaneously and the secondary Will must not revoke the primary Will. The Trustees and the distribution of the assets under each Will may be identical, however if legacies are being provided for they should only be included in one Will. A provision should then be included in the other Will which provides that if the assets under the first Will are insufficient to satisfy the legacies provided for thereunder, that any deficiency should be satisfied from the assets passing under the other Will.

4. WHO MAY MAKE A WILL

(a) Age Requirement

As a general rule, to make a valid Will the testator must be 18 years at the time the Will is executed. Section 8(1) of the *SLRA* sets out four exceptions to this rule.

(b) Testamentary Capacity

In addition to the age requirement, a testator must have testamentary capacity, or in other words, be mentally capable of making a Will at the time the Will is being executed. It is the solicitor's responsibility to satisfy him or herself that the testator has capacity to make a valid Will. This may be difficult as the testator may lack capacity at one moment but be lucid at another, or may be eccentric. No test to determine testamentary capacity is set out in the *SLRA*. One of the leading authorities on the degree of mental capacity necessary to make a valid Will is set out in *Banks v. Goodfellow* (1870), L.R. 5 Q.B. 549, [1861-73] All E.R. Rep. 47, [1871] L.R. 11 Eq. 472, 39 L.J.Q.B. 237, 22 L.T. 813 (Eng. Q.B.). The court held that it is essential that the testator:

- understands the nature of the act (making a Will) and its effect;
- knows and understands the extent of the property of which he or she is disposing; and
- comprehends and appreciates the claims to which he or she ought to give effect.

If the solicitor is uncertain whether the testator has capacity he or she may want to have the testator assessed.

Although the general position is that the testator must have capacity at the time the Will is executed there may be circumstances because of age or illness that the testator had capacity at the time he or she gave instructions to the solicitor for the preparation of his or her Will, but at the time the Will is signed there is an apparent deterioration in the testator's mental capacity. In such a situation, if the Will is executed by the testator, in order for the Will to be valid the testator must be able to appreciate that he or she gave instructions to his or her solicitor regarding the disposition of his or her property following his or her death and that he or she has no doubt that the solicitor has given effect to his or her intentions and that it is carried out in the document. Notwithstanding the foregoing, this principle should be applied with caution.

The solicitor should also be satisfied that the testator is acting on his or her own volition and initiative and that there was no one influencing the testator's decisions.

The solicitor should avoid asking leading questions when obtaining instructions from the testator regarding the disposition of his or her property, but should make enquiries regarding the testator's knowledge of his or her property to ensure that the factors set out in *Banks v. Goodfellow* are satisfied. In the case of an elderly or ill testator, the solicitor should keep notes supporting his or her decision that the testator had capacity, which should include general observations of the testator's mannerisms and what was discussed.

5. GROUNDS FOR INVALIDATING A WILL

(a) Lack of Testamentary Capacity

A Will may be held to be invalid if it can be shown that the testator did not have the requisite testamentary capacity at the time the Will was executed. The burden of proving that a testator did not have the requisite testamentary capacity is on the party alleging the incapacity.

(b) Improper Execution

A Will may be challenged on the grounds that the execution requirements set out in the *SLRA* were not met. An example of an improper execution of a formal Will would occur if initially two witnesses were present in the room, but one left the room when the testator signed and then returned and signed as a witness. Both witnesses must be present when the testator signs the Will.

(c) Undue Influence

As stated above, the solicitor must be satisfied that there was no undue influence exerted on the testator and that he or she acted on his or her own volition. The Will will be held invalid if it is proven on a balance of probabilities that the Will did not reflect the testator's own wishes.

(d) Suspicious Circumstances

The doctrine of suspicious circumstances arises when there is the presence of certain facts or circumstances which make an ordinary person suspicious as to whether the Will reflects the true intentions of the testator. Such circumstances may include a situation where someone may have influenced the testator to change his or her Will, resulting in such person receiving a larger benefit than previously provided under an existing Will. When substantial changes from a previous Will are being made in the distribution of one's estate, the solicitor should enquire into the testator's reasoning for the changes to ensure that changes are being made by the testator on his or her accord. If suspicious circumstances are proven, then the propounder of the Will has the burden of proving that the Will was duly executed with the knowledge and approval of the testator, who had testamentary capacity at the relevant time.

In a situation where a client is distributing his or her estate in a manner that may give rise to suspicious circumstances, in addition to the solicitor's notes regarding this matter, and as a precautionary measure, the solicitor may wish to have the client prepare a letter setting out his or her instructions and the reasoning behind the distribution of his or her estate. This letter can be produced as evidence in the event any of the beneficiaries challenge the Will.

(e) Fraud or Forgery

The grounds of fraud and forgery are self-explanatory. A Will is not valid if the testator's signature was forged by someone claiming to be the testator. As mentioned earlier, it is the practice in Ontario for the testator and each of the witnesses to initial the bottom right hand corner of each Will. This serves as evidence that the testator saw each page of the Will and deters a third party from replacing pages in the Will, thereby changing the disposition to him or herself.

6. REVOCATION OF A WILL

Section 15 of the *SLRA* sets out the various ways in which a Will may be revoked.

(a) Subsequent Will

Execution of a subsequent Will made in accordance with the provisions of Part I of the *SLRA* will revoke a prior Will. However, the fact that a subsequent Will has been made does not necessarily result in the total revocation of an earlier Will unless the subsequent Will expressly or implicitly revokes the earlier Will or the two Wills are incapable of standing together.

(b) Marriage

Generally a Will is revoked by the marriage of the testator. Accordingly, any Will executed by the testator prior to his or her marriage will be revoked and the testator will be deemed to have died intestate. However, s. 16(a) of the *SLRA* provides that the Will executed prior to marriage will not be revoked if it contains a declaration that the Will is made in contemplation of the marriage. Also, s. 16(b) of the *SLRA* provides that a Will is not revoked if the surviving spouse elects to take under the Will, by instrument in writing signed by the spouse and filed within one year after the testator's death in the office of the Estate Registrar for Ontario.

(c) Written Declaration

Pursuant to s. 15(c) of the *SLRA*, a testator may revoke his or her Will in its entirety or in part by signing a written document, prepared in accordance with provisions of Part I of the *SLRA*, which declares his or her intention of revoking the Will or part thereof. Generally, if the testator intends to revoke his or her Will in its entirety a clause will be inserted in a subsequently prepared Will, or if the testator only wishes to revoke a part of the Will, a codicil can be prepared.

(d) Destruction

A testator can revoke his or her Will by burning, tearing or otherwise destroying it by him or herself, or the testator may direct another person to destroy the Will in the testator's presence. The act of destruction of the Will itself is not sufficient to revoke the Will; the testator must intend to revoke the Will by its destruction.

(e) Effect of Divorce

If a testator makes a Will and is subsequently divorced, his or her Will is still in effect; it is not revoked as in the case of marriage. Section 17(2) of the *SLRA* provides that unless a contrary intention appears in the Will, if after a testator makes a Will, his or her marriage is terminated by a judgment absolute of divorce or is declared a nullity, the testators' former spouse is deemed to have predeceased him or her. Accordingly, any gifts to the former spouse will be revoked and the former spouse, if appointed as executor or trustee, will be unable to act. It should be noted that s. 17 does not apply to spouses who are separated at the death of the testator. Therefore, it is extremely important that when spouses separate they enter into a separation agreement which includes a provision that each releases his or her rights to a share in the other's estate and his or her right to act as executor or trustee.

7. ALTERATIONS TO WILLS AND CODICILS

As mentioned above, a Will may be revoked in its entirety or in part. Generally, if a minor change is being made to the Will, the amendment can be made by way of a codicil. A codicil is a separate document which refers to the Will, sets out any changes to the Will, either insertions or deletions, and confirms that all other provisions of the Will remain the same. A codicil must be made in accordance with the formalities set out in Part I of the *SLRA*.

A testator may have more than one codicil, however if a number of changes have already been made to the Will, or need to be made, it is best for a new Will to be prepared. Also, the testator may prefer to make a new Will if he or she does not want others to know of the changes made, such as changes made to the distribution of the estate. Others will have knowledge of any changes made, as a Will, and any codicil thereto, becomes a public document if it is probated or if a copy of it is required to be registered in a Land Registry Office. In addition, the *Rules of Civil Procedure* require that all residual beneficiaries receive a copy of the complete Will and any codicils thereto. Having a new Will prepared may avoid any hard feelings, or any questions arising as to why the changes were made.

If changes are made to the Will when it is being reviewed prior to its execution, the testator and both witnesses should initial the alteration in the margin or in some other part of the Will near the alteration.

If the testator is given the Will after it has been executed, he or she should be cautioned not to make any changes to the document. Section 18 provides that any alterations to a Will after it is executed require the signature of the testator and two witnesses (not necessarily the same two persons who witnessed the Will when it was originally signed), unless it is a holograph Will or a Will of a member of the forces on active service. If these formalities are not complied with, the alterations will be of no effect, or, if as a result of the alterations, the effect of provisions in the Will are no longer apparent, the portion of the Will which has been altered will be of no effect.

8. REVIVAL OF A WILL

If a Will or part thereof has been revoked, the Will or part thereof may be revived by one of the following methods set out in s. 19 of the *SLRA*:

- by the execution of a Will made in accordance with the provisions of Part I of the *SLRA* that shows an intention to give effect to the Will or part that was revoked; or
- by the execution of a codicil made in accordance with the provisions of Part I of the *SLRA* that shows an intention to give effect to the Will or part that was revoked; or
- by re-execution of the revoked Will in accordance with the provisions of Part I of the *SLRA*.

It should be noted that pursuant to s. 21 of the *SLRA*, if a Will has been revived, the Will is deemed to have been made at the time at which it was so revived and not at the time it was originally executed.

9. WILL DRAFTING

(a) Gathering Information

Taking instructions is an integral part of Will drafting. Instructions should be taken directly from the client, however if instructions are taken second-hand, such as from the client's spouse or child, it is imperative that the solicitor confirm the instructions with the client and meet with the client when the Will is signed. The solicitor must be able to satisfy him or herself that the Will accurately expresses the client's intentions and that the client has testamentary capacity. A properly trained clerk is a valuable assistant to a solicitor in gathering information and in the preparation of documents, however the solicitor must be mindful of the Rules of Professional Conduct regarding permissible delegation.

(i) Personal Information

In order for the solicitor to properly advise the testator and prepare his or her Will, the solicitor will require personal information regarding the testator and his or her family, as well as financial information regarding his or her assets and liabilities. Generally a questionnaire will be completed, the first part of which contains personal and financial information and the second half of which contains the Will instructions. The solicitor or clerk taking the instructions should ensure that notes of matters discussed are taken when the instructions are received.

Citizenship

It is very important to ascertain the residence and citizenship of the testator and his or her spouse for tax purposes. In certain jurisdictions, such as the United States, an individual will be taxed based on their citizenship instead of, or in addition to, their residency. In these situations the client should be advised to contact an estate specialist or accountant, as well as a specialist in the other jurisdiction to confirm the tax consequences on death.

Marital Status

It is very important to confirm the client's marital status. A record of the spouse's name, date of marriage, or date of separation or divorce should be kept, as well as a copy of any domestic contract or separation agreement that the client may have obligations under. The solicitor must ensure that any obligations the client has to a spouse or former spouse, under the *FLA* or any agreement, are satisfied under the Will.

Children

The client should be asked if he or she has any children, and if so, their full names and birthdates should be noted. It should also be confirmed whether any children or grandchildren were born outside of marriage (in a common-law relationship where the parents did not subsequently marry) or adopted and whether any child or grandchild has any disability and the nature of his or her disability (it should be noted that these questions should be asked regarding all beneficiaries).

If a child or grandchild has a disability, it is important to ascertain whether such beneficiary is self-sufficient or is receiving government benefits, as well as the possibility of such person's condition deteriorating over time. If the beneficiary is receiving government benefits or is likely to receive them in the future, special trust provisions may have to be included in the Will so as not to jeopardize this government assistance. Special attention will have to be given to this matter to ensure that the solicitor properly advises his or her client of the various options available.

The issue of whether or not a child is born outside of marriage arises if the Will makes reference to distributions to children or issue as a class. Unless the Will states otherwise, such a reference includes children or issue born inside or outside of marriage and the Trustees have an obligation to search the public records to ensure that he or she is dealing with all persons that fall within the class. To avoid the Trustees from having to complete such a search the general practice in Ontario has been to include a provision in the Will that limits gifts to children or issue born within marriage, who were born within a common-law relationship but whose parents subsequently married or children who were adopted. However, with the increasing number of children being born within a common-law relationship whose parents do not subsequently marry, a clause is now being included in Wills that would include these children provided that the parent of the child showed a settled intention to treat the child as his or her own. This is a sensitive issue that clients may not be comfortable discussing, however it must be explained to them and reinforced that the Will may have to be amended depending upon how this matter is to be dealt with.

Assets and Liabilities

A thorough list of the client's assets and liabilities will have to be obtained. How the assets are owned, the type of assets held and the value of the assets, and the extent of the client's liabilities, will all effect the client's estate plan. Once this information has been gathered, it can be ascertained whether the client has sufficient assets, after payment of any liabilities, to distribute his or her estate in the manner he or she intends and whether the client has sufficient assets to meet his or her obligations. With clients with young families it may be evident that additional insurance should be obtained to ensure that the surviving spouse and children will be properly cared for. Consideration should also be given to whether the client owns any special collections or other assets which may necessitate the appointment of a special trustee, or whether the client owns shares in a private corporation which have considerable value. As discussed previously, it may be appropriate to prepare multiple Wills to reduce probate fees.

Type of Ownership

There are various ways that property can be owned. Assets may be owned solely by the client, or with one or more persons as joint tenants with right of survivorship or as tenants-in-common. If assets are owned as joint tenants, on the client's death his or her interest in the assets automatically passes to the surviving owner or owners. If assets are owned as tenants-in-common, the client's interest in the assets will pass to his or her estate (rather than to the other owner or owners) and will be distributed in accordance with the client's Will. One exception to this rule applies with respect to ownership of the matrimonial home. Section 26(1) of the *FLA* provides that if a spouse dies owning an interest in a matrimonial home as a joint tenant with a third person and not with his or her spouse, the joint tenancy is deemed to have been severed immediately before the time of death.

It is also important to determine the nature of the assets the client owns so that the tax consequences that may arise on death can be evaluated. Clients are often very concerned about how much they will have to pay in probate fees and do not consider the taxes that are due on their death. If the client primarily owns assets that produce income (such as term deposits, bonds, etc.), taxes will not be an issue as taxes are paid annually on income earned. However, if the client owns capital property (such as stocks or a cottage) that has substantially increased in value from the time it was purchased substantial monies could be owing on account of capital gains. It should be noted that a principal residence is exempt from capital gains, accordingly even if a client's principal residence increased in value no tax on capital gains will be owing with respect to that residence.

With respect to the client's liabilities, the nature of each of the liabilities should be determined, whether it was secured or unsecured, whether it was incurred for the client's own benefit or whether the client guaranteed a loan for the benefit of someone else. Also, it should be ascertained whether the liability is insured, as insurance may have been taken out at the time the loan application for a mortgage or line of credit was completed.

Location of Assets

As discussed earlier, if a client has property located in other jurisdictions, he or she may wish to prepare a separate Will to deal with those assets or an international Will. Additional reasons for a having a foreign Will or Wills include that the Will prepared in Ontario may not be recognized in the foreign jurisdiction where the property is located, or the foreign jurisdiction may have special rules governing the distribution of property located in its jurisdiction.

Plans, Policies and Insurance

Full particulars should be obtained regarding any registered retirement savings plans, registered retirement income funds, pension plans and life insurance policies owned by the client. The client should confirm whether any beneficiary or beneficiaries have been designated under the plan or policy and if so, who has been designated.

(b) Taking Instructions

After all of the personal and financial information has been gathered, instructions for preparation of the Will are obtained.

(i) Executors and Trustees

The appointment of the Trustees is a very important decision that the client has to make. The terms executor and trustee are usually used together although there is a distinction between the office of "executor" and "trustee". Often the same persons are appointed to hold both offices. The executors are responsible for the administration of the testator's estate following his or her death. The executors are responsible for locating and securing the testator's assets, paying all debts and liabilities of the testator, and distributing the assets of the testator's estate in accordance with the provisions of the testator's Will. Generally if the testator's estate is not too complex and complications do not arise in the administration, the estate may be distributable within one year following the testator's death. This time period is known as the "executor's year".

There will only be a trustee if the testator's estate is not immediately distributed outright to the beneficiaries and the whole or part of the testator's estate is to be held in trust pursuant to the provisions of the Will. It is the trustees' responsibility to administer these on-going trusts. Unlike the executor whose responsibilities end within one year or so after the testator's death, the trustees' responsibilities can go on for years if a trust is held for the lifetime of a beneficiary.

The offices of executor and trustee are sufficiently similar that a detailed discussion of the differences between the two offices is not warranted and the executor and trustee will continue to be referred to as the "Trustees". When deciding who to appoint as the Trustees the client will want to appoint persons who are familiar with the client's personal affairs, but also persons who have an understanding of finances. The client should consider where the person resides and his or her age, particularly if there are trusts to be administered for a long period of time.

As mentioned earlier, there may be one or more persons appointed or a trust company carrying on business in Ontario may be appointed or there may be a combination thereof. However, from a practical point there should probably be no more than four persons appointed, as the Trustees must act unanimously unless the Will provides otherwise. The client can provide that if there are more than two Trustees acting, the decision of the majority of the Trustees is binding, and may further direct that a certain Trustee, such as a spouse, must be one of the majority if he or she is acting as a Trustee at such time. If only one person is being appointed as the Trustee, such as the client's spouse, the client should be advised to appoint someone as an alternate Trustee in the event that the person appointed predeceases the client or is unable to act.

A person must be 18 years of age to act as a Trustee. However, a person under 18 years may still be named in the Will to act upon him or her attaining 18 years provided that an adult or trust company is named together with the minor. The minor may be named to either act together with the adult Trustees or to replace the adult Trustees. If the minor is the sole Trustee appointed or the sole remaining Trustee at the testator's death, s. 26 of the *Estates Act* provides that in such circumstances a Certificate of Appointment of Estate Trustee shall be granted to the guardian of the minor or to such other person as the court thinks fit, until the minor has attained the age of 18 years, at which time the Certificate of Appointment of Estate Trustee may be granted to the minor.

Aside from the practical problems of administering an estate that may arise from appointing a person who resides out of town, if a Trustee resides outside of the Commonwealth, such as in the United States, a bond may be required to be posted as security pursuant to the *Estates Act*.

The client may wish to appoint special trustees whose responsibilities are limited to specific purposes. For example, if the client has an art or stamp collection, a special trustee can be appointed to deal with the disposition of the collection, and the special trustee would then account to the principal Trustee. Further, the client may wish to appoint certain persons to act as his or her Trustees but do not want them to have the added responsibility of administering an ongoing trust. In such a situation, special trustees could be appointed and a provision could be included in the Will providing that the transfer and delivery of the trust property to the special trustees constitutes a full discharge to the Trustees and that the Trustees are under no obligation to see that the terms and conditions of the trust are carried out.

People often think it is an honour to be appointed as a Trustee, however acting as a Trustee is a time consuming position, which is wrought with responsibilities and potential liabilities. Although not legally required, the client should obtain the consent of any person he or she wishes to appoint as a Trustee. It should be noted that a Trustee appointed in a Will is not required to act and may renounce his or her appointment. If more than one Trustee is appointed, the remaining Trustee or Trustees will apply for the Certificate of Appointment of Estate Trustee With a Will, or if the sole Trustee renounces his or her appointment an application will be made to the court and an administrator will be appointed in accordance with the priority set out in s. 29 of the *Estates Act*.

Section 46 of the *Trustee Act*, R.S.O. 1990, c. T.23 (the "*Trustee Act*") provides that where there are several Trustees and one or more of them dies, their powers and duties vest in the survivor or survivors, unless there is some provision to the contrary in the Will. If the sole Trustee, or sole surviving Trustee if there was more than one Trustee appointed, dies before the estate has been fully administered and if an alternate Trustee or Trustees is named in the Will, the alternate Trustee or Trustees will apply for a Certificate of Appointment of Succeeding Estate Trustee. If no alternate Trustee is named in the Will, then on the death of the last surviving Trustee, the Trustee appointed in such deceased Trustee's Will (the "New Trustees") will succeed the deceased Trustee as Trustee of the first Will when the New Trustees obtain probate of the deceased Trustee's Will. The executorship is said to have "devolved".

A Trustee who has been appointed in a Will may be removed from the office or may be prohibited from acting if he or she is incapable of acting because of mental incapacity, conviction for committing an indictable offence, bankruptcy or insolvency. In these situations, ss. 5 and 37 of the *Trustee Act* allow the court to remove any or all of the Trustees and/or appoint replacements.

A Trustee who no longer wishes to continue acting may make an application to the court to be removed as a Trustee. Also, a co-Trustee, or a person interested in the estate of the deceased (generally a beneficiary) may make an application to the court for the removal of a Trustee if the Trustee has breached his or her duties because of misconduct, negligence or inappropriate actions. As a fiduciary, a Trustee must act in the best interests of the beneficiaries and avoid situations that might place them in a conflict of interest. In this regard, the courts have also considered the relationship between the Trustee and the beneficiaries and whether a conflict has developed between them resulting in the Trustee being unable to act as a fiduciary on behalf of a beneficiary. Such a situation may arise where a surviving spouse elects to receive his or her entitlement under the *FLA* instead of the benefits provided under the Will.

The client may wish to provide unlimited powers to the Trustees in administering the estate, or may wish to limit what the Trustees are able to do. Significant amendments to the sections of the *Trustee Act* dealing with investments by Trustees and the liability of Trustees came into effect on July 1, 1999. Previously, Trustees, unless provided otherwise in the Will, were limited to making very conservative type investments which were listed in ss. 26 and 27 of the *Trustee Act*. As a result, a provision was often included in Wills expanding the Trustees' investment power. Section 27 of the *Trustee Act* now establishes a "prudent investor" standard of care, which requires that Trustees exercise the care, skill, diligence and judgment that a prudent investor would exercise in making investments. Subsection 27(5) sets out a list of criteria that Trustees must consider when making investments and subsec. 27(6) makes it obligatory that Trustees diversify investments.

Although Trustees are generally not permitted to delegate their duties, subsec. 27(3) provides that mutual funds are a permitted investment and subsecs. 27(7) and (8) permit Trustees to obtain investment advice and confirm that it is not a breach of trust for the Trustees to rely on that advice if a prudent investor would have done likewise. It should be noted that subsec. 27(9) allows a testator to provide in his or her Will that the provisions of s. 27 do not have to be followed. Accordingly, a testator in his or her Will could direct the Trustees to not diversify investments, but to limit them to income-producing type investments. Section 28 provides that Trustees will not be liable for a loss to the property arising from the investment of the property provided that the investment plan or strategy adopted by the Trustees was a plan or strategy which a prudent investor would have adopted under similar circumstances.

Both individual and corporate Trustees are entitled to compensation. The client may decide to appoint individuals rather than a corporate trustee and if the Trustee is a beneficiary under the Will, he or she may not claim compensation, or may claim a reduced amount. If there is more than one Trustee, the maximum amount of compensation is not generally increased, and the Trustees will determine how the awarded compensation is to be divided between or among them. The subject of executor's compensation is discussed in further detail in the Passing of Accounts chapter.

(ii) Organ Donation and Funeral Arrangements

The client may provide in his or her Will that his or her body or certain organs be donated to medical science for research or transplant purposes. However, the client should be advised that this provision is not legally binding on the Trustees and only serves as an expression of the client's wishes. Similarly, a client may provide in his or her Will whether he or she wishes to be buried or cremated, or particulars regarding his or her funeral. Again these provisions are not legally binding upon the Trustees. As a person's Will is often not read until after the burial, it is best that the client discusses these matters with his or her family members or friends during his or her lifetime.

(iii) Policies and Plans

If the client has not already made beneficiary designations under his or her insurance policies, RRSPs, RRIFs, or pension plans, designations may be made in the Will. These designations will revoke any designations made prior to the execution of the Will. The client must be advised that the designations in the Will only effect policies or plans in place at the date the Will is signed, and will not apply to any policies or plans subsequently taken out. Insurance policy proceeds may be paid outright or held in trust.

(iv) Legacies

A legacy, also known as a bequest, is a disposition of personal property or of a sum of money in a Will. The client should be asked whether he or she wishes to make any specific gifts to any family members, friends or charities. There are three types of legacies that can be made: specific, general and demonstrative.

A specific legacy is a gift of a particular thing which is specified and distinguished from all other of the testator's chattels. An example of a specific legacy is a gift of a wedding ring or a painting.

A general legacy is a pecuniary gift that is payable out of the general assets of the testator's estate. An example of a general legacy is a gift of a specified sum of money.

A demonstrative legacy is a gift of a sum of money with a direction that it is to be paid out of a particular fund. An example of a demonstrative legacy would be a gift of the funds held in a particular bank account.

A disposition of land or realty is known as a "devise".

The type of legacy that is made is relevant in the event that the specific asset cannot be located or if there are insufficient assets in the estate to satisfy all of the legacies.

Ademption

If a specific legacy is provided for in a Will and the asset is not in the deceased's possession or it cannot be located at the time of death either because it was destroyed or disposed of during the testator's lifetime, the doctrine of ademption applies and the gift is said to have adeemed. Subject to the following comments, in this situation the gift fails and no gift is made to the beneficiary in its place.

Section 36 of the *Substitute Decisions Act*, 1992, S.O. 1996, c. 30 as amended from time to time, negates the application of the doctrine of ademption if a guardian of property disposes of property that is subject to a specific testamentary gift unless the deceased's Will includes a provision expressing that a contrary intention is to apply. Therefore, if a specific testamentary gift is disposed of by an attorney, the beneficiary is entitled to receive an amount equal to the proceeds of disposition of the property, without interest, from the residue of the deceased's estate.

Abatement

Abatement is the reduction of legacies occurring when, after payment of debts and liabilities, there are insufficient assets in the residue of the deceased's estate to satisfy all of the gifts provided for in the Will in full.

The type of legacy provided for in the Will is important because it determines the order of abatement. Generally, after the residue has been fully paid, general legacies abate rateably first, followed by demonstrative and specific legacies, which again abate rateably. Further, specific legacies (which are personalty) abate before a devise (a disposition of real property).

If the client is concerned that there may not be sufficient assets to satisfy all of the legacies provided for in his or her Will and he or she does not wish for the general order of abatement to apply, the client can indicate the order of priority of payment of the legacies. The client can direct in his or her Will that all general legacies to family members be paid first and then all general legacies to other beneficiaries, with general legacies to other beneficiaries abating rateably before legacies to family members.

Lapse

It is very important to always ask the client what he or she wishes to happen to a beneficiary's gift, or share of the residue of his or her estate, if the beneficiary predeceases the client.

Generally, if a beneficiary named in a Will predeceases the testator, the gift fails, or is said to lapse. If the gift is a legacy it will fall into the residue of the estate and be dealt with as part thereof. If the beneficiary was entitled to a share of the residue of the estate, there will be an intestacy with respect to that portion of the estate.

However, the doctrine of lapse does not apply in all situations; it depends upon the relationship of the beneficiary to the testator. The doctrine of lapse is avoided if the three criteria set out in s. 31 of the *SLRA*, known as the "anti-lapse provision", are met. Except when a contrary intention is provided for in the Will, if the beneficiary is a child, grandchild, brother or sister of the testator, who predeceases the testator leaving a spouse or issue surviving the testator, the gift will not lapse but instead will be distributed as if it had been made directly to the deceased beneficiary's spouse and/or issue as if he or she had died intestate, except that the preferential share of a surviving spouse is excluded. If the client does not want the anti-lapse provision to apply, a contrary intention can be expressed in the Will by providing that the gift is to the named beneficiary "if he or she survives me" or, a gift over provision can be included which stipulates to whom the gift should be paid if the beneficiary predeceases the client.

Memoranda

Clients often wish to leave specific items of personal property, such as jewellery, art, or furniture to friends and family members. When a client has a fairly lengthy list of items which he or she wishes to distribute, instead of listing these items in the Will, they can be set out in a memorandum. A memorandum is a document which sets out the particular items of personal property and the beneficiary who is to receive it. There are two types of memoranda which can be prepared. Which memorandum will be used will depend upon the client's wishes and circumstances.

A Legal Memorandum: A legal memorandum is legally binding upon the Trustees as it is incorporated by reference into the Will. The memorandum must be prepared and executed prior to the signing of the Will and referred to and clearly identified in the Will. As the memorandum becomes part of the Will, it is subject to the same rules as the Will regarding amendments and revocation. Generally, a client will want to prepare a legal memorandum if the items are of substantial value or if he or she wants to ensure that his or her wishes will be carried out.

A Precatory Memorandum: A precatory memorandum may be prepared and executed at any time after the Will is executed. No specific reference to the memorandum has to be included in the Will, although a provision may be included which provides that it is the testator's wish that the Trustees act in accordance with any memorandum that he or she may subsequently prepare. However, no legal obligation is imposed on the Trustees to do so. As the memorandum is not incorporated by reference into the Will, it may be changed at any time by the testator without the concern that the legal formal requirements have to be met. A precatory memorandum may be used when the client has a number of specific legacies he or she wishes to make which are more in the nature of keepsakes or mementos, items of sentimental value, or in situations where the client is not certain what gifts he or she wishes to make but wishes to finalize his or her Will.

Gifts to Charities

In addition to leaving gifts of cash to family and friends the client may wish to leave legacies to charities. If the client is gifting funds to charities as part of his or her estate plan as a method of reducing income taxes there are number of issues that must be addressed.

The gifts must be to registered Canadian charitable organizations in order for the tax credit to be received. Certain other organizations may also qualify for the tax credit based on specific criteria, such as a Canadian connection, but whether the particular organization qualifies should be confirmed.

Generally the client will specify which charities are to benefit and the amount to be given to each organization, however some clients provide that their Trustees are to select the particular charities. If the client selects the specific charities the tax credit will be available in the year of the testator's death, however if the Trustees select the charities, the tax credit can only be used by the estate. These issues are beyond the scope of this chapter but need to be addressed when developing the client's estate plan.

It is important to confirm with the client what he or she wishes to happen if the organization is no longer in existence when he or she dies. If the organization is no longer in existence the Trustees can apply to the court and it may use its cy-pres jurisdiction to allow the legacy to be paid to an organization with objectives similar to the organization named in the Will. To avoid having to go to court to seek directions, a clause should be inserted in the Will which directs that the cy-pres doctrine be applied if the organization no longer exists, or, alternatively a clause should be inserted that the gift is to fail if the organization no longer exists.

Gifts to Individuals

There are several ways in which a gift of money can be made to an individual. A legacy of a specified sum of money can be left outright to a beneficiary, or, if the gift is for a child, it can be held in trust until the child attains a specified age. Alternatively, the client may wish to provide an annuity for the lifetime of a family member. In such a situation, the Trustees would be directed to set aside a sum of money that would be sufficient to provide a person with guaranteed weekly, monthly, or yearly payments of a specified amount.

(v) Residue

Outright, or in Trust

"Residue" refers to the part of the testator's estate that is remaining after all taxes, debts, liabilities and legacies have been paid. Therefore, the final consideration in preparing a Will is determining how the client wishes to distribute the residue. The whole of the residue may be immediately distributable or the Trustees may be directed to hold it in trust for a period of time, or, alternatively part of the residue may be immediately distributable and part held in trust.

Distributing the residue outright to the beneficiary or beneficiaries is the easiest way of disposing of an estate and therefore clauses dealing with an immediate distribution do not often cause a problem. It should also be kept in mind when advising a client that distributing an estate outright results in an estate which is less expensive and less time consuming to administer. Notwithstanding the foregoing, it always necessary to consider whether the beneficiary would be better served if his or her shares were held in trust instead of distributed outright. Further, as mentioned earlier, consideration should always be given to whether a gift over provision should be used in the Will to deal with the possibility of the residual beneficiary predeceasing the testator and preventing a possible intestacy with respect to the whole or a part of the residue of the testator's estate.

An aside is necessary to comment on the often misused expression *"per stirpes"*. Reference to "my children alive at my death in equal shares *per stirpes*" is often used incorrectly and can be confusing as to whether the testator intended to limit gifts to his or her children, and ignore the issue of any deceased child. The meaning of "children" is normally limited to the testator's first generation descendants, while "issue" includes not only children, but all other descendants in whatever degree. The term *"among my issue in equal shares per stirpes"* indicates that the share of the testator's estate to which the deceased beneficiary would have been entitled if he or she had survived the testator is to be divided equally among the deceased beneficiary's issue by right of representation. Accordingly, if the beneficiary predeceases the testator the share of the estate to which he or she would have been entitled will be divided equally among the beneficiary's surviving children, if the beneficiary has no surviving children it will be divided equally among his or her grandchildren, and so on. A good rule to follow is that *"per stirpes"* should only be used in conjunction with "issue". If it is the client's intention to only benefit his or her children alive at his or her death, the term *"among my children in equal shares per capita"* may be used.

One other drafting note: if the residue is to be divided among several beneficiaries, it is best not to provide at the outset for the residue to be divided into the total number of shares that the client intends. This may result in part or all of the residue failing to be dealt with by the Will and result in a full or partial intestacy. Accordingly, instead of providing that *"my Trustees should divide the residue of my estate into six equal shares and deal with such shares as follows"* it is preferable to provide that *"my Trustees shall divide the residue of my estate into as many equal shares as may be necessary to carry out the following provisions and shall deal with such shares as follows"*. This note applies to any division of the estate when it is not being divided equally among the beneficiaries, whether you are dealing with the residue, or the remainder of property held in trust.

Holding the whole or part of the residue in trust has many benefits, but also requires consideration of matters that do not need to be dealt with when distributing the residue outright. The more common uses of trusts in estate planning include:

- providing for maintenance and education of minors or other beneficiaries to give them the enjoyment of the property while postponing full control over the property until an appropriate time;
- providing for the care of beneficiaries who cannot manage their own financial

affairs (for example, for medical reasons);
- preserving one's estate and allowing for succession of interests in the same assets, for example, in second marriages by providing the surviving spouse with a life interest in the income and/or capital of the assets, and the children with a remainder interest in the assets; or
- implementing legitimate tax plans such as income splitting.

For whatever purpose a testator decides to make use of a trust in his or her Will, the following considerations must be addressed:
- if property is to be held in trust for a beneficiary until he or she attains a certain age, instructions must be provided as to how that property is to be distributed if the beneficiary dies before attaining that age;
- keeping in mind accumulation rules, income must be distributed or accumulated, or both, during the term of the trust;
- if income is payable to more than one beneficiary, the testator must decide whether it shall be payable in fixed proportions or as determined by the Trustees;
- consideration must also be given to whether the Trustees should be empowered to make payments out of the capital of the trust (at the Trustees' discretion or limited to payments for specific purposes such as medical or educational expenses);
- whether the capital should be held for a fixed period after the testator's death or divided immediately into shares for the various beneficiaries (the shares may then be held for a specified time, including for the life of a beneficiary); and
- consideration should be given to the effects of the 21-year deemed disposition of capital property held in trusts pursuant to the *Income Tax Act* (Canada).

Dispositions to a Spouse or a "Spousal Trust"

The taxes which would otherwise be payable on the death of a testator (deemed disposition on capital and depreciable properties) are deferred where such property is left to the testator's spouse or to a "qualifying spousal trust" under the *Income Tax Act*. Property so transferred will be taxable on the earlier of the death of the testator's spouse and the disposition by the testator's spouse of such property.

Survivorship Clause

When property is left outright, or a bequest is made, consideration should always be given to whether it is appropriate to provide for a survivorship period. Most commonly it is used for gifts between spouses. A clause providing that the property is only to be transferred to the spouse if he or she survives the testator by a period of 30 clear days is an example of a survivorship clause.

There are primarily two reasons for using a survivorship period. First, it avoids the duplication of probate fees and other expenses connected with administering the same assets twice. For example, a testator's Will involves a gift of the residue of the estate to his spouse. As it is not uncommon for spouses to travel together, assume the two spouses are involved in a serious car accident. The testator dies en route to the hospital and his spouse is in a coma for ten days before succumbing to her injuries. If the testator's Will requires probate, probate fees will have to be paid on the value of the assets in his estate prior to the assets being transferred to the surviving spouse. When the surviving spouse dies ten days later (and assuming probate is required), the assets which she acquired from the testator's estate will also be included for the purpose of calculating probate fees payable as part of the value of her estate.

The above example also illustrates the second reason for having a survivorship period. Assume that the surviving spouse in the above example is the testator's second spouse. What may occur is a possible unintended distribution if the beneficiaries under the Will of the second spouse to die are not the same beneficiaries whom the testator intended to receive his assets. In such a situation, a survivorship clause allows the testator to direct that his family members (or other beneficiaries of his choice) receive his assets, rather than the family members/other beneficiaries of his spouse.

If the decision is made to include a survivorship period in the Will, the next step is determining an appropriate period of time. The most common periods are ten and 30 days. In our example above, if the surviving spouse had survived for 30 days, it is less likely that she would have then died as a result of the accident.

In circumstances where there is no survivorship provision and where it is impossible to determine who died first, s. 55(1) of the *SLRA* provides that the estate of each person shall be disposed of as if the person had survived the other or others.

Common Accident

A variation of the survivorship issue discussed above involves the situation where the testator and his or her spouse and children are killed in a common accident, or in circumstances where all the beneficiaries die before the estate has been fully administered. The common accident provision provides for alternate beneficiaries in the event that any portion of the testator's estate cannot vest indefeasibly in his or her spouse, children, or other beneficiaries provided for in the Will. A common accident provision may also provide for gifts of any personal property that is still a part of the estate, and for general legacies to specific individuals.

It is very important to include a common accident provision when a client has young children as the family often travels together, whether on daily errands or on family vacations. Often, a client will leave his or her estate to his or her spouse and then to his or her children if the spouse is not alive. If the client and his or her immediate family are involved in a common accident, none of the client's beneficiaries will survive the client and an intestacy will occur. Under such circumstances the client's estate will be distributed in accordance with the provisions of Part II of the *SLRA*, which may result in the client's estate being distributed among family members whom the client would not have chosen.

(c) Limitations on Freedom to Dispose of Property

As mentioned earlier, when taking instructions from a client as to the distribution of his or her estate, it is important to consider whether there are any limitations on the testator's ability to freely dispose of property. The existence of any of the following factors should be considered.

(i) Jointly-Owned Property with Right of Survivorship

As previously discussed, when assets are held jointly with a right of survivorship, the testator does not have the ability to deal with those assets in his or her Will. These assets will automatically pass, by operation of law, to the surviving joint tenant or tenants.

(ii) The *Family Law Act*

If a client is leaving all of his or her estate to his or her spouse outright, the provisions of the *FLA* do not need to be considered. However, if a client who is married intends to leave a large portion of his or her estate to someone other than his or her spouse, or plans to leave some or all his or her spouse's share of the estate in trust, it is essential to consider whether the surviving spouse may have a potential equalization claim under the *FLA*.

Pursuant to s. 5(2) of the *FLA*, when a spouse dies, if the net family property of the deceased spouse exceeds the net family property of the surviving spouse, the surviving spouse is entitled to one-half the difference between them. Therefore, the surviving spouse will only have the right to make an equalization claim if the net family property of the deceased spouse exceeds the net family property of the surviving spouse.

Briefly, net family property is defined as the value of all property owned by a spouse on the day before the date of death less debts and liabilities and less the value of property, other than the matrimonial home, that the spouse owned at the date of the marriage after deducting debts and liabilities calculated as of the date of the marriage. It is important to note that certain property is excluded from the definition of net family property.

If the deceased spouse died leaving a Will, pursuant to s. 6(1), the surviving spouse can choose to elect to receive either the entitlement under s. 5 or the gifts provided for him or her under the deceased spouse's Will. Unless the Will expressly states that the gifts under the Will are in addition to the surviving spouse's entitlement under s. 5, an election in favour of the *FLA* entitlement revokes gifts made to the surviving spouse in the Will and the Will is read as if the surviving spouse had predeceased the testator. In addition, if an election is made by the surviving spouse in favour of the *FLA* entitlement, life insurance owned by the deceased spouse and lump sum pension payments payable on the deceased spouse's death to the surviving spouse are considered credits against the surviving spouse's *FLA* entitlement unless a written declaration by the deceased spouse provides that the surviving spouse is to receive payments under the plan or policy in addition to the *FLA* entitlement, and any excess amount received from any such plan or policy is recoverable by the deceased spouse's personal representative(s).

If the deceased spouse dies without a Will, pursuant to s. 6(2) of the *FLA*, the surviving spouse has the right to elect to receive the entitlement under Part II of the *SLRA* or to receive the entitlement under s. 5.

If there is a partial intestacy, the surviving spouse has the right to elect to take both under the Will and the entitlement under the *SLRA*, or to receive the entitlement under s. 5 of the *FLA*.

An election to take the entitlement pursuant to the provisions of the *FLA* must be filed in the office of the Estate Registrar for Ontario within six months after the first spouse's death. If no election is filed within this time period, the surviving spouse will be deemed to have elected to take under the Will, or to receive any entitlement under the *SLRA*, or both, as the case may be.

In circumstances where the client wishes to leave a large portion of his or her estate to someone other than his or her spouse, or to leave the spouse's share of the estate in trust, and the client's net family property is likely to exceed his or her spouse's, the client should be advised to consider entering into a domestic agreement with his or her spouse. Without entering into an agreement, there is no guarantee that the spouse will not elect to receive the entitlement under the *FLA*, which may result in the client's estate plan being thwarted. The agreement would simply provide that neither spouse will elect to take his or her entitlement under the provisions of the *FLA* upon the death of the other spouse. Further, the agreement may include a copy of each spouse's Will, attached as a schedule, and include a provision that each spouse cannot change his or her Will without the other's consent, or alternatively that if a spouse amends his or her Will or makes a new Will, benefits of at least equal value must be provided for the other spouse. When entering into such an agreement, each spouse will require independent legal advice and be required to provide full financial disclosure to the other spouse. The agreement will ensure that the provisions of each spouse's Will will govern the distribution of their estates.

The rights of the surviving spouse to make an equalization claim under the *FLA* is presently not available to "common-law partners" which include heterosexuals living in a common-law relationship and same-sex spouses. However, the legislation limiting these rights to married spouses has been ruled unconstitutional by the Nova Scotia Court of Appeal in *Walsh v. Bona*, 5 R.F.L. (5th) 188, 2000 NSCA 53, 186 D.L.R. (4th) 50, 183 N.S.R. (2d) 74, 568 A.P.R. 74, [2000] N.S.J. No. 117, 2000 CarswellNS 112 (N.S. C.A.), additional reasons at 2000 NSCA 73, 186 D.L.R. (4th) 50 at 83, 7 R.F.L. (5th) 451, 185 N.S.R. (2d) 190, 575 A.P.R. 190, 2000 CarswellNS 159 (N.S. C.A.), leave to appeal allowed 192 N.S.R. (2d) 200 (note), 599 A.P.R. 200 (note), 267 N.R. 391 (note), 2001 CarswellNS 70, 2001 CarswellNS 71 (S.C.C.), and practitioners should be aware of further changes in this area when receiving Will instructions from clients.

(iii) Dependants' Relief

Part V of the *SLRA* provides an avenue for a dependant of a deceased to make a claim for support. The definition of a "dependant" is two-tiered. First, the dependant must be a spouse, parent, child or sibling of the deceased, and second, the dependant must be someone to whom the deceased was providing support or was under a legal obligation to provide support at the time of his or her death. For the purposes of a support claim under the *SLRA*, "spouse" includes a former spouse and a common-law spouse with whom the deceased was cohabiting continuously for a period of not less than three years, or with whom the deceased was in a relationship of some permanence if they are the natural or adoptive parents of a child. "Child" includes a grandchild and any person whom the deceased has demonstrated a settled intention to treat as a child of his or her family (other than a foster child).

An application for support must be made within six months from the date on which a Certificate of Appointment of Estate Trustee is issued. A dependant support claim is commenced by notice of application to the Superior Court of Justice in the jurisdiction where the Certificate of Appointment has been issued, along with the required supporting documents.

The service of the notice of application on the Trustees results in an automatic stay in the distribution of the estate, other than reasonable advances made to dependants who are beneficiaries of the estate. The Trustees will be personally liable for distributing assets of the estate in violation of this stay if support is ultimately awarded. An award of interim support is also possible.

The list of criteria which the court must consider in determining the amount and duration, if any, of support is extensive and provides the court with a very wide scope to determine the issue of support. In addition, certain assets are deemed to be part of the estate for the purposes of a dependant support claim which would otherwise not be so considered, such as gifts *mortis causa* (gifts made in contemplation of death), joint bank accounts held by the deceased and a third party and the proceeds of any life insurance effected on the life of, and owned by, the deceased, regardless of whether the proceeds are payable to a designated beneficiary. Because they may frustrate the intent of a testator to distribute his or her assets in a certain manner, dependant support claims must always be considered.

(iv) Contractual Obligations

Contracts which the client may have entered into during his or her lifetime may also limit his or her ability to dispose of assets. If the client has entered into any type of domestic agreement, the provisions of that agreement should be carefully reviewed before preparing or amending a Will. Domestic agreements often require that a Will provide certain benefits or assets to the other spouse.

When a client owns shares of a company, his or her ability to dispose of those shares may be affected by survivorship or buy/sell provisions in a shareholders' agreement to which the client is a party. Alternatively, the articles of a company, or an agreement, may provide limitations on the ability to transfer the shares. Similarly, the ability to dispose of an interest in a partnership may be affected by a partnership agreement.

The ability to freely dispose of real estate may be affected by a co-tenancy agreement.

(v) Other Restrictions on Alienation

In addition, consideration should be had to the following situations which may also affect the client's ability to dispose of his or her property:

- any applicable laws relating to community of property;
- limited interests such as life interest in a property, and joint bank accounts;
- franchises;
- rules of professional or business associations;
- agreements relating to any assets of the client;
- property subject to a lien or charge;
- court order following a divorce; and
- constructive/resulting trust.

10. CONCLUSION

The purpose of a client preparing a Will is to allow the client to decide by whom and among whom his or her estate will be distributed and to ensure that a proper estate plan is put into place, regardless of how simple or complex. This can only be achieved if a complete review of the client's personal and financial affairs is completed and the client is advised of any legal obligations he or she may have which may affect his or her ability to dispose of his or her estate, or part thereof. The lawyer must ensure that the Will accurately reflects the client's intentions and addresses any concerns the client may have regarding the distribution or administration of his or her estate. If the Will is prepared by a clerk it is imperative that it be reviewed by the lawyer prior to its execution and that it is executed in accordance with the formal requirements set out in the *SLRA*.

Figure 1-1: Example of Last Will and Testament

THIS IS THE LAST WILL AND TESTAMENT of me, **SUSAN JONES**, of the City of Toronto, in the Province of Ontario.

1. I revoke all prior Wills and testamentary dispositions of every nature and kind made by me.

2. I appoint my spouse, **JOHN DOE** (hereinafter referred to as "my spouse"), to be the sole Executor and Trustee of this Will, provided that if my spouse dies before or after me, but before the trusts hereof shall have terminated, or is or becomes at any time unable or unwilling to act or to continue to act in the office of Executor and Trustee, then I appoint my sister, **CAROL JONES**, and my brother, **DAVID JONES**, to be the Executors and Trustees of this Will in the place and stead of my spouse, and I declare the expression "my Trustees" used throughout this Will shall mean the Executors and Trustees for the time being and from time to time of this Will, whether original or substituted, singular or plural.

3. Unless otherwise specifically provided, any reference in this my Will to a person in terms of a relationship to another person determined by blood or marriage shall not include a person born outside marriage nor a person who comes within the description traced through another person who was born outside marriage, provided that any person who has been legally adopted shall be regarded as having been born in marriage to his or her adopting parent(s) and any person who is born outside marriage and

   (a) whose natural parents subsequently marry; or

   (b) the parent of such person who is related by blood or marriage to me or to a prospective beneficiary of this my Will, and who, in the unfettered and absolute discretion of my Trustees, during most of the minority of such person prior to such parent's death, if deceased, has demonstrated a settled intention to treat such person as his or her child,

shall be regarded as having been born in lawful wedlock to such parents or parent, as the case may be. All decisions by my Trustees, in this regard, shall be made by them in their absolute discretion and shall be final and binding upon all concerned.

4. I direct that:

   (a) any succession, legacy, gift or inheritance, whether as to income or capital, to which any person is or shall become entitled in accordance with the provisions of this my Will or any property substituted therefor ("Substituted Property");

   (b) any fruits, revenues or income at any time subsequently derived from such succession, legacy, gift, inheritance or Substituted Property;

   (c) any accretion in value to such succession, legacy, gift, inheritance or Substituted Property; and

   (d) any property into which property referred to in Paragraphs (a) through (c), above, can be traced,

— continued next page

Figure 1-1: Example of Last Will and Testament (continued)

shall be excluded from such person's net family property, as such term is defined in the *Family Law Act,* R.S.O. 1990, c. F.3, as amended from time to time, and shall not fall into any community of property or partnership of acquests which may exist between any such person and his or her spouse or consort under the provisions of the *Civil Code of Quebec*, or under the laws of any other jurisdiction, but shall remain the private property of such person, free from the control or interests of his or her spouse or consort.

5.   I give the whole of my property of every nature and kind and wheresoever situate, including any property over which I may have a general power of appointment, to my said Trustees upon the following trusts:

(a)   I direct my Trustees to deal with all my articles of personal, domestic, household and garden use or ornament belonging to me at my death, including without limitation, consumable stores, automobiles and accessories thereto (hereinafter referred to as "my Personal Property") in the following manner:

(i)   If my spouse survives me for a period of 30 clear days, I direct my Trustees to deliver to my spouse as my spouse's absolute property all of my Personal Property and notwithstanding the foregoing condition of survivorship, during the said period, my spouse shall have use of all of my Personal Property.

(ii)   If my spouse predeceases me, or survives me but dies within a period of 30 clear days after my death, on the death of the survivor of me and my spouse I direct my Trustees to transfer and deliver my Personal Property to those of my children who are then alive to be divided between or among them in such manner as they may agree or, failing agreement or in the event that any of my children should then be under the age of majority, in such manner as my Trustees in their absolute and uncontrolled discretion consider reasonably equal. If any of my children should become entitled to any articles of my Personal Property while under the age of majority, I authorize my Trustees to transfer and deliver the articles to which such child is entitled to such child at such time or times as my Trustees in their absolute discretion consider advisable and to accept the receipt of such child as a sufficient discharge therefor notwithstanding that such child may be under the age of majority when the said articles or any of them are so transferred and delivered, or to retain the articles to which such child is entitled and to store the same and to transfer and deliver such articles to such child when such child attains the age of majority, or to sell the said articles and hold the proceeds of such sale for such child, or to deal with some of the said articles in one way and some in another as my Trustees in their absolute and uncontrolled discretion consider advisable. I direct my Trustees to pay all necessary packing, insurance and delivery charges, if any, incurred in connection with giving effect to the provisions of this Subparagraph, and also the costs (if any) of insuring and storing the same pending such delivery out of the share of the residue of my estate held for such child pursuant to Subparagraph 5(e)(ii) of this Will.

(b)   To exercise one or more of the following powers in the administration of my estate:

— continued next page

*Figure 1-1: **Example of Last Will and Testament** (continued)*

>   (i)   to retain any asset of my estate regardless of whether such asset is personalty, realty, moveable, immoveable, intangible or of any other form whatsoever, (notwithstanding that it may not be in the form of an investment in which trustees are authorized to invest trust funds and whether or not there is a liability attached to any such asset) for such length of time as my Trustees in their absolute discretion deem advisable, including the entire term of the administration of my estate. Provided that it is not intended that this power contradict or delay any direction or authority to my Trustees to distribute any asset or portion of my estate to any beneficiary at any particular time;
>
>   (ii) to sell, call in and convert into money any asset of my estate not consisting of money, whether such asset is personalty, realty, moveable, immoveable, intangible or of any other form whatsoever, at such time or times, in such manner and upon such terms, and either for cash or credit, or part cash and part credit, as my Trustees in their absolute discretion decide upon;
>
>   (iii) to partition or appropriate, and distribute in specie, any part of my estate in its then actual condition or state of investment in or towards the partial or total satisfaction of the interest of any beneficiary in my estate. No beneficiary shall have the right to insist that my Trustees first sell, and convert any asset of my estate into cash or any other form of investment prior to satisfying such beneficiary's interest in my estate. All decisions by my Trustees, in this regard, shall be made by them in their absolute discretion, and shall be final and binding upon all of the beneficiaries of my estate. And for these purposes, my Trustees shall have the power to determine the value of my estate and any part or parts thereof in any manner that my Trustees shall see fit. Any such valuation as aforesaid shall be made as of the date of distribution of any such part of my estate and, notwithstanding any fluctuation in market value, shall be final and binding upon all the beneficiaries of my estate, notwithstanding that one or more of my Trustees may be beneficially interested in the property or any part thereof so valued.
>
> In addition, the following provisions shall govern the administration of my estate:
>
>   (iv) no reversionary interest shall be sold prior to falling into possession unless my Trustees in their absolute discretion see reason to the contrary; and
>
>   (v)   no property not in fact producing income shall be treated as producing income.
>
> (c) To pay out of and charge to the capital of my general estate, my just debts, funeral and testamentary expenses and all succession duties and estate, inheritance and death taxes, whether imposed by this or any other jurisdiction whatsoever that may be payable in connection with any property passing on my death or any property which does not actually pass on my death but is merely deemed so to pass by any governing law (but not including any property transferred to or acquired by a purchaser or transferee upon or after my death pursuant to any agreement with respect to such property) or in connection with any insurance on my life and/or annuities on my life or any gift or benefit given or conferred by me either during my lifetime or by survivorship or by this my Will, and whether such duties and taxes be payable in respect of estates or

— continued next page

*Figure 1-1: **Example of Last Will and Testament*** (continued)

> interests which fall into possession at my death or at any subsequent time; and I hereby authorize my Trustees in their uncontrolled discretion to commute or prepay any such taxes or duties. Any duties or taxes so paid shall be treated as an ordinary debt of my estate.
>
> (d) I direct my Trustees to pay or transfer the residue of my estate to my spouse, if he survives me for a period of 30 clear days. Notwithstanding the foregoing condition of survivorship, during the said period my Trustees may pay to or for my spouse such amount or amounts out of the capital of the residue of my estate as they in their absolute discretion consider advisable without him being bound to the repayment thereof under any circumstances.
>
> (e) If my spouse predeceases me, or survives me but dies within a period of 30 clear days after the date of my death, on the death of the survivor of me and my spouse (hereinafter referred to as the "Division Date"), I direct my Trustees to divide the residue of my estate into as many equal shares as may be necessary to carry out the following provisions and to deal with such shares as follows:
>
>> (i) My Trustees shall pay or transfer one (1) of such equal shares to each child of mine alive at the Division Date who has then attained the age of thirty-five (35) years, for his or her own use absolutely.
>>
>> (ii) My Trustees shall set aside and hold one (1) of such equal shares for each child of mine alive at the Division Date who has not then attained the age of thirty-five (35) years. If such child has attained the age of 25 years but has not attained the age of 30 years at the Division Date one-quarter (1/4) of such share shall be paid or transferred to him or her. If such child has attained the age of 30 years at the Division Date one-half (2) of such share shall be paid or transferred to him or her. My Trustees may from time to time pay to or apply for the benefit of such child for whom such share is being held the whole or such part of the annual net income derived from such share or from the part thereof from time to time remaining in trust and all or such part or parts of the capital thereof as my Trustees in their absolute and uncontrolled discretion from time to time consider necessary or advisable for the benefit of such child. If in any year that my Trustees hold such share or any part thereof, any portion of the annual net income is not paid to or applied for the benefit of such child, such portion shall be accumulated by my Trustees and added in the following year to the capital of such share and dealt with as part thereof, provided after the expiration of the maximum period for accumulation of income permitted by law, if my Trustees are then holding such share or any part thereof, they shall thereafter pay or apply the whole of the annual net income to or for such child in such annual or more frequent instalments as my Trustees consider advisable. One-quarter (1/4) of such share or of the part thereof then remaining shall be paid or transferred to such child when he or she attains the age of 25 years after the Division Date; one-quarter (1/4) of such share then remaining shall be paid or transferred to such child when he or she attains the age of 30 years after the Division Date; and the remainder of such share shall be paid or transferred to such child when he or she attains the age of thirty-five (35) years. If such child dies before becoming entitled to receive the whole of his or her share my Trustees shall divide

— continued next page

Figure 1-1: Example of Last Will and Testament (continued)

> such share or the part thereof then remaining among such deceased child's issue in equal shares per stirpes; provided if such child dies without leaving issue surviving him or her, such share or the part thereof then remaining shall be divided among my issue in equal shares per stirpes; provided that the portion accruing to any other child of mine then alive and under the age of thirty-five (35) years shall be added to and dealt with as an accretion to the share held by my Trustees for such other child pursuant to the terms of this Subparagraph 5(e)(ii).
>
> (iii) If any child of mine should predecease the Division Date leaving issue alive at the Division Date, my Trustees shall divide one (1) of such equal shares among such deceased child's issue in equal shares per stirpes.
>
> (f) If at any time after my death, any portion of my estate shall not otherwise vest indefeasibly in possession in my spouse or one or more of my issue pursuant to the foregoing provisions, then on the date when it is determined that such portion of my estate will fail so to vest (hereinafter referred to as the "Final Distribution Date") I direct my Trustees to divide such portion into as many equal shares as may be necessary to carry out the following provisions and to deal with such shares as follows:
>
> (i) One (1) of such equal shares shall be paid or transferred to my brother, **STEPHEN JONES,** if he is alive on the Final Distribution Date, provided that if my brother predeceases the Final Distribution Date leaving issue then alive, such share shall be divided among my deceased brother's issue in equal shares per stirpes.
>
> (ii) One (1) of such equal shares shall be paid or transferred to my spouse's sister, **MARY DOE**, if she is alive on the Final Distribution Date, provided that if my spouse's sister predeceases the Final Distribution Date leaving issue then alive, such share shall be divided among my spouse's deceased sister's issue in equal shares per stirpes.
>
> 6. Except as may be otherwise hereinbefore provided, if any person should become entitled indefeasibly to any share in my estate before attaining the age of majority, the share of such person and any income derived therefrom may be held and kept invested by my Trustees, and the income and capital, or so much thereof as my Trustees, in their absolute discretion consider necessary or advisable, may be used for the benefit of such person until he or she attains the age of majority.
>
> 7. I authorize my Trustees to make any payments or transfers for any person under the age of majority or otherwise under disability to a parent or guardian or person acting as such of such person, whose receipt shall be a sufficient discharge of my Trustees in respect of such payments.
>
> 8. I hereby declare that my Trustees when making investments for my estate shall not be limited to investments authorized by law for trustees but may make any investments which in their uncontrolled discretion they consider to be to the advantage of my estate and my said Trustees shall not be liable for any loss that may happen to my estate in connection with any such investments made by them in good faith.

— continued next page

Figure 1-1: Example of Last Will and Testament (continued)

9. My said Trustees shall have the right to let or lease any real or leasehold property forming part of my estate, from month to month, or from year to year or for any term of years, subject to such covenants and conditions as they shall think fit, to accept surrenders of leases and tenancies, to expend money in repairs, improvements and, generally, to manage any such property. My Trustees shall also have the right to renew and keep renewed any mortgage or mortgages upon any real estate forming part of my estate, or any part thereof, to borrow money on any such real estate upon the security of any mortgage or mortgages, and to pay off any mortgage or mortgages which may be in existence at any time forming part of my estate.

10. I authorize and empower my Trustees to lend the whole or any part of my estate upon any security which they may deem sufficient or upon no security whatever; to enter into guarantees or indemnifications for the benefit of the beneficiaries of this my Will and persons, firms or corporations other than the beneficiaries of this my Will and to give security therefor as my Trustees may in their discretion decide; and to renew and keep renewed such guarantees and indemnifications as my Trustees see fit; to borrow money from themselves individually or from others, either without security or upon the security of any of the property, real or personal entrusted to them or from time to time held by them under this my Will, for such purposes and upon such terms and conditions as they shall deem advisable, and without limiting the generality of the foregoing, for the payment of taxes, debts, duties, legacies or expenses and to mortgage, pledge, hypothecate or otherwise encumber, any or all of such property to secure the repayment of money borrowed; and to extend or modify any such encumbrance.

11. I authorize and empower my Trustees to compromise, settle, waive or pay, as the case may be, any claim or claims at any time owing or alleged to be owing by my estate, or which my estate may have against others, for such consideration or no consideration, and upon such terms and conditions as my Trustees may deem advisable, and to refer to arbitration all such claims if my Trustees deem same advisable.

12. I authorize any one or more of the beneficiaries of this my Will, (notwithstanding that such beneficiary or beneficiaries may be a Trustee or Trustees of this my Will), to purchase any part or parts of my estate, real or personal, either at public auction or by private contract, provided in the latter case that the sale shall be conducted by my Trustees (or by the disinterested Trustee or Trustees of this my Will, in the event that a beneficiary or beneficiaries so purchasing is also a Trustee or Trustees of this my Will), and shall be at such price or prices and subject to such terms and conditions and either for cash or credit or for part cash and part credit as the Trustee or Trustees of this my Will conducting the sale shall consider fair and reasonable.

13. I hereby declare that my Trustees shall not be liable for any loss that may happen to my estate or to any beneficiary hereunder resulting from the exercise by my Trustees in good faith of any discretion given them in this my Will.

— continued next page

Figure 1-1: Example of Last Will and Testament (continued)

14. Notwithstanding any of the trusts, terms and conditions herein contained, my Trustees shall have the power at any time, if they in their absolute discretion deem it advisable so to do, to settle by any irrevocable deed or deeds the whole of my estate upon such other trustee or trustees as my Trustees in their absolute discretion shall determine, whether such trustee or trustees are or are not resident or domiciled in Canada, for the benefit of the same beneficiary or beneficiaries herein and upon the same trusts, terms and conditions as are contained herein, including, without limiting the generality of the foregoing, any provisions for the respective advancement and maintenance and education of the beneficiaries herein, save only for such changes of the trusts, terms and conditions hereof as may be required for the proper administration of my estate in accordance with the proper law of any such settlement or for the purpose of complying with the relevant laws, including any rule against perpetuities or accumulations, as determined by the proper law of such settlement; and upon such settlement the trusts herein provided shall forthwith cease and determine.

15. I give to my Trustees full, absolute and unfettered discretion from time to time and at any time or times to make or not to make any election or elections, determinations, distributions and/or allocations for the purposes of the *Income Tax Act* (Canada), R.S.C. 1985, c. 1 (5th Supp.) or any similar legislation of any province or other jurisdiction in force from time to time as they in their absolute discretion deem to be in the best interests of my estate and/or the beneficiaries, whether or not such election or elections, determinations, distributions and/or allocations may or would have the effect of conferring an advantage on any one or more of the beneficiaries or could otherwise be considered but for the foregoing as not being an impartial exercise by my Trustees of their duties hereunder or as not being the maintaining of an even hand among the beneficiaries. Where any specific funds, shares or residue are created under this my Will my Trustees shall have the absolute power to determine which specific assets shall form such fund, share or residue, as the case may be, unless otherwise expressly provided in my Will. I specifically exonerate my Trustees from any responsibility with respect to any such elections, determinations, distributions and/or allocations if they act bona fide in the exercise of such power.

16. This my Will may contain one or more bequests to a class or classes of persons, or to particular persons, subject to a provision that if any of the said persons is not alive at the date of my death or other relevant date, then the gift to which such deceased person would otherwise be entitled if then alive shall instead be given to one or more other specified beneficiaries. Unless otherwise specifically indicated, I hereby declare that, if any such person is not alive at the date of execution of this my Will, he or she shall be deemed to be so alive at the date of such execution for purposes of construing any such provision and consequently giving effect to the relevant substitutionary gifts.

17. I authorize any or all of my Trustees to take and transfer at reasonable intervals from the income and/or capital of my estate amounts on account of compensation which such Trustees reasonably anticipate will be requested at the end of the accounting period in progress, either upon the audit of the estate accounts or on approval by the adult beneficiaries of my estate.

— continued next page

Figure 1-1: Example of Last Will and Testament (continued)

If the amount subsequently awarded on court audit or agreed to by the beneficiaries is less than the amount taken, the excess shall be repaid to my estate without interest.

18. If my spouse predeceases me and if I die before any child of mine has attained the age of majority, I appoint my sister, **CAROL JONES**, to have custody of the person of such child and act as the guardian of the property of such child. It is my wish that before the expiration of 90 days from the date of my death the person who I have herein appointed apply to the court of competent jurisdiction to have custody of the person of such child and act as the guardian of the property of such child pursuant to the provisions of the *Children's Law Reform Act*, R.S.O. 1990, c. c. 12, as from time to time amended, without being required to give any bond or security.

IN TESTIMONY WHEREOF I have to this my last Will and Testament, written upon this and twelve (12) preceding pages of paper, subscribed my name this _____ day of _____, 2001.

SIGNED, PUBLISHED AND DECLARED)
by the said Testatrix, **SUSAN JONES**, as and)
for her Last Will and Testament, in the pres-)
ence of us, both present at the same time, who)
at her request, in her presence, and in the pres-)
ence of each other have hereunto subscribed) _____
our names as witnesses.) **SUSAN JONES**
)
)

_____ _____
Signature   Signature

_____ _____
Name   Name

_____ _____
Address   Address

2

PRIOR TO THE GRANT

Karen M. Gibbs

1. Differing Roles of the Personal Representative and Solicitor
   (a) Personal Representative's Responsibilities
   (b) Solicitor's Responsibilities
2. Location of Will
3. Locating Assets
4. Locating Liabilities
5. To Obtain a Court Grant or Not
   (a) Real Estate
       (i) Real Estate Registered under the Registry System
       (ii) Real Estate Registered under the Land Titles System
   (b) Shareholdings
       (i) Private Corporations
       (ii) Public Corporations
   (c) Money on Deposit
   (d) Safety Deposit Box
   (e) Canada Savings Bonds
   (f) Other Assets
6. Valuing the Estate
7. Intestacy
   (a) Distribution on an Intestacy
   (b) Who is Entitled to Apply as Estate Trustee Without a Will
   (c) Posting Security
8. Forms
   Figure 2-1: Letter to Solicitor re: Location of Deceased's Will and Authorization of Personal Representative
   Figure 2-2: General Letter to a Bank
   Figure 2-3: Letter to the Bank of Canada re: Search
   Figure 2-4: Letter to the Bank where Deceased Held Assets
   Figure 2-5: Letter to Transfer Agent Requesting Waiver of Requirement of the Court Certificate
   Figure 2-6: Notarial Certificate
   Figure 2-7: Sample of Information Required for Statement of Assets

1. DIFFERING ROLES OF THE PERSONAL REPRESENTATIVE AND SOLICITOR

It is the personal representative's responsibility to carry out the terms of the deceased's Will, or in the case of an intestacy to gather in and distribute the estate pursuant to the relevant statutes. In order to do this, it is necessary first to determine the deceased's assets, as well as all liabilities that have to be paid, before any distributions set out in the Will or required by statute can be made.

Your first contact with the personal representative may be almost immediately after the death. This is often the best-case scenario, especially if your office is holding the Last Will and Testament of the deceased for safekeeping. One of the worst mistakes a testator can make is not informing the named executor or executors that they are named as such in the Will and of the whereabouts of the Will. If the deceased's true wishes are to be carried out, the executors must be put in a position as quickly as possible to manage the estate. Often burial wishes and the donation of body parts are contained in the Will or in a memorandum provided to the solicitor. However, the executor does not have an opportunity to consider these wishes if not advised in advance by the deceased regarding such wishes or the Will's location. As there are very strict guidelines and time restraints on the donation of organs, it is unfortunate if the personal representative is unable to fulfil the deceased's wishes only through not being aware of them in sufficient time. It is also of great assistance to the executor if the testator has advised whether he owns a funeral plot.

It should be noted that where there is an executor, it is the executor's responsibility to arrange the funeral and burial. In certain circumstances, the executor is not an immediate family member, and the solicitor may have to explain this to the family. If the funeral has been prearranged and prepaid this lifts a certain amount of responsibility from the executor. If the deceased had limited assets and the executor chooses a very costly and elaborate funeral, the executor can be held personally liable should it be determined that there are insufficient assets to satisfy the creditors of the deceased. However, in the case where the deceased's assets may not be sufficient to cover his liabilities, the executor is allowed to arrange and pay for a simple funeral and burial.

Where there is an intestacy, the funeral would usually be arranged by the next of kin.

Generally, after the funeral has taken place, the solicitor will advise the personal representative of his responsibilities as well as those of the solicitor and, if available, they will review the contents of the deceased's Will.

The personal representative should be advised that one of his most important duties, and one that should not be taken lightly, is the preservation of the deceased's assets. It is important that all relevant parties be advised as soon as possible of the death, and that new instructions be given regarding assets as a result of the death. For example, if the deceased held mortgages and has been receiving monthly payments, it is important that the mortgagor be contacted, advised of the death and given the new address, if there is a change, for forwarding all future payments.

(a) Personal Representative's Responsibilities

- Locate Will (see Location of Will, below);
- Arrange for the donation of organs if directed by testator;
- Arrange for the funeral and burial, together with memorial, where appropriate;
- Determine assets and liabilities and make all necessary contacts in order to preserve the assets;
- Retain a solicitor for advice;

- File tax returns, pay taxes owing and obtain appropriate clearance certificates and/or release;
- Maintain proper accounting records and statements;
- Distribute assets as directed by Will;
- Invest assets for establishment of on-going trust if so directed by Will;
- Locate inventory, value and secure the assets;
- Regular reports to beneficiaries.

(b) Solicitor's Responsibilities

- Review the contents of the Will with the personal representative. Determine if it is a valid Will or advise how the Will might be located (See Chapter 1 for Will requirements);
- Provide a sufficient number of notarial copies of the Will (see Figure 2-6)* and notarial copies of proof of death to the personal representative to enable the personal representative to start delving into the deceased's assets;
- Assist the personal representative in locating assets, preparing Statement of Assets (see Figure 2-7) and determining liabilities;
- Explain how the administration of an estate usually proceeds;
- Complete the necessary forms, including applications for the Court Certificate and Canada Pension Plan Death and Survivor Benefits, and insurance claim forms and the forms necessary to arrange for the transfer of the estate assets and distributions to beneficiaries, including releases;
- If the personal representative knows of a financial institution where the deceased held a bank account, explain that although access to the deceased's money will not generally be granted prior to a Court Certificate being issued or alternate arrangements being made, the institution will normally allow two bank drafts to be issued; one for the funeral costs and one for the cost of the application to be made to court for probate;
- Consider the *Family Law Act*, R.S.O. 1990, c. F.3, with the personal representative;
- Compile client information sheet and all required information regarding the deceased. As you become familiar with the forms generally required in administering estates you will begin to realize the very detailed nature of the information required. The information being obtained should generally include the following (however, the material itself may take several meetings with the client in order to compile):
    — all information required to complete the application for the Court Certificate;
    — all pension information, including deceased's social insurance number; and
    — information as to the deceased's assets which should be very detailed and include interest rates earned, when interest is payable and maturity dates where applicable;
- As the solicitor will be looked to for guidance, it is a good practice at this point to

---
* All figures referred to are located at the end of this chapter.

provide the personal representative with a letter detailing the different steps in an estate's administration including what the personal representative's obligations and responsibilities are and where it is appropriate for the solicitor to assist. The letter may include the following:
— detailed summary of the Last Will and Testament;
— summary of estate administration, the *Trustee Act*, R.S.O. 1990, c. T.23, and how it is applicable to personal representatives;
— review of the *Family Law Act* and how it is applicable;
— summary of when and why the personal representative will be required to obtain a Court Grant;
— explanation of preparing inventory of assets and determining liabilities and advertisement for creditors;
— possible benefits received under the Canada Pension Plan;
— how different assets will be dealt with;
— the requirement of filing income tax returns and the different returns to be filed;
— the concept of executor's compensation and when estate accounts are passed by the court together with the special format required for these accounts;
— the law firm's billing practice, and advice that separate bills may be rendered to the executor personally, not the estate, should the solicitor be doing what is considered executor's work as opposed to solicitor's work;
• Arrange to appear in Court to pass executor's accounts, if necessary.

2. LOCATION OF WILL

As previously mentioned, the testator does not always advise where the Will can be located in the event of death.

Hopefully, the Will is in your law firm's vault for safekeeping. However, you may not have it, or, if you do, it may be felt that the Will is not in fact the Last Will and Testament of the deceased. If this is the case the following possibilities should be considered:

• Is it with the deceased's personal papers at the deceased's home?
• Is it with the executor or a family member for safekeeping?
• Could it be at another solicitor's office (see Figure 2-1)? A family member may be of assistance in advising of other solicitors with whom the deceased may have had dealings;
• Did the deceased have a safety deposit box? This can often be a difficult situation, as the executor is entitled to enter a safety deposit box for the purpose of listing the contents. However, often a financial institution will advise that they will not release the contents of the box until the Court Grant is obtained. Obviously, the application to the court cannot be made until the testamentary document is received, so a certain amount of tact may be required to obtain it. As the original Will is not available, the bank will want to be satisfied that it is appropriate for them to open the box for the person claiming to believe they are the executor.

- Is it on deposit with the Superior Court of Justice? Rule 74.02 of the Rules of Civil Procedure, R.R.O. 1990, Reg. 194, provides the circumstances in which the court is to act as a depository for a Will or codicil. For further discussion of depositing Wills with the court, see Chapter 3.

If no Will is located through the above, the solicitor should consider placing an advertisement in the Ontario Reports.

It should be the practice of a law firm to check their Wills vaults whenever these advertisements appear in the Ontario Reports.

3. LOCATING ASSETS

In a perfect world the personal representative is aware of the assets and liabilities of the deceased and where they can be located. This is the case if one of the personal representatives was the deceased's accountant or financial advisor or if the deceased maintained an up-to-date listing of assets and liabilities. However, as this is generally not the case, the solicitor's office will often be requested to assist or provide guidance.

The following are often considered when trying to locate assets:

- Review deceased's income tax returns for the last couple of years to determine the sources of all income. This will also often provide you with additional information such as the broker used by the deceased, and banking information.
- Review all deceased's papers (both at deceased's home and office). This can often be quite tedious and time-consuming but can turn up previously unknown assets.
- Search of banks where it is thought the deceased may have had a relationship (see Figure 2-2).
- A search can also be done through the Bank of Canada if it is suspected that there have been misplaced Canada Savings Bonds or if old bank passbooks are found for bank accounts that may have become dormant (see Figure 2-3).
- Ask any asset holders to check and make sure the deceased did not have any other assets with them. For example, when writing to the bank in connection with a bank account, you might ask them to check for other assets such as other accounts, guaranteed investment certificates, bank deposit certificates and safety deposit boxes (see Figure 2-4).

4. LOCATING LIABILITIES

It is also important to determine the liabilities of the estate. This will include determining any payments made by the deceased that may not have been honoured by the bank as yet. If the deceased was the sole owner of a home and there was a mortgage on the home, it is important to contact the mortgage company as soon as possible to determine when the payments are due and if they have any postdated cheques. It is also important to advise the creditor if the payments will not be made pending obtaining the Court Certificate. However the personal representative must be aware that it is his or her duty to arrange for the payment of debts as quickly as possible. If the personal representative does not deal with these matters diligently, assets can be lost. Again, using the example of the deceased being the sole owner of a home, if appropriate arrangements are not made, the mortgage company could commence sale proceedings as a result of the payments not being made.

5. TO OBTAIN A COURT GRANT OR NOT

As will be seen in Chapter 3, the cost of applying for the grant of a Certificate of Appointment of Estate Trustee with a Will (or Without a Will) can be substantial as it is based on the value of the deceased's assets. For that reason, just as someone preparing a Will will often use certain estate planning techniques to avoid the need to obtain a Court Grant at death, we will often attempt to administer an estate without having obtained the grant by dealing with the various asset holders. All assets do not require the Court Certificate or grant to enable the personal representative to deal with them. However, where someone has died without a Will, the Certificate of Appointment of Estate Trustee without a Will is almost always required.

Assets held "on joint account with right of survivorship" can be transferred to the surviving joint owner upon providing proof of death and without any Court Certificate.

The following is a listing of certain types of assets which could be registered solely in the deceased's name, each of which would have to be considered when determining whether the certificate of appointment will be necessary:

(a) Real Estate

(i) Real Estate Registered under the Registry System

The *Registry Act*, R.S.O. 1990, c. R.20, s. 53(a), provides as follows:

> 53.(1) A will shall be registered by registering,
> (a) the original will or a notarial copy of it with,
> (i) in the case of a will that is not a holograph will,
> (A) a statement by one of the subscribing witnesses to the will proving the due execution of it by the testator,
> (B) a statement by a person well acquainted with the testator attesting to the signature of the testator on the will, or
> (C) a notarial copy of a statement described in sub-subclause (A) or (B),
> (ii) in the case of a holograph will,
> (A) a statement by a person well acquainted with the testator attesting to the handwriting and the signature of the testator on the will, or
> (B) a notarial copy of a statement described in sub-subclause (A), and
> (iii) one of the following:
> 1. A statement that the testator died on or about a specified date, made by any person who has personal knowledge of that fact.
> 1.1 A notarial copy of a statement described in paragraph 1.
> 2. A death certificate under the *Vital Statistics Act* in respect of the death of the testator or a notarial copy of the certificate.
> 3. A certificate in respect of the death of the testator issued by a funeral director who has provided funeral services in respect of the death or a notarial copy of the certificate;

PRIOR TO THE GRANT 45

If it is determined that the grant is not required for any other asset, it is therefore possible to register a copy of the Will and proof of death on title pursuant to the above to carry out the wishes of the deceased without a Court Certificate.

Any properties located in Ontario under the Registry System are being moved to the Land Titles System.

(ii) Real Estate Registered under the Land Titles System

Pursuant to the *Land Titles Act*, R.S.O. 1990, c. L.5, it is necessary in the case of an estate for the Estate Trustee to file a transmission application to transmit the property into the Estate Trustee's name. However, it is possible in certain circumstances to transmit the property without the need for the Certificate of Appointment of the Estate Trustee. The waiver is subject to the value of the estate being under the prescribed value, which amount may change from time to time by regulation. This amount is currently $25,000. It would be very rare today to find an estate valued at $25,000 or less that has an interest in real estate.

If jointly held property is located in Land Titles, it is necessary to file an application under the *Land Titles Act* to delete the name of the deceased joint tenant.

However, in dealing with real estate held as an asset of an estate one should remember s. 9(1) of the *Estates Administration Act*, R.S.O. 1990, c. E.22, provides as follows:

> **9.**(1) Real property not disposed of, conveyed to, divided or distributed among the persons beneficially entitled thereto under section 17 by the personal representative within three years after the death of the deceased is, subject to the *Land Titles Act* in the case of land registered under that Act and subject to subsections 53(3) and (5) of the *Registry Act*, and subject as hereinafter provided, at the expiration of that period, whether probate or letters of administration have or have not been taken, thenceforth vested in the persons beneficially entitled thereto under the will or upon the intestacy or their assigns without any conveyance by the personal representative, unless such personal representative, if any, has signed and registered, in the proper land registry office, a caution in Form 1, and, if a caution is so registered, the real property mentioned therein does not so vest for three years from the time of the registration of the caution or of the last caution if more than one was registered.

After three years have passed from the date of death, if no power of sale in favour of the personal representative exists in the deceased's Will, and no caution was registered by the personal representative, then the property may vest in the beneficiary pursuant to the above and they can then apply to be registered as owners, upon filing the necessary documents, without filing the Certificate Appointment of Estate Trustee With a Will.

If the property in question has been converted to the Land Titles System from the Registry System, there is an exemption for the requirement of obtaining the Certificate of Appointment of Estate Trustee if it is a first registration after the conversion and certain requirements are met. A supporting Affidavit will be required by the Land Titles Office and a query should be made to the Director of Titles.

(b) Shareholdings

Notwithstanding very small monetary values that are set out in the *Business Corporations Act*, R.S.O. 1990, c. B.16, that allow shares held by a deceased to be transferred without the requirement of a Court Certificate, it is possible in certain circumstances when the value of the shares are over the limit to obtain the waiver of the requirement for the certificate.

(i) Private Corporations

A letter should be forwarded to the person maintaining the minute books for the corporation, often a solicitor, explaining why it is not desirous to obtain the Court Certificate. If the transfer is approved you are generally required to provide the standard estate transfer documents (see Chapter 4 on Estate Administration) which will be amended to reflect that no certificate was obtained.

(ii) Public Corporations

The practice is similar when dealing with public corporations. However, the letter (see Figure 2-5) will be sent to the transfer agent for the corporation. Transfer agents generally have certain limits they have set wherein they will allow transfers to take place without the Court Certificate. The transfer agent will ask for a bond of indemnity to be posted which will cost the estate a one-time premium based on the value of the shares.

(c) Money on Deposit

Each of the chartered banks has set a maximum amount of value of assets it will release without obtaining a court grant. This amount is generally very low. However, the final determination of whether a bank will allow the payment out of assets without the certificate being obtained lies with the bank manager or, often, the head office of the bank, so it is always wise to ask the bank to consider your request when it is desired that the cost of the court application be avoided.

The personal representative should be advised that, even if the bank agrees to release the funds without a court application, it may require a form of indemnification from the beneficiary and/or the personal representative. Personal representatives may not feel comfortable under certain circumstances, especially when dealing with a non-family member, to arrange for the payment out of funds and then be held responsible should it be determined subsequently that there was a subsequent Will, and different beneficiaries are designated.

A second hurdle may be encountered after having obtained the waiver by the bank of the requirement of the certificate: the need to open an estate bank account in order to deposit all the monies received on behalf of the estate, attend to the payment of all liabilities and arrange for all distributions under the Will.

(d) Safety Deposit Box

When a request is sent to the bank to determine if the bank accounts and other deposits held with its branch may be released without the certificate, a request to empty the safety deposit box should also be included. However, you must remember that you will have to make a similar request for the waiver of the requirement of the Court Certificate in connection with each of the items held in the box (*e.g.*, transfer agents in connection with shares held in public corporations).

(e) Canada Savings Bonds

The Bank of Canada has set the following limits for the transfer of Canada Savings Bonds and Government of Canada Bonds in an estate without requiring the Court Certificate:

- If the bonds are to be transferred to a spouse, $200,000 face value. As you will see later, this amount is equivalent to a spouse's preferential share under the *Succession Law Reform Act*, R.S.O. 1990, c. S.26, as amended (the *"SLRA"*), s. 45.
- If the bonds are to be transferred to someone other than a spouse, $20,000 face value.

(f) Other Assets

In the case of any other type of asset located (but not listed) above, a letter should go to the institution requesting the waiver of the requirement of obtaining the Court Certificate.

6. VALUING THE ESTATE

When determining the value of the estate for purposes of either determining the cost of obtaining the Court Certificate or when completing the application for the certificate, the values used are as at the date of death. You do not include the value of insurance payable to a named beneficiary or assigned for value or property held jointly and therefore passing by right of survivorship. You also do not include the value of real estate located outside the Province of Ontario.

It is also important to realize that when determining the value for purposes of the court application, the only debt that is to be deducted from the gross value of the assets is any mortgage held against real estate. In other words, the value used in the application for real estate is the equity held in the property. This does not apply to any assets other than real estate.

As you can see from the above, the cost of obtaining the waiver of the requirement of the Court Certificate can be high, both with additional legal fees and administrative requirements requested by the different organizations being dealt with. The personal representative should be made aware of these costs which they will have to weigh against the fees charged by the court for the Court Certificate.

7. INTESTACY

When a person dies without a will, the person is said to have died intestate. The person who applies for the Certificate of the Court is known as an administrator. One distinct difference between the role of an executor and an administrator, is that an executor takes his authority from the Will, and upon the death of the testator steps into that role, but the administrator requires the Certificate of the Court from which to derive his authority.

(a) Distribution on an Intestacy

Part II of the *SLRA* provides the guidelines for administering an estate on an "intestacy". The distribution is as follows:

1. If the deceased is survived by only the spouse, the entire estate goes to the spouse;
2. If the deceased is survived by a spouse and issue,
   (a) the first $200,000 goes to the spouse after the payment of debts. This is known as the "preferential share".
   (b) the remainder of the estate is divided equally between the spouse and child, if there is only one child.
   (c) If the deceased is survived by more than one child, the spouse receives the first $200,000 remaining after payment of debts and the remainder is paid one-third to the spouse and two-thirds is divided among the children. If a child has predeceased a parent but left issue, the deceased child's interest is divided among that child's issue equally.
3. If the deceased is survived by only his or her children, the estate is divided among the children equally. If one of the intestate's children has predeceased the parent but left issue, the deceased child's share goes among the deceased child's issue equally.
4. If the deceased died leaving no spouse or issue, the estate is distributed as follows:
   (a) if survived by one or both parents the estate is paid to both parents or the surviving parent;
   (b) if no parent has survived the deceased, then the estate is distributed among the brothers and sisters. If any of the brothers and sisters predeceased the deceased, then that brother or sister's share shall be distributed among that brother or sister's children equally;
   (c) if no parent or brother or sister survived the deceased, then the estate is distributed among the nephews and nieces equally;
   (d) if none of the above survive the deceased, the estate is distributed among "the next of kin of equal degree of consanguinity to the intestate equally without representation";[1]
   (e) if there are no next of kin the estate goes to the Crown.

Under s. 47(9) of the *SLRA*, "descendants and relatives of the deceased conceived before and born alive after the death of the deceased shall inherit as if they had been born in the lifetime of the deceased and had survived him or her."

As it is possible to have a partial intestacy on an estate, one must remember that a spouse's preferential share on an intestacy is reduced by the value of the assets received under the Will.

---

[1] *SLRA*, s. 47(6).

PRIOR TO THE GRANT 49

(b) Who is Entitled to Apply as Estate Trustee Without a Will

Again, reference is to Part II of the *SLRA*. The right to apply is based on one's interest in the estate. However, the applicant must be a resident of Ontario. The applicant is usually that person having the majority interest in the estate or that person's nominee. For example, if the deceased is survived by a spouse, whether there are children or not, the spouse would be the first in line as applicant. However, if the applicant is not the person entitled to apply, those persons entitled to share in the distribution of the estate and who together have a majority interest must consent to the appointment of the applicant.

Section 1 of the *SLRA* defines a spouse as follows:

> Spouse means either of a man and woman who,
> a) are married to each other, or
> b) have together entered into a marriage that is voidable or void, in good faith on the part of the person asserting a right under this Act,

As stated in *Estate Administration*[2]

> the certificate is usually granted in the following order of preference:
> 1. spouse (including common-law spouse or same-sex partner);
> 2. child or children;
> 3. grandchild or grandchildren;
> 4. great-grandchild or great grandchildren or other descendants;
> 5. father;
> 6. mother;
> 7. brothers and sisters;
> 8. grandparents;
> 9. uncles, aunts, nephews and nieces;
> 10. collateral relatives of more remote degree; and
> 11. where there are no known relatives living and competent to take the grant, the Public Guardian and Trustee.

(c) Posting Security

Sections 35 and 36 of the *Estates Act*, R.S.O. 1990, c. E.21, provide as follows:

> **35.** Except where otherwise provided by law, every person to whom a grant of administration, including administration with the will annexed, is committed shall give a bond to the judge of the court by which the grant is made, to enure for the benefit of the Accountant of the Ontario Court, with a surety or sureties as may be required by the judge, conditioned for the due collecting, getting in, administering and accounting for the property of the deceased, and the bond shall be in the form prescribed by the rules of court, and in cases not provided for by the rules, the bond shall be in such form as the judge by special order may direct.
>
> **36.**(1) It is not necessary for the Government of Ontario or any ministry thereof or any Provincial commission or board created under any Act of the Legislature to give any security for the due performance of its duty as executor, administrator, trustee, committee, or in any other office to which it may be appointed by order of the court or under any Act.
>
> (2) A bond shall not be required where the administration on an intestacy is granted to the surviving spouse of the deceased and where,

---

2 Anne E.P. Armstrong, *Estate Administration: A Solicitor's Reference Manual*, vol. 1 (Toronto: Carswell, 1994) (looseleaf) at section 2.6.2.

(a) the net value of the estate as computed for the purposes of section 45 of the *Succession Law Reform Act* does not exceed the preferential share prescribed under subsection 45(6) of that Act; and

(b) there is filed with the application for administration an affidavit setting forth the debts of the estate.

It should be noted that the above-cited s. 45 of the *SLRA* was amended by the *Statute Law Amendment Act (Government Management and Services) 1994*, S.O. 1994, c. 27, s. 63(1-3). On April 1, 1995, O. Reg. 54/95 (under the *SLRA*) came into force. This regulation increased the amount of the preferential share from $75,000 to $200,000.

Rule 74.11 of the Rules of Civil Procedure provides that the bond can be obtained through an insurance or guarantee company licensed to carry on business in Ontario or two personal sureties where the value of the estate is greater than $100,000, but by only one surety when the value does not exceed $100,000. Any personal surety must be 18 years of age or older and must be a resident of Ontario and must be prepared to provide evidence of his or her net worth. Neither the registrar of the court nor a solicitor will be accepted as a personal surety.

Security is also required when an application is being made for a Certificate of Appointment of Succeeding Estate Trustee. However, in this case the bond is in the amount of the value of the estate remaining unadministered. In the case of an application for a Certificate of Ancillary Appointment of Estate Trustee, the security is to be equal to the value of the Ontario estate. For additional information on these two applications, see Chapter 3.

A bond is not required if the applicant is a trust company registered to carry on business in Ontario.

For the form of the bond and additional information regarding dispensing with the bond requirements, see Chapter 3.

Figure 2-1: Letter to Solicitor re: Location of Deceased's Will and Authorization of Personal Representative

---

[address of solicitor]

Dear   :

Re: Estate of *[name of deceased]*

We represent the personal representative(s) of the above-mentioned estate and wish to advise that *[name of deceased]* died on or about the *[date of death]*.

We understand that you *[may have]* prepared the last Will of the late *[named of deceased]* and we would appreciate your advising if you are holding the original Will for safekeeping. In anticipation that you are holding the original Will and Codicils, we are taking this opportunity to enclose herewith the written authorization signed by the personal representative to release all testamentary documents to us. We would also appreciate you providing us with the Affidavit of Execution to each of the testamentary documents and contacting the undersigned when the documents are available to be picked up.

Yours very truly,

_____

AUTHORIZATION

To: *[name of solicitor]*
Re: Testamentary documents of *[name of deceased]*

I, *[name of the personal representative]*, am Personal Representative of the Estate of *[name of deceased]* and as such do hereby authorize and direct you to deliver forthwith to my solicitors *[name of firm]*, all original testamentary documents which are in your possession.

DATED at Toronto this   day of   ,   .

_____*[signature]*_____
[name of personal representative]

Figure 2-2: General Letter to a Bank

[name of bank at head office]

Attention: Customer Service

Re: Estate of *[name of deceased]*

I am the solicitor for the personal representative(s) of the above-mentioned estate and I would appreciate your advising if you can search your banking records to determine if the above-mentioned had an account or safety deposit box with your bank at any branch located in *[put area in which you wish search done]*.

I look forward to hearing from you at your earliest possible convenience.

Yours very truly,

Note: There is a charge levied by banks for this service and therefore it is less costly if you indicate an area.

Figure 2-3: Letter to the Bank of Canada re: Search

Bank of Canada — Bond Dept.
150 King Street West, Suite 2000
Toronto, ON M5H 1J9

Gentlemen:

　　　　　　　　　Re: Estate of *[name of deceased]*
　　　　　　　　Social Insurance Number: _____
　　　　　　　　Last known address: _____

We represent the personal representative(s) of the above-mentioned estate and as such have located certain information indicating the deceased may have had several bank accounts that have become dormant. We would ask that you search your records and advise if your search locates any of these accounts. Also, we understand the deceased held Canada Savings Bonds. However, to date, we have not been able to locate same and we would appreciate you also checking your records to determine if the deceased purchased bonds.

Yours very truly,

Figure 2-4: Letter to the Bank where Deceased Held Assets

[name of bank and address]

Dear Sirs:

Re: Estate of <u>*[name of deceased]*</u>

We represent the personal representative(s) of the above-mentioned estate and as such we wish to advise *[name of deceased]* died on the *[date of death]*.

We understand that the deceased maintained a number of accounts with your branch. We would therefore appreciate your providing us with the following information:

    (a)   account numbers and how accounts held;
    (b)   the balance in any such bank accounts at the date of death (excluding accrued interest);
    (c)   the amount of accrued interest on such bank accounts to the date of death;
    (d)   the current balance in each of the accounts.

We believe that the deceased may have also maintained a number of term deposits and investment certificates at your branch. We will require the following information with respect to each such investment:

    (f)   date of death value;
    (g)   accrued interest to date of death;
    (h)   issue date;
    (i)   interest rate;
    (j)   maturity date; and
    (k)   registration of the investment.

We also believe the deceased may have retained a safety deposit box with your branch and we would appreciate your advising if this is the case.

Would you also please advise if your records indicate if the deceased personally guaranteed any loans at your branch or if there are any existing liabilities of the deceased at your branch. We would also appreciate your advising if your branch is holding any securities in safekeeping or as collateral for any loans.

Yours very truly,

Figure 2-5: Letter to Transfer Agent Requesting Waiver of Requirement of the Court Certificate

---

[name of transfer agent and address]

Dear Sirs:

>Re: Estate of [name of deceased]
>Account No. _____

We represent the personal representative(s) of the above-mentioned estate and as such we wish to advise that the deceased died on the [date of death]. It is our understanding that the deceased held [type of shares] totalling [number of shares] in [name of company].

It would appear from searches completed by the personal representative(s) that these shares are the only asset of the estate and we would appreciate your advising if the shares can be administered pursuant to the terms of the Will without the requirement of obtaining a Certificate of Estate Trustee with a Will from the Court.

We look forward to hearing from you at your earliest convenience.

Yours very truly,

Figure 2-6: Notarial Certificate

CANADA

Province of Ontario

To Wit   )
)   To all whom these Presents
)
)   may come, be seen or known
)

I, [NAME OF NOTARY],
a Notary Public, in and for the Province of Ontario, by Royal Authority duly appointed, residing at the City of North York in said Province,

Do Certify and Attest that the paper-writing hereto annexed is a true copy of a document produced and shown to me and purporting to be a Last Will and Testament for [NAME OF TESTATOR] dated [DATE OF WILL], and Codicil to the Last Will and Testament of [NAME OF TESTATOR] dated [DATE OF CODICIL], the said copy having been compared by me with the original document, an act whereof being requested I have granted under my Notarial Form and Seal of Office to serve and avail as occasion shall or may require.

In Testimony Whereof I have hereto subscribed my name and affixed my Notarial Seal of Office at Toronto this day of January, 1996.

        [NAME OF NOTARY]

        A Notary Public in and for the Province of Ontario.

"Seal"

Figure 2-7: Sample of Information Required for Statement of Assets

Date of Amendment:

ESTATE OF: _____

DATE OF DEATH: _____
DATE OF BIRTH: _____
SIN: _____

STATEMENT OF ASSETS

ASSETS | PROBATE VALUE

Bank Accounts

1. Bank
   Bank Address
   (i) Savings account no.
   (ii) Savings account no.
   (iii) Chequing account no.
2. Bank
   Bank address
   (i) Savings account no.

Registered Retirement Savings Plans

1. Name of company
   Plan no.
   Beneficiary
   Amount

Guaranteed Investment Certificates

1. Name of company
   Address
   Certificate no.
   Principal amount
   Interest rate
   Interest from date of death
   Registration

Insurance

1. Name of company
   Address
   Insured
   Beneficiary (Note: If named beneficiary, value for probate is nil)
   Amount of policy
   Type of policy

Real Estate

1. Address
   Legal description
   Ownership
   Assessment no.

— *continued next page*

Figure 2-7: Sample of Information Required for Statement of Assets (continued)

Shareholdings

1. Name of company
   No. of shares
   Type of shares
   Value per share
   Certificate no.
   Registration

Miscellaneous

1. Bank
   Address
   (i) Safety deposit box no.
   Listing of contents
2. Canada Pension Plan Death Benefit
3. 20__ income tax refund
4. For Personal Effects:
   (a) automobiles;
   (b) paintings;
   (c) furniture;
   (d) jewellery;
   (e) [as determined]

Total assets: $

COURT FEES

Value for probate purposes $

On the first $50,000 — $5/1,000
On the remainder (total less $50,000) $15/1,000

3
LETTERS TESTAMENTARY

Karen M. Gibbs

1. Jurisdiction to File Grant
2. Calculating Court Fees on Applications for Estate Trustee
3. Role of the Court as a Will Depository
4. Notice of Applications
5. Application for Certificate of Appointment of Estate Trustee With a Will
   (a) Generally
   (b) Documents to be Filed with Court
   (c) Other Documents that may be Required
6. Application for Certificate of Appointment of Estate Trustee With a Will Limited to Assets Referred to in the Will
   (a) Generally
   (b) Documents to be Filed with Court
   (c) Other Documents that may be Required
7. Application for Certificate of Appointment of Estate Trustee Without a Will
   (a) Generally
   (b) Documents to be Filed with Court
   (c) Other Documents that may be Required
8. Application for Certificate of Appointment as Succeeding Estate Trustee With a Will
   (a) Generally
   (b) Documents to be Filed with Court
   (c) Other Documents that may be Required
9. Application for Certificate of Appointment as Succeeding Trustee Without a Will
   (a) Generally
   (b) Documents to be Filed with Court
   (c) Other Documents that may be Required
10. Confirmation By Resealing of Appointment of Estate Trustee With or Without a Will
    (a) Generally
    (b) Documents to be Filed with Court
    (c) Other Documents that may be Required
11. Certificate of Ancillary Appointment of Estate Trustee With a Will
    (a) Generally
    (b) Documents to be Filed with Court
    (c) Other Documents that may be Required
12. Certificate of Foreign Estate Trustee's Nominee as Estate Trustee Without a Will
    (a) Generally
    (b) Documents to be Filed with Court
13. Certificate of Estate Trustee During Litigation
    (a) Generally

(b) Documents to be Filed with Court
(c) Other Documents that may be Required
14. Forms
    Figure 3-1: Letter to Court Enclosing Application for Certificate of Appointment of Estate Trustee With a Will
    Figure 3-2: Letter to Court Enclosing Application for Certificate of Appointment of Estate Trustee Without a Will
    Figure 3-3: Letter to Court Enclosing Application for Certificate of Appointment of Succeeding Estate Trustee With a Will
    Figure 3-4: Letter to Court Enclosing Application for Certificate of Appointment of Succeeding Estate Trustee Without a Will
    Figure 3-5: Letter to Court Enclosing Application for Confirmation by Resealing of Appointment of Estate Trustee (With or Without a Will)
    Figure 3-6: Letter to Court Enclosing Application for Certificate of Ancillary Appointment of Estate Trustee With a Will
    Figure 3-7: Letter to Court Enclosing Application for Certificate of Appointment of Estate Trustee During Litigation
    Figure 3-8: Notice of Deposit to Estate Registrar (Form 74.1)
    Figure 3-9: Notice of the Withdrawal to Estate Registrar (Form 74.2)
    Figure 3-10: Application for Certificate of Appointment of Estate Trustee With a Will (Individual Applicant) (Form 74.4)
    Figure 3-11: Application for Certificate of Appointment of Estate Trustee With a Will (Individual Applicant) Limited to Assets Referred to in the Will (Form 74.4.1)
    Figure 3-12: Application for Certificate of Appointment of Estate Trustee With a Will (Corporate Applicant) (Form 74.5)
    Figure 3-13: Application for Certificate of Appointment of Estate Trustee With a Will (Corporate Applicant) Limited to Assets Referred to in the Will (Form 74.5.1)
    Figure 3-14: Affidavit of Service of Notice (With a Will) (Form 74.6)
    Figure 3-15: Notice of an Application for a Certificate of Appointment of Estate Trustee With a Will (Form 74.7)
    Figure 3-16: Affidavit of Execution of Will or Codicil (Form 74.8)
    Figure 3-17: Affidavit Attesting to the Handwriting and Signature of a Holograph Will or Codicil (Form 74.9)
    Figure 3-18: Affidavit of Condition of Will or Codicil (Form 74.10)
    Figure 3-19: Renunciation of Right to a Certificate of Appointment of Estate Trustee (or Succeeding Estate Trustee) With a Will (Form 74.11)
    Figure 3-20: Consent to Applicant's Appointment as Estate Trustee With a Will (Form 74.12)
    Figure 3-21: Certificate of Appointment of Estate Trustee With a Will (Form 74.13)
    Figure 3-22: Certificate of Appointment of Estate Trustee With a Will Limited to the Assets Referred to in the Will (Form 74.13.1)
    Figure 3-23: Application for Certificate of Appointment of Estate Trustee Without a Will (Individual Applicant) (Form 74.14)
    Figure 3-24: Application for Certificate of Appointment of Estate Trustee Without a Will (Corporate Applicant) (Form 74.15)
    Figure 3-25: Affidavit of Service of Notice (Without a Will) (Form 74.16)
    Figure 3-26: Notice of an Application for a Certificate of Appointment of Estate Trustee Without a Will (Form 74.17)
    Figure 3-27: Renunciation of Prior Right to a Certificate of Appointment of Estate Trustee Without a Will (Form 74.18)
    Figure 3-28: Consent to Applicant's Appointment as Estate Trustee Without a Will (Form 74.19)
    Figure 3-29: Certificate of Appointment of Estate Trustee Without a Will (Form 74.20)
    Figure 3-30: Application for Certificate of Appointment of a Foreign Estate Trustee's Nominee as Estate Trustee Without a Will (Form 74.20.1)
    Figure 3-31: Nomination of Applicant by Foreign Estate Trustee (Form 74.20.2)

Figure 3-32: Certificate of Appointment of Foreign Estate Trustee's Nominee as Estate Trustee Without a Will (Form 74.20.3)
Figure 3-33: Application for Certificate of Appointment as Succeeding Estate Trustee With a Will (Form 74.21)
Figure 3-34: Consent to Applicant's Appointment as Succeeding Estate Trustee With a Will (Form 74.22)
Figure 3-35: Certificate of Appointment of Succeeding Estate Trustee With a Will (Form 74.23)
Figure 3-36: Application for Certificate of Appointment as Succeeding Estate Trustee Without a Will (Form 74.24)
Figure 3-37: Consent to Applicant's Appointment as Succeeding Estate Trustee Without a Will (Form 74.25)
Figure 3-38: Certificate of Appointment of Succeeding Estate Trustee Without a Will (Form 74.26)
Figure 3-39: Application for Confirmation by Resealing of Appointment or Certificate of Ancillary Appointment of Estate Trustee (Form 74.27)
Figure 3-40: Application for Confirmation by Resealing of Appointment or Certificate of Ancillary Appointment of Estate Trustee (Form 74.27)
Figure 3-41: Confirmation by Resealing of Appointment of Estate Trustee (Form 74.28)
Figure 3-42: Certificate of Ancillary Appointment of Estate Trustee With a Will (Form 74.29)
Figure 3-43: Application for Certificate of Appointment of Estate Trustee During Litigation (Form 74.30)
Figure 3-44: Certificate of Appointment of Estate Trustee During Litigation (Form 74.31)
Figure 3-45: Bond — Insurance or Guarantee Company (Form 74.32)
Figure 3-46: Bond — Personal Sureties (Form 74.33)
Figure 3-47: Registrar's Notice of Application With a Will (Form 74.34)
Figure 3-48: Registrar's Notice of Application Without a Will (Form 74.35)
Figure 3-49: Affidavit in Support of Request for an Order that the Requirement of Posting a Bond be Dispensed With
Figure 3-50: Order to Dispense With Bond
Figure 3-51: Affidavit as to Evidence of Signature
Figure 3-52: Undertaking
Figure 3-53: Affidavit re Multiple Wills
Figure 3-54: Order
List of Addresses of Offices of Superior Court of Justice

1. JURISDICTION TO FILE GRANT

The *Estates Act*, R.S.O. 1990, c. E.21, s. 7, provides that the application for Certificate of Appointment of Estate Trustee With or Without a Will (formerly Letters Probate or Letters of Administration) shall be filed in the court office for the district where the deceased had a fixed place of abode. If the deceased resided out of Ontario or had no fixed place of abode in Ontario, the application is to be filed in the court office for the district where the deceased had property at the time of his or her death. In other cases the application can be filed in any court office. A list of addresses of offices of the Superior Court of Justice is located at the end of this chapter.

2. CALCULATING COURT FEES ON APPLICATIONS FOR ESTATE TRUSTEE

The fees of the court are as prescribed by regulation. As of January 28, 2000, O. Reg. 293/92, s. 2 provides for the following:

2. (1) The following fees are payable in estate matters:
1. For a certificate of succeeding estate trustee or a certificate of estate trustee during litigation $65.00
2. For an application of an estate trustee to pass accounts, including all services in connection with it $280.00
3. For a notice of objection to accounts $60.00
4. For an application other than an application to pass accounts, including an application for proof of lost or destroyed will, a revocation of a certificate of appointment, an application for directions or the filing of a claim and notice of contestation $150.00
5. For a notice of objection other than a notice of objection to accounts, including the filing of a notice of appearance $60.00
6. For a request for notice of commencement of proceedings $60.00
7. For the deposit of a will or codicil for safekeeping $17.00
8. For an assessment of costs, including the certificate $40.00

Keep in mind that applications for court grants filed prior to June, 1994 were calculated at the rate of $5 per $1,000 of assets and if additional payments are being made on these estates, they are paid at the lesser rate.

3. ROLE OF THE COURT AS A WILL DEPOSITORY

The *Estates Act*, s. 2, provides as follows:

> **2.** The office of the local registrar of the Ontario Court (General Division) is a depository for all wills of living persons given there for safekeeping, and the local registrar shall receive and keep those wills under such regulations as are prescribed by the rules of court.

Rule 74.02 of the Rules of Civil Procedure, R.R.O. 1990, Reg. 194 (the "Rules"), provides the circumstances in which the Court is to act as a depository for a Will or codicil. The deposit is to be made by the following:

(a) the testator;
(b) a person authorized by the testator in writing;
(c) a solicitor who held the will or codicil at the time of retirement from practice;
(d) the estate trustee of a solicitor who held the will or codicil at the time of the solicitor's death;
(e) the representative of a trust corporation that held the will or codicil when it ceased to do business in Ontario; or
(f) a person authorized by the court to deposit the will or codicil.

At the time the deposit is made, an Affidavit of Execution of Will or Codicil (Form 74.8, see Figure 3-16)* can also be deposited. In response to the recent Eurig decision, which held that probate "fees" were a tax and not a fee, the Province of Ontario enacted the *Estates Administration Tax Act, 1998* (the "Act"), which imposes a tax on an estate when an estate certificate is issued. The tax is applicable with respect to all estate certificates issued after May 14, 1950, and is retroactive May 15, 1950. The amount of tax payable under the Act mirrors the fees that were payable for the certificate under the *Surrogate*

---

* In this chapter, a *form* number given in parentheses refers to number of the form as stated in the Rules; the *figure* number refers to the order of its representation at the end of this chapter.

Courts Act and the *Administration of Justice Act*. The Act provides that the fees paid under the unauthorized regulations are to be applied to discharge the liability for taxes under the Act. Similar amendments were made where necessary to the *Estates Act*.

At the time a Will or codicil is being deposited with the court, the Registrar of the Court is to seal the document, in the presence of the depositor, in an envelope endorsed with the date of deposit, the name and address of the depositor, the testator, the testator's date of birth, the Estate Trustee(s) named, and the date of the Will. Within seven days of the deposit being made the Registrar of the Court is to send notice (Form 74.1, see Figure 3-8) to the Estate Registrar for Ontario that the deposit was made.

The Estate Registrar for Ontario is located at the Toronto office of the court, which is currently 393 University Avenue, 10th floor, Toronto, Ontario M5G 1E8.

Only the testator or a guardian of the estate of the testator, unless a court order is obtained, can remove, copy or inspect the document during the testator's lifetime. Upon the death of the testator, any person may inspect or copy the Will or codicil held by the Court, upon filing a written request which includes the date of birth of the testator and a Funeral Director's Statement of Death or a Death Certificate issued by the Registrar General. The Funeral Director's Statement of Death is generally the quickest and easiest certificate to obtain. However, it will often be provided only to the next of kin of the deceased.

The Will or codicil on deposit with the Registrar will be provided to the Estate Trustee upon the Estate Trustee providing a written request stating the date of birth and date of death of the testator together with a Funeral Director's Statement of Death or a Death Certificate issued by the Registrar General. The Court Registrar will then retain a copy of the Will or codicil which is certified by the Registrar together with the receipt for the Will or codicil signed by the person who received it. A Notice of the Withdrawal (Form 74.2, see Figure 3-9) is then sent by the Registrar to the Estate Registrar for Ontario.

Wills and codicils that have been held for safekeeping for 125 years or more are sent to the Archivist for Ontario.

Where an application for Certificate of Appointment of Estate Trustee With a Will is filed and it is determined by the court that there is a Will and/or codicil on deposit with the court office dated after the date of the Will being submitted with the certificate, a notice (Form 74.34, see Figure 3-47) will be sent by the Registrar to the person named as executor in the Will or codicil on deposit. If an application for Certificate of Appointment of Estate Trustee Without a Will is brought and it is found that there is a Will and/or codicil on deposit with the court, a notice (Form 74.35, see Figure 3-48) will be sent to the person named as executor in the Will and/or codicil.

4. NOTICE OF APPLICATIONS

As a result of the amendments to the rules governing estates, one of the biggest changes in applying for a grant from the court is the requirement of serving notice on all beneficiaries, with the exception of the applicant if the applicant is also a beneficiary, and potential beneficiaries. Although there is no time limit for the service and filing of this notice, you will see that evidence of the service must be provided to the court at the time the application is made for the certificate. You must serve this notice of an entitlement in an estate on all beneficiaries, including contingent beneficiaries. If minors have an interest or a potential interest in an estate that notice is served on their parent or guardian and the Children's Lawyer. If there are unborn or unascertained beneficiaries to an estate, the notice is served only on the Children's Lawyer. For mentally incapable beneficiaries, the notice is served on the guardian or attorney for the mentally incapable person, or if there is no guardian or attorney, the Public Guardian and Trustee. If a charity has an interest in an estate, the notice is sent to the charity.

The concept of serving notice on all beneficiaries has caused concern to many as the notice must have copies of the Will and any codicils attached thereto if being sent to residual beneficiaries. In the case of a specified gift of property on an amount of money, only an extract of the relevant sections of the Will and/or Codicil is included. However, one must remember that once the Will and codicils were submitted to the court in the past, the documents did become public record, although many people did not realize this.

5. APPLICATION FOR CERTIFICATE OF APPOINTMENT OF ESTATE TRUSTEE WITH A WILL*

(a) Generally

Rule 74.04 provides as follows:

74.04 (1) An application for a certificate of appointment of estate trustee with a will (Form 74.4 or 74.5 or, if the application is for a certificate limited to assets referred to in the will, Form 74.4.1 or 74.5.1) shall be accompanied by,

(a) the original of the will and of every codicil;
(b) an affidavit (Form 74.6) attesting that notice of the application (Form 74.7) has been served in accordance with subrules (2) to (7);
(c) an affidavit of execution (Form 74.8) of the will and of every codicil, or if neither of the witnesses to the will or the codicil can be found, or both have died, such other evidence of due execution as the court may require;
(d) if the will or a codicil is in holograph form, an affidavit (Form 74.9) attesting that the handwriting and signature in the will or codicil are those of the deceased;
(e) if the will or a codicil is not in holograph form but contains an alteration, erasure, obliteration or interlineation that has not been attested, an affidavit as to the condition of the will or codicil at the time of execution (Form 74.10);
(f) a renunciation (Form 74.11) from every living person who is named in the will or codicil as estate trustee who has not joined in the application and is entitled to do so;
(g) if the applicant is not named as an estate trustee in the will or codicil, a consent to the applicant's appointment (Form 74.12) by persons who are entitled to share in the distribution of the estate and who together have a majority interest in the value of the assets of the estate at the date of death;
(h) the security required by the *Estates Act*; and
(i) such additional or other material as the court directs.

(2) Notice of the application shall be served on all persons entitled to share in the distribution of the estate, including charities and contingent beneficiaries; however, notice need not be served on the applicant.

(3) [Revoked O. Reg. 24/00, s. 12.].

---

* Formerly Letters Probate and Letters of Administration with Will Annexed

(4) If a person who is entitled to share in the distribution of the estate is less than 18 years of age, notice of the application shall not be served on the person, despite subrule (2), but shall be served on a parent or guardian and on the Children's Lawyer.

(5) If there may be unborn or unascertained beneficiaries, notice of the application shall be served on the Children's Lawyer.

(6) If a person who is entitled to share in the distribution of the estate is mentally incapable within the meaning of section 6 of the *Substitute Decisions Act, 1992* in respect of an issue in the proceeding, notice of the application shall also be served,
- (a) if there is a guardian with authority to act in the proceeding, on the guardian;
- (b) if there is no guardian with authority to act in the proceeding but there is an attorney under a power of attorney with authority to act in the proceeding, on the attorney;
- (c) if there is neither a guardian nor an attorney with authority to act in the proceeding, on the Public Guardian and Trustee.

(7) Notice under this rule shall be served on all persons, including charities, the Children's Lawyer and the Public Guardian and Trustee, by regular lettermail sent to the person's last known address.

(8) The certificate of appointment of estate trustee with a will shall be in Form 74.13.

(9) The certificate of appointment of estate trustee with a will limited to the assets referred to in the will shall be in Form 74.13.1.

The Certificate of Appointment of Estate Trustee With a Will is the certificate applied for when the deceased left a Will, even though there may be no executor named in the Will or the named executor(s) are not the applicants.

Should anyone have a prior right to apply as Estate Trustee, the party with the prior right must execute a Renunciation. If someone named as an executor in a Will does not intend to apply for the certificate and does not respond to a request for a Renunciation, you can obtain an Order to Accept or Refuse Appointment as Estate Trustee (see Chapter 5, Court Disputes). If no response is received to the order, a Renunciation is then not required.

If the applicant is not named in the Will of the deceased as the executor, consents must be obtained from the beneficiaries having a majority interest in the Estate.

Pursuant to r. 74.04(e), if the Will or codicil contains "an alteration, erasure, obliteration or interliniation that has not been attested, an affidavit as to the condition of the will or codicil at the time of execution" is required.

(b) Documents to be Filed with Court

1. Application for a Certificate of Appointment of Estate Trustee With a Will, either for Individual Applicant (Form 74.4, see Figure 3-10) or Corporate Applicant (if one of the applicants is a trust company) (Form 74.5, see Figure 3-12).
2. Original of the Will and all codicils, together with a copy of each.
   It should be noted that there is no longer a requirement that the applicant identify the Will and codicils by placing his signature on the back of the last page of the Will and any codicils thereto.
3. Affidavit of Service of Notice of Application With a Will (Form 74.6, see Figure 3-14) with Notice (Form 74.7, see Figure 3-15) attached as exhibit thereto.
   If the applicant is not able to give notice as required, it is necessary to obtain an order dispensing with such notice or accepting alternate notice pursuant to the Rules (currently under r. 16).

4. Affidavit of Execution of Will and Affidavit of Execution of Codicils for any codicils thereto (Form 74.8, see Figure 3-16).
5. Certificate of Appointment of Estate Trustee With a Will (Form 74.13, see Figure 3-21) where required by the local registrar of the court.
6. Applicable court fees.
7. Letter to court (see Figure 3-1).

(c) Other Documents that may be Required

1. Renunciation of Right to a Certificate of Appointment of Estate Trustee With a Will (Form 74.11, see Figure 3-19), to be completed by all living persons named in the Will or codicils as Estate Trustee, but who are not joining in the application, although entitled.
2. Consent to Applicant's Appointment as Estate Trustee With a Will where applicant not named (Form 74.12, see Figure 3-20) to be completed by all persons entitled to share in the distribution of the estate who have a majority interest in the value of the assets.
3. Security as required under the *Estates Act* if the applicant is not resident in Ontario or is not named as Estate Trustee. The security is in the form of a bond either by personal sureties (Form 74.33, see Figure 3-46) or an insurance or guarantee company (Form 74.32, see Figure 3-45).
4. Affidavit in Support of Request for an Order that the Requirement of Posting a Bond be Dispensed With (see Figure 3-49) and draft Order to Dispense With Bond (see Figure 3-50).
5. Affidavit of Condition of Will or Codicil (Form 74.10, see Figure 3-18). Many firms will prepare this shortly after execution of the Will, if amendments have been made to the Will and it is unclear to the reader if they were made in the presence of the testator and witness or if they were made at a later date.
6. Affidavit Attesting to the Handwriting and Signature of a Holograph Will or Codicil (Form 74.9, see Figure 3-17).
7. If witnesses to the Will or codicil cannot be located, such other evidence as the court may require; Affidavit as to Evidence of Signature (see Figure 3-51).
8. Pursuant to r. 74.13 the applicant may also file an affidavit as to the estimated value of the estate and pay the court fees on the estimated value provided an Undertaking (see Figure 3-52) is also filed stating that the applicant will file a sworn statement of the total value of the estate and pay the balance of fees within six months of the filing of the Undertaking.

It should be noted, however, that if the Undertaking is not fulfilled, the Registrar of the Court may request an Order for Compliance of which the end result could be that the Estate Trustee could be found to be in contempt.

LETTERS TESTAMENTARY 67

6. APPLICATION FOR CERTIFICATE OF APPOINTMENT OF ESTATE TRUSTEE WITH A WILL LIMITED TO ASSETS REFERRED TO IN THE WILL

(a) Generally

It is important to note that as a result of recent changes it is now possible to have multiple Wills, however, only apply for a Certificate to be issued in connection with one of the Wills, which application is limited to the assets dealt with in that particular Will. Although the concept of multiple Wills is dealt with in the Will chapter, the simplest description is one Will deals with the testator's assets that will require probate and the other Will deals with those assets that do not require probate and usually include shares in a private corporation.

All the documents referred to in Rule 74.04 above are required to be filed with the application for Certificate of Appointment of Estate Trustee With a Will limited to assets referred to in the Will. However, there are additional documents to be filed with this application and reference should be made to section (b) below.

(b) Documents to be Filed with Court

1. Application for Certificate of Appointment of Estate Trustee With a Will Limited to Assets referred to in the Will (Form 74.4.1, see Figure 3-11).
2. Original of the Will and all Codicils, together with a copy of each.
3. Affidavit of Service of Notice of Application With a Will Limited to Assets referred to in the Will (Form 74.6, see Figure 3-14) with Notice (Form 74.7, see Figure 3-15) attached as exhibit hereto.
4. Affidavit of Execution of Will and Affidavit of Execution of Codicils for any codicils thereto (Form 74.8, see Figure 3-16).
5. Certificate of Appointment of Estate Trustee with a Will Limited to the Assets referred to in the Will (Form 74.13.1, see Figure 3-22).
6. Applicable court fees.
7. Affidavit of applicant detailing other Will and providing the Court with a copy of same (see Figure 3-53).
8. Order (see Figure 3-54).

(c) Other Documents that may be Required

See Section 5, above.

7. APPLICATION FOR CERTIFICATE OF APPOINTMENT OF ESTATE TRUSTEE WITHOUT A WILL*

(a) Generally

Rule 74.05 provides as follows:

---
* Formerly Letters of Administration.

74.05 (1) An application for a certificate of appointment of estate trustee without a will (Form 74.14 or 74.15) shall be accompanied by,
- (a) an affidavit (Form 74.16) attesting that notice of the application (Form 74.17) has been served in accordance with subrules (2) to (5);
- (b) a renunciation (Form 74.18) from every person who is entitled in priority to be named as estate trustee and who has not joined in the application;
- (c) a consent to the applicant's appointment (Form 74.19) by persons who are entitled to share in the distribution of the estate and who together have a majority interest in the value of the assets of the estate at the date of death;
- (d) the security required by the *Estates Act*; and
- (e) such additional or other material as the court directs.

(2) Notice of the application shall be served on all persons entitled to share in the distribution of the estate; however, notice need not be served on the applicant.

(3) If a person who is entitled to share in the distribution of the estate is less than 18 years of age, notice of the application shall not be served on the person, despite subrule (2), but shall be served on a parent or guardian and on the Children's Lawyer.

(4) If a person who is entitled to share in the distribution of the estate is mentally incapable within the meaning of section 6 of the *Substitute Decisions Act, 1992* in respect of an issue in the proceeding, notice of the application shall also be served,
- (a) if there is a guardian with authority to act in the proceeding, on the guardian;
- (b) if there is no guardian with authority to act in the proceeding but there is an attorney under a power of attorney with authority to act in the proceeding, on the attorney;
- (c) if there is neither a guardian nor an attorney with authority to act in the proceeding, on the Public Guardian and Trustee.

(5) Notice under this rule shall be served on all persons, including the Children's Lawyer and the Public Guardian and Trustee, by regular lettermail sent to the person's last known address.

(6) The certificate of appointment of estate trustee without a will shall be in Form 74.20.

The Certificate of Appointment of Estate Trustee Without a Will is the application that is filed when a person dies intestate (without a Will). It should be noted that this certificate can only be issued to a resident of Ontario and the applicant must be of the age of majority. This certificate provides the Estate Trustee with his or her authority. In the case of the Estate Trustee with a will his or her authority comes from the Will itself, not the certificate.

The right to apply for this certificate is given in the order of interest in the estate. The *Succession Law Reform Act*, R.S.O. 1990, c. S.26 (the *"SLRA"*), determines the beneficiary or beneficiaries of the intestate estate and from that the list of applicants is determined as follows:

1. spouse;
2. children;
3. grandchildren;
4. great grandchildren or other descendants;
5. parents;
6. brothers and sisters;
7. grandparents;
8. uncles, aunts, nephews and nieces;
9. collateral relatives of more remote degree; and

LETTERS TESTAMENTARY 69

10. where no relatives are found or there are no living relatives or only persons found to be incompetent, then the Public Guardian and Trustee.

The applicant can be the nominee of a majority of beneficiaries of equal standing in which case the beneficiaries of a majority interest of the residue should execute consents. Renunciations must be provided for any party with a prior right that does not wish to apply.

(b) Documents to be Filed with Court

1. Application for Certificate of Appointment of Estate Trustee Without a Will, either for an Individual Applicant (Form 74.14, see Figure 3-23) or a Corporate Applicant (Form 74.15, see Figure 3-24).
2. Affidavit of Service of Notice of Application (Without a Will) (Form 74.16, see Figure 3-25) with Notice of an Application for Certificate of Appointment of Estate Trustee Without a Will (Form 74.17, see Figure 3-26) attached as exhibit.
   If the applicant is not able to give notice as required, it is necessary to obtain an order dispensing with such notice or accepting alternate notice pursuant to the Rules (currently under r. 16).
3. Certificate of Appointment of Estate Trustee Without a Will (Form 74.20, see Figure 3-29) where required by the local Registrar.
4. Applicable court fees.
5. Letter to court (see Figure 3-2).

(c) Other Documents that may be Required

1. Renunciation of Prior Right to a Certificate of Appointment of Estate Trustee Without a Will (Form 74.18, see Figure 3-27).
   A Renunciation is to be completed by every person who is entitled in priority to be named as Estate Trustee without a Will, but is not an applicant.
2. Consent to Applicant's Appointment as Estate Trustee Without a Will (Form 74.19, see Figure 3-28).
   A consent to the appointment is to be completed by persons entitled to share in the distribution of the estate who together have a majority interest.
3. Security as required under the *Estates Act*.
   The security is in the form of a bond either by personal sureties (Form 74.33, see Figure 3-46) or an insurance or guarantee company (Form 74.32, see Figure 3-45).
4. Affidavit in Support of Request for an Order that the Requirement of Posting a Bond be Dispensed With (see Figure 3-49) and draft Order to Dispense With Bond (see Figure 3-50).
5. Pursuant to r. 74.13, the applicant may also file an affidavit as to the estimated value of the estate and pay the court fees on the estimated value provided an Undertaking (see Figure 3-52) is also filed stating that the applicant will file a sworn statement of the total value of the estate and pay the balance of fees within six months of the filing of the Undertaking.

8. APPLICATION FOR CERTIFICATE OF APPOINTMENT AS SUCCEEDING ESTATE TRUSTEE WITH A WILL*

(a) Generally

Rule 74.06 provides as follows:

> **74.06** (1) An application for a certificate of appointment of estate trustee to succeed an estate trustee with a will (Form 74.21) shall be accompanied by,
> - (a) the original certificate of appointment or, if the original certificate has been lost, a copy of it certified by the court;
> - (b) a renunciation (Form 74.11) from every living person who is named in the will or codicil as an estate trustee and who has not joined in the application and is entitled to do so;
> - (c) if the applicant is not named as an estate trustee in the will or codicil, a consent (Form 74.22) to the application by persons who are entitled to share in the distribution of the remaining estate and who together have a majority interest in the value of the assets remaining in the estate at the date of the application;
> - (d) the security required by the *Estates Act*; and
> - (e) such additional or other material as the court directs.
>
> (2) The certificate of appointment of a succeeding estate trustee with a will shall be in Form 74.23.

When an Estate Trustee with a Will resigns or is removed before the administration of the estate is complete, or dies without leaving a Will, this certificate is applied for to enable the administration to be completed. Often a Will names alternate or succeeding Estate Trustees. Generally, if the Will does not provide for alternates, and there is only one Estate Trustee, or one Estate Trustee surviving, the personal representatives of the estate of the deceased Estate Trustee are first in line to apply.

(b) Documents to be Filed with Court

1. Application for Certificate of Appointment as Succeeding Estate Trustee With a Will (Form 74.21, see Figure 3-33).
2. The original certificate, or if original cannot be located, a certified copy.
3. Certificate of Appointment of Succeeding Estate Trustee With a Will (Form 74.23, see Figure 3-35).
4. Letter to court (see Figure 3-3).
5. Applicable fees based on the current value of the estate.

(c) Other Documents that may be Required

1. Renunciation (Form 74.11, see Figure 3-19) from all living persons named in the Will or codicil as succeeding Estate Trustees who are not applicants.
2. Consent (Form 74.22, see Figure 3-34) to applicant's appointment (if applicant is not named as replacement Estate Trustee in Will or codicils) is to be completed by persons entitled to share in the distribution of the remainder of the estate and who together have a majority interest in the remaining assets.

---

* Formerly Double Letters Probate and Letters of Administration Bonis Non With Will Annexed.

3. Security as required by the *Estates Act* based on the value of the remaining estate. The security is in the form of a bond as previously described.
4. Affidavit in Support of Request for an Order that the Requirement of Posting a Bond be Dispensed With (see Figure 3-49) and draft Order to Dispense with Bond (see Figure 3-50).
5. As previously mentioned, the applicant may also file an affidavit as to the estimated value of the estate and pay the court fees on the estimated value provided an Undertaking (see Figure 3-52) is also filed stating that the applicant will file a sworn statement of the total value of the estate and pay the balance of fees within six months of the filing of the Undertaking.

9. APPLICATION FOR CERTIFICATE OF APPOINTMENT AS SUCCEEDING TRUSTEE WITHOUT A WILL*

(a) Generally

Rule 74.07 provides as follows:

> **74.07** (1) An application for a certificate of appointment of estate trustee to succeed an estate trustee without a will (Form 74.24) shall be accompanied by,
> (a) the original certificate of appointment or, if the original certificate has been lost, a copy of it certified by the court;
> (b) a consent (Form 74.25) to the application by persons who are entitled to share in the distribution of the remaining estate and who together have a majority interest in the value of the assets remaining in the estate at the date of the application;
> (c) the security required by the *Estates Act*; and
> (d) such additional or other material as the court directs.
> (2) The certificate of appointment of a succeeding estate trustee without a will shall be in Form 74.26.

When an Estate Trustee without a Will resigns or is removed or dies before the administration of the estate is complete, this certificate is applied for to enable the administration to be completed. Generally this certificate is granted to someone having a beneficial interest in the estate or the nominee of that person.

(b) Documents to be Filed with Court

1. Application for Certificate of Appointment as Succeeding Estate Trustee Without a Will (Form 74.24, see Figure 3-36).
2. The original certificate, or if original cannot be located, a certified copy.
3. Certificate of Appointment of Succeeding Estate Trustee Without a Will (Form 74.26, see Figure 3-38).
4. Letter to court (see Figure 3-4).
5. Applicable fees based on the current value of the estate.

---

* Formerly Letters of Administration de Bonis Non Administratis.

(c) Other Documents that may be Required

1. Consent (Form 74.25, see Figure 3-37) to Applicant's appointment. If the applicant is not a beneficiary, this is to be completed by persons entitled to share in the distribution of the remainder of the estate and who together have a majority interest in the remaining assets.
2. Security as required by the *Estates Act* based on the value of the remaining estate. Again, the security is in the form of a bond either by personal Sureties or an insurance or guarantee company.
3. Affidavit in Support of Request for an Order that the Requirement of Posting a Bond be Dispensed With (see Figure 3-49) and draft Order to Dispense with Bond (see Figure 3-50).
4. Again, the applicant may also file an affidavit as to the estimated value of the estate and pay the court fees on the estimated value provided an Undertaking (see Figure 3-52) is also filed stating that the applicant will file a sworn statement of the total value of the estate and pay the balance of fees within six months of the filing of the Undertaking.

10. CONFIRMATION BY RESEALING OF APPOINTMENT OF ESTATE TRUSTEE WITH OR WITHOUT A WILL*

(a) Generally

Rule 74.08 provides as follows:

> **74.08** (1) An application for confirmation by resealing of the appointment of an estate trustee with or without a will that was granted by a court of competent jurisdiction in the United Kingdom, in a province or territory of Canada or in any British possession (Form 74.27) shall be accompanied by,
> (a) two certified copies of the document under the seal of the court that granted it, or the original document and one certified copy under the seal of the court that granted it;
> (b) the security required by the *Estates Act*; and
> (c) such additional or other material as the court directs.
> (2) A confirmation by resealing of the appointment of an estate trustee with or without a will shall be in Form 74.28.

Where a certificate or grant has been issued by a "court of competent jurisdiction in the United Kingdom, in a province or territory of Canada or in any British possession"[1] and a person is determined to have assets in Ontario, this application is filed.

Although security is generally required by the court, if it can be proven by evidence from the court issuing the original certificate that the security posted with them was sufficient to cover the assets in Ontario, the applicant does not have to be an Ontario resident nor does he or she have to nominate an Ontario resident to act in his or her place.

---

* Formerly Resealing of Letters Probate or Letters of Administration.
1 Rule 74.08(1).

LETTERS TESTAMENTARY 73

(b) Documents to be Filed with Court

Note: as the same form is used, whether for an application for resealing or an ancillary appointment, you must designate on the form which application is being made.

1. Two certified copies of the original appointment granted by the originating court of competent jurisdiction in the United Kingdom, a province or territory of Canada or any British possession under court seal.
2. Security required by the *Estates Act* on the assets in Ontario.

    The security is in the form of a bond either by personal sureties or an insurance or guarantee company.

    Where there is no Will, a certificate is required by the Registrar of the court which issued the original document, indicating sufficient security has been given to cover the value of all estate assets, including those in Ontario. If this certificate is not available, a bond must be posted.
3. Application for Confirmation by Resealing of Appointment (Form 74.27, see Figure 3-39).
4. Confirmation by Resealing of Appointment of an Estate Trustee (Form 74.28, see Figure 3-41).
5. Applicable court fees on the Ontario assets.
6. Letter to court (see Figure 3-5).

(c) Other Documents that may be Required

1. Affidavit in Support of Request for an Order that the Requirement of Posting a Bond be Dispensed With (see Figure 3-49) and draft Order to Dispense With Bond (see Figure 3-50).
2. The applicant may also file an affidavit as to the estimated value of the estate and pay the court fees on the estimated value provided an Undertaking (see Figure 3-52) is also filed stating that the applicant will file a sworn statement of the total value of the estate and pay the balance of fees within six months of the filing of the Undertaking.

11. CERTIFICATE OF ANCILLARY APPOINTMENT OF ESTATE TRUSTEE WITH A WILL*

(a) Generally

Rule 74.09 provides as follows:

74.09 (1) An application for a certificate of ancillary appointment of an estate trustee with a will where the applicant has been appointed by a court having jurisdiction outside Ontario, other than a jurisdiction referred to in rule 74.08. (Form 74.27) shall be accompanied by,

(a) two certified copies of the document under the seal of the court that granted it;

---

* Formerly Ancillary Letters Probate.

(b) the security required by the *Estates Act*; and
(c) such additional or other material as the court directs.

(2) A certificate of ancillary appointment of an estate trustee with a will shall be in Form 74.29.

While it is similar to the process of resealing as described above, this process, however, is used when the grant was issued by a court outside Ontario, other than "in the United Kingdom, in a province or territory of Canada or in any British possession".

This is only available where there is a Will.

(b) Documents to be Filed with Court

1. Two certified copies of the original grant by the originating court under that court's seal.
2. Security required by the *Estates Act* on the assets in Ontario.
   The security is in the form of a bond either by personal sureties or an insurance or guarantee company.
3. Application for Certificate of Ancillary Appointment of Estate Trustee (Form 74.27, see Figure 3-40).
4. Certificate of Ancillary Appointment of Estate Trustee With a Will (Form 74.29, see Figure 3-42).
5. Applicable court fees on the Ontario assets.
6. Letter to court (see Figure 3-6).

(c) Other Documents that may be Required

1. Affidavit in Support of Request for an Order that the Requirement of Posting a Bond be Dispensed With (see Figure 3-49) and draft Order to Dispense with Bond (see Figure 3-50).
2. The applicant may also wish to file an affidavit as to the estimated value of the estate and pay the court fees on the estimated value provided an Undertaking (see Figure 3-52) is also filed stating that the applicant will file a sworn statement of the total value of the estate and pay the balance of fees within six months of the filing of the Undertaking.

12. CERTIFICATE OF FOREIGN ESTATE TRUSTEE'S NOMINEE AS ESTATE TRUSTEE WITHOUT A WILL

(a) Generally

Rule 74.05.1(1) provides as follows:

74.05.1 (1) An application for a certificate of appointment of a foreign estate trustee's nominee as estate trustee without a will (Form 74.20.1) shall be accompanied by,
   (a) a nomination (Form 74.20.2) of the applicant by the estate trustee appointed in the jurisdiction where the deceased was domiciled at the date of death;
   (b) a copy of the document appointing the foreign estate trustee, certified under the seal

of the court that granted it;
- (c) a certificate under the seal of the court that granted the foreign document, issued within a reasonable amount of time before the date of the application and stating that the foreign document remains effective as of the date of the certificate;
- (d) the security required by the *Estates Act*; and
- (e) such additional or other material as the court directs.

(2) The certificate of appointment of a foreign estate trustee's nominee as estate trustee without a will shall be in Form 74.20.3. [en. O. Reg. 332/96, s.3]

As a certificate of any appointment without a will will not be issued to a person resident outside of Ontario, it is necessary for a foreign estate trustee without a will to nominate an estate trustee within the Province.

(b) Documents to be Filed with Court

1. Application for Certificate of Appointment of Foreign Estate Trustee's Nominee without a Will (Form 74.20.3, see Figure 3-30).
2. Nomination of the Applicant executed by the estate trustee who was appointed in the jurisdiction where the deceased was domiciliated (Form 74.20.2, see Figure 3-31).
3. Court certified copy of the document appointing the foreign estate trustee.
4. Certificate under the seal of the court that granted the foreign document, issued within a reasonable amount of time before the date of the application and stating that the foreign document remains effective as at the date of the certificate.
5. Security required by the *Estates Act* on the assets in Ontario in the form of a bond either by personal sureties or an insurance or guarantee company.
6. Certificate of Appointment of Foreign Estate Trustee's Nominee without a Will (Form 74.20.3, see Figure 3-32).
7. Applicable court fee.
8. Letter to the court.

13. CERTIFICATE OF ESTATE TRUSTEE DURING LITIGATION*

(a) Generally

Rule 74.10 provides as follows:

74.10 (1) An application for a certificate of appointment of an estate trustee during litigation (Form 74.30) shall be accompanied by,
- (a) a copy of the order appointing the applicant as estate trustee during litigation;
- (b) the security required by the *Estates Act*; and
- (c) such additional or other material as the court directs.

(2) A certificate of appointment of an estate trustee during litigation shall be in Form 74.31.

Often it is not possible to immediately apply for the certificate of Estate Trustee. A question of whether a Will is valid, or whether the determination of the court is required,

---

* Formerly Administrator Pendente Lite.

may arise. It is therefore necessary to have someone appointed to preserve the assets of the estate pending the outcome of the litigation. The Estate Trustee during litigation has the same rights and powers as an Estate Trustee, other than that they cannot distribute the estate without leave of the court.

(b) Documents to be Filed with Court

1. Application for the Certificate of Appointment of Estate Trustee During Litigation (Form 74.30, see Figure 3-30).
2. Certificate of Appointment of Estate Trustee During Litigation (Form 74.31, see Figure 3-31).
3. Security required by the *Estates Act* on the assets in Ontario in the form of a bond either by personal sureties or an insurance or guarantee company.
4. A copy of the order appointing the applicant as Estate Trustee during litigation.
5. Applicable court fees on the Ontario assets.
6. Letter to court (see Figure 3-7).

(c) Other Documents that may be Required

1. The applicant may also file an affidavit as to the estimated value of the estate and pay the court fees on the estimated value provided an Undertaking (see Figure 3-52) is also filed stating that the applicant will file a sworn statement of the total value of the estate and pay the balance of fees within six months of the filing of the Undertaking.

LETTERS TESTAMENTARY 77

Figure 3-1: Letter to Court Enclosing Application for Certificate of Appointment of Estate Trustee With a Will

Local Registrar
Superior Court of Justice
  at *[area]*
Estates Division
[address]

Dear Sirs:

<u>Re: Estate of *[name]*</u>

We represent the Executor(s) of the Estate of *[name]*, who died on *[date of death]*. We enclose the following documents in order to apply for a Certificate of Appointment of Estate Trustee with a Will:

1. Affidavit of Service of Notice with Notice of Application attached as an Exhibit thereto;
2. Application for Certificate of Appointment of Estate Trustee with a Will;
3. Certificate of Appointment of Estate Trustee with a Will;
4. Original Last Will and Testament of *[deceased's name]* dated the *[date of Will]* and a copy thereof;
5. Affidavit of Execution of Will;
6. Certified cheque in the amount of $*[amount of fees]* in payment of the Court fees;

*

We would appreciate receiving the Certificate as soon as possible.

Yours very truly,

---

* Other possible enclosures as mentioned in the section dealing with the Certificate of Appointment of Estate Trustee With a Will.

Figure 3-2: Letter to Court Enclosing Application for Certificate of Appointment of Estate Trustee Without a Will

Local Registrar
Superior Court of Justice
  at
Estates Division
[address]

Dear Sirs:

Re: Estate of *[name]*

We represent the Administrator(s) of the Estate of *[name]*, who died on *[date of death]*. We enclose the following documents in order to apply for a Certificate of Appointment of Estate Trustee without a Will:

1. Affidavit of Service of Notice;
2. Application for Certificate of Appointment of Estate Trustee without a Will;
3. Certificate of Appointment of Estate Trustee without a Will;
4. Certified cheque in the amount of $*[court fees]* in payment of the Court fees;
5. Undertaking by the Estate Trustee(s) to pay any additional Court fees.

*

We would appreciate receiving the Certificate as soon as possible.

Yours very truly,

---

* Other possible enclosures as mentioned in the section dealing with the Certificate of Appointment of Estate Trustee Without a Will.

Figure 3-3: Letter to Court Enclosing Application for Certificate of Appointment of Succeeding Estate Trustee With a Will

Local Registrar
Superior Court of Justice
  at
Estates Division
[address]

Dear Sirs:

<u>Re: Estate of *[name]*</u>

We represent the Executor(s) of the Estate of *[name]*, who died on *[date of death]*. We enclose the following documents in order to apply for a Certificate of Appointment of Succeeding Estate Trustee with a Will:

1. Original Court grant;
2. Application for Certificate of Appointment of Succeeding Estate Trustee with a Will;
3. Certificate of Appointment of Succeeding Estate Trustee with a Will;
4. Renunciation of Right to Certificate of Appointment of Succeeding Estate Trustee (if applicable);
5. Consent to Applicant's appointment as Succeeding Estate Trustee with a Will (if applicable);
6. Certified cheque in the amount of $*[Court fees]* in payment of the Court fees;

*

We would appreciate receiving the Certificate as soon as possible.

Yours very truly,

---

* Other possible enclosures as mentioned in the section dealing with the Certificate of Appointment of Succeeding Estate Trustee With a Will.

Figure 3-4: Letter to Court Enclosing Application for Certificate of Appointment of Succeeding Estate Trustee Without a Will

---

Local Registrar
Superior Court of Justice
 at
Estates Division
[address]

Dear Sirs:

Re: Estate of <u>*[name]*</u>

We represent the Administrator(s) of the Estate of *[name]*, who died on *[date of death]*. We enclose the following documents in order to apply for a Certificate of Appointment of Succeeding Estate Trustee without a Will:

1. Original Court grant;
2. Application for Certificate of Appointment of Succeeding Estate Trustee without a Will;
3. Certificate of Appointment of Succeeding Estate Trustee without a Will;
4. Consent to Applicant's appointment as Succeeding Estate Trustee without a Will (if applicable);
5. Affidavit in Support of Dispensing with Security or provide the Court with the Security;
6. Certified cheque in the amount of $*[Court fees]* in payment of the Court fees;

*

We would appreciate receiving the Certificate as soon as possible.

Yours very truly,

---

* Other possible enclosures as mentioned in the section dealing with the Certificate of Appointment of Succeeding Estate Trustee Without a Will.

Figure 3-5: Letter to Court Enclosing Application for Confirmation by Resealing of Appointment of Estate Trustee (With or Without a Will)

Local Registrar
Superior Court of Justice
  at
Estates Division
[address]

Dear Sirs:

<u>Re: Estate of *[name]*</u>

We represent the *[insert type of personal representative]* of the Estate of *[name]*, who died on *[date of death]*. We enclose the following documents in order to apply for Confirmation by Resealing of Appointment of Estate Trustee *[insert with or without]* a Will:

1. Application for Confirmation by Resealing of Appointment of an Estate Trustee *[insert with or without]* a Will;
2. Two certified copies of original Appointment granted by the Court under the seal of that Court;
3. Bond or Affidavit by issuing Court;
4. Confirmation by Resealing of Appointment of Estate Trustee *[insert with or without]* a Will;
5. Certified cheque in the amount of $*[court fees]* in payment of the Court fees;

*

We would appreciate receiving the Certificate as soon as possible.

Yours very truly,

---

* Other possible enclosures as mentioned in the section dealing with Confirmation by Resealing of Appointment of Estate Trustee.

Figure 3-6: Letter to Court Enclosing Application for Certificate of Ancillary Appointment of Estate Trustee With a Will

---

Local Registrar
Superior Court of Justice
  at
Estates Division
[address]

Dear Sirs:

Re: Estate of [name of estate]

We represent the Executor(s) of the Estate of *[name]*, who died on *[date of death]*. We enclose the following documents in order to apply for a Certificate of Ancillary Appointment of Estate Trustee with a Will:

1. Application for a Certificate of Ancillary Appointment of Estate Trustee with a Will;
2. Two certified copies of original Appointment granted by the Court under the seal of that Court;
3. Affidavit Dispensing with Security or bond;
4. Certificate of Ancillary Appointment of Estate Trustee with a Will;
5. Certified cheque in the amount of $*[court fees]* in payment of the Court fees;

*

We would appreciate receiving the Certificate as soon as possible.

Yours very truly,

* Other possible enclosures as mentioned in the section dealing with Certificate of Ancillary Appointment of Estate Trustee with a Will.

Figure 3-7: Letter to Court Enclosing Application for Certificate of Appointment of Estate Trustee During Litigation

Superior Court of Justice
  at
Estates Division
[address]

Dear Sirs:

Re: Estate of <u>*[name]*</u>

We represent the Applicant for a Certificate of Appointment of Estate Trustee during Litigation of the Estate of *[name]*. We enclose the following documents in order to apply for a Certificate of Appointment of Estate Trustee during Litigation:

1. Application for Certificate of Appointment of Estate Trustee during Litigation;
2. Certificate of Estate Trustee during Litigation;
3. Court Order for appointment of *[name of Estate Trustee]* as Estate Trustee during Litigation;
4. Certified cheque in the amount of $*[amount of court fees]* in payment of the Court fees.

We would appreciate receiving the Certificate of Appointment of Estate Trustee during Litigation as soon as possible.

Yours very truly,

84 THE PRACTICAL GUIDE TO ONTARIO ESTATE ADMINISTRATION

Figure 3-8: Notice of Deposit to Estate Registrar (Form 74.1)

ONTARIO
SUPERIOR COURT OF JUSTICE

NOTICE

TO THE ESTATE REGISTRAR FOR ONTARIO:

A will or codicil has been deposited in this office. Particulars of the document follow.

Details about the Testator

Complete in full as applicable	And if the testator is known by any other name, state below the full names used
First given name William	Given name or names N/A
Second given name N/A	
Third given name N/A	Surname N/A
Surname ADAMS	

Birth date of testator: 17   07   45
                          (day month year)

Date of will or codicil: 14   03   88
                          (day month year)

Estate trustees named in will or codicil:

1. Name: Adams, Barbara

   Address: 123 Alphabet Drive, Toronto, Ontario M3H 1R2

Date of deposit: 2   01   00
                  (day month year)

Office of deposit: City of Toronto

   DATE: 6   01   00
                  (day month year)

                                                                            Registrar

Address of court office
393 University Avenue
10th Floor
Toronto, ON M5G 1E6

LETTERS TESTAMENTARY 85

Figure 3-9: Notice of the Withdrawal to Estate Registrar (Form 74.2)

ONTARIO
SUPERIOR COURT OF JUSTICE

NOTICE

TO THE ESTATE REGISTRAR FOR ONTARIO:

A will or codicil has been withdrawn from this office. Particulars of the document follow.

Details about the Testator

Complete in full as applicable

And if the testator is known by any other name, state below the full names used

First given name William	Given name or names N/A
Second given name N/A	
Third given name N/A	Surname N/A
Surname ADAMS	

Birth date of testator: 17   07   45
                         (day month year)

Date of will or codicil: 14   03   88
                         (day month year)

Date of deposit: 02   01   00
                         (day month year)

Date of withdrawal: 06   01   00
                         (day month year)

Office of deposit: City of Toronto

DATE: 07   01   00
                         (day month year)

_____
Registrar

Address of court office
393 University Avenue
10th Floor
Toronto, ON M5G 1E6

Figure 3-10: Application for Certificate of Appointment of Estate Trustee With a Will (Individual Applicant) (Form 74.4)

ONTARIO Superior Court of Justice at City of Toronto	APPLICATION FOR CERTIFICATE OF APPOINTMENT OF ESTATE TRUSTEE WITH A WILL (INDIVIDUAL APPLICANT)
This application is filed by *(insert name, address and fax number)* Brown & Brown, 678 Driveway Street, Toronto, ON M3R 2H1	

DETAILS ABOUT THE DECEASED PERSON

Complete in full as applicable		And if the deceased was known by any other name, state below the full names used
First given name William		Given name or names N/A
Second given name N/A		
Third given name N/A		Surname N/A
Surname Adams		
Address of fixed place of abode *(street or postal address) (city or town)* 123 Alphabet Drive, Toronto, ON M3H 1R2		*(county, district, regional or metropolitan municipality)* City of Toronto, Province of Ontario
If the deceased person had no fixed place of abode in Ontario, did he or she have property in Ontario? [] No [] Yes N/A		**Last occupation of deceased person** Psychiatrist
Place of death *(city or town: county, district, regional or metropolitan municipality)* City of Toronto, Province of Ontario	**Date of death** *(day, month, year)* 01 June 1999	**Date of last will** (marked as Exhibit "A") *(day, month, year)* 14 March 1988
Was the deceased person 18 years of age or older at the date of the will (or 21 years of age or older if the will is dated earlier than September 1, 1971)? [] No [x] Yes If not, explain why certificate is being sought. Give details in an attached schedule.		
Date of codicil (marked as Exhibit "B") *(day, month, year)* N/A	**Date of codicil** (marked as Exhibit "C") *(day, month, year)* N/A	
Marital status [] Unmarried [] Widowed [x] Married [] Divorced	Did the deceased person marry after the date of the will? [x] No [] Yes If yes, explain why certificate is being sought. Give details in an attached schedule.	
Was a marriage of the deceased person terminated by a judgment absolute of divorce, or declared a nullity, after the date of the will? [x] No [] Yes If yes, give details in an attached schedule.	Is any person who signed the will or a codicil as witness or for the testator, or the spouse of such person, a beneficiary under the will? [x] No [] Yes If yes, give details in an attached schedule.	

VALUE OF ASSETS OF ESTATE

Do not include in the total amount: insurance payable to a named beneficiary or assigned for value, property held jointly and passing by survivorship, or real estate outside Ontario.

Personal property	Real estate, net of encumbrances	Total
$250,000.00	$150,000.00	$400,000.00

Is there any person entitled to an interest in the estate who is not an applicant? [] No [x] Yes
If a person named in the will or a codicil as estate trustee is not an applicant, explain.

— continued next page

Figure 3-10: Application for Certificate of Appointment of Estate Trustee With a Will (Individual Applicant) (Form 74.4) (continued)

If a person not named in the will or a codicil as estate trustee is an applicant, explain why that person is entitled to apply.

If the spouse of the deceased is an applicant, has the spouse elected to receive the entitlement under section 5 of the *Family Law Act*?   [ ] No [ ] Yes N/A

If yes, explain why the spouse is entitled to apply

AFFIDAVIT(S) OF APPLICANT(S)
(Attach a separate sheet for additional affidavits, if necessary.)

I, an applicant named in this application, make oath and say/affirm:

1. I am 18 years of age or older. 2. The exhibit(s) referred to in this application are the last will and each codicil (where applicable) of the deceased person and I do not know of any later will or codicil. 3. I will faithfully administer the deceased person's property according to law and render a complete and true account of my administration when lawfully required.	4. If I am not named as estate trustee in the will or codicil, consents of persons who together have a majority interest in the value of the assets of the estate at the date of death are attached. 5. The information contained in this application and in any attached schedules is true, to the best of my knowledge and belief.

Name *(surname and forename(s))* Adams, Barbara	**Occupation** Hairdresser	
Address *(street or postal address) (city or town)* 123 Alphabet Drive, Toronto, ON M3H 1R2	*(province)*	*(postal code)*

Sworn/Affirmed before me at the
City of Toronto
in the Province of Ontario
this 4th day of January, 2000

                                            "Barbara Adams"
                                          Signature of applicant

A Commissioner for Taking Affidavits

I, an applicant named in this application, make oath and say/affirm:

1. I am 18 years of age or older. 2. The exhibit(s) referred to in this application are the last will and each codicil (where applicable) of the deceased person and I do not know of any later will or codicil. 3. I will faithfully administer the deceased person's property according to law and render a complete and true account of my administration when lawfully required.	4. If I am not named as estate trustee in the will or codicil, consents of persons who together have a majority interest in the value of the assets of the estate at the date of death are attached. 5. The information contained in this application and in any attached schedules is true, to the best of my knowledge and belief.

Name *(surname and forename(s))*	**Occupation**	
Address *(street or postal address) (city or town)*	*(province)*	*(postal code)*

Sworn/Affirmed before me at the
City of Toronto
in the Province of Ontario
this   day of   , 2000

                                            Signature of applicant

A Commissioner for Taking Affidavits

Figure 3-11: Application for Certificate of Appointment of Estate Trustee With a Will (Individual Applicant) Limited to Assets Referred to in the Will (Form 74.4.1)

ONTARIO
Superior Court of Justice
at

APPLICATION FOR CERTIFICATE OF APPOINTMENT OF ESTATE TRUSTEE WITH A WILL (INDIVIDUAL APPLICANT) LIMITED TO ASSETS REFERRED TO IN THE WILL

This application is filed by *(insert name and address)*

DETAILS ABOUT THE DECEASED PERSON

Complete in full as applicable	And if the deceased was known by any other name, state below the full names used
First given name William	Given name or names N/A
Second given name N/A	
Third given name N/A	Surname
Surname ADAMS	N/A

Address of fixed place of abode *(street or postal address) (city or town)*
123 Alphabet Drive, Toronto, ON M3H 1R2

(county, district, regional or metropolitan municipality)
City of Toronto, Province of Ontario

If the deceased person had no fixed place of abode in Ontario, did he or she have property in Ontario? [ ] No [ ] Yes N/A	**Last occupation of deceased person** Psychiatrist

Place of death *(city or town; county, district, regional or metropolitan municipality)* City of Toronto, Province of Ontario	**Date of death** *(day, month, year)* 01 June 1999	**Date of last will** (marked as Exhibit "A") *(day, month, year)* 14 March 1988

Was the deceased person 18 years of age or older at the date of the will (or 21 years of age or older if the will is dated earlier than September 1, 1971)? [ ] No [X] Yes
If not, explain why certificate is being sought. Give details in an attached schedule.

Date of codicil (marked as Exhibit "B") *(day, month, year)* N/A	**Date of codicil** (marked as Exhibit "C") *(day, month, year)* N/A
Marital status [ ] Unmarried [ ] Widowed [X] Married [ ] Divorced	Did the deceased person marry after the date of the will? [X] No [ ] Yes If yes, explain why certificate is being sought. Give details in an attached schedule.
Was a marriage of the deceased person terminated by a judgment absolute of divorce, or declared a nullity, after the date of the will? [X] No [ ] Yes If yes, give details in an attached schedule.	Is any person who signed the will or a codicil as witness or for the testator, or the spouse of such person, a beneficiary under the will? [X] No [ ] Yes If yes, give details in an attached schedule.

VALUE OF ASSETS OF ESTATE

Do not include in the total amount: insurance payable to a named beneficiary or assigned for value, property held jointly and passing by survivorship, or real estate outside Ontario.

Personal property	Real estate, net of encumbrances	Total
250,000.00	150,000.00	$400,000.00

Is there any person entitled to an interest in the estate who is not an applicant? [ ] No [X] Yes

If a person named in the will or a codicil as estate trustee is not an applicant, explain.

If a person not named in the will or a codicil as estate trustee is an applicant, explain why that person is entitled to apply.

— continued next page

LETTERS TESTAMENTARY 89

Figure 3-11: Application for Certificate of Appointment of Estate Trustee With a Will (Individual Applicant) Limited to Assets Referred to in the Will (Form 74.4.1) (continued)

If the spouse of the deceased is an applicant, has the spouse elected to receive the entitlement under section 5 of the *Family Law Act*?
[ ] No [ ] Yes
If yes, explain why the spouse is entitled to apply   N/A

AFFIDAVIT(S) OF APPLICANT(S)
(Attach a separate sheet for additional affidavits, if necessary.)
I, an applicant named in this application, make oath and say/affirm:

1. I am 18 years of age or older. 2. The exhibit(s) referred to in this application are the last will and each codicil (where applicable) of the deceased person relating to the assets referred to in the will and I do not know of any later will or codicil affecting those assets. 3. I will faithfully administer the deceased person's property according to law and render a complete and true account of my administration when lawfully required.	4. If I am not named as estate trustee in the will or codicil, consents of persons who together have a majority interest in the value of the assets of the estate at the date of death are attached. 5. The information contained in this application and in any attached schedules is true, to the best of my knowledge and belief.

Name *(surname and forename(s))* Adams, Barbara		**Occupation** Hairdresser	
Address *(street or postal address) (city or town)* 123 Alphabet Drive, Toronto,	*(province)* ON		*(postal code)* M3H 1R2

Sworn/Affirmed before me at the
City of Toronto
in the Province of Ontario
this 4th day of January, 2000   "Barbara Adams"
_____
                                                               Signature of applicant

A Commissioner for Taking Affidavits
(or as may be)

Figure 3-12: Application for Certificate of Appointment of Estate Trustee With a Will (Corporate Applicant) (Form 74.5)

ONTARIO
Superior Court of Justice
at City of Toronto

APPLICATION FOR CERTIFICATE OF APPOINTMENT OF ESTATE TRUSTEE WITH A WILL (CORPORATE APPLICANT)

This application is filed by *(insert name and address)*
Brown & Brown, 678 Driveway Street, Toronto, ON M3R 2H1

DETAILS ABOUT THE DECEASED PERSON

Complete in full as applicable	*And if the deceased was known by any other name, state below the full names used*
First given name William	Given name or names N/A
Second given name N/A	
Third given name N/A	Surname N/A
Surname Adams	

Address of fixed place of abode *(street or postal address) (city or town)* 123 Alphabet Drive, Toronto, ON M3H 1R2	*(county, district, regional or metropolitan municipality)* City of Toronto, Province of Ontario

If the deceased person had no fixed place of abode in Ontario, did he or she have property in Ontario? [] No [] Yes N/A	**Last occupation of deceased person** Psychiatrist	
Place of death *(city or town; county, district, regional or metropolitan municipality)* City of Toronto, Province of Ontario	**Date of death** *(day, month, year)* 01 June 1999	**Date of last will** (marked as Exhibit "A") *(day, month, year)* 14 March 1988

Was the deceased person 18 years of age or older at the date of the will (or 21 years of age or older if the will is dated earlier than September 1, 1971)?   [] No [x] Yes
If not, explain why certificate is being sought. Give details in an attached schedule.

Date of codicil (marked as Exhibit "B") *(day, month, year)* N/A	**Date of codicil** (marked as Exhibit "C") *(day, month, year)* N/A
Marital status [] Unmarried [] Widowed [x] Married [] Divorced	Did the deceased person marry after the date of the will? [x] No [] Yes If yes, explain why certificate is being sought. Give details in an attached schedule.
Was a marriage of the deceased person terminated by a judgment absolute of divorce, or declared a nullity, after the date of the will? [x] No [] Yes If yes, give details in an attached schedule.	Is any person who signed the will or a codicil as witness or for the testator, or the spouse of such person, a beneficiary under the will? [x] No [] Yes If yes, give details in an attached schedule.

VALUE OF ASSETS OF ESTATE

Do not include in the total amount: insurance payable to a named beneficiary or assigned for value, property held jointly and passing by survivorship, or real estate outside Ontario.

Personal property	**Real estate, net of encumbrances**	**Total**
$250,000.00	$150,000.00	$400,000.00

Is there any person interested in the estate who is not an applicant?	[] No [x] Yes
If a person named in the will or a codicil as estate trustee is not an applicant, explain.	

— *continued next page*

Figure 3-12: Application for Certificate of Appointment of Estate Trustee With a Will (Corporate Applicant) (Form 74.5) (continued)

If a person not named in the will or a codicil as estate trustee is an applicant, explain why that person is entitled to apply.   ***In_will***

If the spouse of the deceased is an applicant, has the spouse elected to receive the entitlement under section 5 of the *Family Law Act*?   [ ] No [ ]Yes N/A

If yes, explain why the spouse is entitled to apply

AFFIDAVIT(S) OF APPLICANT(S)
(Attach a separate sheet for additional affidavits, if necessary.)

I, a trust officer named in this application, make oath and say/affirm:

1. I am a trust officer of the corporate applicant.	lawfully required.
2. I am 18 years of age or older.	5. If the corporate applicant is not named as estate trustee in the will or codicil, consents of persons who together have a majority interest in the value of the assets of the estate at the date of death are attached.
3. The exhibit(s) referred to in this application are the last will and each codicil (where applicable) of the deceased person and I do not know of any later will or codicil.	
4. The corporate applicant will faithfully administer the deceased person's property according to law and render a complete and true account of its administration when	6. The information contained in this application and in any attached schedules is true, to the best of my knowledge and belief.
Name of corporate applicant The Canada Trust Company	**Name of trust officer** John Smith

Address of corporate applicant *(street or postal address)   (city or town)   (province)   (postal code)*
111 Your Street, Toronto, ON M5C 1R2

Sworn/Affirmed before me at the
City of Toronto
in the Province of Ontario
this 4th day of January, 2000

A Commissioner for Taking Affidavits

"John Smith"
Signature of trust officer

I, an applicant named in this application, make oath and say/affirm:

1. I am 18 years of age or older.	4. If I am not named as estate trustee in the will or codicil, consents of persons who together have a majority interest in the value of the assets of the estate at the date of death are attached.
2. The exhibit(s) referred to in this application are the last will and each codicil (where applicable) of the deceased person and I do not know of any later will or codicil.	
3. I will faithfully administer the deceased person's property according to law and render a complete and true account of my administration when lawfully required.	5. The information contained in this application and in any attached schedules is true, to the best of my knowledge and belief.
Name *(surname and forename(s))*	**Occupation**

Address *(street or postal address)   (city or town)*   *(province)*   *(postal code)*

Sworn/Affirmed before me at the

in the
this   day of   , 2000

A Commissioner for Taking Affidavits

Signature of applicant

Figure 3-13: Application for Certificate of Appointment of Estate Trustee With a Will (Corporate Applicant) Limited to Assets Referred to in the Will (Form 74.5.1)

ONTARIO	
Superior Court of Justice at	APPLICATION FOR CERTIFICATE OF APPOINTMENT OF ESTATE TRUSTEE WITH A WILL (CORPORATE APPLICANT) LIMITED TO ASSETS REFERRED TO IN THE WILL

This application is filed by *(insert name and address)*

DETAILS ABOUT THE DECEASED PERSON

Complete in full as applicable	And if the deceased was known by any other name, state below the full names used
First given name William	Given name or names N/A
Second given name N/A	
Third given name N/A	Surname N/A
Surname Adams	

Address of fixed place of abode *(street or postal address) (city or town)* 123 Alphabet Drive, Toronto, ON M3H 1R2	*(county, district, regional or metropolitan municipality)* City of Toronto, Province of Ontario

If the deceased person had no fixed place of abode in Ontario, did he or she have property in Ontario? [ ] No [ ] Yes N/A	Last occupation of deceased person Psychiatrist	
Place of death *(city or town; county, district, regional or metropolitan municipality)* City of Toronto, Province of Ontario	Date of death *(day, month, year)* 01 June 1999	Date of last will (marked as Exhibit "A") *(day, month, year)* 14 March 1988

Was the deceased person 18 years of age or older at the date of the will (or 21 years of age or older if the will is dated earlier than September 1, 1971)?   [ ] No   [X] Yes
If not, explain why certificate is being sought. Give details in an attached schedule.

Date of codicil (marked as Exhibit "B") *(day, month, year)* N/A	Date of codicil (marked as Exhibit "C") *(day, month, year)* N/A
Marital status [ ] Unmarried [ ] Widowed [X] Married [ ] Divorced	Did the deceased person marry after the date of the will? [X] No [ ] Yes If yes, explain why certificate is being sought. Give details in an attached schedule.
Was a marriage of the deceased person terminated by a judgment absolute of divorce, or declared a nullity, after the date of the will? [X] No [ ] Yes If yes, give details in an attached schedule.	Is any person who signed the will or a codicil as witness or for the testator, or the spouse of such person, a beneficiary under the will? [X] No [ ] Yes If yes, give details in an attached schedule.

VALUE OF ASSETS OF ESTATE

Do not include in the total amount: insurance payable to a named beneficiary or assigned for value, property held jointly and passing by survivorship, or real estate outside Ontario.

Personal property	Real estate, net of encumbrances	Total
250,000.00	150,000.00	$400,000.00

Is there any person interested in the estate who is not an applicant?	[ ] No [ ] Yes

If a person named in the will or a codicil as estate trustee is not an applicant, explain.

If a person not named in the will or a codicil as estate trustee is an applicant, explain why that person is entitled to apply.

— continued next page

LETTERS TESTAMENTARY 93

Figure 3-13: Application for Certificate of Appointment of Estate Trustee With a Will (Corporate Applicant) Limited to Assets Referred to in the Will (Form 74.5.1) (continued)

If the spouse of the deceased is an applicant, has the spouse elected to receive the entitlement under section 5 of the *Family Law Act*?	
[ ] No [ ] Yes	
If yes, explain why the spouse is entitled to apply	N/A

AFFIDAVIT(S) OF APPLICANT(S)
(Attach a separate sheet for additional affidavits, if necessary.)
I, a trust officer named in this application, make oath and say/affirm:

1. I am a trust officer of the corporate applicant.	lawfully required.
2. I am 18 years of age or older.	5. If the corporate applicant is not named as estate trustee in the will or codicil, consents of persons who together have a majority interest in the value of the assets of the estate at the date of death are attached.
3. The exhibit(s) referred to in this application are the last will and each codicil (where applicable) of the deceased person relating to the assets referred to in the will and I do not know of any later will or codicil affecting those assets.	
	6. The information contained in this application and in any attached schedules is true, to the best of my knowledge and belief.
4. The corporate applicant will faithfully administer the deceased person's property according to law and render a complete and true account of its administration when	
Name of corporate applicant	**Name of trust officer**

Address of corporate applicant *(street or postal address)   (city or town)   (province)   (postal code)*

Sworn/Affirmed before me at the
City of Toronto,
in the Province of Ontario
this   4th day of January, 2000

A Commissioner for Taking Affidavits   Signature of trust officer
(or as may be)

Figure 3-14: Affidavit of Service of Notice (With a Will) (Form 74.6)

ONTARIO

SUPERIOR COURT OF JUSTICE

IN THE ESTATE OF WILLIAM ADAMS, deceased.

AFFIDAVIT OF SERVICE OF NOTICE

I, John Smith, of the City of Toronto, Province of Ontario, MAKE OATH AND SAY/AFFIRM:

1. I am a Trust Officer of the Corporate Applicant, The Canada Trust Company, one of the applicants for a certificate of appointment of estate trustee with a will in the estate.

2. I have sent or caused to be sent a notice in Form 74.7, a copy of which is marked as Exhibit "A" to this affidavit, to all adult persons and charities named in the notice (except to an applicant who is entitled to share in the distribution of the estate), to the Public Guardian and Trustee if paragraph 6 of the notice applies, to a parent or guardian of the minor and to the Children's Lawyer if paragraph 4 applies, to the guardian or attorney if paragraph 5 applies, and to the Children's Lawyer if paragraph 7 applies, all by regular lettermail sent to the person's last known address.

3. I attached or caused to be attached to each notice the following:
   (A) In the case of a notice sent to or in respect of a person entitled only to a specified item of property or stated amount of money, an extract of the part

— continued next page

Figure 3-14: Affidavit of Service of Notice (With a Will) (Form 74.6) (continued)

        or parts of the will or codicil relating to the gift, or a copy of the will (and codicil(s), if any).

    (B)   In case of a notice sent to or in respect of any other beneficiary, a copy of the will (and codicil(s), if any).

    (C)   In the case of a notice sent to the Children's Lawyer or the Public Guardian and Trustee, a copy of the will (and codicil(s), if any) and a statement of the estimated value of the interest of the person represented.

4.   To the best of my knowledge and belief, the persons named in the notice are all the persons who are entitled to share in the distribution of the estate.

Sworn/Affirmed before me at the   )
City of Toronto   )
in the Province of Ontario   )
this 4th day of January, 2000   )
)   "John Smith"
)   Signature of applicant
)
A Commissioner for Taking Affidavits   )

NOTE: If any person cannot be served, add at the end of paragraph 4 "except for (insert name) who cannot be served because (give explanation)".

Figure 3-15: Notice of an Application for a Certificate of Appointment of Estate Trustee With a Will (Form 74.7)

ONTARIO

SUPERIOR COURT OF JUSTICE

IN THE ESTATE OF WILLIAM ADAMS, deceased.

**NOTICE OF AN APPLICATION FOR A
CERTIFICATE OF APPOINTMENT OF ESTATE TRUSTEE WITH A WILL**

1. The deceased died on June 1, 1995.

2. Attached to this notice are:

   (A) If the notice is sent to or in respect of a person entitled only to a specified item of property or stated amount of money, an extract of the part or parts of the will or codicil relating to the gift, or a copy of the will (and codicil(s), if any).

   (B) If the notice is sent to or in respect of any other beneficiary, a copy of the will (and codicil(s), if any).

   (C) If the notice is sent to the Children's Lawyer or the Public Guardian and Trustee, a copy of the will (and codicil(s), if any) and if it is not included in the notice, a statement of the estimated value of the interest of the person represented.

3. The applicant named in this notice is applying for a certificate of appointment of estate trustee with a will.

— continued next page

Figure 3-15: *Notice of an Application for a Certificate of Appointment of Estate Trustee With a Will (Form 74.7)* (continued)

APPLICANT	
NAME	**ADDRESS**
The Canada Trust Company	111 Your Street, Toronto ON M5C 1R2
Barbara Adams	123 Alphabet Drive, Toronto ON M3H 1R2

4. The following persons who are less than 18 years of age are entitled, whether their interest is contingent or vested, to share in the distribution of the estate:

Name	Date of Birth *(day/month/year)*	Name and Address of Parent or Guardian	Estimated Value of Interest in Estate*
N/A			

*Note: The Estimated Value of Interest in Estate may be omitted in the form if it is included in a separate schedule attached to the notice sent to the Children's Lawyer.

5. The following persons who are mentally incapable within the meaning of section 6 of the *Substitute Decisions Act, 1992* in respect of an issue in the proceeding, and who have guardians or attorneys acting under powers of attorney with authority to act in the proceeding, are entitled, whether their interest is contingent or vested, to share in the distribution of the estate:

Name and Address of Person	Name and Address of Guardian or Attorney*
N/A	

* Specify whether guardian or attorney

6. The following persons who are mentally incapable within the meaning of section 6 of the *Substitute Decisions Act, 1992* in respect of an issue in the proceeding, and who do not have guardians or attorneys acting under powers of attorney with authority to act in the proceeding, are entitled, whether their interest is contingent or vested, to share in the distribution of the estate:

— continued next page

Figure 3-15: Notice of an Application for a Certificate of Appointment of Estate Trustee With a Will (Form 74.7) (continued)

Name and Address of Person	Estimated Value of Interest in Estate*
N/A	

*Note: *The Estimated Value of Interest in Estate may be omitted in the form if it is included in a separate schedule attached to the notice sent to the Public Guardian and Trustee.*

7. Unborn or unascertained persons may be entitled to share in the distribution of the estate. *(Delete if inapplicable)*

8. All other persons and charities entitled, whether their interest is contingent or vested, to share in the distribution of the estate are as follows:

Name	Address
Barbara Adams	123 Alphabet Drive, Toronto, ON M3H 1R2
Troy Adams	761 Your Street, Toronto, ON M5H 3P1
The Canadian Cancer Society	222 Their Street, Toronto, ON M7P 5M6

9. This notice is being sent, by regular lettermail, to all adult persons and charities named in this notice (except to an applicant who is entitled to share in the distribution of the estate), to the Public Guardian and Trustee if paragraph 6 applies, to a parent or guardian of the minor and to the Children's Lawyer if paragraph 4 applies, to the guardian or attorney if paragraph 5 applies and to the Children's Lawyer if paragraph 7 applies.

DATE: August 12, 2000

Figure 3-16: Affidavit of Execution of Will or Codicil (Form 74.8)

ONTARIO

SUPERIOR COURT OF JUSTICE

In the matter of the execution of a will or codicil of WILLIAM ADAMS.

AFFIDAVIT

I, JOHN SMITH, of the City of Toronto, Province of Ontario, MAKE OATH AND SAY/AFFIRM:

1. On March 14, 1988, I was present and saw the document marked as Exhibit "A" to this affidavit executed by WILLIAM ADAMS.

2. WILLIAM ADAMS executed the document in the presence of myself and of Betty Jones of the City of Toronto, Province of Ontario. We were both present at the same time, and signed the document in the testator's presence as attesting witnesses.

Sworn or Affirmed before me at the)
City of Toronto)
)
in the Province of Ontario)
)
on January 4, 2000)
)
) "John Smith"_____
)
)
)
)
)
A Commissioner for Taking Affidavits)

NOTE: If the testator was blind or signed by making his or her mark, add the following paragraph:
3. Before its execution, the document was read over to the testator, who (was blind)(signed by marking his or her mark). The testator appeared to understand the contents.

WARNING: A beneficiary or the spouse of a beneficiary should not be a witness.

(Fax number of solicitor or person filing this document)
Fax number:

Figure 3-17: Affidavit Attesting to the Handwriting and Signature of a Holograph Will or Codicil (Form 74.9)

ONTARIO
SUPERIOR COURT OF JUSTICE

IN THE ESTATE OF WILLIAM ADAMS, deceased.

**AFFIDAVIT ATTESTING TO THE HANDWRITING
AND SIGNATURE OF A HOLOGRAPH WILL OR CODICIL**

I, BETTY JONES, of the City of Toronto, MAKE OATH AND SAY/AFFIRM:

1. I was well acquainted with the deceased and have frequently seen the deceased's signature and handwriting.

2. I believe the whole of the document dated March 14, 1988, now shown to me and marked as Exhibit "A" to this affidavit, including the signature, is in the handwriting of the deceased.

Sworn or Affirmed before me at the	)
City of Toronto	)
in the Province of Ontario	)
on January 4, 2000	)
	) "Betty Jones"
	)
	)
A Commissioner for Taking Affidavits	)

(Fax number of solicitor or person filing this document)

Fax-number:

Figure 3-18: Affidavit of Condition of Will or Codicil (Form 74.10)

ONTARIO
SUPERIOR COURT OF JUSTICE

IN THE ESTATE OF [insert name], deceased.

AFFIDAVIT OF CONDITION OF WILL OR CODICIL

I, [insert name], of the [insert city or town and country or district, metropolitan or regional municipality of residence], MAKE OATH AND SAY/AFFIRM:

1. On   , I was present and saw the document marked as Exhibit "A" to this affidavit executed by the deceased, in the presence of myself and [insert name of other witness].

2. The following alterations, erasures, obliterations or interlineations that have not been attested appear in the document:

3. The document is now in the same condition as when it was executed.

Sworn or Affirmed before me at the	)
City of Toronto	)
in the Province of Ontario	)
on August , 2000	)
	)_____
	) [name of deponent]
	)
A Commissioner for Taking Affidavits	)

(Fax number of solicitor or person filing this document)
Fax number:

NOTE: If paragraph 3 is not correct, and the words "except that" and give details of the exceptions.

Figure 3-19: Renunciation of Right to a Certificate of Appointment of Estate Trustee (or Succeeding Estate Trustee) With a Will (Form 74.11)

ONTARIO

Court file no.

SUPERIOR COURT OF JUSTICE

IN THE ESTATE OF WILLIAM ADAMS, deceased.

RENUNCIATION OF RIGHT TO A CERTIFICATE OF APPOINTMENT OF ESTATE TRUSTEE (OR SUCCEEDING ESTATE TRUSTEE) WITH A WILL

The deceased died on June 1, 1999.

In that person's testamentary document dated March 15, 1988, I, LOUIS ADAMS, was named an estate trustee.

I renounce my right to a certificate of appointment of succeeding estate trustee with a will.

DATE: January 4, 2000

"Signature of Witness"   "Louis Adams"
Signature of witness   *Signature of person renouncing*

(Fax number of solicitor or person filing this document)
Fax number:

Figure 3-20: Consent to Applicant's Appointment as Estate Trustee With a Will (Form 74.12)

ONTARIO

Court file no.

SUPERIOR COURT OF JUSTICE

IN THE ESTATE OF WILLIAM ADAMS, deceased.

**CONSENT TO APPLICANT'S
APPOINTMENT AS ESTATE TRUSTEE WITH A WILL**

The deceased died on June 1, 1999.

No estate trustee named in a testamentary document of that person is applying for a certificate of appointment of estate trustee with a will.

I, LOUIS ADAMS, am entitled to share in the distribution of the estate.

I consent to the application by BARBARA ADAMS for a certificate of appointment of estate trustee with a will.

(Delete the following paragraph if it is inapplicable) I consent to an order dispensing with the filing of a bond by the applicant.

DATE: January 4, 2000

"Signature of Witness"   "Louis Adams"
Signature of witness   *Signature of person consenting*

(Fax number of solicitor or person filing this document)
Fax number:

Figure 3-21: Certificate of Appointment of Estate Trustee With a Will (Form 74.13)

ONTARIO

Court file no.

SUPERIOR COURT OF JUSTICE

IN THE ESTATE OF WILLIAM ADAMS, deceased.

late of City of Toronto, Province of Ontario

occupation Psychiatrist

who died on June 1, 1999

**CERTIFICATE OF APPOINTMENT
OF ESTATE TRUSTEE WITH A WILL**

Applicant	Address	Occupation
Barbara Adams	123 Alphabet Drive Toronto, ON M3H 1R2	Hairdresser

This CERTIFICATE OF APPOINTMENT OF ESTATE TRUSTEE WITH A WILL is hereby issued under the seal of the court to the applicant named above. A copy of the deceased's last will (and codicil(s), if any) is attached.

DATE:

_____
Registrar

Address of court office
393 University Avenue
10th Floor
Toronto, ON M5G 1E6

— continued next page

Figure 3-21: Certificate of Appointment of Estate Trustee With a Will (Form 74.13)
    (continued)

Court file no.

Ontario
Superior Court of Justice

Proceeding commenced at Toronto
IN THE ESTATE OF

WILLIAM ADAMS, deceased

**CERTIFICATE OF APPOINTMENT
OF ESTATE TRUSTEE
WITH A WILL**
(Form 74.13 under the Rules)

Name, address and telephone number of solicitor, party or person

Brown & Brown
678 Driveway Street
Toronto, ON M3R 2H1

Tel: (416) 111-2222
Fax: (416) 333-4444

Solicitor for the Applicants

Figure 3-22: Certificate of Appointment of Estate Trustee With a Will Limited to the Assets Referred to in the Will (Form 74.13.1)

Court file no.

SUPERIOR COURT OF JUSTICE

IN THE ESTATE OF William Adams

late of the City of Toronto,

occupation Psychiatrist

who died on June 1, 1999

CERTIFICATE OF APPOINTMENT OF ESTATE TRUSTEE WITH A WILL LIMITED TO THE ASSETS REFERRED TO IN THE WILL

Applicant:	Address:	Occupation:
Barbara Adams	123 Alphabet Drive	Hairdresser
	Toronto, ON M3H 1R2	

By Order of a Judge of the Superior Court of Justice this grant of a Certificate of Appointment of Estate Trustee with a Will is limited to the Assets Referred to in the Will dated May 14, 1988, a copy of which is attached. This will is the last will of the deceased dealing with those assets.

This CERTIFICATE OF APPOINTMENT OF ESTATE TRUSTEE WITH A WILL LIMITED TO THE ASSETS REFERRED TO IN THE WILL is hereby issued under the seal of the court to the applicant named above.

DATE:

_____
Registrar

Address of court office
393 University Avenue
10th Floor
Toronto, ON M5G 1E6

— continued next page

LETTERS TESTAMENTARY 107

Figure 3-22: Certificate of Appointment of Estate Trustee With a Will Limited to the Assets Referred to in the Will (Form 74.13.1) (continued)

Court file no.

Ontario
Superior Court of Justice

Proceeding commenced at Toronto
IN THE ESTATE OF

WILLIAM ADAMS, deceased

**CERTIFICATE OF APPOINTMENT
OF ESTATE TRUSTEE
WITH A WILL
LIMITED TO THE ASSETS
REFERRED TO IN THE WILL**

Name, address and telephone number of solicitor, party or person

Brown & Brown
678 Driveway Street
Toronto, ON M3R 2H1

Tel: (416) 111-2222
Fax: (416) 333-4444

Solicitor for the Applicants

Figure 3-23: Application for Certificate of Appointment of Estate Trustee Without a Will (Individual Applicant) (Form 74.14)

ONTARIO **Superior Court of Justice** at Toronto	APPLICATION FOR CERTIFICATE OF APPOINTMENT OF ESTATE TRUSTEE WITHOUT A WILL (INDIVIDUAL APPLICANT)
This application is filed by *(insert name, address and fax number)* Brown & Brown, 678 Driveway Street, Toronto, ON M3R 2H1	

DETAILS ABOUT THE DECEASED PERSON

Complete in full as applicable	*And if the deceased was known by any other name, state below the full names used*	
First given name WILLIAM	Given name or names N/A	
Second given name N/A		
Third given name N/A	Surname N/A	
Surname ADAMS		
Address of fixed place of abode *(street or postal address) (city or town)* 123 Alphabet Drive, Toronto, ON M3H 1R2	*(county, district, regional or metropolitan municipality)* City of Toronto, Province of Ontario	
If the deceased person had no fixed place of abode in Ontario, did he or she have property in Ontario? [] No [] Yes N/A	**Last occupation of deceased person** Psychiatrist	
Place of death *(city or town; county, district, regional or metropolitan municipality)* Toronto	**Date of death** *(day, month, year)* 1 June 1999	
Marital status [x] Unmarried [] Widowed [] Married [] Divorced	Was the deceased person's marriage terminated by a judgment absolute of divorce, or declared a nullity? [] No [] Yes N/A If yes, give details in an attached schedule.	
Did the deceased person go through a form of marriage with another person where it appears uncertain whether an earlier marriage of the deceased person had been terminated by divorce or declared a nullity? [x] No [] Yes If yes, give the other person's name and address, and the names and addresses of any children (including deceased children) of the marriage, in an attached schedule.		
Was any earlier marriage of another person with whom the deceased person went through a form of marriage terminated by divorce or declared a nullity? [x] No [] Yes If yes, give details in an attached schedule.	Was the deceased person immediately before his or her death, living in a conjugal relationship outside marriage with a person of the opposite sex or of the same sex? [x] No [] Yes If yes, give the person's name and address in an attached schedule.	

PERSONS ENTITLED TO SHARE IN THE ESTATE

(Attach a schedule if more space is needed. If a person entitled to share in the estate is not a spouse, child, parent, brother or sister of the deceased person, show how the relationship is traced.)

Name	Address	Relationship to deceased person	Age if under 18
Troy Adams	761 Your Street, Toronto, ON M5H 3P1	Brother	N/A

— continued next page

Figure 3-23: Application for Certificate of Appointment of Estate Trustee Without a Will (Individual Applicant) (Form 74.14) (continued)

Stacy Adams	167 Her Street, Toronto ON M5P 7R2	Niece	N/A

VALUE OF ASSETS OF ESTATE

Do not include in the total amount: insurance payable to a named beneficiary or assigned for value, property held jointly and passing by survivorship, or real estate outside Ontario.

Personal property	Real estate, net of encumbrances	Total
$250,000.00	$150,000.00	$400,000.00

Explain why the applicant is entitled to apply.
Niece of deceased and nominee of other next-of-kin.

AFFIDAVIT(S) OF APPLICANT(S)
(Attach a separate sheet for additional affidavits, if necessary.)
I, an applicant named in this application, make oath and say/affirm:

1. I am 18 years of age or older and a resident of Ontario.	a complete and true account of my administration when lawfully required.
2. I have made a careful search and inquiry for a will or other testamentary document of the deceased person, but none has been found. I believe that the person did not leave a will or other testamentary document.	4. Consents of persons who together have a majority interest in the value of the assets of the estate at the date of death are attached.
3. I will faithfully administer the deceased person's property according to law and render	5. The information contained in this application and in any attached schedules is true, to the best of my knowledge and belief.

Name *(surname and forename(s))*	**Occupation**
Adams Stacy	Salesperson

Address *(street or postal address) (city or town)*   *(province)*   *(postal code)*

167 Her Street, Toronto, ON M5P 7R2

Sworn/Affirmed before me at the
City of Toronto
in the Province of Ontario
this 6th day of January, 2000

                                             "Stacy Adams"
A Commissioner for Taking Affidavits   Signature of applicant

Name *(surname and forename(s))*	**Occupation**

Address *(street or postal address) (city or town)*   *(province)*   *(postal code)*

Sworn/Affirmed before me at the

in the
this   day of   , 2000

A Commissioner for Taking Affidavits   Signature of applicant

Figure 3-24: Application for Certificate of Appointment of Estate Trustee Without a Will (Corporate Applicant) (Form 74.15)

ONTARIO Superior Court of Justice at Toronto	APPLICATION FOR CERTIFICATE OF APPOINTMENT OF ESTATE TRUSTEE WITHOUT A WILL (CORPORATE APPLICANT)

This application is filed by *(insert name, address and fax number)*
Brown & Brown, 678 Driveway Street, Toronto, ON M3R 2H1

DETAILS ABOUT THE DECEASED PERSON

Complete in full as applicable	*And if the deceased was known by any other name, state below the full names used*
First given name WILLIAM	Given name or names N/A
Second given name N/A	
Third given name N/A	Surname N/A
Surname ADAMS	
Address of fixed place of abode *(street or postal address)* *(city or town)* 123 Alphabet Drive, Toronto, ON M3H 1R2	*(county, district, regional or metropolitan municipality)* City of Toronto, Province of Ontario
If the deceased person had no fixed place of abode in Ontario, did he or she have property in Ontario? [] No [] Yes N/A	**Last occupation of deceased person** Psychiatrist
Place of death *(city or town; county, district, regional or metropolitan municipality)* Toronto	**Date of death** *(day, month, year)* 1 June 1999
Marital status [x] Unmarried [] Widowed [] Married [] Divorced	Was the deceased person's marriage terminated by a judgment absolute of divorce, or declared a nullity? [] No [] Yes N/A If yes, give details in an attached schedule.
Did the deceased person go through a form of marriage with another person where it appears uncertain whether an earlier marriage of the deceased person had been terminated by divorce or declared a nullity? [x] No [] Yes If yes, give the other person's name and address, and the names and addresses of any children (including deceased children) of the marriage, in an attached schedule.	
Was any earlier marriage of another person with whom the deceased person went through a form of marriage terminated by divorce or declared a nullity? [x] No [] Yes If yes, give details in an attached schedule.	Was the deceased person immediately before his or her death, living in a conjugal relationship outside marriage with a person of the opposite sex or of the same sex? [x] No [] Yes If yes, give the person's name and address in an attached schedule.

PERSONS ENTITLED TO SHARE IN THE ESTATE

(Attach a schedule if more space is needed. If a person entitled to share in the estate is not a spouse, child, parent, brother or sister of the deceased person, show how the relationship is traced.)

Name	Address	Relationship to deceased person	Age if under 18
Troy Adams	761 Your Street, Toronto, ON M5H 3P1	Brother	N/A

— continued next page

LETTERS TESTAMENTARY 111

Figure 3-24: Application for Certificate of Appointment of Estate Trustee Without a Will (Corporate Applicant) (Form 74.15) (continued)

Stacy Adams	167 Her Street, Toronto ON M5P 7R2	Niece	N/A

VALUE OF ASSETS OF ESTATE

Do not include in the total amount: insurance payable to a named beneficiary or assigned for value, property held jointly and passing by survivorship, or real estate outside Ontario.

Personal property	Real estate, net of encumbrances	Total
$250,000.00	$150,000.00	$400,000.00

Explain why the applicant is entitled to apply.
Nominee of next-of-kin.

AFFIDAVIT(S) OF APPLICANT(S)
(Attach a separate sheet for additional affidavits, if necessary.)
I, an applicant named in this application, make oath and say/affirm:

1. I am a trust officer of the corporate applicant. 2. I am 18 years of age or older. 3. I have made a careful search and inquiry for a will or other testamentary document of the deceased person, but none has been found. I believe that the person did not leave a will or other testamentary document. 4. The corporate applicant will faithfully administer the deceased person's property according to law and render a complete and true account of its administration when lawfully required.	5. Consents of persons who together have a majority interest in the value of the assets of the estate at the date of death are attached. 6. The information contained in this application and in any attached schedules is true, to the best of my knowledge and belief.
Name of Corporate Applicant The Canada Trust Company	**Name of trust officer** John Smith
Address of corporate applicant 111 Your Street, Toronto, ON M5C 1R2	*(province)* *(postal code)*

Sworn/Affirmed before me at the
City of Toronto
in the Province of Ontario
this 6th day of January, 2000

A Commissioner for Taking Affidavits

_____"John Smith"_____
Signature of trust officer

Figure 3-25: Affidavit of Service of Notice (Without a Will) (Form 74.16)

ONTARIO
SUPERIOR COURT OF JUSTICE

IN THE ESTATE OF WILLIAM ADAMS, deceased.

AFFIDAVIT OF SERVICE OF NOTICE

I, Stacy Adams, of the City of Toronto, MAKE OATH AND SAY/AFFIRM:

1. I am an applicant for a certificate of appointment of estate trustee without a will in the estate.

2. I have sent or caused to be sent a notice in Form 74.17, a copy of which is marked as Exhibit "A" to this affidavit, to all adult persons named in the notice (except to an applicant who is entitled to share in the distribution of the estate), to a parent or guardian of the minor and to the Children's Lawyer if paragraph 3 of the notice applies, to the guardian or attorney if paragraph 4 applies and to the Public Guardian and Trustee if paragraph 5 applies, all by regular lettermail sent to the person's last known address.

3. To the best of my knowledge and belief, the persons named in the notice are all the persons who are entitled to share in the distribution of the estate.

Sworn/Affirmed before me at the	)
City of Toronto	)
in the Province of Ontario	)
this 4th day of January, 2000	)
	) "Stacy Adams"
A Commissioner for Taking Affidavits	)

NOTE: If any person cannot be served, add at the end of paragraph 3 "except for *(insert name)* who cannot be served because *(give explanation)*".

Figure 3-26: Notice of an Application for a Certificate of Appointment of Estate Trustee Without a Will (Form 74.17)

ONTARIO

SUPERIOR COURT OF JUSTICE

IN THE ESTATE OF WILLIAM ADAMS, deceased.

NOTICE OF AN APPLICATION FOR A
CERTIFICATE OF APPOINTMENT OF ESTATE TRUSTEE WITHOUT A WILL

1. The deceased died on June 1, 1999, without a will.

2. The applicant named in this notice is applying for a certificate of appointment of estate trustee without a will.

APPLICANT

NAME	**ADDRESS** (and fax number of solicitor or applicant)
Stacy Adams	167 Her Street, Toronto, ON M5P 7R2

3. The following persons who are less than 18 years of age are entitled to share in the distribution of the estate:

Name	Date of birth (day/month/year)	Name and address of Parent or guardian	Estimated value of interest in estate
N/A			

4. The following persons who are mentally incapable within the meaning of section 6 of the *Substitute Decisions Act, 1992* in respect of an issue in the proceeding, and who have guardians or attorneys acting under powers of attorney with authority to act in the proceeding, are entitled to share in the distribution of the estate:

— continued next page

Figure 3-26: Notice of an Application for a Certificate of Appointment of Estate Trustee Without a Will (Form 74.17) (continued)

Name and address of person	Name and address of guardian or attorney*	Estimated value of interest in estate
N/A		

* Specify whether guardian or attorney.

5. The following persons who are mentally incapable within the meaning of section 6 of the *Substitute Decisions Act, 1992* in respect of an issue in the proceeding, and who do not have guardians or attorneys acting under powers of attorney with authority to act in the proceeding, are entitled to share in the distribution of the estate:

Name and address of person	Estimated value of interest in estate
N/A	

6. All other persons entitled to share in the distribution of the estate are as follows:

Name	Address
Barbara Adams	123 Alphabet Drive, Toronto, ON M3H 1R2
Troy Adams	761 Your Street, Toronto, ON M5H 3P1

7. This notice is being sent, by regular lettermail, to all adult persons named in this notice (except to an applicant who is entitled to share in the distribution of the estate), to a parent or guardian of the minor and to the Children's Lawyer if paragraph 3 applies, to the guardian or attorney if paragraph 4 applies, and to the Public Guardian and Trustee if paragraph 5 applies.

DATE:

Figure 3-27: Renunciation of Prior Right to a Certificate of Appointment of Estate Trustee Without a Will (Form 74.18)

ONTARIO

Court file no.

SUPERIOR COURT OF JUSTICE

IN THE ESTATE OF WILLIAM ADAMS, deceased.

RENUNCIATION OF PRIOR RIGHT TO A CERTIFICATE OF APPOINTMENT OF ESTATE TRUSTEE WITHOUT A WILL

The deceased died on June 1, 1999, without a will.

I, Troy Adams, am entitled to apply for a certificate of appointment of estate trustee without a will in priority to Stacy Adams.

I renounce my right to a certificate of appointment of estate trustee without a will in priority to (insert name).

DATE: January 4, 2000

"Signature of Witness" "Troy Adams"
Signature of witness   *Signature of person renouncing*

(Fax number of solicitor or person filing this document)
Fax number:

116 THE PRACTICAL GUIDE TO ONTARIO ESTATE ADMINISTRATION

Figure 3-28: Consent to Applicant's Appointment as Estate Trustee Without a Will (Form 74.19)

ONTARIO

Court file no.

SUPERIOR COURT OF JUSTICE

IN THE ESTATE OF WILLIAM ADAMS, deceased.

**CONSENT TO APPLICANT'S
APPOINTMENT AS ESTATE TRUSTEE WITHOUT A WILL**

The deceased died on June 1, 1999, without a will.

I, Troy Adams, am entitled to share in the distribution of the estate.

I consent to the application by Stacy Adams for a certificate of appointment of estate trustee without a will.

I consent to an order dispensing with the filing of a bond by the applicant. *(Delete the following paragraph if it is inapplicable)*

DATE: January 4, 2000

"Signature of Witness"   "Troy Adams"
Signature of witness   Signature of person consenting

(Fax number of solicitor or person filing this document)
Fax number:

Figure 3-29: Certificate of Appointment of Estate Trustee Without a Will (Form 74.20)

Court file no.

SUPERIOR COURT OF JUSTICE

IN THE ESTATE OF WILLIAM ADAMS, deceased.

late of City of Toronto, Province of Ontario

occupation Psychiatrist

who died on June 1, 1999

CERTIFICATE OF APPOINTMENT
OF ESTATE TRUSTEE WITHOUT A WILL

Applicant	Address	Occupation
Stacy Adams	167 Her Street, Toronto, ON M5P 7R2	Doctor

This CERTIFICATE OF APPOINTMENT OF ESTATE TRUSTEE WITHOUT A WILL is hereby issued under the seal of the court to the applicant named above.

DATE : _____

Registrar

Address of court office
393 University Avenue
10th Floor
Toronto, ON M5G 1E6

— continued next page

118 THE PRACTICAL GUIDE TO ONTARIO ESTATE ADMINISTRATION

Figure 3-29: Certificate of Appointment of Estate Trustee Without a Will (Form 74.20) (continued)

Court file no.

Ontario
Superior Court of Justice

Proceeding commenced at Toronto
IN THE ESTATE OF

WILLIAM ADAMS, deceased

CERTIFICATE OF APPOINTMENT OF ESTATE TRUSTEE WITHOUT A WILL
(Form 74.20 under the Rules)

Name, address and telephone number of solicitor, party or person

Brown & Brown
678 Driveway Street
Toronto, ON M3R 2H1

Tel: (416) 111-2222
Fax: (416) 333-4444

Solicitor for the Applicants

Figure 3-30: Application for Certificate of Appointment of a Foreign Estate Trustee's Nominee as Estate Trustee Without a Will (Form 74.20.1)

ONTARIO

Superior Court of Justice

APPLICATION FOR CERTIFICATE OF APPOINTMENT OF A FOREIGN ESTATE TRUSTEE'S NOMINEE AS ESTATE TRUSTEE WITHOUT A WILL

This application is filed by *(insert name and fax number)*
Barbara Adams, 502 American Way, New York, NY, USA 90075

DETAILS ABOUT THE DECEASED PERSON

Complete in full as applicable	And if the deceased was known by any other name, state below the full names used
First given name WILLIAM	Given name or names N/A
Second given name N/A	
Third given name N/A	Surname N/A
Surname ADAMS	
Address *(street or postal address) (city or town) (country)* New York City, New York, USA	*(province or state)*
Place of death *(city or town; country)* New York	Date of death *(day, month, year)* 1 January 1996

Country of domicile
United States

PARTICULARS OF FOREIGN CERTIFICATE

Country (and province or state if applicable) where issued	Issuing court	Date issued *(day, month, year)*
United States	Monroe County Surrogate Court	6 March 1996

TOTAL VALUE OF ASSETS OF ESTATE	Total
	$ 650,000.00

VALUE OF ASSETS LOCATED IN ONTARIO

Personal property	Real estate, net of encumbrances	Total
$ NIL	$150,000.00	$150,000.00

— continued next page

Figure 3-30: Application for Certificate of Appointment of a Foreign Estate Trustee's Nominee as Estate Trustee Without a Will (Form 74.20.1) (continued)

AFFIDAVIT(S) OF APPLICANT(S)
(Attach a separate sheet for additional affidavits, if necessary.)

I, an applicant named in this application, make oath and say/affirm:

1. I am the nominee of the foreign estate trustee appointed in the jurisdiction where the deceased was domiciled at the date of death. 2. A copy of the document appointing the foreign estate trustee, certified by the court that issued it, is marked as Exhibit "A" to this affidavit. 3. I am 18 years of age or older.	4. I will faithfully administer the deceased person's property according to law and render a complete and true account of my administration when lawfully required. 5. The information contained in this application and in any attached schedules is true, to the best of my knowledge and belief.
Name *(surname and forename(s))* Adams Joan	**Occupation** Homemaker
Address *(street or postal address)* *(city or town)* *(province)* *(postal code)* 12 Her Street, Toronto, ON M1M 1M1	

Sworn/Affirmed before me at the
City of Toronto
in the Province of Ontario
this 6th day of January, 2000

                                              "Joan Adams"

A Commissioner for Taking Affidavits   Signature of applicant

I, an applicant named in this application, make oath and say/affirm:

1. I am the nominee of the foreign estate trustee appointed in the jurisdiction where the deceased was domiciled at the date of death. 2. A copy of the document appointing the foreign estate trustee, certified by the court that issued it, is marked as Exhibit "A" to this affidavit. 3. I am 18 years of age or older.	4. I will faithfully administer the deceased person's property according to law and render a complete and true account of my administration when lawfully required. 5. The information contained in this application and in any attached schedules is true, to the best of my knowledge and belief.
Name *(surname and forename(s))*	**Occupation**
Address *(street or postal address)* *(city or town)* *(province)* *(postal code)*	

Sworn/Affirmed before me at the
of
in the
of
this   day of   , 2000

A Commissioner for Taking Affidavits   Signature of applicant

Figure 3-31: Nomination of Applicant by Foreign Estate Trustee (Form 74.20.2)

ONTARIO

SUPERIOR COURT OF JUSTICE

IN THE ESTATE OF WILLIAM ADAMS, deceased.

NOMINATION OF APPLICANT BY FOREIGN ESTATE TRUSTEE

1. The deceased died on January 6, 1996, without a will.

2. I, Barbara Adams was appointed estate trustee by the Monroe County Surrogate Court, in the jurisdiction where the deceased was domiciled at the date of death, on the 6th day of March, 1996.

3. I nominate Joan Adams to apply in Ontario for a certificate of estate trustee without a will.

DATE:

_____   _____
Signature of witness   Signature of person nominating

Figure 3-32: Certificate of Appointment of Foreign Estate Trustee's Nominee as Estate Trustee Without a Will (Form 74.20.3)

ONTARIO

Court file no.

SUPERIOR COURT OF JUSTICE

IN THE ESTATE OF WILLIAM ADAMS, deceased,

late of City of New York, in the State of New York.

occupation Psychiatrist

who died on January 1, 1996

CERTIFICATE OF APPOINTMENT OF FOREIGN ESTATE TRUSTEE'S NOMINEE AS ESTATE TRUSTEE WITHOUT A WILL

Applicant	Address	Occupation
Joan Adams	12 Her Street, Toronto, ON M1M 1M1	Homemaker

This CERTIFICATE OF APPOINTMENT OF FOREIGN ESTATE TRUSTEE'S NOMINEE AS ESTATE TRUSTEE WITHOUT A WILL is hereby issued under the seal of the court to the applicant named above.

DATE: March 16, 2000

Registrar

Address of court office
393 University Avenue
10th Floor
Toronto, ON M5G 1E6

Figure 3-33: Application for Certificate of Appointment as Succeeding Estate Trustee With a Will (Form 74.21)

ONTARIO
Superior Court of Justice
at Toronto

APPLICATION FOR CERTIFICATE OF APPOINTMENT AS SUCCEEDING ESTATE TRUSTEE WITH A WILL

This application is filed by *(insert name, address and fax number)*
Brown & Brown, 678 Driveway Street, Toronto, ON M3R 2H1

DETAILS ABOUT THE DECEASED PERSON

Complete in full as applicable	And if the deceased was known by any other name, state below the full names used
First given name WILLIAM	Given name or names N/A
Second given name N/A	
Third given name N/A	Surname N/A
Surname ADAMS	

PARTICULARS OF FIRST CERTIFICATE

Name(s) of estate trustee(s)	Date issued *(day, month, year)*
James Hammel	1 June 1999

VALUE OF UNDISTRIBUTED ASSETS OF ESTATE

Personal property	Real estate, net of encumbrances	Total
$250,000.00	$150,000.00	$400,000.00

Explain why the applicant is entitled to apply.
Previous trustee was removed by the Court.

AFFIDAVIT(S) OF APPLICANT(S)
(Attach a separate sheet for additional affidavits, if necessary.)
I, a trust officer named in this application, make oath and say/affirm:

1. I am a trust officer of the corporate applicant. 2. I am 18 years of age or older. 3. The corporate applicant will faithfully administer the deceased person's property according to law and render a complete and true account of its administration when lawfully required. 4. If the corporate applicant is not named as	Estate trustee in the will or codicil, consents of persons who together have a majority interest in the value of the undistributed assets of the estate at the date of this application are attached. 5. The information contained in this application and in any attached schedules is true, to the best of my knowledge and belief.
Name of corporate applicant The Canada Trust Company	Name of trust officer John Smith

Address of corporate applicant *(street or postal address) (city or town) (province) (postal code)*
111 Your Street, Toronto, ON M5C 1R2

Sworn/Affirmed before me at the
City of Toronto
in the Province of Ontario
this 6th day of January, 2000

"John Smith"
A Commissioner for Taking Affidavits   Signature of trust officer

— continued next page

Figure 3-33: Application for Certificate of Appointment as Succeeding Estate Trustee With a Will (Form 74.21) (continued)

I, an applicant named in this application, make oath and say/affirm:	
1. I am 18 years of age or older. 2. I will faithfully administer the deceased person's property according to law and render a complete and true account of my administration when lawfully required. 3. If I am not named as estate trustee in the will or codicil, consents of persons who together	have a majority interest in the value of the undistributed assets of the estate at the date of this application are attached. 4. The information contained in this application and in any attached schedules is true, to the best of my knowledge and belief.
Name *(surname and forename(s))*	**Occupation**
Address *(street or postal address(city or town))* (province) (postal code)	

Sworn/Affirmed before me at the
    of
in the
this   day of   , 2000

A Commissioner for Taking Affidavits   Signature of applicant

Figure 3-34: Consent to Applicant's Appointment as Succeeding Estate Trustee With a Will (Form 74.22)

Court file no.

ONTARIO

SUPERIOR COURT OF JUSTICE

IN THE ESTATE OF WILLIAM ADAMS, deceased.

**CONSENT TO APPLICANT'S APPOINTMENT
AS SUCCEEDING ESTATE TRUSTEE WITH A WILL**

The deceased died on June 1, 1999.

I, Troy Adams, am entitled to share in the distribution of the remaining estate.

I consent to the application by The Canada Trust Company for a certificate of appointment of succeeding estate trustee with a will.

I consent to an order dispensing with the filing of a bond by the applicant. *(Delete if inapplicable)*

DATE:

　"Signature of witness"　　　　　　　　　　"Troy Adams"
Signature of witness　　　　　　　　　　　　[Signature of person consenting]

(Fax number of solicitor or person filing this document)
Fax number:

Figure 3-35: *Certificate of Appointment of Succeeding Estate Trustee With a Will (Form 74.23)*

Court file no.

SUPERIOR COURT OF JUSTICE

IN THE ESTATE OF WILLIAM ADAMS, deceased.

late of City of Toronto, Province of Ontario

occupation Psychiatrist

who died on June 1, 1999

**CERTIFICATE OF APPOINTMENT
OF SUCCEEDING ESTATE TRUSTEE WITH A WILL**

Applicant	Address	Occupation
The Canada Trust Company	111 Your Street, Toronto ON M5C 1R2	

This CERTIFICATE OF APPOINTMENT OF SUCCEEDING ESTATE TRUSTEE WITH A WILL is hereby issued under the seal of the court to the applicant named above. A copy of the deceased's last will (and codicil(s), if any) is attached.

DATE:

_____
Registrar

Address of court office
393 University Avenue
10th Floor
Toronto, ON M5G 1E6

— continued next page

LETTERS TESTAMENTARY 127

Figure 3-35: Certificate of Appointment of Succeeding Estate Trustee With a Will (Form 74.23) (continued)

Court file no.

Ontario
Superior Court of Justice

Proceeding commenced at Toronto
IN THE ESTATE OF

WILLIAM ADAMS, deceased

**CERTIFICATE OF APPOINTMENT
OF SUCCEEDING ESTATE TRUSTEE
WITH A WILL**
(Form 74.23 under the Rules)

Name, address and telephone number of solicitor, party or person

Brown & Brown
678 Driveway Street
Toronto, ON M3R 2H1

Tel: (416) 111-2222
Fax: (416) 333-4444

Solicitor for the Applicants

Figure 3-36: Application for Certificate of Appointment as Succeeding Estate Trustee Without a Will (Form 74.24)

ONTARIO

Superior Court of Justice
at Toronto

APPLICATION FOR CERTIFICATE OF APPOINTMENT AS SUCCEEDING ESTATE TRUSTEE WITHOUT A WILL

This application is filed by *(insert name, address and fax number)*

Brown & Brown, 678 Driveway Street, Toronto, ON M3R 2H1

DETAILS ABOUT THE DECEASED PERSON

Complete in full as applicable	And if the deceased was known by any other name, state below the full names used
First given name WILLIAM	Given name or names N/A
Second given name N/A	
Third given name N/A	Surname N/A
Surname ADAMS	

PARTICULARS OF FIRST CERTIFICATE

Name(s) of estate trustee(s) or administrator(s)	Date issued *(day, month, year)*
Stacy Adams	01 June 1999

PERSONS ENTITLED TO SHARE IN THE ESTATE (at date of this application)

(Attach a schedule if more space is needed. If a person entitled to share in the estate is not a spouse, child, parent, brother or sister of the deceased person, show how the relationship is traced.)

Name	Address	Relationship to deceased person	Age if under 18
David Adams	127 Long Street, Toronto, ON M2N 2H1	Son	N/A
Jennifer Adams	721 Short Street, Toronto ON M2N 3H1	Daughter	N/A

VALUE OF UNDISTRIBUTED ASSETS OF ESTATE

Personal property	Real estate, net of encumbrances	Total
$250,000.00	$150,000.00	$400,000.00

Explain why the applicant is entitled to apply.
Stacy Adams to whom a Certificate of Estate Trustee Without a Will was granted on June 1, 1999 died on August 3, 2000, the applicant is the nominee of the next-of-kin.

— continued next page

LETTERS TESTAMENTARY 129

Figure 3-36: Application for Certificate of Appointment as Succeeding Estate Trustee Without a Will (Form 74.24) (continued)

AFFIDAVIT(S) OF APPLICANT(S)
(Attach a separate sheet for additional affidavits, if necessary.)

I, a trust officer named in this application, make oath and say/affirm:

1. I am a trust officer of the corporate applicant. 2. I am 18 years of age or older. 3. The corporate applicant will faithfully administer the deceased person's property according to law and render a complete and true account of its administration when lawfully required.	4. Consents of persons who together have a majority interest in the value of the undistributed assets of the estate at the date of this application are attached. 5. The information contained in this application and in any attached schedules is true, to the best of my knowledge and belief.
Name of corporate applicant The Canada Trust Company	**Name of trust officer** John Smith
Address of corporate applicant *(street or postal address) (city or town) (province) (postal code)* 111 Your Street, Toronto, ON M5C 1R2	

Sworn/Affirmed before me at the
City of Toronto
in the Province of Ontario
this 6th day of January, 2000

_____   <u>"John Smith"</u>
A Commissioner for Taking Affidavits   Signature of trust officer

I, an applicant named in this application, make oath and say/affirm:

1. I am 18 years of age or older and a resident of Ontario. 2. I will faithfully administer the deceased person's property according to law and render a complete and true account of my administration when lawfully required. 3. Consents of persons who together have a	majority interest in the value of the undistributed assets of the estate at the date of this application are attached. 4. The information contained in this application and in any attached schedules is true, to the best of my knowledge and belief.
Name *(surname and forename(s))*	**Occupation**
Address *(street or postal address) (city or town)*	*(province) (postal code)*

Sworn/Affirmed before me at the
         of
,in the   ,
this   day of   , 2000.

_____   _____
A Commissioner for Taking Affidavits   Signature of applicant

Figure 3-37: Consent to Applicant's Appointment as Succeeding Estate Trustee Without a Will (Form 74.25)

ONTARIO

Court file no.

SUPERIOR COURT OF JUSTICE

IN THE ESTATE OF WILLIAM ADAMS, deceased.

**CONSENT TO APPLICANT'S APPOINTMENT
AS SUCCEEDING ESTATE TRUSTEE WITHOUT A WILL**

The deceased died on January 6, 1999, without a will.

I, David Adams, am entitled to share in the distribution of the remaining estate.

I consent to the application by The Canada Trust Company for a certificate of appointment of succeeding estate trustee without a will.

*(Delete the following paragraph if it is inapplicable)*I consent to an order dispensing with the filing of a bond by the applicant.

DATE:

"Signature of witness"   "David Adams"
Signature of witness   *Signature of person consenting*

(Fax number of solicitor or person filing this document)
Fax number:

LETTERS TESTAMENTARY 131

Figure 3-38: Certificate of Appointment of Succeeding Estate Trustee Without a Will (Form 74.26)

Court file no.

ONTARIO

SUPERIOR COURT OF JUSTICE

IN THE ESTATE OF WILLIAM ADAMS, deceased.

late of City of Toronto, Province of Ontario

occupation Psychiatrist

who died on June 1, 1999

**CERTIFICATE OF APPOINTMENT
OF SUCCEEDING ESTATE TRUSTEE WITHOUT A WILL**

Applicant	Address	Occupation
The Canada Trust Company	111 Your Street, Toronto, ON M5C 1E2	

This CERTIFICATE OF APPOINTMENT OF SUCCEEDING ESTATE TRUSTEE WITHOUT A WILL is hereby issued under the seal of the court to the applicant named above.

DATE:

_____
Registrar

Address of court office
393 University Avenue
10th Floor
Toronto, ON M5G 1E6

— continued next page

132 THE PRACTICAL GUIDE TO ONTARIO ESTATE ADMINISTRATION

Figure 3-38: Certificate of Appointment of Succeeding Estate Trustee Without a Will (Form 74.26) (continued)

Court file no.			
Ontario **Superior Court of Justice** Proceeding commenced at Toronto IN THE ESTATE OF WILLIAM ADAMS, deceased	**CERTIFICATE OF APPOINTMENT OF SUCCEEDING ESTATE TRUSTEE WITH A WILL** *(Form 74.25 under the Rules)*	*Name, address and telephone number of solicitor, party or person* Brown & Brown 678 Driveway Street Toronto, ON M3R 2H1 Tel: (416) 111-2222 Fax: (416) 333-4444 Solicitor for the Applicants	

LETTERS TESTAMENTARY 133

Figure 3-39: Application for Confirmation by Resealing of Appointment or Certificate of Ancillary Appointment of Estate Trustee (Form 74.27)

ONTARIO
Superior Court of Justice
at Toronto

APPLICATION FOR CONFIRMATION BY RESEALING OF APPOINTMENT OR CERTIFICATE OF ANCILLARY APPOINTMENT OF ESTATE TRUSTEE

This is an application for (*check one*)

[x] confirmation by resealing of the appointment of an estate trustee with (*or* without) a will.

[ ] a certificate of ancillary appointment of an estate trustee with a will.

This application is filed by (*insert name and address*)
Brown & Brown, 678 Driveway Street, Toronto, ON M3R 2H1

DETAILS ABOUT THE DECEASED PERSON

Complete in full as applicable	And if the deceased was known by any other name, state below the full names used
First given name WILLIAM	Given name or names N/A
Second given name N/A	
Third given name N/A	Surname N/A
Surname ADAMS	

Address (*street or postal address*)   (*city or town*)   (*province or state*)   (*country*)
113 Black Street, St. John's, NB, Canada

Place of death (*city or town, country*) St. John's, Canada	Date of death (*day, month, year*) 1 January 1996

PARTICULARS OF PRIMARY CERTIFICATE OR GRANT

Country (*and province or state if applicable*) where issued New Brunswick, Canada	Issuing court Court of Queen's Bench	Date issued (*day, month, year*) 1 March 1996

VALUE OF ASSETS LOCATED IN ONTARIO

Personal property	Real estate, net of encumbrances	Total
$ NIL	$200,000.00	$200,000.00

— continued next page

134 THE PRACTICAL GUIDE TO ONTARIO ESTATE ADMINISTRATION

Figure 3-39: Application for Confirmation by Resealing of Appointment or Certificate of Ancillary Appointment of Estate Trustee (Form 74.27) (continued)

AFFIDAVIT(S) OF APPLICANT(S)
(Attach a separate sheet for additional affidavits, if necessary.)

I, an applicant named in this application, make oath and say/affirm:

1. I am an estate trustee named in the primary certificate (*or* primary grant of letters probate *or* letters of administration), a copy of which, certified by the court that issued it, is Exhibit "A" to this affidavit. 2. I am 18 years of age or older. 3. I will faithfully administer the deceased person's property according to law and render	a complete and true account of my administration when lawfully required. 4. The primary certificate (*or* primary grant of letters probate *or* letters of administration) is still effective. 5. The information contained in this application and in any attached schedules is true, to the best of my knowledge and belief.

Name *(surname and forename(s))* — **Occupation**

Adams, Barbara — Hairdresser

Address *(street or postal address) (city or town)   (province)   (postal code)*

502 American Way, New York, NY, USA 90075

Sworn/Affirmed before me at the
City of Toronto
in the in the Province of Ontario
this 6th day of January, 2000

_____   "Barbara Adams"
A Commissioner for Taking Affidavits   Signature of applicant
(or as may be)

LETTERS TESTAMENTARY 135

Figure 3-40: Application for Confirmation by Resealing of Appointment or Certificate of Ancillary Appointment of Estate Trustee (Form 74.27)

ONTARIO
Superior Court of Justice
at Toronto

APPLICATION FOR CONFIRMATION BY RESEALING OF APPOINTMENT OR CERTIFICATE OF ANCILLARY APPOINTMENT OF ESTATE TRUSTEE

This is an application for (*check one*)

[ ] confirmation by resealing of the appointment of an estate trustee with (*or* without) a will.

[x] a certificate of ancillary appointment of an estate trustee with a will.

This application is filed by *(insert name and address)*
Barbara Adams, 502 American Way, New York, NY, USA 900075

DETAILS ABOUT THE DECEASED PERSON

Complete in full as applicable	And if the deceased was known by any other name, state below the full names used
First given name WILLIAM	Given name or names N/A
Second given name N/A	
Third given name N/A	Surname N/A
Surname ADAMS	

Address *(street or postal address)* *(city or town)* *(province or state)* *(country)*
New York City, New York, USA

Place of death *(city or town, country)*	Date of death *(day, month, year)* 1 January 1996

PARTICULARS OF PRIMARY CERTIFICATE OR GRANT

Country (*and province or state if applicable*) where issued	Issuing court Monroe County Surrogate Court	Date issued *(day, month, year)* 6 March 1996

VALUE OF ASSETS LOCATED IN ONTARIO

Personal property	Real estate, net of encumbrances	Total
$ NIL	$150,000.00	$150,000.00

— continued next page

Figure 3-40: Application for Confirmation by Resealing of Appointment or Certificate of Ancillary Appointment of Estate Trustee (Form 74.27) (continued)

AFFIDAVIT(S) OF APPLICANT(S)
(Attach a separate sheet for additional affidavits, if necessary.)

I, an applicant named in this application, make oath and say/affirm:

1. I am an estate trustee named in the primary certificate (*or* primary grant of letters probate *or* letters of administration), a copy of which, certified by the court that issued it, is Exhibit "A" to this affidavit. 2. I am 18 years of age or older. 3. I will faithfully administer the deceased person's property according to law and render	a complete and true account of my administration when lawfully required. 4. The primary certificate (*or* primary grant of letters probate *or* letters of administration) is still effective. 5. The information contained in this application and in any attached schedules is true, to the best of my knowledge and belief.
Name *(surname and forename(s))*	**Occupation**
Adams, Barbara	Hairdresser
Address *(street or postal address) (city or town)*	*(province)* *(postal code)*
113 Black Street, St. John's, NB L0K 2G0	

Sworn/Affirmed before me at the
City of Toronto
in the Province of Ontario
this 6th day of January, 2000

                                                            "Barbara Adams"
A Commissioner for Taking Affidavits   Signature of applicant
(or as may be)

Figure 3-41: Confirmation by Resealing of Appointment of Estate Trustee (Form 74.28)

**CONFIRMATION BY RESEALING OF APPOINTMENT OF
ESTATE TRUSTEE**

Sealed with the seal of the Superior Court of Justice by order of that court dated

, under subsection 52(1) of the *Estates Act*.

DATE:

_____
Registrar

Address of court office
393 University Avenue 10th Floor
Toronto, ON M5G 1E6

Figure 3-42: Certificate of Ancillary Appointment of Estate Trustee With a Will (Form 74.29)

ONTARIO

Court file no.

SUPERIOR COURT OF JUSTICE

IN THE ESTATE OF WILLIAM ADAMS, deceased.

late of New York, NY, USA

occupation Psychiatrist

who died on January 1, 1996

**CERTIFICATE OF ANCILLARY APPOINTMENT
OF ESTATE TRUSTEE WITH A WILL**

Applicant	Address	Occupation
Barbara Adams	502 American Way, New York, NY, USA 90075	Hairdresser

Court of foreign grant Monroe County Surrogate's Court

Date of foreign grant March 6, 1996

This CERTIFICATE OF ANCILLARY APPOINTMENT OF ESTATE TRUSTEE WITH A WILL is hereby issued under the seal of the court to the applicant named above.

A certified copy of the foreign grant, to which this certificate is ancillary, is attached.

DATE:

———————————————
Registrar

Address of court office
393 University Avenue
10th Floor
Toronto, ON M5G 1E6

— *continued next page*

Figure 3-42: Certificate of Ancillary Appointment of Estate Trustee With a Will (Form 74.29) (continued)

Court file no. _____

Ontario
Superior Court of Justice

Proceeding commenced at Toronto
IN THE ESTATE OF

WILLIAM ADAMS, deceased

CERTIFICATE OF ANCILLARY APPOINTMENT OF ESTATE TRUSTEE WITH A WILL
(Form 74.23 under the Rules)

Name, address and telephone number of solicitor, party or person

Brown & Brown
678 Driveway Street
Toronto, ON M3R 2H1

Tel: (416) 111-2222
Fax: (416) 333-4444

Solicitor for the Applicants

140 THE PRACTICAL GUIDE TO ONTARIO ESTATE ADMINISTRATION

Figure 3-43: Application for Certificate of Appointment of Estate Trustee During Litigation (Form 74.30)

ONTARIO

Superior Court of Justice
at Toronto

APPLICATION FOR CERTIFICATE OF APPOINTMENT OF ESTATE TRUSTEE DURING LITIGATION

This application is filed by *(insert name, address and fax number)*
Brown & Brown, 678 Driveway Street, Toronto, ON M3R 2H1

DETAILS ABOUT THE DECEASED PERSON

Name *(insert surname and forename(s), and, if applicable, any other name by which the deceased person was known)*
ADAMS WILLIAM

Address of fixed place of abode *(street or postal address) (city or town)* 123 Alphabet Drive, Toronto, ON M3H 1R2	*(county, district, regional or metropolitan municipality)* City of Toronto, Province of Ontario
If the deceased person had no fixed place of abode in Ontario, did he or she have property in Ontario? [] No [] Yes N/A	**Last occupation of deceased person** Psychiatrist
Place of death *(city or town; county, district, regional or metropolitan municipality)* City of Toronto	**Date of death** *(day, month, year)* 1 June 1999

VALUE OF ASSETS OF ESTATE

Do not include in the total amount: insurance payable to a named beneficiary or assigned for value, property held jointly and passing by survivorship, or real estate outside Ontario.

Personal property	**Real estate, net of Encumbrances**	**Total**
$250,000.00	$150,000.00	$400,000.00

This application is made pursuant to an order for the appointment of an estate trustee during litigation, made by
(name of judge) *(day, month, year)*

Len Bird	12 December 1999

— continued next page

Figure 3-43: Application for Certificate of Appointment of Estate Trustee During Litigation (Form 74.30) (continued)

AFFIDAVIT(S) OF APPLICANT(S)
(Attach a separate sheet for additional affidavits, if necessary.)

I, a trust officer named in this application, make oath and say/affirm:

1. I am a trust officer of the corporate applicant. 2. I am 18 years of age or older. 3. The corporate applicant will faithfully administer the deceased person's property according to law, make no distribution without a court order, and render a complete and true	account of its administration when lawfully required. 4. The information contained in this application and in any attached schedules is true, to the best of my knowledge and belief.
Name of corporate applicant The Canada Trust Company	**Name of trust officer** John Smith
Address of corporate applicant *(street or postal address)* *(city or town)* *(province)* *(postal code)* 111 Your Street, Toronto, ON M5C 1R2	

Sworn/Affirmed before me at the
City of Toronto
in the Province of Ontario
this 6 day of March, 2000

_____   "John Smith"_____
A Commissioner for Taking Affidavits   Signature of trust officer

I, an applicant named in this application, make oath and say/affirm:

1. I am 18 years of age or older. 2. I will faithfully administer the deceased person's property according to law, make no distribution without a court order, and render a complete and true account of my	Administration when lawfully required. 3. The information contained in this application and in any attached schedules is true, to the best of my knowledge and belief.
Name *(surname and forename(s))*	**Occupation**
Address *(street or postal address)* *(city or town)*	*(province)* *(postal code)*

Sworn/Affirmed before me at the

in the
this   day of   , 2000

_____   _____
A Commissioner for Taking Affidavits   Signature of applicant

Figure 3-44: Certificate of Appointment of Estate Trustee During Litigation (Form 74.31)

Court file no.

SUPERIOR COURT OF JUSTICE

IN THE ESTATE OF WILLIAM ADAMS, deceased.

late of City of Toronto

occupation Psychiatrist

who died on June 1, 1999

CERTIFICATE OF APPOINTMENT
OF ESTATE TRUSTEE DURING LITIGATION

Applicant	Address	Occupation
The Canada Trust Company	111 Your Street, Toronto, ON M5C 1R2	

By order of the Superior Court of Justice, this **CERTIFICATE OF APPOINTMENT OF ESTATE TRUSTEE DURING LITIGATION** to determine the validity of a testamentary document of the deceased is hereby issued under the seal of the court to the applicant named above.

DATE:

_____
Registrar

Address of court office
393 University Avenue
10th Floor
Toronto, ON M5G 1E6

— continued next page

Figure 3-44: Certificate of Appointment of Estate Trustee During Litigation (Form 74.31) (continued)

Court file no.

Ontario
Superior Court of Justice

Proceeding commenced at Toronto
IN THE ESTATE OF

WILLIAM ADAMS, deceased

**CERTIFICATE OF APPOINTMENT
OF ESTATE TRUSTEE
DURING LITIGATION**
(Form 74.23 under the Rules)

Name, address and telephone number of solicitor, party or person

Brown & Brown
678 Driveway Street
Toronto, ON M3R 2H1

Tel: (416) 111-2222
Fax: (416) 333-4444

Solicitor for the Applicants

144 THE PRACTICAL GUIDE TO ONTARIO ESTATE ADMINISTRATION

Figure 3-45: Bond — Insurance or Guarantee Company (Form 74.32)

ONTARIO
SUPERIOR COURT OF JUSTICE

BOND NO. $ 400,000.00

IN THE ESTATE OF WILLIAM ADAMS, deceased.

The principal in this bond is BARBARA ADAMS

The surety in this bond is (name of Bonding Company), an insurer licensed under the *Insurance Act* to write surety and fidelity insurance in Ontario.

The obligee in this bond is the Accountant of the Superior Court of Justice acting for the benefit of creditors and persons entitled to share in the estate of the deceased.

The principal and the surety bind themselves, their heirs, executors, successors and assigns jointly and severally to the Accountant of the Superior Court of Justice in the amount of FOUR HUNDRED THOUSAND DOLLARS ($400,000).

The principal as an estate trustee is required to prepare a complete and true inventory of all the property of the deceased, collect the assets of the estate, pay the debts of the estate, distribute the property of the deceased according to law, and render a complete and true accounting of these activities when lawfully required.

The primary obligation under this bond belongs to the principal. The principal is liable under this bond for any amount found by the court to be owing to any creditors of the estate and persons entitled to share in the estate to whom proper payment has not been made.

The surety, provided it has been given reasonable notice of any proceeding in which judgment may be given against the principal for failure to perform the obligations of this bond shall, on order of the court, and on default of the principal to pay any final judgment made against the principal in the proceeding, pay to the obligee the amount of any deficiency

---

— continued next page

Figure 3-45: Bond — Insurance or Guarantee Company (Form 74.32)
    (continued)

>
> in the payment by the principal, but the surety shall not be liable to pay more than the amount of the bond.
>
> The amount of this bond shall be reduced by and to the extent of any payment made under the bond pursuant to an order of the court.
>
> The surety is entitled to an assignment of the rights of any person who receives payment or benefit from the proceeds of this bond, to the extent of such payment or benefit received.
>
> DATE: January 5, 2000
>
> SIGNED, SEALED AND DELIVERED
> in the presence of:
>
>
>   __"BARBARA ADAMS"__
>   Principal
>
> __"WITNESS TO PRINCIPAL"__
>
>
>   _____
>   Surety
>
>
> *(Fax number of solicitor or person filing this document)*
> Fax number: (416) 333-4444

Figure 3-46: Bond — Personal Sureties (Form 74.33)

ONTARIO

SUPERIOR COURT OF JUSTICE

BOND NO.   AMOUNT $800,000.00

IN THE ESTATE OF WILLIAM ADAMS, deceased.

The principal in this bond is EIGHT HUNDRED THOUSAND DOLLARS

The sureties in this bond are ALLAN ADAMS and SALLY ADAMS

The obligee in this bond is the Accountant of the Superior Court of Justice acting for the benefit of creditors and persons entitled to share in the estate of the deceased.

The principal and the sureties bind themselves, their heirs, executors, successors and assigns jointly and severally to the Accountant of the Superior Court of Justice in the amount of EIGHT HUNDRED THOUSAND Dollars ($800,000.00).

The principal as an estate trustee is required to prepare a complete and true inventory of all the property of the deceased, collect the assets of the estate, pay the debts of the estate, distribute the property of the deceased according to law, and render a complete and true accounting of these activities when lawfully required.

The primary obligation under this bond belongs to the principal. The principal is liable under this bond for any amount found by the court to be owing to any creditors of the estate and persons entitled to share in the estate to whom proper payment has not been made.

The sureties, provided they have been given reasonable notice of any proceeding in which judgment may be given against the principal for failure to perform the obligations of this bond shall, on order of the court, and on default of the principal to pay any final judgment made against the principal in the proceeding, pay to the obligee the

— continued next page

Figure 3-46: Bond — Personal Sureties (Form 74.33) (continued)

> amount of any deficiency in the payment by the principal, but the sureties shall not be liable to pay more than the amount of the bond.
>
> The amount of this bond shall be reduced by and to the extent of any payment made under the bond pursuant to an order of the court.
>
> The sureties are entitled to an assignment of the rights of any person who receives payment or benefit from the proceeds of this bond, to the extent of such payment or benefit received.
>
> DATE:
>
> SIGNED, SEALED AND DELIVERED
> in the presence of:
>
>   "Barbara Adams"
>   Principal
>
> "Witness"   "Allan Adams"
>   Surety
>
>   "Sally Adams"
>   Surety
>
> *(Fax number of solicitor or person filing this document)*
> Fax number:

— continued next page

Figure 3-46: Bond — Personal Sureties (Form 74.33) (continued)

AFFIDAVIT OF SURETY

I, ALLAN ADAMS, of the City of Toronto, Province of Ontario, MAKE OATH AND SAY/AFFIRM:

I am a proposed surety on behalf of the intended estate trustees of the property of WILLIAM ADAMS, deceased, named in the attached bond.

I am eighteen years of age or over and own property worth $400,000.00 over and above all encumbrances, and over and above what will pay my just debts and every sum for which I am now bail or for which I am liable as surety or endorser or otherwise.

Sworn *or* Affirmed before me at the	)
City of Toronto	)
in the in the Province of Ontario	)
on 4th day of January, 2000	)
	) "ALLAN ADAMS"
	)
A Commissioner for Taking Affidavits	)

— continued next page

Figure 3-46: Bond — Personal Sureties (Form 74.33) (continued)

AFFIDAVIT OF SURETY

I, SALLY ADAMS, of the City of Toronto, in the Province of Ontario, MAKE OATH AND SAY/AFFIRM:

I am a proposed surety on behalf of the intended estate trustees of the property of WILLIAM ADAMS, deceased, named in the attached bond.

I am eighteen years of age or over and own property worth $400,000.00 over and above all encumbrances, and over and above what will pay my just debts and every sum for which I am now bail or for which I am liable as surety or endorser or otherwise.

Sworn *or* Affirmed before me at the	)
City of Toronto	)
in the Province of Ontario	)
on January 4, 2000	)
	) "SALLY ADAMS"
	)
A Commissioner for Taking Affidavits	)

Figure 3-47: Registrar's Notice of Application With a Will (Form 74.34)

ONTARIO

SUPERIOR COURT OF JUSTICE

NOTICE

Attached are a copy of an application for appointment of an estate trustee with a will in the estate of William Adams, deceased, and a copy of a certificate of the Estate Registrar indicating that you were named as an estate trustee in a later will or codicil of the deceased that is on deposit in the Superior Court of Justice.

DATE: August 12, 2000

_____
Registrar

Address of court office
393 University Avenue
10th Floor
Toronto, ON M5G 1E6

TO: Barbara Adams
    123 Alphabet Drive
    Toronto, ON M3H 1R2

Figure 3-48: Registrar's Notice of Application Without a Will (Form 74.35)

ONTARIO
SUPERIOR COURT OF JUSTICE

NOTICE

Attached are a copy of an application for appointment of an estate trustee without a will in the estate of William Adams, deceased, and a copy of a certificate of the Estate Registrar indicating that you were named as an estate trustee in a later will or codicil of the deceased that is on deposit in the Superior Court of Justice.

DATE: August 12, 2000

_____
Registrar

Address of court office
393 University Avenue
10th Floor
Toronto, ON M5G 1E6

TO: Barbara Adams
    123 Alphabet Drive
    Toronto, ON M3H 1R2

Figure 3-49: Affidavit in Support of Request for an Order that the Requirement of Posting a Bond be Dispensed With

ONTARIO
SUPERIOR COURT OF JUSTICE

IN THE ESTATE OF   , deceased.

AFFIDAVIT

I,   , of the   of   in the   of   , MAKE OATH AND SAY/AFFIRM:

1. I am the surviving spouse of the late   who died on the   day of   , 200 .

2. I had intimate knowledge of my husband's affairs prior to his death.

3. At the time of his death, he was employed by   as an   and was never engaged in business.

4. There are no debts of my late husband presently outstanding as I have personally arranged for payment of the funeral account. I believe that if my husband had left debts, I would know of them.

5. At the time of his death, the next of kin of my husband were as follows:

    All the next of kin are the full age of eighteen years.

6. Attached hereto as Exhibits   and   are the Consents of the next of kin to my appointment as Estate Trustee without the need to post security.

7. I make this Affidavit in support of an Application for Certificate of Appointment of Estate Trustee with(out) a Will, without the need to post security and for no improper purpose.

Sworn or Affirmed before me at the   )
)
City of Toronto   )
)
in the Province of Ontario   )
)
on   , 2000   )
)_____
)
)
)
A Commissioner for Taking Affidavits   )

(Fax number of solicitor or person filing this document)
Fax number:

Figure 3-50: Order to Dispense With Bond

ONTARIO

SUPERIOR COURT OF JUSTICE

In the Estate of
late of the City of
in the
deceased

The Honourable) THE DAY
) OF , 2000
)
)

ORDER TO DISPENSE WITH BOND

UPON THE APPLICATION of, , solicitor for the Applicants herein for a Certificate of Appointment of Estate Trustee with(out) a Will, and upon reading the Affidavit of , and exhibits thereto, filed.

IT IS ORDERED that the requirement for the filing of a Bond by the Applicants shall be dispensed with.

DATED at this day of , 2000.

———————————————

— continued next page

Figure 3-50: ***Order to Dispense With Bond*** (continued)

Court file no.	**ONTARIO SUPERIOR COURT OF JUSTICE** Proceeding commenced at Toronto IN THE ESTATE OF deceased	**ORDER TO DISPENSE WITH BOND**	*Name, address and telephone number of solicitor, party or person*

Figure 3-51: Affidavit as to Evidence of Signature

ONTARIO
SUPERIOR COURT OF JUSTICE

IN THE ESTATE OF   , deceased.

AFFIDAVIT

I,   , of the   , in the   , of Bank Manager, MAKE OATH AND SAY/AFFIRM:

1. I have been the Manager of the   Branch of   since the day of   , and as such have knowledge of the matters herein deposed to.

2. I am familiar with the signature of   , late of   who held   account no.   at the said bank branch and signed an account signature card in connection therewith.

3. Now shown to me and marked as Exhibit "B" to this my Affidavit is a copy of the said account signature card. To the best of my knowledge, information and belief, the signature on the said card is the signature of   .

4. The signature of   on his Last Will and Testament now produced and shown to me and marked as Exhibit "A", to this my Affidavit and the signature on Exhibit "A", to the best of my knowledge, information and belief are identical and are both the signature of the deceased.

Sworn or Affirmed before me at the	)
City of Toronto	)
in the Province of Ontario	)
on , 2000	)
	)_____
	) [name of deponent]
A Commissioner for Taking Affidavits	)

(Fax number of solicitor or person filing this document)
Fax number:

Figure 3-52: Undertaking

ONTARIO
SUPERIOR COURT OF JUSTICE

IN THE ESTATE OF   , deceased.

UNDERTAKING

I/WE   and   , are the Applicants for Certificate of Appointment of Estate Trustee with(out) a Will in connection with the above Estate.

The values of the assets of the Estate have not, as yet, been wholly determined as (GIVE DETAILED EXPLANATION - SUITABLE TO COURT OFFICE - AS TO WHY VALUES NOT AVAILABLE).

I/We hereby undertake to inform the Ontario Superior Court of Justice at Toronto of the values of the assets within six months and we further undertake to pay any additional Court fees that may become due when the said values have been ascertained.

DATED the   day of   , 2000

                                                        _____
                                                        Executor

                                                        _____
                                                        Executor

Figure 3-53: Affidavit re Multiple Wills

Court File No.

IN THE ONTARIO COURT OF JUSTICE AT TORONTO

IN THE MATTER OF THE ESTATE OF
WILLIAM ADAMS
OF THE CITY OF TORONTO, IN THE PROVINCE OF ONTARIO

AFFIDAVIT

I, **BARBARA ADAMS**, of the City of Toronto, in the Province of Ontario, MAKE OATH AND SAY AS FOLLOWS:

1. My husband, William Adams ("Adams") died on or about the 1st day of June, 1999, having left a Last Will and Testament dated the 14th day of March, 1998, (the "● Will"), dealing with the assets of his Estate, with certain specific exclusions, which assets are referred to as "the ● Estate", a copy of which ● Will is attached hereto as Exhibit "A".

2. Adams executed a second Will, a copy of which is attached as Exhibit "B" subsequently executed but also on the 14th day of March, 1998 (the "● Will"), which deals only with those specific assets which were excluded from the ● Estate. The assets excluded from the ● Estate, which are subject to the provisions of the ● Will are defined in the ● Will as being:

   > "The term "my ● Estate" for all purposes of this my Will shall refer only to my shares in the capitals of ALPHABET LIMITED AND NUMBER LIMITED (hereinafter collectively referred to as the "Corporations"), those of my assets which are held in trust for me by any one or more of the Corporation, and all amounts owing to me from any of the Corporations or from any other corporation controlled directly or indirectly by me, my wife and/or our issue or by any combination of us. It is my intention to include these assets in my ● Estate."

   and known as the "● Estate".

3. Pursuant to the ● Will and ● Will (the "Wills) the Deceased named me as the Executrix and Trustee of his Estate.

— continued next page

Figure 3-53: Affidavit re Multiple Wills (continued)

4. I am the Applicant to the Superior Court of Justice at Toronto for a Certificate of Appointment of Estate Trustee with a Will, with respect to the ● Will only.

5. The ● Will, does not revoke any of the provisions of the ● Will and the revocation clause of the ● Will is limited to the ● Estate and reads as follows:

    "I hereby revoke all Wills and Testamentary dispositions of every nature and kind whatsoever by me heretofore made regarding those of my assets which form part of my ● Estate."

    "I declare that I have an existing Will (my "● Will") executed on this same day, which Will, deals with certain of my assets (defined in such Will to be my ● Estate and which Will I do not intend to revoke by the provisions of this Will."

6. I make this Affidavit in support of an Application for a Certificate of Appointment of Estate Trustee with a Will with respect to the ● Will, which is being brought by myself, which only deals with the ● Estate, and for no improper purpose.

SWORN before me at the   )
City of Toronto   )
in the Province of Ontario   )
this   day of   , 2000.)
)
)   **BARBARA ADAMS**
_____   )
A Commissioner, etc.   )

Figure 3-54: Order

ONTARIO SUPERIOR COURT OF JUSTICE

THE HONOURABLE

IN THE ESTATE OF WILLIAM ADAMS, Deceased

ORDER

UPON reading the Application and Affidavit of Barbara Adams, the applicant for a Certificate of Appointment of Estate Trustee With A Will of the ● Estate of William Adams dated March 1, 1998.

IT IS HEREBY ORDERED that this Certificate of Appointment of Estate Trustee With A Will of the ● Estate, a copy of which is attached as Schedule A, being a limited grant, limited to the assets under the ● Will, be issued to the applicant.

DATED this   day of   , 2000.

_____
Justice

— continued next page

Figure 3-54: Order (continued)

Court file no. _____

Ontario
Superior Court of Justice
Proceeding commenced at Toronto
IN THE ESTATE OF
WILLIAM ADAMS, deceased

ORDER

Name, address and telephone number of solicitor, party or person

Brown & Brown
678 Driveway Street
Toronto, ON M3R 2H1

TEL: (416) 111-2222
FAX: (416) 333-4444

Solicitor for the applicant

LIST OF ADDRESSES OF OFFICES OF SUPERIOR COURT OF JUSTICE

AREA	ADDRESS	TELEPHONE	FAX
Estate Registrar for Ontario	Estates Administration Office Estates List Superior Court of Justice 303 University Avenue 10th Floor Toronto, Ontario, M5G 1Y8	(416) 326-2940	(416) 326-2939
Algoma District	Local Registrar Superior Court of Justice Estates Division Court House 426 Queen Street East Sault Ste. Marie, Ontario, P6A 1Z7	(705) 945-8000 ext. 521	(705) 945-5044
Brant County	Local Registrar Superior Court of Justice Estates Division Court House 70 Wellington Street Brantford, Ontario, N3T 2L9	(519) 752-7828	
Bruce County	Local Registrar Superior Court of Justice Estates Division Court House 215 Cayley Street Walkerton, Ontario, N0G 2V0	(519) 881-0211	
Cochrane District	Local Registrar Superior Court of Justice Estates Division Court House 149-4th Avenue P.O. Box 638 Cochrane, Ontario, P0L 1C0	(705) 272-4256	
Dufferin County	Local Registrar Superior Court of Justice Estates Division Court House 10 Louisa Street Orangeville, Ontario, L9W 3P9	(519) 941-4744	(519) 941-6941
Durham	Local Registrar Superior Court of Justice Estates Division Court House 605 Rossland Road East, P.O. Box 640 Whitby, Ontario, L1N 9G7	(905) 430-5800	(905) 430-5802
Elgin County	Local Registrar Superior Court of Justice Estates Division Court House 145 Curtis Street, P.O. Box 310 St. Thomas, Ontario, N5P 3T9	(519) 633-1720	(519) 633-7629
Essex County	Local Registrar Superior Court of Justice Estates Division Court House 245 Windsor Avenue Windsor, Ontario, N9A 1J2	(519) 973-6620	(519) 973-6614

AREA	ADDRESS	TELEPHONE	FAX
Frontenac County	Local Registrar Superior Court of Justice Estates Division Court House 5 Court Street Kingston, Ontario, K7L 2N4	(613) 548-6811	
Grey County	Local Registrar Superior Court of Justice Estates Division Court House 595-9th Avenue East Owen Sound, Ontario, N4K 3E3	(519) 376-1461	(519) 376-7101
Regional Mun. of Haldimand Norfolk	Local Registrar Superior Court of Justice Estates Division Court House Box 399 55 Munroe Street North Cayuga, Ontario, N0A 1E0	(905) 772-3335	
Hamilton-Wentworth	Local Registrar Superior Court of Justice Estates Division Court House 50 Main Street East Hamilton, Ontario, L8N 1E9	(905) 308-7218	
Hastings County	Local Registrar Superior Court of Justice Estates Division Court House 235 Pinnacle Street, Room 204 Belleville, Ontario, K8N 3A9	(613) 962-9106	
Huron County	Local Registrar Superior Court of Justice Estates Division Court House P.O. Box 400 Goderich, Ontario, N7A 4C6	(519) 524-7322	(519) 524-5670
Kenora District	Local Registrar Superior Court of Justice Estates Division Court House 216 Water Street Kenora, Ontario, P9N 1S4	(807) 468-2842	(807) 468-2840
Kent County	Local Registrar Superior Court of Justice Estates Division Court House 21 Seventh Street 3rd Floor Chatham, Ontario, N7M 5L1	(519) 354-4450	(519) 354-6292
Lambton County	Local Registrar Superior Court of Justice Estates Division Court House 700 North Christina Street Sarnia, Ontario, N7V 3C2	(519) 337-5314	(519) 332-3411

AREA	ADDRESS	TELEPHONE	FAX
Lanark County	Local Registrar Superior Court of Justice Estates Division Court House 43 Drummond Street East Perth, Ontario, K7H 1G1	(613) 267-2021	(613) 264-8315
Leeds & Grenville Counties	Local Registrar Superior Court of Justice Estates Division District Court House 10 Wall Street Brockville, Ontario, K6V 7A8	(613) 342-2288	
Lennox & Addington	Local Registrar Superior Court of Justice Estates Division Court House 41 Dundas Street West Napanee, Ontario, K7R 1Z5	(613) 354-3845	
Manitoulin District	Local Registrar Superior Court of Justice Estates Division Court House Gore Bay, Ontario, P0P 1H0	(705) 282-2461	(705) 282-3245
City of Toronto	Local Registrar Superior Court of Justice Estates Division Phoenix House 393 University Avenue 10th Floor Toronto, Ontario, M5G 1E6	(416) 326-2940	
Middlesex County	Local Registrar Superior Court of Justice Estates Division Court House Ground Floor A 80 Dundas Street London, Ontario, N6A 6A3	(519) 660-3027	(519) 660-3053
Muskoka	Local Registrar Superior Court of Justice Estates Division Court House 3 Dominion Street North Bracebridge, Ontario, P1L 2E6	(705) 645-8793	(705) 645-7901
Niagara North	Local Registrar Superior Court of Justice Estates Division Court House 4th Floor 59 Church Street St. Catharines, Ontario, L2R 7N8	(905) 988-6200	
Niagara at Welland	Local Registrar Superior Court of Justice Estates Division Court House 200 Dain Avenue Welland, Ontario, L3B 3E6	(905) 735-0010	(905) 734-9119

AREA	ADDRESS	TELEPHONE	FAX
Nipissing District	Local Registrar Superior Court of Justice Estates Division Court House 360 Plouffe Street North Bay, Ontario, P1B 9L5	(705) 495-8308	(705) 495-8368
Norfolk	Local Registrar Superior Court of Justice Estates Division Court House 530 Queensway West Box 308 Simcoe, Ontario, N3Y 4L2	(519) 426-6550	
Northumberland Country	Local Registrar Superior Court of Justice Estates Division Court House 860 William Street Cobourg, Ontario, K9A 3A9	(905) 372-3751	(905) 372-9952
Ottawa-Carleton	Local Registrar Superior Court of Justice Estates Division, Court House 161 Elgin Street Ottawa, Ontario, K2P 2K1	(613) 239-1024	
Oxford County	Local Registrar Superior Court of Justice Estates Division Court House P.O. Box 70 415 Hunter Street Woodstock, Ontario, N4S 7W5	(519) 539-6187	(519) 539-4579
Parry Sound District	Local Registrar Superior Court of Justice Estates Division Court House 89 James Street Parry Sound, Ontario, P2A 1T7	(705) 746-4251	(705) 746-6179
Peel	Local Registrar Superior Court of Justice Estates Division Court House 7755 Hurontario Street Brampton, Ontario, L6V 2M7	(905) 452-6685	(905) 452-6678
Perth County	Local Registrar Superior Court of Justice Estates Division Administration of Justice Blding 17 George Street West Stratford, Ontario, N5A 1A6	(519) 271-2572	(519) 271-8080
Peterborough County	Local Registrar Superior Court of Justice Estates Division Court House 70 Simcoe Street Peterborough, Ontario, K9H 7G9	(705) 876-3810	(705) 876-3813

LETTERS TESTAMENTARY 165

AREA	ADDRESS	TELEPHONE	FAX
Prescott & Russell Counties	Local Registrar Superior Court of Justice Estates Division, Court House 59 Court Street L'Orignal, Ontario, K0B 1K0	(613) 675-4567	(613) 675-4507
Prince Edward County	Local Registrar Superior Court of Justice Estates Division Court House 44 Union Street Box 680 Picton, Ontario, K0K 2T0	(613) 476-6236	(613) 476-7297
Rainy River District	Local Registrar Superior Court of Justice Estates Division Court House Box 8 333 Church Street Fort Frances, Ontario, P9A 1C9	(807) 274-5961	(807) 274-0516
Renfrew County	Local Registrar Superior Court of Justice Estates Division Court House 297 Pembroke Street East Pembroke, Ontario, K8A 3K2	(613) 732-8581	(613) 732-1766
Simcoe County	Local Registrar Superior Court of Justice Estates Division Court House 114 Worsley Street, Room 301 Barrie, Ontario, L4M 1M1	(705) 739-6144	
Stormont, Dundas & Glengarry Counties	Local Registrar Superior Court of Justice Estates Division Court House 340 Pitt Street, 4th Floor Cornwall, Ontario, K6J 3P9	(613) 932-1290	
Sudbury District	Local Registrar Superior Court of Justice Estates Division Court House 155 Elm Street West Sudbury, Ontario, P3C 1T9	(705) 671-5958	(705) 671-5979
Thunder Bay District	Local Registrar Superior Court of Justice Estates Division Court House 277 Camelot Street Thunder Bay, Ontario, P7A 4B3	(807) 343-2725	(807) 343-2704
Timiskaming District	Local Registrar Superior Court of Justice Estates Division Court House Box 609 393 Main Street Haileybury, Ontario, P0J 1K0	(705) 672-3321	(705) 672-3360

AREA	ADDRESS	TELEPHONE	FAX
Victoria & Haliburton Counties	Local Registrar Superior Court of Justice Estates Division Court House 440 Kent Street West Box 4000 Lindsay, Ontario, K9V 5P2	(705) 324-2425	(705) 324-1401
Waterloo, Regional Municipality of	Local Registrar Superior Court of Justice Estates Division Court House 20 Weber Street East Kitchener, Ontario, N2H 1C3	(519) 741-3204	
Wellington County	Local Registrar Superior Court of Justice Estates Division Court House 74 Woolwich Street Box 247 Guelph, Ontario, N1H 3T9	(519) 824-4100	(519) 824-5449
York Region	Local Registrar Superior Court of Justice Estates Division Court House 50 Eagle Street West Room 2025 Newmarket, Ontario, L3Y 6B1	(905) 853-4809	

4

ADMINISTERING AN ESTATE

Karen M. Gibbs

1. Locating and Dealing With Assets
    (a) Proof of Death
    (b) Opening the Estate Bank Account
    (c) Dealing with the Safety Deposit Box
    (d) Dealing with Money on Deposit
    (e) Without a Court Certificate
    (f) With the Court Certificate
    (g) Dealing with Term Deposits and Guaranteed Investment Certificates
    (h) Dealing with Real Estate
        (i) Under the *Registry Act*, R.S.O. 1990, c. R.20
            Joint Property
            Without a Court Certificate
            With a Court Certificate
        (ii) Under the *Land Titles Act*, R.S.O. 1990, c. L.5
            Joint Property
            Without a Court Certificate
            With a Court Certificate
        (iii) Possible Difficulties Dealing with Real Estate
    (i) Dealing with Canada Savings Bonds and other Government of Canada Securities
        (i) Without a Court Certificate
        (ii) With a Court Certificate
    (j) Dealing with other Bonds and Shares
        (i) Valuing Public Shares
        (ii) Valuing Bonds
        (iii) Without a Certificate
        (iv) With a Certificate
    (k) Dealing with Life Insurance
        (i) Where there is a Named Beneficiary
        (ii) Estate as Beneficiary
    (l) Dealing with Registered Retirement Savings Plans
        (i) Dealing with Registered Retirement Savings Plans and Spouses
            Named Beneficiary
            Estate is Beneficiary, or No Beneficiary Named
    (m) Dealing with Pension Plans
    (n) Dealing with Canada Pension Plan Benefits
        (i) Death Benefit
        (ii) Survivor's Benefit
        (iii) Orphan's Benefit

168   THE PRACTICAL GUIDE TO ONTARIO ESTATE ADMINISTRATION

    (o) Dealing with Motor Vehicles
    (p) Dealing with Other Assets
2. Locating and Dealing with Liabilities
    (a) *Family Law Act* Election
    (b) Payment of Debts
    (c) Advertisement for Creditors
    (d) Insolvent Estates
3. Finalizing the Estate
    (a) Finalizing the Value of the Estate with the Court
    (b) Documents to be Filed
    (c) Arranging Return of Security from Court
    (d) Distributions
    (e) Ongoing Estates
    (f) Payment of Money into Court
    (g) Keeping a Tickler System
    (h) Obtaining Status Certificates
    (i) Succession Duty
4. Forms
    Figure 4-1: Letter to Registrar General Requesting Birth, Marriage and Death Certificates
    Figure 4-2: Letter to Insurance Company Requesting Particulars on a Claim
    Figure 4-3: Letter to Insurance Company Proving Claim for Named Beneficiary
    Figure 4-4: Letter to Broker Requesting Information on Securities and What Commission Costs Will be to Sell Securities
    Figure 4-5: Letter to Transfer Agent Requesting Transfer of Shares
    Figure 4-6: Letter to Newspaper with Notice to Creditors
    Figure 4-7: Letter to Revenue Canada Requesting Final Clearance Certificate (Terminal, Partial and Final)
    Figure 4-8: Letter to Canada Pension Plan Applying for Death Benefit, Survivors' Benefits, Orphan's Benefit
    Figure 4-9: Letter to Canada Pension Plan to Cancel Pension Cheques
    Figure 4-10: Letter to Old Age Security to Cancel Cheques
    Figure 4-11: Letter Instructing Bank to Issue Cheque for Probate Fees
    Figure 4-12: Letter to Bank Without a Certificate
    Figure 4-13: Letter to Bank With a Certificate
    Figure 4-14: Letter to Bank of Canada to Transfer Bonds to Beneficiary (or Cash Bonds)
    Figure 4-15: Letter to Beneficiaries re: FLA Clause
    Figure 4-16: Letter to Court, Toronto Region, re: Filing of FLA Election
    Figure 4-17: Letter to Court re: Probate Fees Owing
    Figure 4-18: Letter to Court re: Refund of Probate Fees
    Figure 4-19: Letter to Court re: No Additional Probate Fees Owing
    Figure 4-20: Authorization re: Safety Deposit Box
    Figure 4-21: Power of Attorney to Transfer Bonds - Shares
    Figure 4-22: Declaration of Transmission (re: Shares)
    Figure 4-23: Declaration of Transmission (re: Bonds and Debentures)
    Figure 4-24: Election under the *Family Law Act, 1986*
    Figure 4-25: Consent
    Figure 4-26: Affidavit re: Increase in Probate Value
    Figure 4-27: Affidavit re: Decrease in Probate Value

As discussed in previous chapters, the administration of the estate will commence prior to obtaining any certificate from the court. However, once the certificate is received, or it has been determined the certificate will not be required, the administering of the assets begins.

ADMINISTERING AN ESTATE 169

1. LOCATING AND DEALING WITH ASSETS

Working together, the personal representative and the solicitor's office will commence the preparation and eventual completion of the Statement of Assets of the deceased as the asset information is received. Depending on the terms of the deceased's Will, prior commitments or terms of agreements made by the deceased in his or her lifetime, certain assets may be transferred directly to a beneficiary. This is known as transferring "in specie". However, certain assets may be "called in" or redeemed in favour of the estate by the personal representative in order to arrange for the payment of liabilities and to make distributions. The decision, subject to the terms of the Will, as to which assets should be retained in the form the deceased left them and which assets should be redeemed as soon as possible is that of the personal representative. In the interim, it is important for control of all the assets to be taken by the personal representative and therefore contact should be made in connection with all the known assets.

The personal representative should attend to the following:

- Change of address should be filed at the post office, if necessary. This, of course, is not necessary if the spouse is the personal representative and resided with the deceased.
- Make sure there is adequate insurance held for real estate, vehicles and other insurable assets. Make sure vacancy certificates have been placed on real estate remaining vacant.
- Arrange for valuation of all assets as at the date of death.
- If rental property is held, make contact with tenants and advise where cheques should be forwarded and that they should be made payable to the estate.
- Contact all creditors to advise of death and when personal representative might be in a position to satisfy payment.
- Return any Canada Pension Plan and Old Age Security monthly cheques that the deceased was not entitled to. If these payments were being automatically deposited into the bank account of the deceased, arrange for their cancellation. The estate is entitled to any cheques up to and including the month of death. Notify both the Canada Pension Plan and Old Age Security office of the death (See Figures 4-9 and 4-10).*
- Arrange the return of any other cheques the estate may not be entitled to. A request should be forwarded with the cheques to determine if a portion of the payment should be paid to the estate.
- Determine any pre-authorized chequing arrangements or post-dated cheques the deceased may have provided and make alternate arrangements.
- Cancel all credit cards, making sure not to cancel a card that the deceased's spouse may have held a secondary card for, without notifying the spouse.
- Return the deceased's driver's licence for cancellation and request a return of any unearned fee paid for the licence.
- Open estate bank account (see below).

---

* All figures referred to are located at the end of this chapter.

(a) Proof of Death

Although a Funeral Director's Statement of Death is generally accepted as proof of a death, certain companies have set monetary limits to the amount of assets for which they will accept the Funeral Director's Statement of Death and under certain circumstances they will require a Provincial Death Certificate to be produced. By way of example, life insurance companies have such monetary limits, although under certain circumstances a company may waive this requirement.

If it is necessary to obtain the Provincial Death Certificate, contact the Registrar General either in person or by mail (see Figure 4-1). Upon filing the completed application form required by the Registrar General's Office and the applicable fee, the certificate will be issued. This certificate is only available once the death has been registered with the province. The currently prescribed application to obtain the Province of Ontario death certificate is also used to obtain a Birth or Marriage Certificate.

(b) Opening the Estate Bank Account

The personal representative should arrange to open an estate bank account as quickly as possible. This account can generally be opened by providing proof of death, a notarial copy of the Last Will and Testament of the deceased, if one exists, a signed bank signature card and bank account application form. However, the personal representative should be advised that although deposits can generally be made to the account prior to the issuance of the Court Certificate, no withdrawals can be made.

The cost of the funeral and the court fees (see Figure 4-11) will usually be paid by the bank, by bank draft, from funds left by the deceased in his or her bank accounts. However, if there are not sufficient monies on deposit at the bank you may have to consider filing your court application based on an estimated value.

The personal representative should be advised of the appropriate way in which records should be kept in connection with the administration of the estate and particularly the estate bank account. As the personal representative may be called upon to present his or her accounts to the court, or the personal representative may wish to do so in order to claim compensation (see Chapter 6, Passing of Accounts) a very detailed record of the receipts and disbursements broken down between capital and revenue, if the distribution of the estate is allocated between capital and revenue, should be kept.

(c) Dealing with the Safety Deposit Box

Unless arrangements were made with the bank for the closing of the safety deposit box without the requirement of the Court Certificate, it is necessary to provide the bank with the certificate in order to close out the safety deposit box and arrange for the return of any unearned fees for the rental of the box.

Although not always the case, the personal representative may wish to retain the box to hold the estate securities and he or she would therefore arrange to change the name of

ADMINISTERING AN ESTATE 171

the owner on the box to the personal representative. (*e.g.*, "John Smith, Estate Trustee for the estate of June Smith").

However, when it is necessary to enter the box for the purpose of listing the assets, it is generally possible for the personal representative to provide authorization for the bank to allow the solicitor's office to attend with a banking official to prepare the listing (See Figure 4-20). There are no prescribed formal listing requirements; however, the bank official may use a form similar to the prescribed form previously required under the now repealed *Succession Duty Act*, R.S.O. 1970, c. 449.

(d) Dealing with Money on Deposit

Monies held on joint account can be transferred to the surviving joint owner by providing the bank with a notarial copy of proof of death.

If there is a concern that the deceased had not meant the account to be joint or was not competent to make the decision to make the account a joint account, the account could be frozen pending resolution of this dispute, in the case where the surviving joint owner has not already dealt with the monies.

(e) Without a Court Certificate

If the personal representative has been successful in having the bank or trust company waive the requirement for the Court Certificate, the following is generally required in order to close out bank accounts:

- Letter to bank (see Figure 4-12).
- Notarial copy of the Last Will and Testament and any codicils thereto.
- Notarial copy of proof of death.
- Indemnity in favour of the bank, in a form acceptable to the bank, provided by the personal representative or beneficiary or both.

Certain banks may also request their form of Declaration of Transmission, in order to deal with an account.

Remember, that the bank draft issued to close out an account cannot be dealt with if it is made payable to the estate as you have no estate bank account, unless you have made special arrangements. You may have been able to have one bank agree to deposit the cheque payable to the estate into the deceased's account and at that point that bank will close out the account. For this reason, among others, you must be very careful and thorough in assisting the personal representative in determining if an estate can be administered without the Court Certificate.

(f) With the Court Certificate

If it has been determined that the Court Certificate was required, then when it is time to arrange to close out an account the following is generally required:

- Letter to the bank (see Figure 4-13).
- Notarial copy of the certificate issued by the court.
- Notarial copy of proof of death.

As mentioned above, a bank may request their form, Declaration of Transmission.

(g) Dealing with Term Deposits and Guaranteed Investment Certificates

Although each institution has its own requirements, certain institutions may render a penalty for transferring ownership from the deceased into the name of the estate or may consider it appropriate to amend the certificate to reflect the current rate of interest being paid at the time of the transfer. There can also be a penalty when a certificate is cashed prior to its maturity date so a full review of the certificate and the purchase agreement is recommended prior to requesting an early redemption.

In certain circumstances and depending on the particular institution's requirements you may also be asked to provide a Declaration of Transmission; either the standard form or the bank's prescribed form may be requested. The Declaration of Transmission can be used in two ways. The one is to "transmit" the asset into the name of the personal representative and the second transmits the asset to the personal representative and then immediately to the beneficiary if this is the desired result.

The forms required in order to deal with these deposits or certificates are:

- Notarial copy of Court Certificate.
- Notarial copy of proof of death.
- Declaration of Transmission (see Figure 4-22), if requested.
- Letter to institution or bank (see Figure 4-13 or 4-14).
- Power of Attorney to Transfer Bonds — Shares (see Figure 4-21), if requested.

If the Power of Attorney to Transfer Bonds — Shares is required, the personal representative's signature must be guaranteed. The institution may also request a Letter of Direction, although this and additional forms would be at the discretion of the individual institutions.

(h) Dealing with Real Estate

(i) Under the *Registry Act*, R.S.O. 1990, c. R.20

Joint Property

Generally, proof of death of the deceased joint tenant is deposited on the title to the property and when the surviving owner deals with the property the registration particulars are recited in the Deed/Transfer of Land.

Without a Court Certificate

The original Will and any codicils thereto or a notarial copy thereof, together with a notarial copy of proof of death, are registered against the title to the property. When the personal representative sells or is ready to deal with the land, an Executor's Deed will be completed, which document will include recitals of the registration particulars of both the Will and proof of death.

It is also necessary to deposit an original Affidavit of Execution on the title. However, please note the Affidavit normally refers to the original Will being marked as Exhibit "A" to the Affidavit and therefore the form of Affidavit of Execution must be amended to refer to the notarial copy being marked as Exhibit "A".

With a Court Certificate

The procedure is the same as without the certificate; however, a notarial copy of the Court Certificate will be registered instead of just the Will and any codicils. The Affidavit of Execution is not required in this instance as the original Affidavit of Execution was provided to the Court with the Application and the original Will.

(ii) Under the *Land Titles Act*, R.S.O. 1990, c. L.5

Joint Property

It is necessary for the surviving joint tenant to file an application under the *Land Titles Act* to have the deceased joint tenant's name deleted from the parcel register. This application will contain a notarial copy of the proof of death and the affidavit of the applicant confirming how the property was held and the confirmation of the death.

Without a Court Certificate

If the approval of the Director of Titles has been obtained (see Chapter 2), a Transmission Application containing the original or a notarial copy of the Will and any codicils thereto, proof of death and the applicant's affidavit as outlined under the *Land Titles Act* must be registered.

With a Court Certificate

The personal representative cannot deal with property registered under the land titles system without having the property transmitted into his or her name. Therefore, a Transmission Application containing a notarial copy of the Court Certificate, proof of death and the affidavit of the applicant pursuant to the *Land Titles Act* must be registered. Upon registration of the Transmission Application, the personal representative is considered the owner as the personal representative of the estate and can deal with the property.

(iii) Possible Difficulties Dealing with Real Estate

- Unless the Will or other document allows to the contrary, a personal representative should not purchase any assets from the estate including real estate without obtaining

the consent of the court and the beneficiaries. However, this is not applicable if the personal representative is the named beneficiary of the property in question.
- There are very specific limitations when a minor has an interest in real estate.
- Whether in the Registry Office or Land Titles Office there is a possible requirement for the registration of a Succession Duty Consent if succession duty was applicable or payable at the time of death (see Succession Duty, *infra*).

(i) Dealing with Canada Savings Bonds and other Government of Canada Securities

(i) Without a Court Certificate

Whether a testate or intestate estate, Canada Savings Bonds or Government of Canada securities can be dealt with without a Court Certificate, if:

- The total of the Government of Canada securities or bonds held is $20,000, or less; or
- The total of the Government of Canada securities or bonds held is $200,000, or less and the spouse is the recipient.

The forms required are the following:

- Letter to the Bank of Canada (see Figure 4-14).
- The securities, or, if the securities are lost, evidence as requested by the Bank of Canada.
- Transfer of Registered Government Securities — Bank of Canada Form 534.
- Bank of Canada Transfer/Exchange Request Form No. 351A.
- Notarial copy of the Last Will and Testament and any codicils thereto in the case of a testate estate.
- Notarial copy of proof of death.

(ii) With a Court Certificate

The following forms are required:

- Letter to the Bank of Canada (see Figure 4-14).
- The securities or if the securities are lost, evidence as requested by the Bank of Canada.
- Bank of Canada Form 533 with the signature of the transferor guaranteed.
- Bank of Canada Transfer\Exchange Request Form No. 351A.
- Notarial copy of the Court Certificate.
- Notarial copy of proof of death.

ADMINISTERING AN ESTATE 175

(j) Dealing with other Bonds and Shares

(i) Valuing Public Shares

In valuing public shares, the following steps should be taken:

- Request the value of the shares as at the date of death from a stock broker. The values are required for both the purposes of completing the application to the court and for income tax purposes. For this reason, it is best to obtain the valuations in writing. If the personal representative does not have a stockbroker or the deceased did not have a relationship with a broker, most law firms have developed relationships with stock brokers which can be used for these purposes.
- The Statistics Department of the Toronto Stock Exchange will provide you with the values. However, there is a charge for this and they will only provide a certain number of quotations for each phone call.
- Obtain the quotations from the financial section of the newspaper.

(ii) Valuing Bonds

This valuation is usually easier to obtain. A review of a bond or debenture will provide you with the interest rate and state when the interest is to be paid. Generally, the value of a bond at the date of death is the face value together with the interest calculated from the time of the last interest payment date prior to death, up to the date of death.

(iii) Without a Certificate

If you have determined that you will be able to deal with the estate without the certificate requirement, the following procedures are required:

- Obtain notarial copy of the Last Will and Testament and any codicil thereto.
- Obtain notarial copy of proof of death.
- The bond or share certificate must be endorsed by the personal representative and his or her signature guaranteed thereon. In lieu of the bond or certificate being endorsed, the personal representative can complete a Power of Attorney to Transfer Bonds — Shares, and again his or her signature must be guaranteed (see Figure 4-21).
- The return of the original certificates. If it is found that the certificates have been lost, affidavit evidence is generally required as to the loss and confirmation that should the certificate be located, it will be returned.
- An Indemnity Bond may be requested and a one-time premium will be paid by the estate based on the value of the bond or shares.
- A Declaration of Transmission (see Figure 4-22) revised based on the fact that the Court Certificate will not be obtained.

If the deceased held his or her securities in a brokerage account and the broker has agreed to deal with the account without the need for the certificate, all of the above documents

176   THE PRACTICAL GUIDE TO ONTARIO ESTATE ADMINISTRATION

would be required with the exception of the return of the certificates affidavit as the bond or share certificates are held by the broker and were not in the deceased's possession.

If the shares are in "street form" they have already been endorsed on the back of the certificate by the registered owner for transfer and therefore are considered the property of the holder or bearer of the certificate so estate documentation is not required.

(iv) With a Certificate

The following steps should be taken:

- Obtain notarial copy of the Court Certificate.
- Obtain notarial copy of proof of death.
- Return of the certificates with the personal representative's signature guaranteed thereon or, if the certificates cannot be located, Affidavit of Loss requirements as provided by the transfer agent. Again, the Power of Attorney to Transfer Bonds — Shares can be provided in lieu of the certificate being endorsed on the reverse.
- Covering letter to transfer agent or broker (see Figure 4-4).
- Obtain Declaration of Transmission (In the case of shares see Figure 4-22; or, if bonds or debentures see Figure 4-23).

The Declaration of Transmission provides the evidence which allows the asset to be transmitted into the name of the personal representative, or it can be used to go the additional step of transferring the asset outright to the beneficiary or beneficiaries entitled thereto. If it is the intention of the personal representative to sell the shares, this is generally done through a stockbroker. The transfer agent registers any transfers and keeps the records for the corporation up to date.

(k)   Dealing with Life Insurance

If it is suspected that the deceased held life insurance, but no policies have been located, contact should be made with the deceased's employer or employer prior to retirement. The deceased's last tax return should also be reviewed to determine if dividends were possibly being paid from a life insurance policy or if there is any other reference to life insurance.

If during your search you locate information regarding a life insurance policy, a letter should be forwarded to the insurance company requesting particulars of the policy, which include, among other things, whether there is a named beneficiary. If there is a named beneficiary, the value of the policy is not included for purposes of your evaluation for the application for the Court Certificate. If there is not a named beneficiary, or the beneficiary is the estate, the proceeds are payable to the estate and it is necessary to determine the value as at the date of death (see Figure 4-2).

(i)   Where there is a Named Beneficiary

It should be kept in mind that when the spouse is the beneficiary, the proceeds of any life insurance policy received by the spouse are deductible from the spouse's entitlement under the *Family Law Act*, R.S.O. 1990, c. F.3, if the spouse elects under that Act.

If the policy is payable to a named beneficiary, the claimant's statement, provided by the insurance company, will be completed by the claimant beneficiary and not the personal representative. The following documents are required:

- Letter to the insurance company (see Figure 4-3).
- Return of the original policy or proof of loss if the policy cannot be located.
- Completed claimant's statement for the proof of death.

If the named beneficiary of the policy is deceased, the personal representative should review the terms of the insurance policy in order to determine if there are alternative provisions set out. If there are no other named beneficiaries to the policy, the policy will then form part of the insured's estate upon providing the above documentation together with proof of death of the deceased's beneficiary and upon providing additional documents listed below.

(ii) Estate as Beneficiary

The following are the documents required:

- Letter to the insurance company enclosing four documents listed immediately below (see Figure 4-3).
- Proof of death, which may be by way of a proof of death form completed by the attending physician, which form is provided by the insurance company, or a notarial copy of the funeral director's statement of death or provincial death certificate, as will be requested by the insurance company.
- Claimant's statement completed by the personal representative.
- General insurance policy or proof of loss if policy is not available.
- Notarial copy of the Court Certificate.

(l) Dealing with Registered Retirement Savings Plans

There are very specific tax consequences when dealing with Registered Retirement Savings Plans ("RRSPs"), and for a summary of these and certain matters you should be aware of when you are dealing with the transfer, please see Chapters 7 and 8.

(i) Dealing with Registered Retirement Savings Plans and Spouses

Although a rollover is allowed (pursuant to the *Income Tax Act*) to the spouse of a deceased person, any other named beneficiary will receive the proceeds of the plan and not the transfer of a plan. The entire proceeds of the plan may be taxable in the hands of the estate and not the beneficiary.

Named Beneficiary

In the case of a named beneficiary, the following are required:

- Proof of death of the deceased.
- Completed claimant's statement.

- If the beneficiary designation is contained in the Will and not on the plan itself, a notarial copy of the Will or a notarial copy of the Court Certificate should be provided.

Estate is Beneficiary, or No Beneficiary Named

When the estate is a beneficiary or there is no named beneficiary, the following are required:

- Proof of death of the deceased.
- Completed claimant's statement.
- Notarial copy of the Court Certificate, unless the insurance company has agreed to accept a notarial copy of the Will and any codicils.

In certain circumstances, additional forms may be required. For example, if a joint election is being executed by the personal representative and the surviving spouse to transfer the RRSP to the surviving spouse, additional transfer forms will be required.

(m) Dealing with Pension Plans

If the deceased was receiving a pension or was contributing to a pension plan through employment, a certain amount is generally payable to the estate of the deceased or to a named beneficiary. Contact should be made with the administrator of the plan to determine what benefits are payable and to whom. You may be requested to provide a notarial copy of the Court Certificate if there is not a named beneficiary under the plan.

(n) Dealing with Canada Pension Plan Benefits

The Canada Pension Plan was introduced in 1963 with the contributing period commencing in 1966. There are different benefits paid under the plan, all of which are based on contributions made by the deceased contributor. If the deceased did not contribute to the plan then no benefits are payable.

Although Health and Welfare Canada does return any original documents submitted with the applications, notarized or certified copies of the originals are accepted.

(i) Death Benefit

This is a one time lump sum payment paid to the estate. The maximum death benefit currently paid is just over $2,500, and this amount is increased from time to time. The following documents are required when applying for the benefit:

- Letter to Health and Welfare Canada (see Figure 4-8).
- If the deceased was under the age of 65, or not receiving benefits under the Canada Pension Plan, proof of age is required.
- If the deceased was under the age of 65, or not receiving benefits under the Canada Pension Plan, the social insurance number for the deceased must be provided.

- Application in the form provided by Health and Welfare Canada.
- Proof of death together with proof of payment of funeral expenses.

Although the application would generally be made by the personal representative, it can be made by someone who paid for the funeral of the deceased. In the case of very small estates or where there is no estate, the Director of the Canada Pension Plan may determine what person is entitled to the Death Benefit. In the case where it is not the personal representative applying, completion of an additional form setting out why the person is entitled to apply is required.

(ii) Survivor's Benefit

This is a monthly payment payable to the spouse of the deceased and the application is made by the spouse. However, there are maximum amounts payable to an individual under the Canada Pension Plan so if the spouse is already receiving a monthly pension payment or disability payment under the Canada Pension Plan, the maximum allowed as Survivor's Benefit may be reduced. There are also certain age restrictions, which are currently as follows:

- If, at the time of death, the spouse is under the age of 35, has no dependent children and is not disabled, the spouse will not be entitled to the Survivor's Benefit at that time, but may become entitled at a later date.
- If, at the time of death, the spouse is between the ages of 35 and 45 and has no dependent children, the spouse will be entitled to a reduced amount.

The following documents are required when applying for the benefit:

1. Letter to Health and Welfare Canada (see Figure 4-8).
2. Proof of age for the deceased.
3. Social insurance number for the deceased.
4. Birth Certificate and the social insurance number for the applicant.
5. Application in the form provided by Health and Welfare Canada.
6. Proof of death for the deceased spouse.
7. Birth Certificates for all dependent children.
8. Marriage Certificate.

If an application for the Death Benefit has been filed or is being filed at the same time, numbers 2, 3 and 6 (above) are not required.

(iii) Orphan's Benefit

This is a monthly payment payable to a child of the deceased contributor provided he or she is not married, is under the age of 18, or is under the age of 25 but in full-time attendance at a school or university. The applicant can only receive one orphan's pension notwithstanding both parents may have died. Again, there is a maximum amount payable and it is paid to the person having custody of the child or, if the child is over 18 it can be paid directly to the child. The following documents are required when applying for the benefit:

1. Letter to Health and Welfare Canada (see Figure 4-8).

2. Proof of age of the deceased.
3. Social insurance number of the deceased.
4. Application in the form provided by Health and Welfare Canada.
5. Birth Certificate for the applicant.
6. Social insurance number for the applicant.
7. Proof of death for the deceased contributor.

If the application for the Death Benefit has been filed or is being filed at the same time as this application, numbers 2, 3 and 7 (above) are not required.

(o) Dealing with Motor Vehicles

Where it is not necessary to obtain a Court Certificate to deal with other assets, it is recommended that a letter be sent to the Ministry of Transportation outlining this and obtaining approval for the transfer of the ownership of the vehicle.

In order for the personal representative to take over ownership of the car for sale purposes, he or she would complete the car ownership registered in the deceased's name transferring it to himself or herself as personal representative and would also complete an application for registration. This type of vehicle transfer does not require a Certificate of Mechanical Fitness for the vehicle; however, when the vehicle is sold for fair market value the Certificate of Mechanical Fitness and payment of applicable provincial sales tax are required.

If the transfer is to take place to a beneficiary named in the Will, the personal representative will sign the registration as transferor and the beneficiary will complete the registration as transferee.

Although the Ministry of Transportation will generally accept a solicitor's letter detailing the particulars of death and the relevant information regarding the personal representative, they may make a request to see proof of death and, in the case where there is no named beneficiary, a copy of the Will; however these documents will not be kept but will be immediately returned.

(p) Dealing with Other Assets

The above reflects the general type of assets found, but in the case of unusual assets, it is suggested that you contact the institution where the asset is held and request a value for the asset as at the date of death together with what documentation will be required in order to transfer the asset to the personal representative and then to a subsequent owner, given the possible sale or redemption of the asset thereafter.

2. LOCATING AND DEALING WITH LIABILITIES

(a) *Family Law Act* Election

Section 4(1) of the *Family Law Act* (the "*FLA*") defines "net family property" as follows:

... means the value of all the property, except property described in subsection (2), that a spouse owns on the valuation date, after deducting,
  (a) the spouse's debts and other liabilities, and
  (b) the value of property, other than a matrimonial home, that the spouse owned on the date of the marriage, after deducting the spouse's debts and other liabilities, calculated as of the date of the marriage;

Upon the death of a spouse, there is an "equalization of net family properties" that is to take place. If the deceased spouse's net family property is determined to have a higher value than the net family property of the surviving spouse, the surviving spouse is entitled to one-half of the difference, thus providing an equal distribution of the net family property (*FLA*, s. 5). If the deceased spouse left a will, pursuant to s. 6(l) of the *FLA*, the surviving spouse is to elect to either take the entitlement under the Will or under the *FLA*. If the election (see Figure 4-24) is not filed within six months of the date of death, or by the expiry of any extension period granted by the court, the surviving spouse is deemed to take his or her entitlement under the Will, or, in the case of an intestacy, the *Succession Law Reform Act*, R.S.O. 1990, c. S.26 (the *SLRA*).

If the surviving spouse elects to take under s. 5 of the *FLA*, the surviving spouse is deemed to have predeceased the deceased spouse for the purposes of the deceased spouse's Will.

Section 6 of the *FLA* also provides for the following:

- Where the spouse dies intestate, the election to be made by the surviving spouse is to either take his or her entitlement under the *SLRA* or under s. 5 of the *FLA*.
- In the case of a partial intestacy, the surviving spouse may elect to take under the Will and the *SLRA* or s. 5 of the *FLA*.
- A Will can expressly provide that gifts to a surviving spouse are in addition to any entitlement under s. 5 of the *FLA*.
- If the surviving spouse was the beneficiary of a life insurance policy or a lump sum payment under a pension or similar plan and if the election is made to take the entitlement under s. 5 of the *FLA*, the aforementioned payments under the life insurance policy, pension or similar plan shall be credited towards the entitlement. If, as a result of this there results an overpayment in the hands of the surviving spouse, the personal representative of the deceased spouse's estate "may recover the excess from the surviving spouse."
- The surviving spouse's s. 5 entitlement is a priority over gifts made under the Will, with the exception of a gift in the Will made in accordance with a contract entered into by the deceased "in good faith and for valuable consideration, except to the extent that the value of the gift, in the court's opinion, exceeds the consideration." The entitlement is also a priority to a person's right to share in an intestacy under the *SLRA* and an order made under Part V of the *SLRA* for support of dependants, except an order in favour of a child of the deceased.

If no election has been made by the spouse during the first six month period, any distribution made from the estate should only be made upon obtaining the consent (see Figure 4-25) of the surviving spouse unless the court authorizes a distribution.

If the surviving spouse is a personal representative for the estate, he or she should be made aware that he or she would be in a conflict position should the decision be made to elect to take under the *FLA*. As a result of the possible conflicts that can exist it is often recommended that the spouse obtain independent legal advice.

(b) Payment of Debts

Prior to the distribution of the estate and once the assets have been realized or are under the control of the personal representative, the personal representative must attend to the payment of the liabilities of the deceased and the estate. Unless the Will provides to the contrary, liabilities are generally paid from the residue of the estate.

Prior to the payment of debts, verification of the debt and the amount should be obtained from the creditor.

(c) Advertisement for Creditors

Often, although not required by law, the personal representative will arrange for a formal advertisement for creditors. The general accepted practice in Ontario is to insert the notice (see Figure 4-6) three times in a newspaper in the area where the deceased resided or carried on business. There is generally a period of at least one month from the time the notice is first published to the date set out in the notice for filing all claims.

If the personal representative does not feel that he or she is aware of all the deceased's debts, or if the deceased carried on a business, it is generally recommended that the advertisement be placed to enable the personal representative to distribute the estate without personal liability should a claim be determined after the distribution of the deceased's assets.

(d) Insolvent Estates

When it is determined that an estate does not have sufficient assets to satisfy the liabilities, the estate is said to be insolvent. In such a case, it is necessary to look at both the common law and statutes, including the *Trustee Act*, R.S.O. 1990, c. T.23, to determine which assets are to be applied to the debts. The order is as follows:[1]

1. personalty which has not been bequeathed;
2. real estate devised to pay debts;
3. real estate not so designated; and
4. legacies (general legacies first, then specific legacies).

Dealing with an insolvent estate gives rise to an additional problem. As previously mentioned, when determining the value of the estate for purposes of submitting your application, the only liability to be deducted is the value of any mortgage against real property.

---

[1] Anne E.P. Armstrong, *Estate Administration: A Solicitor's Reference Manual*, vol. 1 (Toronto: Carswell, 1994) (looseleaf) at section 3.13.6.

3. FINALIZING THE ESTATE

Prior to the personal representative completing the estate by making final distributions, there are several items that one must make sure have been completed. The following is a list of those general matters; however, it is important to remember that each estate is different and particular attention must be made to the individual file and what has transpired to date. For this reason it is a good practice to keep a continuing checklist of those items in an estate that have not yet been finalized in order that they not be overlooked.

(a) Finalizing the Value of the Estate with the Court

Always review the value of the estate at the date of death, once the administration of the assets has taken place. Possibly, only estimates were used at the time the application was filed with the court or perhaps additional assets were found after the application was filed. It is a good practice to review the value of the Statement of Assets from time to time, as the personal representative is required to provide the court with a new statement of the total value within six months of having located new property.

Section 32 of the *Estates Act*, R.S.O. 1990, c. E.21, provide as follows:

> **32.**(1) The person applying for a grant of probate or administration shall before it is granted make or cause to be made and delivered to the registrar a true statement of the total value, verified by the oath or affirmation of the applicant, of all the property that belonged to the deceased at the time of his or her death.
>
> (2) When after the grant of probate or letters of administration any property belonging to the deceased at the time of his or her death and not included in such statement of total value is discovered by the executor or administrator, they shall, within six months thereafter, deliver to the registrar a true statement of the total value, duly verified by oath or affirmation, of such newly discovered property.
>
> (3) Where the application or grant is limited to part only of the property of the deceased, it is sufficient to set forth in the statement of value only the property and value thereof intended to be affected by such application or grant.

(b) Documents to be Filed

The following are the documents to be filed:

- Letter to the court advising of increase in assets (see Figure 4-17) or decrease in assets (see Figure 4-18);
- Affidavit stating the new values of the estate including the amount of additional court fees being paid (see Figure 4-26) or amount of court fees to be refunded (see Figure 4-27).

No formal Statement of Assets is filed with the court, other than a breakdown of the assets into personalty and real estate.

It is also a good practice to forward a letter to the court advising of no change in the value of the estate. Therefore if an undertaking had been filed with the court, the court can now close the file and will not have to forward a notice requesting a final value. The court has the authority to issue an Order for Compliance pursuant to r. 74.13(3) of the

Rules of Civil Procedure, R.R.O. 1990, Reg. 194, so any request for additional asset information received from the court should be responded to on a timely basis.

(c) Arranging Return of Security from Court

If it was necessary to provide the court with security at the time the application for the certificate was filed, it is necessary to apply to the court for the release of the bond prior to finalizing the estate. The insurance company holding the bond will generally request an annual premium from the personal representative and the bond itself cannot be cancelled without the agreement of the court.

The application for the release of the bond is filed with the court and contains the following:

- Supporting affidavit containing the particulars of the court appointment, confirmation that all debts were paid and the estate has been administered.
- Confirmation of the advertisement for creditors. This is generally in the form of a declaration provided by the newspaper where the advertisement was published.
- All beneficiaries must execute releases.
- Draft Order sought.

Notice of your application must be provided to the Office of the Children's Lawyer if a minor has an interest in the estate and/or to the Office of the Public Guardian and Trustee where an incompetent has an interest in the estate.

(d) Distributions

During the first year of the estate, the personal representative arranges to call in the assets and arranges for the payment of debts. This period is known as the "executor's year" which in the case of an intestacy runs from the date the certificate is issued by the court or, in the case where the personal representative was named in the Will, from the date of death. At the expiration of this period, the personal representative should be in a position to distribute the estate, unless there is a contrary intention provided in the Will. If the distributions cannot be made at this time, and in the absence of special circumstances, interest is payable on legacies.

Distributions are made pursuant to the terms of the Will of the deceased or in the case of an intestacy under the *Succession Law Reform Act*, subject to a spouse having elected under the *Family Law Act*. In the absence of the *Family Law Act* election being filed, no distribution is to take place without the consent of the spouse or direction of the court. Pursuant to the provisions of the *Estates Administration Act*, R.S.O. 1990, c. E.22, no distribution is to take place on an intestacy for the period of one year. Generally, specific gifts are dealt with before distribution of the residue takes place. As it can be some time before a personal representative is in a position to make final distribution of the estate, it is often wise to make interim distributions to the residual beneficiaries.

Generally, the following is the procedure followed leading up to the distribution:

1. Convert assets to cash or transferrable assets.
2. Pay all debts and obtain receipts.
3. Pay all legacies and obtain receipts.
4. Make interest distributions to residual beneficiaries.
5. File final tax returns and once the Notice of Assessment is received, request Final Clearance Certificate.
6. Arrange to pass accounts or circulate estate accounts to the beneficiaries and obtain their consent and release.
7. Make final distributions and obtain the release and indemnity of each beneficiary.
8. Although reports should be sent to the personal representative regularly, a final reporting letter should be forwarded detailing the administration.

(e) Ongoing Estates

Often a Will does not provide for an outright distribution, or it establishes testamentary trusts for the benefit of a spouse or other beneficiary. In these cases, the personal representative moves into the role of a Trustee whereby he or she holds certain assets in trust, attends to the continued investment of those assets and looks to the powers provided to the personal representative in the Will. If the Will is absent as to certain powers, the personal representative should look to the *Trustee Act* for direction.

The personal representative must deal with the filing of the annual Trust Information Tax Return, often referred to as a T3 Return. This particular return must be filed within 90 days of the year end of the estate.

The solicitor's office may be called on from time to time to assist the personal representative with some of these administrative matters, including the circulation of the estate accounts. It is recommended in the case of an ongoing estate that the personal representative formally pass the accounts for the estate to enable the "closing of the books" of the estate for the period in question. At the very least, the personal representative should consider circulating the accounts in draft form for the approval of the beneficiaries.

(f) Payment of Money into Court

Although a Will generally provides the personal representative with certain direction as to the dealing with monies which will be held in trust for some time, such as in the case of minor beneficiaries, when this direction is absent from the Will or in the case where there is no Will and therefore no power to hold funds in trust, the personal representative must bring an application to pay money into court.

Sections 36(6)-(9) of the *Trustee Act* provide the following information and requirements in connection with the payment of money into court:

> **Payment into court of money to which minor or mentally incapable person entitled**
> (6) If a minor or mentally incapable person is entitled to any money, the person by whom the money is payable may pay it into court to the credit of the minor or mentally incapable person.
> **Same**
> (6.1) The payment shall be made to the Accountant of the Superior Court of Justice.

Accompanying affidavit, minor

(6.2) If the person entitled to the money is a minor, the person by whom it is payable shall deliver an affidavit containing the following to the Accountant at the time of the payment into court:

1. A statement that the money is being paid into court under subsection (6).
2. A statement of the facts entitling the minor to the money.
3. If the affidavit deals with more than one minor beneficiary's entitlement, the amount of each individual entitlement.
4. If the amount being paid into court differs from an amount specified in a document that establishes the minor's entitlement, an explanation of the difference.
5. The minor's date of birth.
6. The full name and postal address of,
    i. the minor,
    ii. the minor's parents, or the parent with lawful custody if it is known that only one parent has lawful custody,
    iii. any person, if known, who has lawful custody of the minor but is not his or her parent, and
    iv. any guardian of property, if known, appointed under section 47 of the *Children's Law Reform Act*.

Accompanying affidavit, mentally incapable person

(6.3) If the person entitled to the money is a mentally incapable person, the person by whom it is payable shall deliver an affidavit containing the following to the Accountant at the time of the payment into court:

1. A statement that the money is being paid into court under subsection (6).
2. A statement of the facts entitling the mentally incapable person to the money.
3. The mentally incapable person's date of birth.
4. The full name and postal address of,
    i. the mentally incapable person,
    ii. the mentally incapable person's guardian of property, if any, under the *Substitute Decisions Act, 1992*,
    iii. the person, if known, who holds a continuing power of attorney for property for the mentally incapable person.

Copy of document

(6.4) An affidavit under subsection (6.2) or (6.3) shall have attached to it, as a schedule, a copy of any document that establishes,

(a) the person's entitlement to the money;
(b) the amount to which the person is entitled;
(c) any conditions to be met before the person is entitled to receive the money, including, in the case of a minor, the attainment of a specified age.

Discharge

(6.5) Payment into court in accordance with subsection (6), (6.2) or (6.3), as the case may be, and with subsection (6.4) is a sufficient discharge for the money paid into court.

(7) Where a trustee desires to be relieved from the trust, the court may order all property held for the trust to be transferred to the Public Trustee.

(8) Money paid into court is subject to the order of the court.

(9) Where, however, the Public Guardian and Trustee is the guardian of property of the person to whom the money is due, as mentioned in subsections (4) and (6), the money shall be paid to the Public Guardian and Trustee.

(g) Keeping a Tickler System

Although every estate has different deadlines, it is very important to keep a follow-up system. Your system should include the following, among other things:

- *Family Law Act* election — within six months of the date of death unless an extension has been granted by the court.
- Filing the terminal year tax return — the later of six months from the date of death or April 30 of the year following death.
- Trust Information Tax Returns (T3s) — 90 days from the year-end of the estate.
- Advertise for creditors — when can distribution be made?
- Such other dates as are applicable to the file.

(h) Obtaining Status Certificates

When it is necessary to provide confirmation of the history of an estate, it is possible to obtain a certificate from the court which details the chain of events. This is particularly helpful in older estates where possibly several executors have resigned or died and replacements have stepped in, either those named as alternate personal representatives in a deceased's Will or the personal representatives of the last surviving personal representative of an estate.

Although a Will generally provides for the appointment of an "Executor and Trustee" in certain instances different persons are provided with the different duties. Although the removal of an executor is dealt with through the courts, a person in the position of Trustee can be dealt with pursuant to the provisions of the *Trustee Act*.

This certificate detailing the chain of events can be obtained by providing the court with the applicable fee (currently $18) together with copies of the relevant documents required by the court to prove the chain of events.

(i) Succession Duty

If a person died between January, 1950 and April 11, 1979, their estate was subject to succession duties under the *Succession Duty Act*. Under that Act a Succession Duty Return was filed, the relevant duties paid and the consents to transfer of assets obtained from the Minister of Revenue. Under certain circumstances, it was possible to defer the duty to a later date.

It was quite common for the Succession Duty Department, now a branch of the Ministry of Finance, to follow up to review the value of the assets of the estate as to whether any capital encroachments were made. This allowed the Succession Duty Department to determine if sufficient security had been posted to cover the potential duty. As Succession Duty has now been repealed, a final review is now being undertaken by that office which will result in the files currently held by them being closed and any security posted being returned where appropriate.

Queries regarding lost consents, returns filed or the status of the Succession Duty levy on a file can be forwarded to The Succession Duty Assessor, Ministry of Finance, P.O. Box 625, 33 King Street West, Oshawa, Ontario, L1H 8H9.

Figure 4-1: Letter to Registrar General Requesting Birth, Marriage and Death Certificates

MAIL ONLY OR	**DELIVERY ONLY**
The Office of the Registrar General	Office of the Registrar General
Ministry of Consumer and Commercial Relations	MacDonald Block
P.O. Box 4600	Parliament Buildings
189 Red River Road	Toronto, Ontario
Thunder Bay, Ontario	M7A 1Y5
P7B 6L8	

Dear Sirs:

<u>Re: Estate of *[enter name of deceased]*</u>

We represent the executor(s) of the Estate of *[enter name of deceased]* who died on *[enter date]*.

We enclose an application for a death certificate, together with our firm cheque in the amount of $*[insert applicable fee]* in payment of the applicable fee.

We look forward to receiving the death certificate as soon as possible.

Yours very truly,

Enclosures

Figure 4-2: Letter to Insurance Company Requesting Particulars on a Claim

---

[enter address of insurance company]

Dear Sirs:

Re: Estate of *[enter name of deceased]*
Policy No. *[enter policy number]*

We represent the executor(s) of the Estate of *[enter name of estate]* who died on *[enter date]*.

We understand that the deceased was insured under the above-noted insurance policy. Would you please check your records and provide us with the following information concerning the policy:

   (a)   face value;
   (b)   value at the date of death;
   (c)   named beneficiary (if any);
   (d)   interest rate payable until the date of distribution of the policy proceeds; and
   (e)   the amount of any outstanding loans against the policy.

In addition, please check your records to ensure that the deceased was not insured under any other policies with your company.

Lastly, would you please advise us of your requirements to pay the policy proceeds to the Estate of *[beneficiary]* and provide us with the necessary claim forms.

Yours very truly,

Figure 4-3: Letter to Insurance Company Proving Claim for Named Beneficiary

[enter address of insurance company]

Attention: Claims Department
            Deceased Persons

Dear Sirs:

Re: Estate of *[enter name of deceased]*
Policy No. *[enter policy number]*

We represent the executor(s) of the Estate of *[enter name of deceased]* who died on *[enter date]*.

We enclose the following documents in order to prove the claim under the above-noted policy:

1. original policy contract no. *[enter policy number]*;
2. Claimant's Statement completed by *[enter name of claimant]*; and
3. notarial copy of deceased's death certificate.

We trust the enclosed will allow you to process the claim under the policy. In due course, please provide us with a cheque payable to *[enter name of claimant]* for the amount of the total proceeds payable under the policy.

Yours very truly,

Enclosures

Figure 4-4: Letter to Broker Requesting Information on Securities and What Commission Costs Will be to Sell Securities

[enter address of broker]

Dear Sirs:

Re: Estate of *[enter name of deceased]*
<u>Account No. *[enter account number]*</u>

We represent the executor(s) of the Estate of *[enter name of deceased]* who died on *[enter date]*.

We understand that the deceased maintained the above-noted investment account with your company. Accordingly, we would appreciate your providing us with the following information:

    (a)   account balance at the date of death;
    (b)   full particulars of all securities held in the account at the date of death; and
    (c)   the market values of each of the securities in the account as at the date of death.

Yours very truly,

Figure 4-5: Letter to Transfer Agent Requesting Transfer of Shares

[enter address of trust company (transfer agent)]

Attention: Stock Transfer Department

Dear Sirs:

Re: Estate of *[enter name of deceased]*

We represent the executor(s) of the Estate of *[enter name of deceased]* who died on *[enter date]*. The deceased held *[_____]*. We enclose the following documents to transfer the shares from the name of the deceased into the names of *[enter executor]* and *[enter executor]*, Executors of the Estate of *[enter name of deceased]* *[or enter beneficiary, beneficiary entitled thereto]*:

(a) certificate no(s). _____ representing *[no. of shares]* *[class]* shares of *[enter name of company]*;
(b) Declaration of Transmission;
(c) Power of Attorney to transfer the securities; and
(d) notarial copy of Certificate of Estate Trustee *[insert with or without a Will]*.

Once the transfers have been completed, please forward the new certificate(s) to the attention of the undersigned.

Yours very truly,

Enclosures

Figure 4-6: Letter to Newspaper with Notice to Creditors

The Globe and Mail
444 Front Street West
Toronto, Ontario
M5V 2S9

Attention: Display Advertising

Dear Sirs:

<u>Re: Estate of *[enter name of deceased]*</u>

We represent the executor(s) of the Estate of *[enter name of deceased]* who died on *[enter date]*.

We enclose two copies of a Notice to Creditors and Others. Please arrange to publish the enclosed Notice in three consecutive weekly issues of your newspaper.

In due course, please provide us with an Affidavit of Proof of Publication together with your statement of account. Please forward all correspondence to the attention of the undersigned.

Yours very truly,

NOTICE TO CREDITORS AND OTHERS

All claims against the Estate of *[enter name of deceased]*, late of City of Toronto, Province of Ontario, who died on *[enter date]*, must be filed with the undersigned personal representative on or before the *[enter date]*, after which date the estate will be distributed having regard only to the claims of which the Administrator then shall have notice.

DATED at Toronto, this   day of   , 19*[enter year]*.

[enter executor], Estate Trustee
of the estate of *[enter name of deceased]*
by his\her solicitors
[enter solicitor]
[enter solicitor's address]

Figure 4-7: Letter to Revenue Canada Requesting Final Clearance Certificate (Terminal, Partial and Final)

Revenue Canada
District Taxation Office
36 Adelaide Street East
Toronto, Ontario
M5C 1J6

Dear Sirs:

Re: The Estate of *[enter name of deceased]*
Account No. *[enter number] [or S.I.N. No.]*

We represent the executor(s) of the Estate of the above-named who died on *[enter date]*, 19*[enter year]*. To date the Accountants have filed a T.1 general Income Tax Return for the taxation year *[enter year]*, a T.1 General Terminal Return for the period *[enter date]*, 19*[enter year]* to *[enter date]*, 19*[enter year]* and a T.3 Trust Information and Income Tax Return for the period *[enter date]*, 19*[enter year]* to *[date of death]*, 19*[enter year]*. *[as applicable]*

We enclose copies of Assessment Notices for the 19*[enter year]* and 19*[enter year]* taxation years.

[The estate is being terminated as of the [enter day] of [enter month], 19[enter year] and the assets distributed to the beneficiaries.

OR

A partial distribution of the assets of the estate to the beneficiaries will be made as follows:

[enter name[s] of beneficiaries]

Therefore, would you please provide us with a *[Form TX21 [final]* **or** *Form TX21A [partial to date to death]* **or** *Form TX21B [partial to date of partial distribution]]* clearance certificate pursuant to section 159(2) of the Income Tax Act stating that all taxes, interest or penalties assessed against the estate have been paid. If you have any questions, please do not hesitate to contact us.

Yours very truly,

Enclosures

P.S. We also take this opportunity to enclose herewith the completed request for clearance certificate form.

***Figure 4-8:** Letter to Canada Pension Plan Applying for Death Benefit, Survivors' Benefits, Orphan's Benefit*

Canada Pension Plan
Income Security Programs
Health and Welfare Canada
P.O. Box 5100
Station "D"
Scarborough, Ontario
M1R 5C8

Dear Sirs:

Re: [enter name of deceased], deceased
<u>S.I.N.</u> [enter SIN number]

We represent the executor(s) of the Estate of *[enter name of deceased]* who passed away on *[enter date]*, 19*[enter year]*.

Enclosed are the following documents:

1. An Application for Death Benefit, together with the following enclosures:
   (a) Proof of Age of deceased.
   (b) Social Insurance Card for the deceased.
   (c) Proof of Payment of Funeral Expenses.
   (d) Death Certificate.
2. An Application for Survivors' Benefits, together with the following enclosures:
   (a) Social Insurance Card for the deceased's widow, *[enter name of widow]*, together with Social Insurance Card for each of the dependents, *[enter dependents]*.
   (b) Proof of Age for the deceased's widow, *[enter name of widow]*, together with Proof of Age for each of the dependents, *[enter dependents]*.
   (c) Marriage Certificate for the deceased and his widow.
[3. An Application for Orphan's Benefit and a Declaration of Attendance at School or University, with a photocopy of [enter dependents] birth certificate attached.]

Would you please process the above applications and send the proceeds directly to *[enter name(s) of widow or dependents]* at her/his home address.

Yours very truly,

Enclosures

Note: This letter has been drafted to include all applications under the Canada Pension Plan, but applications are often submitted individually and the letter is amended accordingly.

Figure 4-9: Letter to Canada Pension Plan to Cancel Pension Cheques

---

Canada Pension Plan
Income Security Programs
Health and Welfare Canada
P.O. Box 5100, Station "D"
Scarborough, Ontario
M1R 5C8

Dear Sirs:

Re: *[enter name of deceased]*, deceased
S.I.N. *[enter SIN]*

We represent the Executor(s) of the Estate of *[enter name of deceased]* who passed away on *[enter date]*, 19*[enter year]*.

We enclose herewith pension cheque(s) for the month(s) of *[enter months]* and we would ask that you amend the payee to the Estate of *[enter name of estate]* and return to us.

Please cancel *[enter name of the deceased]*'s pension cheques from the month after the date of death.

Yours very truly,

Figure 4-10: Letter to Old Age Security to Cancel Cheques

Old Age Security
Income Security Programs
Health and Welfare Canada
P.O. Box 5555, Station D
Scarborough, Ontario
M1R 5E1

Dear Sirs:

Re: *[enter name of deceased]*, deceased
S.I.N. *[enter SIN]*

We represent the Executor(s) of the Estate of *[enter name of deceased]* who passed away on *[enter date]*, 19*[enter year]*.

[We are returning the Old Age Security cheque for the month of [enter month] and we would ask that you amend the cheque to show the payee as the Estate of [enter name of deceased] and return same to us.]

Please cancel *[enter name of deceased]*'s Old Age Security cheques from the month following the date of death onward.

Yours very truly,

Figure 4-11: Letter Instructing Bank to Issue Cheque for Probate Fees

[enter address of bank]

Dear Sirs:

Re: Estate of *[enter name of deceased]*
Account No. *[enter account number]*

We represent the executor(s) of the Estate of *[enter name of deceased]* who died on *[enter date]*.

In order to apply for the Court grant, we require a bank draft payable to the "Minister of Finance" in the amount of $*[enter amount]* in payment of the applicable Court fees. We trust there are sufficient funds in the above-noted bank account to cover this bank draft.

Accordingly, would you please provide us with the requested bank draft as soon as possible. If you will telephone the undersigned when the bank draft has been issued, we will arrange to have it picked up.

Yours very truly,

Figure 4-12: Letter to Bank Without a Certificate

[date]

[contact and bank address]

Dear *[contact]*:

> Re: *[name of estate]* — Account No. *[account information]*

Further to our telephone conversation, wherein you have confirmed that you will allow the release of the funds held at your branch upon receipt of certain documents, I am pleased to enclose herewith the following:

1. Notarial copy of Funeral Director's Statement of Death for the above-mentioned.
2. Notarial copy of the Last Will and Testament *[name of deceased]* dated *[date of Will]*.
3. Indemnity which has been executed as requested.

I would appreciate your contacting my office to advise when I can arrange to pick up the proceeds of the accounts held by your branch payable to *[the Estate or possibly named beneficiary]*.

Yours very truly,

Enclosures

Figure 4-13: Letter to Bank With a Certificate

[date]

[contact and bank address]

Dear *[contact]*:

Re: <u>*[name of estate]* — Account No. *[account information]*</u>

Further to our telephone conversation, I am pleased to enclose herewith the following:

1. Notarial copy of Funeral Director's Statement of Death for the above-mentioned.
2. Notarial copy of the Certificate of Appointment of Estate Trustee with a Will dated *[date of Court certificate]*.

I would appreciate your contacting my office to advise when I can arrange to pick up the proceeds of the accounts held by your branch payable to *[the Estate or possibly named beneficiary]*.

Yours very truly,

Enclosures

Figure 4-14: Letter to Bank of Canada to Transfer Bonds to Beneficiary (or Cash Bonds)

REGISTERED MAIL OR DELIVERED

Bank of Canada
250 University Avenue
Toronto, Ontario
M5H 3E5

Attention: Bond Transfer Department

Dear Sirs:

Re: Estate of [enter name of estate]

We represent the executor(s) of the Estate of *[enter name of deceased]* who died on *[enter date]*.

The deceased owned $*[enter amount]* Canada Savings Bonds, *[enter series]* Series, due *[enter date]*. The executors would like to transfer the bonds into the name of the beneficiary entitled thereto. Accordingly, we enclose the following documents:

(a) Certificate No. *[enter number]*, representing $*[enter amount]* Canada Savings Bonds, *[enter series]* Series, due *[enter date]*;
(b) power of attorney to transfer the bonds, on which the signature[s] of the executor(s) has/have been guaranteed by the *[_____]*;
(c) notarial copy of Certificate of Estate Trustee *[insert with or without a Will]*; and
(d) four copies of your form of Receipt.

Would you please acknowledge receipt of the enclosed bonds by signing and returning one copy of the enclosed Receipt to the undersigned.

Please proceed to transfer the bonds as requested. If you will telephone the undersigned when the bonds have been re-registered, we will make arrangements to have them picked up by our messengers.

Yours very truly,

Figure 4-15: Letter to Beneficiaries re: FLA Clause

[enter inside address]

Dear *[name of beneficiary]*:

Re: Estate of <u>*[enter name of estate]*</u>

We represent the Executor of the Estate of *[name of deceased]*. The deceased's Last Will and Testament provides that you are a beneficiary/potential beneficiary. In addition, the Will contains the following clause which we think you should be aware of:

> "I direct that any gift, including any income at any time subsequently derived therefrom or any accretion in value thereto, to which any person is or shall become entitled in accordance with the provisions of this my Will shall be excluded from such person's net family property, as such term is defined in the Family Law Act, 1986."

In the event that you are or become married, the above direction contained in the Will is relevant upon the breakdown of your marriage or upon your death or upon the death of your spouse, because it may affect your net family property for purposes of the Family Law Act. The consequences may differ depending on whether you become entitled to the gift before or after marriage. We suggest that you retain this letter with your records and, in addition, that you discuss this matter further with your solicitor who can advise you fully of the consequences in accordance with the provisions of the Family Law Act.

Yours very truly,

Figure 4-16: Letter to Court, Toronto Region, re: Filing of FLA Election

The Registrar
Superior Court of Justice
  at Toronto, Estates Division
Phoenix House
393 University Avenue, 10th Floor
Toronto, Ontario
M5G 1E6

Dear Sirs:

Re: Estate of [enter name of estate]

We represent *[enter name of spouse]*, the spouse of the late *[enter name of deceased]* who died on *[enter date]*, 19*[enter year]*.

We enclose an Election under Section 6 of the Family Law Act, 1986 signed by *[enter name of spouse]*, together with an Affidavit of Subscribing Witness.

Yours very truly,

Enclosures

Figure 4-17: Letter to Court re: Probate Fees Owing

DELIVERED

The Registrar
Superior Court of Justice
  at Toronto, Estates Division
Phoenix House
393 University Avenue, 10th Floor
Toronto, Ontario
M5G 1E6

Dear Sirs:

Re: Estate of *[enter name of estate]*

We represent the Executor(s) of the Estate of *[enter name of deceased]*, who died on *[enter date]*. The Court grant was issued on *[enter date]* and numbered *[enter number]*.

At the time the grant was applied for, the Estate assets were valued at $*[enter amount]*. A proper inventory of the estate assets has since been carried out and the value of the Estate assets has been determined to be $*[enter amount]*.

We enclose an Affidavit from the Executor(s) together with a certified cheque in the amount of $*[enter amount]* payable to the Minister of Finance for additional Court fees. Please forward the receipt to the undersigned.

Yours very truly,

Enclosures

Figure 4-18: Letter to Court re: Refund of Probate Fees

DELIVERED

The Registrar
Superior Court of Justice
　at Toronto, Estates Division
Phoenix House
393 University Avenue, 10th Floor
Toronto, Ontario
M5G 1E6

Dear Sirs:

Re: Estate of [enter name of estate]

We represent the Executor(s) of the Estate of *[enter name of deceased]*, who died on *[enter date]*. The Court grant was issued on *[enter date]* and numbered *[enter number(s)]*.

At the time the grant was applied for, the Estate assets were valued at $*[enter amount]*. A proper inventory of the Estate assets has since been carried out and the value of the Estate assets has been determined to be $*[enter amount]*.

Please issue a refund cheque for the overpayment of Court fees in the amount of *[enter amount]* to the Estate of *[enter name of deceased]* and forward it to the undersigned.

Yours very truly,

Enclosures

Figure 4-19: Letter to Court re: No Additional Probate Fees Owing

DELIVERED

The Registrar
Superior Court of Justice
　at Toronto, Estates Division
Phoenix House
393 University Avenue, 10th Floor
Toronto, Ontario
M5G 1E6

Dear Sirs:

Re: Estate of [enter name of estate]

We represent the Executor(s) of the Estate of *[enter name of deceased]*, who died on *[enter date]*. The Court grant was issued on *[enter date]* and numbered *[enter number(s)]*.

At the time the grant was applied for, the Estate assets were valued at $*[enter amount]*. A proper inventory of the Estate assets has since been carried out and the value of the Estate assets remained the same.

Consequently, please be advised that there are no additional Court fees owing.

Yours very truly,

Enclosures

Figure 4-20: Authorization re: Safety Deposit Box

TO:

AUTHORIZATION

I/We the undersigned, am/are the Executor(s) of the Estate of   .

This is your authorization to permit   , from the law firm of   to attend on my/our behalf to list the contents of the above-numbered safety-deposit box registered in the name of the deceased.

I/We further authorize to remove from the box any testamentary documents and such other documents as may be necessary to permit the proper administration of the Estate and protection of assets. Attached is a notarial copy of the Will and death certificate.

This Authorization shall be your good and sufficient authority for so doing.

   DATED AT   , this   day of   , 19   .

Figure 4-21: Power of Attorney to Transfer Bonds - Shares

POWER OF ATTORNEY TO TRANSFER
BONDS - SHARES

KNOW ALL MEN BY THESE PRESENTS that for value received

I/we [NAME OF PERSONAL REPRESENTATIVE(S), ESTATE TRUSTEE(S) (WITH OR WITHOUT A WILL) FOR THE ESTATE OF (NAME OF ESTATE), ADDRESS]

have bargained, sold, assigned and transferred unto [NAME AND ADDRESS OF TRANSFEREE IF APPLICABLE]

the following bonds/shares of [NAME OF INSTITUTION]

Certificate or Bond No.	Maturity Date	No. of Shares	Par Value	Registration
[Certificate or Bond No.]	[If Applicable]	[If Applicable]	[If Applicable]	[Exact Name as it appears on Certificate]

AND do hereby constitute and appoint

true and lawful Attorney, irrevocably, for and in name and stead to transfer the said bonds/shares, and for that purpose to make and execute all necessary acts of assignment and transfer thereof and to substitute one or more persons with like full power, hereby ratifying and confirming all that the said Attorney or substitutes shall lawfully do by virtue hereof.

Dated at   this day of   , 19 .

Witness to signature of Transferor.

Signature must correspond exactly with name as registered

SIGNATURE OF PERSONAL REPRESENTATIVE
_____

Signature of Transferor is hereby guaranteed.

_____
_____

Figure 4-22: Declaration of Transmission (re: Shares)

Declaration of Transmission

IN THE MATTER OF THE ESTATE OF   [FULL NAME OF DECEASED] late of Deceased.

I/WE [ENTER FULL NAMES AND ADDRESS OF EXECUTORS OR ADMINISTRATORS]

herein referred to as the "personal representatives",

DO SOLEMNLY DECLARE THAT:

(1) The Deceased died at   on the   day of , 19 , [ENTER TESTATE OR INTESTATE] and at the date of death was resident and domiciled in the Province of

(2) Letters [ENTER PROBATE, ADMINISTRATION OR ADMINISTRATION WITH WILL ANNEXED)   were granted to the personal representative(s) on the day of , 19 , by the [ENTER NAME OF COURT] Court .

- OR -

I/We is/are the Personal Representative named in the Will of [NAME OF DECEASED] and I/We do not intend to apply to the Ontario Court (General Division) for a Court Certificate.

(3) There are registered in the name of the Deceased on the books of [ENTER FULL NAME OF COMPANY] herein referred to as "the Company" [ENTER NUMBER AND CLASS OF SHARES] Shares of its Capital Stock, represented by certificates numbered   .

(4) The Deceased and [ENTER NAME ON CERTIFICATE(S)] named in the said certificates was one and the same person.

(5) At the date of death of the Deceased, all of the said certificates were physically situate in the Province of   .

(6) At the date of death of the Deceased, none of the beneficiaries of the Deceased was resident or domiciled in the Province of Quebec.

(7) By virtue of the foregoing the said shares have devolved upon and become vested in [ENTER ME OR US] , being (all of) the personal representative(s) of the Deceased, who desire to have the same recorded in the name(s) of the personal representative(s) upon the books of the Company
[DELETE IF NOT REQUIRED] and immediately thereafter transferred to the beneficiary(ies) properly entitled by law to receive the said shares, namely: --

[ENTER NAMES AND ADDRESSES OF BENEFICIARY(IES)]

And I/We make this solemn Declaration conscientiously believing it to be true, and knowing that it is of the same force and effect as if made under oath.

(SEVERALLY) DECLARED before me   )
at   )
) _____
)
this   day of   , 19   )

A Commissioner for Oaths, Notary Public.

Figure 4-23: Declaration of Transmission (re: Bonds and Debentures)

Declaration of Transmission

IN THE MATTER OF THE ESTATE OF [NAME OF DECEASED]   late of Deceased.

I/We [FULL NAMES AND ADDRESS OF EXECUTORS OR ADMINISTRATORS] herein referred to as the "personal representatives",

DO SOLEMNLY DECLARE THAT:

(1) The Deceased died at   on the   day of   , 19   , [TESTATE\INTESTATE] and at the date of death was resident and domiciled in the Province of

(2) Letters [PROBATE\ADMINISTRATION\ADMINISTRATION WITH WILL ANNEXED] were granted to the personal representative(s) on the   day of , 19 , by the [FULL NAME OF COURT] Court   .

- OR -

I/We is/are the Personal Representative named in the Will of [NAME OF DECEASED] and I/We do not intend to apply to the Ontario Court (General Division) for a Court Certificate.

(3) There are registered in the name of the Deceased on register of [FULL NAME OF COMPANY] herein referred to as "the Company" [PROPER DESCRIPTION OF BONDS\DEBENTURES] dollars ($) principal amount of the bonds/debentures represented by certificates bearing the serial numbers

(4) All of the said certificates are executed under seal and at the date of death of the Deceased, were physically situate in the Province of   .

(5) The Deceased and   named in the certificates was one and the same person.

(6) At the date of death of the Deceased, none of the beneficiaries of the Deceased was resident or domiciled in the Province of Quebec.

(7) By virtue of the foregoing the said bonds/debentures have devolved upon and become vested in me/us , being (all of) the personal representative(s) of the Deceased, who desire to have the same recorded in the name(s) of the personal representative(s) upon the register of the Company
[DELETE IF NOT REQUIRED] and immediately thereafter transferred to the beneficiary(ies) properly entitled by law to receive the said bonds/debentures, namely:

[ENTER NAMES AND ADDRESSES OF BENEFICIARY(IES)]

And I/We make this solemn Declaration conscientiously believing it to be true, and knowing that it is of the same force and effect as if made under oath.

(SEVERALLY) DECLARED before me   )
at   )
)   _____
)
this   day of   , 19   )

A Commissioner for Oaths, Notary Public.

Figure 4-24: Election under the Family Law Act, 1986

ELECTION UNDER THE FAMILY LAW ACT, 1986
CHOIX DU CONJOINT FAIT EN VERTU DE LA
LOI DE 1986 SUR LE DROIT DE LA FAMILLE

Court File No. / *Dossier de la cour n°*

This election is filed by (solicitors) / *Déposé par (procureurs)*

Name of deceased / *Nom du défunt* Surname / *Nom de famille*   Given name(s) / *Prénom(s)*

Last address of deceased / *Dernière adresse du défunt* Street or postal address / *Rue et numéro ou adresse postale* City, town, etc. / *Cité, ville, etc.*

Date of death / *Date du décès* Day, month, year / *Jour, mois, année*

Surviving spouse / *Conjoint survivant* Surname / *Nom de famille*   Given name(s) / *Prénom(s)*

Address of spouse / *Adresse du conjoint* Street or postal address / *rue et numéro ou adresse postale* City, town, etc. / *Cité, ville, etc.* Postal Code / *Code postal*

I, ... the surviving spouse elect:
Je soussigné(e)   (Please print) / *(écrire en caractères d'imprimerie)*   *conjoint survivant, fais le choix suivant:*

☐ to receive the entitlement under section 5 of the Family Law Act, 1986;
    jouir du droit prévu à l'article 5 de la Loi de 1986 sur le droit de la famille;

OR (check one box only) /
OU (cocher une seule case)

☐ to receive the entitlement under the will, or under Part II of the Succession Law Reform Act, if there is an intestacy, or both, if there is a partial intestacy. /
    bénéficier des dispositions testamentaires; s'il n'y a pas de testament, jouir du droit prévu à la partie II de la Loi portant réforme du droit des successions; s'il s'agit d'une succession en partie testamentaire et en partie sans testament, se prévaloir de ces deux options.

Signature of surviving spouse / *Signature du conjoint survivant*   Date

NOTE: THIS ELECTION HAS IMPORTANT EFFECTS ON YOUR RIGHTS. YOU SHOULD HAVE LEGAL ADVICE BEFORE SIGNING IT /
REMARQUE: *LE PRÉSENT CHOIX ENTRAÎNERA DES EFFETS IMPORTANTS SUR VOS DROITS. VOUS DEVRIEZ OBTENIR DES CONSEILS JURIDIQUES AVANT DE LE SIGNER.*

Figure 4-25: Consent

> IN THE ESTATE OF *[name of estate]*
>
> THE FAMILY LAW ACT, 1986
>
> CONSENT
>
> PARAGRAPH 6(13)(a)
>
> I, *[name of spouse]*, the spouse of the late *[name of deceased]*, hereby consent pursuant to the provisions of Paragraph 6(13)(a) of the Family Law Act, 1986 to any one or more distributions being made in the administration of the Estate of *[name of deceased]* in accordance with the provisions of paragraph *[specify paragraphs from Will]* of the Last Will and Testament of *[name of deceased]* by *[name of Estate Trustees]*, Estate Trustees of the Estate, within the six (6) month period following the death of my late *[husband/wife]*, *[name of deceased]*.
>
> I acknowledge that I have been advised to seek independent legal representation prior to executing this Consent.

Figure 4-26: Affidavit re: Increase in Probate Value

IN THE ONTARIO SUPERIOR COURT OF JUSTICE AT

IN THE MATTER OF THE ESTATE OF

AFFIDAVIT

, and , of the Province of Ontario, Executor(s) of the Estate of , make oath and say as follows:

1. issued on the day of , 19 and numbered .

2. At the time the Application was submitted, an Undertaking was filed stating that the undersigned would inform the Superior Court of Justice at of the values of the assets as soon as they had been ascertained and pay any additional Court fees that may become due when the said values had been ascertained.

3. The value of the estate assets included on the application was $ on which Court fees of $ were paid. A proper inventory of the estate assets has been carried out and the value of the estate assets has been determined to be $, on which aggregate fees in the amount of $ are payable. As a result, additional fees of $ are now due and payable to the Court.

```
SWORN before me at the          )
of                              )
in the                          )
this day of                     )
19    .                         ) _____
                                )
_____         )
A Commissioner, etc.            )

SWORN before me at the          )
of                              )
in the                          )
this day of                     )
19    .                         ) _____
                                )
_____         )
A Commissioner, etc.            )

SWORN before me at the          )
of                              )
in the                          )
this day of                     )
19    .                         ) _____
                                )
_____         )
A Commissioner, etc.            )
```

Figure 4-27: Affidavit re: Decrease in Probate Value

IN THE ONTARIO SUPERIOR COURT OF JUSTICE AT
IN THE MATTER OF THE ESTATE OF

AFFIDAVIT

I/We,   and   , of the Province of Ontario, Executor(s) of the Estate of   , make oath and say as follows:

1.   were issued on the   day of   , 19   and numbered

2. At the time the Application was submitted, an Undertaking was filed stating that the undersigned would inform the Superior Court of Justice at   of the values of the assets as soon as they had been ascertained and pay any additional Court fees that may become due when the said values had been ascertained.

3. The value of the estate assets included on the application was $ on which fees of $ were paid. A proper inventory of the estate assets has been carried out and the value of the estate assets has been determined to be $, on which aggregate fees in the amount of are payable. As a result, a refund in the amount of   is now due and payable to the Estate of   .

SWORN before me at the   )
of   )
in the   )
this day of   )
19   .   ) _____
)
_____)
A Commissioner, etc.   )

SWORN before me at the   )
of   )
in the   )
this day of   )
19   .   ) _____
)
_____)
A Commissioner, etc.   )

SWORN before me at the   )
of   )
in the   )
this day of   )
19   .   ) _____
)
_____)
A Commissioner, etc.   )

5
COURT DISPUTES

Archie J. Rabinowitz

1. Request for Notice of Commencement of Proceeding — Rule 74.03
2. Orders for Assistance
    (a) Order to Accept or Refuse Appointment — Rule 74.15(1)(a) and (b)
    (b) Order to Consent or Object to Proposed Appointment — Rule 74.15(1)(c)
    (c) Order to File Statement of Assets of the Estate — Rule 74.15(1)(d)
    (d) Order for Further Details — Rule 74.15(1)(e)
    (e) Order to Beneficiary Witness — Rule 74.15(1)(f)
    (f) Order to Former Spouse — Rule 74.15(1)(g)
    (g) Order to Pass Accounts — Rule 74.15(1)(h)
    (h) Order for Other Matters — Rule 74.15(1)(i)
3. Contentious Proceedings
        (i) Notice to the Profession — Toronto Region — Estates List
        (ii) Mandatory Mediation — Estates, Trusts and Substitute Decisions
        (iii) *Courts Improvement Act, 1996*
        (iv) Case Management in Estates and Related Matters
        (v) Rule 75 — Contentious Proceedings in Estate Matters
    (a) Objection to Issuing a Certificate of Appointment — Rule 75.03
    (b) Revocation of Certificate of Appointment
    (c) Return of Certificate — Rule 75.05(1)
    (d) Application or Motion for Directions
    (e) Statement of Submission of Rights
4. Additional Prescribed Forms
5. Claims Against Estate
6. Dependant's Relief Claims
7. *Family Law Act* Claims
8. Forms
    Figure 5-1: Request for Notice of Commencement of Proceeding (Form 74.3)
    Figure 5-2: Order to Accept or Refuse Appointment as Estate Trustee With a Will (Form 74.36)
    Figure 5-3: Order to Accept or Refuse Appointment as Estate Trustee Without a Will (Form 74.37)
    Figure 5-4: Order to Consent or Object to a Proposed Appointment of an Estate Trustee With or Without a Will (Form 74.38)
    Figure 5-5: Order to File a Statement of Assets of the Estate (Form 74.39)
    Figure 5-6: Order to Beneficiary Witness (Form 74.40)
    Figure 5-7: Order to Former Spouse (Form 74.41)
    Figure 5-8: Order to Pass Accounts (Form 74.42)
    Figure 5-9: Notice of Objection (to Issuing a Certificate of Appointment) (Form 75.1)

Figure 5-10: Request for Assignment of Mediator (Form 75.1A)
Figure 5-11: Notice by Mediator (Form 75.1B)
Figure 5-12: Statement of Issues (Form 75.1C)
Figure 5-13: Certificate of Non-Compliance (Form 75.1D)
Figure 5-14: Notice that Objection Has Been Filed (Form 75.2)
Figure 5-15: Notice to Objector (Form 75.3)
Figure 5-16: Notice of Appearance (Form 75.4)
Figure 5-17: Notice of Application for Directions (Form 75.5)
Figure 5-18: Notice of Motion for Directions (Form 75.6)
Figure 5-19: Statement of Claim Pursuant to Order Giving Directions (Form 75.7)
Figure 5-20: Order Giving Directions (Form 75.8) — Whether by Application or Motion
Figure 5-21: Order Giving Directions (Trial of Issue-Motion) (Form 75.9)
Figure 5-22: Statement of Submission of Rights to the Court (Form 75.10)
Figure 5-23: Notice of Settlement (Form 75.11)
Figure 5-24: Rejection of Settlement (Form 75.12)
Figure 5-25: Notice of Contestation (Form 75.13)
Figure 5-26: Claim Against Estate (Form 75.14)
Figure 5-27: Election under the *Family Law Act, 1986* (Form 210)

Rule 74 of the Rules of Civil Procedure, R.R.O. 1990, Reg. 194 (the "Rules") establishes the various procedures to be used in non-contentious proceedings under estates. Although not necessarily contentious, it may be necessary to bring certain applications described under r. 74 on behalf of persons having a financial interest in an estate.

1. REQUEST FOR NOTICE OF COMMENCEMENT OF PROCEEDING — RULE 74.03

Before a certificate of appointment of estate trustee is issued, a person having a financial interest in an estate and who desires to be informed of the commencement of a proceeding may file a request for notice of commencement of proceeding (Form 74.3, see Figure 5-1).* The person filing the notice will receive notification of the commencement of any proceeding in the estate up to the time a Certificate of Appointment of Estate Trustee is issued, unless ordered otherwise. The request for notice expires three years after it is filed but a further request may be filed at any time prior to the Certificate of Appointment of Estate Trustee being issued. This type of request for notice might be used by persons who aren't challenging the validity of a will, but who are creditors of the estate and who wish to keep abreast of any proceedings within the estate.

2. ORDERS FOR ASSISTANCE

Requests for orders for assistance may be brought by persons who appear to have a financial interest in an estate. Before the recent additions to the Rules, an order for assistance was formally known as a Citation. These requests for orders for assistance are generally done on an *ex parte* (without notice) basis and are generally obtained by filing two copies of the draft order you wish to obtain, one copy of a sworn supporting affidavit which will set out the facts, along with a Notice of Motion. Once an order for assistance

---

* In this chapter, a *form* number given in parentheses refers to number of the form as stated in the Rules; the *figure* number refers to the order of its representation at the end of this chapter.

is obtained it is then generally served by personal service or an alternate to personal service as prescribed by the Rules or otherwise if, for example, a motion is brought pursuant to Rule 16 of the Rules of Civil Procedure for substituted service.

(a) Order to Accept or Refuse Appointment — Rule 74.15(1)(a) and (b)

Where a person has an interest, or believes they have an interest in an estate and is aware that there is a Will, and has searched the court records to find that no application for a Certificate of Appointment of Estate Trustee has been brought, that person may move for an order (Form 74.36, see Figure 5-2) requiring that the person they believe is named as Estate Trustee in the Will either accept or refuse the appointment as an Estate Trustee with a Will. If there is an intestacy and a search reveals that no application for a Certificate of Appointment of Estate Trustee Without a Will has been brought, again, a request for an order (Form 74.37, see Figure 5-3) may be brought ordering that the person entitled to apply as the administrator (*e.g.*, surviving spouse) accept or refuse the appointment.

Once the order is obtained it is personally served on the person who is to accept or refuse the appointment of estate trustee. Should they not file the application for the certificate of appointment within the time prescribed by the order, the person is deemed to have renounced their right to be appointed.

(b) Order to Consent or Object to Proposed Appointment — Rule 74.15(1)(c)

Where the consent of a party is required to the appointment of an Estate Trustee, for example, an Estate Trustee without a Will, a request for this order (Form 74.38, see Figure 5-4) will result in the person either having to consent or file a notice of objection to the appointment within a prescribed time failing which the person failing to consent will be deemed to have consented to the appointment. The form of notice of objection to appointment of Estate Trustee is attached as Schedule "A" to the order and then served on the party failing to file their consent.

(c) Order to File Statement of Assets of the Estate — Rule 74.15(1)(d)

The applicant for a Certificate of Appointment of Estate Trustee is only required to give the value of the total estate broken down into the real estate holdings of the deceased (in Ontario), and personalty (wherever located). If the Estate Trustee is not forthcoming in providing asset information to a person with an entitlement in an estate, an order may be requested (Form 74.39, see Figure 5-5) requiring the Estate Trustee to file a Statement of Assets of the Estate with the court within a prescribed time limit. Again, once the order is obtained it is then generally personally served on the Estate Trustee.

(d) Order for Further Details — Rule 74.15(1)(e)

If the party is not satisfied with the financial information received after obtaining an order under r. 74.15(1)(d), an order for further information and details about the assets of the estate may then be requested.

A motion under this rule requires ten days' notice to the Estate Trustee.

(e) Order to Beneficiary Witness — Rule 74.15(1)(f)

This is an order (Form 74.40, see Figure 5-6) that either a beneficiary or the spouse of a beneficiary who witnessed a Will or codicil, or signed the Will or codicil for the testator, must satisfy the court that the beneficiary or spouse of the beneficiary did not exercise improper or undue influence on the testator.

Pursuant to s. 12 of the *Succession Law Reform Act*, R.S.O. 1990, c. S.26, if the beneficiary or spouse of the beneficiary fails to provide satisfactory evidence that there was no improper or undue influence exercised over the testator the gift to the beneficiary under the Will is void. However, the balance of the Will is generally still valid unless the Court orders otherwise.

This motion will be brought by the Estate Trustee and the order usually states that if the beneficiary does not bring the motion and provide satisfactory evidence to the court the applicant for the Certificate of Appointment of Estate Trustee may obtain the certificate of appointment and an endorsement will be made that the beneficiary's benefits under the Will are void pursuant to s. 12 of the *Succession Law Reform Act*.

(f) Order to Former Spouse — Rule 74.15(1)(g)

If a Will names a former spouse as an Estate Trustee, it is necessary that a request for this order (Form 74.41, see Figure 5-7) be brought requiring the former spouse to enter an appearance if they wish to take part in the determination as to whether they are in fact entitled to apply as Estate Trustee.

Pursuant to s. 17(2) of the *Succession Law Reform Act*, unless there is a contrary intention appearing by the Will where, after the date of the Will, a marriage is terminated or declared a nullity, a devise or bequest, an appointment as executor or trustee or the conferring of a general or special power of appointment to a former spouse are all revoked and the Will shall be construed as if the former spouse had predeceased the testator.

(g) Order to Pass Accounts — Rule 74.15(1)(h)

This allows a person who has an interest in an estate to require that the Estate Trustee file the accounts of the estate and an application to pass accounts within a certain period of time. The order (Form 74.42, see Figure 5-8) is then personally served upon the Estate Trustee and sets out the period for which the accounting is to be for.

For the form of the accounts and application see Chapter 6 on Passing of Accounts.

COURT DISPUTES 219

(h) Order for Other Matters — Rule 74.15(1)(i)

This rule provides the court with the authority to make an order providing for any other matter that the court directs.

3. CONTENTIOUS PROCEEDINGS

There have been significant and recent developments in The Rules of Civil Procedure which impact on contentious estate matters.

(i) Notice to the Profession — Toronto Region — Estates List

Contentious estate matters in Toronto are now subject to this recent Notice to the Profession which expands the list of matters to be heard on the Estates List in Toronto (*e.g.* applications to extend the time for making an FLA election, variations of trusts, guardianship applications, *etc.*). In addition, the Notice defines and clarifies the scope of matters to be placed upon the Estates List. The Notice provides:

> "The profession is notified of additions to the list of matters to be heard on the Estates List in Toronto.
> 1. Applications for extension of time for making an election under section 6(1) of the *Family Law Act* regarding the interest of a spouse under section 5(2)
> On and after March 1, 1999, new applications for these extensions will no longer be placed on the Family Law List but will be placed on the Estates List.
> 2. Applications relating to *inter vivos* trusts, whether under the *Variation of Trusts Act*, the rule 14.05 or otherwise
> On and after March 1, 1999, these applications must be placed on the Estates List.
> 3. *Substitute Decisions Act, 1992* proceedings
> All applications brought under the *Substitute Decisions Act, 1992* and related matters falling under the *Health Care Consent Act* are to be placed on the Estates List. This confirms the continuing practice relating to mental incapacity as reflected in the new statutes.
> 4. *Children's Law Reform Act*, s. 47 for appointment of a guardian for the property of a child.
> On and after March 1, 1999, these applications must be placed on the Estates List and not the Family Law List if the application is brought in the Superior Court of Justice.
>
> The profession is also reminded that the correct reference to the administrative vehicle for estate and mental capacity matters is the "Estates List" and not "Estates Court".
> The Estates List is administered through the Estates Office, 10th Floor, 393 University Avenue, Toronto, Ontario, M5G 1E6, telephone number (416) 326-2940 and fax number (416) 326-2939. All filing, issuing and appointment-setting functions relating to Estates List matters are done in the Estates Office. Please note that none of these matters will be heard on the regular motions list. If any is placed on the motions list, it will be adjourned to a date to be fixed by the Estates Registrar. The Estates List deal with the following matters:
> (a) estate passings of accounts
> (b) trials for proof of wills in solemn form
> (c) trials involving issues of testamentary capacity, fraud and undue influence
> (d) matters arising under Rules 74 and 75
> (e) summary procedure for claims against estates, *Estates Act*, s. 44 and s. 45
> (f) applications under Rule 14.05 regarding wills and trusts, including *inter vivos* trusts
> (g) applications under the *Variation of Trusts Act*
> (h) applications under Part V of the *Succession Law Reform Act*
> (i) pre-trials for trials arising out of the above matters

> (j) all proceedings under the *Substitute Decisions Act, 1992* and related matters under the *Health Care Consent Act*
> (k) passing of accounts for persons acting in a trustee capacity, *e.g.* committee of an absentee, guardians of property, persons acting under a power of attorney for property
> (l) applications for extension of time to make an election relating to s. 6(1) of the *Family Law Act*
> (m) applications for the appointment of a guardian of property of a child under s. 47 of the *Children's Law Reform Act*, if brought in the Superior Court of Justice
>
> Where an estate is either plaintiff or defendant in a civil action which does not concern estate law specifically, or where an estate becomes a party in such an action by virtue only of an order to continue under rule 11.02, the action shall proceed as any other action and shall not be placed on the Estates List.
>
> The Estates List will be heard at 393 University Avenue, Toronto, unless notice to the contrary is given. It will be heard the first full week of sitting in every month and, in alternate months, also in the second week in the month. The last two Fridays in each month will be Estates List duty days reserved for emergency matters and as arranged by the Estates Registrar. Pre-trials will be heard at 2:30 p.m. on days during the Estates weeks and at other times, as arranged by the Estates Registrar. Counsel will come to the pre-trial having obtained a date from the Estates Registrar, which will be noted on the record by the pre-trial judge.
>
> Dates for applications motions and passings of accounts will be assigned by the Estates Registrar at the time the record or all supporting material is filed with the Estates Office.
>
> Trial dates will be set by the Estates Registrar. Applications expected to take longer than 2 hours will be heard at a time to be fixed by the Registrar, which may or may not be during an Estates week.
>
> Where a matter is proven to be an emergency to the satisfaction of the Estates Registrar, the matter may be fixed to be heard in a week other than an Estates week or an Estates List duty day, subject to the availability of a judge and a court room.
>
> Gowns will be worn for all proceedings except pre-trials."

Curiously, the expanded list set out in the Notice does not expressly deal with breach of trust actions (except insofar as they arise out of contested passings of accounts). Presumably, one can still commence a proceeding outside of the Estates List for breach of trust, subject to an Order being made requiring the transfer of the matter to the Estates List. Although the Notice refers to "(a) estate passings of accounts", it appears that the Estates Registrar will permit applications for passings in *inter-vivos* trusts and charitable foundations.

It should be noted that as of the date of publication, Toronto Region is the only jurisdiction in Ontario which is subject to a Notice to the Profession issued by the Regional Senior Justice.

(ii) Mandatory Mediation — Estates, Trusts and Substitute Decisions

Effective September 1, 1999, a pilot project for mandatory mediation in Toronto Region and the Regional Municipality of Ottawa-Carleton has been established by Regulation under the *Courts of Justice Act*. The scope of the Rule as it applies to contentious estate proceedings differs from the scope of matters set out in the Notice to Profession concerning the Estates List. As such, not all matters which are within the scope of the Estates List are necessarily subject to mandatory mediation. The provisions for mandatory mediation are set out in new Rule 75.1, which Rule is to be revoked on July 3, 2004.

COURT DISPUTES 221

Hopefully, the pilot will prove to be successful and will be extended and expanded to other Regions in Ontario.

Rule 75.1 (Mandatory Mediation) provides as follows:

75.1.01 This rule establishes a pilot project for mandatory mediation, in the City of Toronto and The Regional Municipality of Ottawa-Carleton, in matters relating to estates, trusts and substitute decisions.

SCOPE

75.1.02 (1) This Rule applies to proceedings,
  (a) that are commenced in the City of Toronto or The Regional Municipality of Ottawa-Carleton on or after September 1, 1999; and
  (b) to which any of the following applies,
      (i) rule 74.18 (application to pass accounts), if the application is contested,
      (ii) rule 75.01 (formal proof of testamentary instrument), 75.03 (objection to issuing certificate of appointment), 75.05 (return of certificate) or 75.08 (claims against an estate),
      (iii) Part V of the *Succession Law Reform Act*,
      (iv) the *Substitute Decisions Act, 1992*,
      (v) the *Absentees Act*, the *Charities Accounting Act*, the *Estates Act*, the *Trustee Act* or the *Variation of Trusts Act*,
      (vi) subrule 14.05(3), if the matters at issue relate to an estate or trust, or
      (vii) subsection 5(2) of the *Family Law Act*.

(2) The fact that an estate or trust is a party to a proceeding, by virtue of an order to continue under Rule 11 or otherwise, is not sufficient to bring the proceeding under this Rule.

DEFINITIONS

75.1.03 In this Rule,

"designated party" means a party whom an order under rule 75.1.05 requires to attend a mediation session in person; ("partie désignée")

"list", when used in reference to a country, means the list maintained for the country under subrule 24.1.08(1); ("liste")

"mediation co-ordinator", when used in reference to a county, means the person designated as mediation co-ordinator for the county under rule 24.1.06. ("coordonnateur de la médiation")

EXEMPTION FROM MEDIATION

75.1.04 The court may make an order, on a party's motion or of its own motion, exempting the proceeding from this Rule.

DIRECTIONS FOR CONDUCT OF MEDIATION

Motion for Directions

75.1.05 (1) In a proceeding described in subrule 75.1.02(1), except a contested passing of accounts under rule 74.18, the applicant shall make a motion, in the same way as under rule 75.06, seeking directions for the conduct of the mediation.

(2) The notice of motion shall be served within 30 days after the last day for serving a notice of appearance.

(3) The motion may be combined with a motion under rule 75.06.

Directions

(4) On the hearing of the motion under this rule, the court may direct,
  (a) the issues to be mediated;
  (b) who has carriage of the mediation and who shall respond;
  (c) within what times the mediation session shall take place;
  (d) which parties are required to attend the mediation session in person, and how they are to be served;
  (e) whether notice to be given to parties submitting their rights to the court under rule 75.07.1;

(f) how the cost of the mediation is to be apportioned among the designated parties; and

(g) any other matter that may be desirable to facilitate the mediation.

(5) In a contested passing of accounts the court shall, on the hearing date specified in the notice of application, deal with the matter as if subrule (4) applied.

Non-Compliance

(6) If there is a non-compliance with a direction given under subrule (4) or (5), the matter shall be referred,

(a) in the City of Toronto, to a judge; and

(b) in The Regional Municipality of Ottawa-Carleton, to a case management master.

MEDIATORS

75.1.06 (1) A mediation under this Rule shall be conducted by,

(a) a person chosen from the list for the county by the agreement of the designated parties;

(b) a person assigned from the list by the mediation co-ordinator for the county, at the request of a designated party; or

(c) a person who is not named on the list if the designated parties consent.

(2) Every person who conducts a mediation under subrule (1), whether named on the list or not, is required to comply with this Rule.

CHOICE OF MEDIATOR

75.1.07 (1) Within 30 days after an order giving directions is made under rule 75.1.05, the designated parties shall choose a mediator under subrule 75.1.06 (1).

(2) When a mediator has been chosen, the party with carriage of the mediation shall give the mediator a copy of the order giving directions.

(3) If the designated parties have not chosen a mediator by the end of the 30-day period, the party with carriage of the mediation shall immediately file with the mediation co-ordinator for the county a request for the assignment of a mediator (Form 75.1A, see Figure 5-10).

(4) A copy of the order giving directions shall be attached to the request.

(5) On receiving the request, the mediation co-ordinator shall immediately assign a mediator from the list and give the mediator a copy of the order giving directions.

(6) If the party with carriage of the mediation fails to file a request, any designated party may file the request.

(7) The mediator shall, immediately on being chosen or assigned, fix a date for the mediation session and shall, at least 20 days before that date, serve on every designated party a notice (Form 75.1B, see Figure 5-11) stating the place, date and time of the session and advising that attendance is obligatory.

PROCEDURE BEFORE MEDIATION SESSION

Statement of Issues

75.1.08 (1) At least seven days before the mediation session, every designated party shall prepare a statement in Form 75.1C (see Figure 5-12) and provide a copy to every other designated party and to the mediator.

(2) The statement shall identify the factual and legal issues in dispute and briefly set out the position and interests of the party making the statement.

(3) The party making the statement shall attach to it any documents that the party considers of central importance in the proceeding.

Non-Compliance

(4) If it is not practical to conduct a mediation session because a designated party fails to comply with subrule (1), the mediator shall cancel the session and immediately file with the court a certificate of non-compliance (Form 75.1D, see Figure 5-13).

ATTENDANCE AT MEDIATION SESSION

Who is Required to Attend

75.1.09 (1) The designated parties, and their lawyers if the designated parties are represented, are required to attend the mediation session.

Authority to Settle

(2) A designated party who requires another person's approval before agreeing to a settlement shall, before the mediation session, arrange to have ready telephone access to the other person throughout the session, whether it takes place during or after regular business hours.

Failure to Attend

(3) If it is not practical to conduct a scheduled mediation session because a designated party fails to attend within the first 30 minutes of the time appointed for the commencement of the session, the mediator shall cancel the session and immediately file with the court a certificate of non-compliance (Form 75.1D, see Figure 5-13).

REMEDY FOR NON-COMPLIANCE

75.1.10 (1) When a certificate of non-compliance is filed, the party with carriage of the mediation shall, within 15 days after the date fixed for the mediation session that was cancelled, bring a motion for further directions before,

    (a) the judge who made the order under rule 75.1.05;
    (b) any other judge who is available; or
    (c) in The Regional Municipality of Ottawa-Carleton, a case management master.

(2) The judge or case management master may require the designated parties to appear before him or her and may,

    (a) establish a timetable for the proceeding;
    (b) strike out any document filed by a designed party;
    (c) order a designated party to pay costs; or
    (d) make any other order that is just.

CONFIDENTIALITY

75.1.11 All communications at a mediation session and the mediator's notes and records shall be deemed to be without prejudice settlement discussions.

OUTCOME OF MEDIATION

Mediator's Report

75.1.12 (1) Within 10 days after the mediation is concluded, the mediator shall give the mediation co-ordinator for the county and the designated parties a report on the mediation.

(2) The mediation co-ordinator may remove from the list the name of a mediator who does not comply with subrule (1).

Agreement

(3) If there is an agreement resolving some or all of the issues in dispute, it shall be signed by the designated parties or their lawyers.

(4) If the agreement resolves all the issues in dispute, the party with carriage of the mediation shall file a notice to that effect with the court,

    (a) in the case of an unconditional agreement, within 10 days after the agreement is signed;
    (b) in the case of a conditional agreement, within 10 days after the condition is satisfied.

(5) Despite subrule (4), if rule 7.08 (person under disability, approval of settlement) also applies to the agreement, the notice shall be filed within 10 days after the event mentioned in clause (4) (a) or (b), or within 10 days after the agreement is approved, whichever is later.

Failure to Comply with Signed Agreement

(6) If a party to a signed agreement fails to comply with its terms, any other party to the agreement may,

    (a) make a motion to a judge for judgment in the terms of the agreement, and the judge may grant judgment accordingly; or
    (b) continue the proceeding as if there had been no agreement.

No Agreement

(7) If no agreement is reached that resolves all the issues in dispute, the matter shall proceed in accordance with any directions given under rule 75.06, or a motion for directions shall be made as soon as possible under that rule.

CONSENT ORDER FOR ADDITIONAL MEDIATION SESSION
  75.1.13 (1) With the consent of the designated parties the court may, at any stage in the proceeding, make an order requiring them to participate in an additional mediation session.
  (2) The court may include any necessary directions in the order.
  (3) Rules 75.1.07 to 75.1.12 apply in respect of the additional session, with necessary modifications.

REVOCATION
  75.1.14 (1) This Rule is revoked on July 3, 2004.
  (2) Despite subsection 3 (2) of Ontario Regulation 290/99, paragraph 2.1 of Form 75.8 is revoked on July 3, 2004.
  (3) Despite subsection 4 (2) of Ontario Regulation 290/99, paragraph 2.1 of Form 75.9 is revoked on July 3, 2004.
  (4) Despite subsection 5 (2) of Ontario Regulation 290/99, Forms 75.1A, 75.1B, 75.1C and 75.1D are revoked on July 3, 2004.
  (5) Item 1.2 of Part I of Tariff A is revoked on July 3, 2004.
  (6) Item 23.2 of Part II of Tariff A is revoked on July 3, 2004.

(iii) *Courts Improvement Act, 1996*

Effective April 19, 1999, Part IV of the *Courts Improvement Act, 1996* was proclaimed in force whereby the Ontario Court (General Division) has been renamed as the Superior Court of Justice. This also applies to matters to be placed on the Estates List.

(iv) Case Management in Estates and Related Matters

While the matters to be heard by the Estates List in the Toronto Region continue to be exempt from the Civil Case Management Rule (*i.e.* Rule 77), there has been some discussion and consideration as to whether a new rule concerning case management in certain, but not all, contentious estate and related matters will be forthcoming. There does not seem to any imminent developments which are expected.

(v) Rule 75 — Contentious Proceedings in Estate Matters

Where r. 74 deals with non-contentious proceedings, r. 75 of the Rules of Civil Procedure deals with contentious proceedings in estate matters:

(a) Objection to Issuing a Certificate of Appointment — Rule 75.03

Prior to the issuing of a Certificate of Appointment of Estate Trustee, any person having a financial interest in the estate may give notice of their objection to the issuance of the certificate by filing with the Registrar or the Estate Registrar for Ontario a Notice of Objection (Form 75.1, see Figure 5-9) which is to be signed by the objector or their solicitor and must state the nature of the objector's interest and of the objection.

The Notice of Objection is what was formally known as a "Caveat". The Notice of Objection expires three years after it is filed but may be withdrawn by the person who filed it at any time before a hearing for directions and an application for the certificate or can be removed by order of the court.

Once a notice is filed, the Registrar will send notice of the filing to the applicant, (see Figure 5-14) or the applicant's solicitor, who filed the application for a Certificate of Appointment of Estate Trustee.

The applicant for a Certificate of Appointment of Estate Trustee must then file a Notice to Objector (Form 75.3, see Figure 5-15) and then file a copy of the notice and proof of service with the court. If the objector does not serve and file a Notice of Appearance (Form 75.4, see Figure 5-16) within 20 days after service of the Notice to Objector, the application for a Certificate of Appointment of Estate Trustee can proceed as if no Notice of Objection had been filed.

If the objector files his Notice of Appearance as mentioned above and the applicant does not move for directions of the court within 30 days after service of the Notice of Appearance, the objector may then move for directions.

(b) Revocation of Certificate of Appointment

Pursuant to r. 75.04, the court may revoke the Certificate of Appointment of Estate Trustee where the court is satisfied that,

(a) the certificate was issued in error or as a result of a fraud on the court;
(b) the appointment is no longer effective; or
(c) the certificate should be revoked for any other reason.

This might be used where, for example, a later Will is subsequently found, and the prior grant by the court was made in error.

(c) Return of Certificate — Rule 75.05(1)

If an application is brought pursuant to r. 75.04, mentioned above, or the moving party seeks the determination of the validity of the Will or of the entitlement of an Estate Trustee to the certificate, the court may, on motion, without notice, order that the certificate of appointment be returned to the court.

The party who obtained the order that the certificate of appointment be returned to the court shall within 30 days of the making of the order move for directions of the court pursuant to r. 75.05(4). The Estate Trustee, as well as anyone else with a financial interest in the estate, may at any time move for directions under r. 75.06.

It should be noted that if the motion for directions is not brought, the Estate Trustee may bring a motion, without notice, ordering the release of the Certificate of Appointment of Estate Trustee.

(d) Application or Motion for Directions

Rule 75.06 provides as follows:

> **75.06**(1) Any person who appears to have a financial interest in an estate may apply for directions, or move for directions in another proceeding under this rule, as to the procedure for bringing any matter before the court.
>
> Service
>
> (2) An application for directions (Form 75.5) [see Figure 5-17] or motion for directions (Form 75.6) [see Figure 5-18] shall be served on all persons appearing to have a financial interest in the estate, or as the court directs, at least 10 days before the hearing of the application or motion.
>
> Order
>
> (3) On an application or motion for directions, the court may direct,
> - (a) the issues to be decided;
> - (b) who are parties, who is plaintiff and defendant and who is submitting rights to the court;
> - (c) who shall be served with the order for directions, and the method and times of service;
> - (d) procedures for bringing the matter before the court in a summary fashion, where appropriate;
> - (e) that the plaintiff file and serve a statement of claim (Form 75.7) [see Figure 5-19];
> - (f) that an estate trustee be appointed during litigation, and file such security as the court directs;
> - (f.1) that a mediation session be conducted under Rule 75.1;
> - (g) such other procedures as are just.
>
> (4) An order giving directions shall be in Form 75.8 or 75.9 [see Figures 5-20, 5-21].

Pursuant to r. 75.07, if a statement of claim is delivered as set out in r. 75.06(3), above, each defendant served may then serve on each party and file with proof of service,

(a) statement of defence or statement of defence and counterclaim; or

(b) a Statement of Submission of Rights to the Court (Form 75.10, see Figure 5-22).

Upon receipt of the statement of defence or statement of defence or counterclaim, the plaintiff may deliver a reply or a reply and defence to counterclaim.

(e) Statement of Submission of Rights

Any party filing a Statement of Submission of Rights to the Court must acknowledge that they are not entitled to receive their costs in the proceeding and will not be liable to pay the costs of any party to the proceeding, except indirectly to the extent costs are ordered by the court to be paid out of the estate. They also acknowledge that they are not entitled to receive notice of any step taken in a proceeding except for the notice of trial and copy of the judgment disposing of the matter if the proceeding is settled by agreement. A judgment on consent will not be given without notice to the party submitting their rights, or without that party's written consent.

Typically the rule permitting a party (*i.e.*, defendant) to file a Statement of Submission of Rights to the Court will be used by a beneficiary who does not wish to become embroiled in costly and protracted litigation. Nevertheless, by filing the Statement of Submission of Rights to the Court the person is protected by ensuring that they receive notice of the trial or, if the matter is being settled, no judgment can be signed without notice to them or without their written consent.

4. ADDITIONAL PRESCRIBED FORMS

1. Notice of Settlement (Form 75.11, see Figure 5-23);
2. Rejection of Settlement (Form 75.12, see Figure 5-24); and
3. Notice of Contestation (pursuant to Section 44 or 45 of the *Estates Act*) (Form 75.13, see Figure 5-25).

5. CLAIMS AGAINST ESTATE

Rule 75.08 relates to ss. 44 and 45 of the *Estates Act*, R.S.O. 1990, c. E.21, which provides for a summary procedure for dealing with claims (oral or written) made against an estate. Unless the court orders otherwise, once a Notice of Contestation is served upon the claimant and the claimant serves a Claim Against Estate (Form 75.14, *not* a Statement of Claim), the Registrar fixes a trial date which then typically proceeds in a summary manner (often without pre-trial discoveries) (Form 75.14, see Figure 5-26). However, the Estate Trustee may request that documentary and oral discovery be held before the trial.

6. DEPENDANT'S RELIEF CLAIMS

Part IV of the *Succession Law Reform Act* (the "*SLRA*") details the procedure in which an award for support of a dependant can be brought. If a deceased has not made adequate provision for the support of all or some of the deceased's dependants, a court application may be brought to obtain an order that appropriate support, which support is determined at the time of the application, be made out of an estate. It does not matter if the deceased died with or without a Will.

Under s. 57 of the *SLRA* a "dependant" means,

(a) the spouse or same-sex partner of the deceased,
(b) a parent of the deceased,
(c) a child of the deceased, or
(d) a brother or sister of the deceased,

to whom the deceased was providing support or was under a legal obligation to provide support immediately before his or her death.

The *SLRA* also provides, in s. 59, for a dependant to bring an application for an order stopping or suspending the administration of part or all of the estate for such period as the court may determine. This order can also include any assets or property transferred or distributed prior to the deceased's death.

An application for support of a dependant may be brought by the following:

(a) the dependant,
(b) the dependant's parent,
(c) the Ministry of Community and Social Services,

(d) a municipal corporation, including a metropolitan, district or regional municipality, but not including an area in municipality,
(e) a district of welfare administration board under the *District Welfare Administration Boards Act*, R.S.O. 1990, c. D.15,
(f) a band approved under s. 15 of the *General Welfare Assistance Act*, R.S.O. 1990, c. G.6, if it is provided a benefit under the *Family Benefits Act*, R.S.O. 1990, c. F.2, or assistance under the *General Welfare Assistance Act* in connection with the support of the dependant.

It should also be noted that an application brought is considered by the court to be brought on behalf of all dependants who might apply.

The application must be brought within six months after the date of the issuance of the Certificate of Estate Trustee (*i.e.*, with or without a Will), or Court Grant, with the exception that the court may allow an application to be brought at any time against any undistributed portion of an estate.

The evidence provided in support of such application will include the financial information of the dependant, both present and potential future, consideration of any property transferred by the deceased prior to his death, any other claims being brought or that could be brought, any agreements between the deceased and the dependant, (although a court order may still be made even if such an agreement exists), and whatever additional information the court may determine.

The court order may result in a payment being made from either the capital or income of the estate, or both and may result in a lump sum or periodic payment to the dependant.

In cases where it is proven the dependant is in need and it will take some time to obtain all the required information, the court can make an interim order for support.

Once an application has been brought under the *SLRA* by or on behalf of the dependant and once notice is received by the personal representative of such application, no distribution or further distribution as the case may be, of the estate assets may be made unless all persons entitled to apply for support consent to the distribution or unless the court orders such distribution be made. The personal representative must be aware that should they make a distribution without consent or a court order they can be held personally liable, to the extent that there is any deficiency between the support award and the balance left in the estate.

Once the order is obtained, a certified copy is to be filed with the court that issued the Certificate of Appointment of Estate Trustee.

7. *FAMILY LAW ACT* CLAIMS

Under the *Family Law Act*, R.S.O. 1990, c. F.3 (the "*FLA*"), a deceased's spouse may elect to take their entitlement under the deceased's Will if there is a Will, or in the case of an intestacy their spouse's entitlement under Part II of the *SLRA* or in either case they may elect to take their entitlement under s. 5 of the *FLA* (equalization of net family properties). In the case of a partial intestacy, the spouse may elect to take under the Will and the entitlement under Part II of the *SLRA* or to receive the entitlement under s. 5 of the *FLA*. However, the deceased's Will can also express that the spouse is to receive all gifts under the Will in addition to their entitlement under s. 5 of the *FLA*.

The entitlement under s. 5 of the *Family Law Act* is an equalizing payment to the spouse of one-half of the difference between the deceased's net family property and the spouse's net family property.

"Net Family Property" is defined by s. 4 of the *FLA* as follows:

> ... the value of all the property, except property described in subsection (2), that a spouse owns on the valuation date, after deducting,
>
> (a) the spouse's debts and other liabilities, and
>
> (b) the value of property, other than a matrimonial home, that the spouse owned on the date of marriage, after deducting the spouse's debts and other liabilities, calculated as of the date of marriage;

Under s. 6(b) of the *FLA*, where a surviving spouse elects to receive the entitlement under s. 5, the payment to the surviving spouse of a life insurance policy or pension plan shall be credited against the surviving spouse's entitlement under s. 5, unless there is a written designation by the deceased that these proceeds are to be received in addition to the s. 5 entitlement.

It should be noted that under s. 6(12) of the *FLA* the spouse's s. 5 entitlement has priority over:

> (a) the gifts made in the deceased spouse's will, if any, subject to subsection (13); [The s. 5 entitlement does not have priority over a gift by Will made in accordance with a contract that the deceased entered into in good faith and for valuable consideration, except to the extent that the value of the gift, in the court's opinion, exceeds this consideration.]
>
> (b) a person's right to a share of the estate under Part II (Intestate Succession) of the *Succession Law Reform Act*;
>
> (c) an order made against the estate under Part V (Support of Dependants) of the *Succession Law Reform Act*, except an order in favour of a child of the deceased spouse.

The election (see Figure 5-27) required to be filed by the spouse under the *FLA* must be filed within six months of the date of death unless the spouse brings an application for an extension of same.

No distributions under the estate are to take place within a six-month period of the spouse's death unless upon the written consent of the spouse or unless a court orders the distribution. The personal representative should be aware that they may be held personally liable for any distribution made after the date of the notice of the claim. If, in fact, the court provides an extension for the spouse's application, any property that is distributed before the date of the order and without notice of the application is not brought into the calculation of the deceased spouse's net family property.

Figure 5-1: Request for Notice of Commencement of Proceeding (Form 74.3)

ONTARIO

SUPERIOR COURT OF JUSTICE

IN THE ESTATE OF SAMUEL SMITH, deceased.

Details about the Deceased Person

Complete in full as applicable   *And if the deceased was known by any other name, state below the full names used*

First given name:	Given name or names:
Second given name:	
Third given name:	Surname:
Surname:	

REQUEST FOR NOTICE OF COMMENCEMENT OF PROCEEDING

    I have or appear to have a financial interest in the estate and desire to be informed of the commencement of any proceeding in the estate.

    Notice of the commencement of any proceeding may be mailed to me at the address shown below.

    DATE: [day, month, year]

NAME OF INTERESTED PARTY: Allan Smith
ADDRESS: 123 Address Road
                 Toronto, Ontario
                 M1X 1X1

Figure 5-2: Order to Accept or Refuse Appointment as Estate Trustee With a Will (Form 74.36)

Court File No. [INSERT]

ONTARIO

SUPERIOR COURT OF JUSTICE

IN THE ESTATE OF SAMUEL SMITH, deceased.

ORDER TO ACCEPT OR REFUSE APPOINTMENT AS ESTATE TRUSTEE WITH A WILL

A motion for this order has been made by JACK SMITH. From an affidavit made by JACK SMITH that has been filed it appears that you are named as estate trustee in a will or codicil of the deceased dated [date].

1. THIS COURT ORDERS THAT you file an application for a certificate of appointment of estate trustee with a will in the court office within [number] days after this order is served on you.

2. THIS COURT ORDERS THAT if you do not do so within that time, you shall be deemed to have renounced your right to be appointed.

_____
Registrar

Address of court office
393 University Avenue
10th Floor
Toronto, Ontario
M5G 1E6

TO: [estate trustee]

— continued next page

Figure 5-2: ***Order to Accept or Refuse Appointment as Estate Trustee With a Will (Form 74.36)*** (continued)

Court file no. [INSERT]

**ONTARIO
SUPERIOR COURT OF JUSTICE**

Proceeding commenced at Toronto
IN THE ESTATE OF

SAMUEL SMITH, deceased

**ORDER TO ACCEPT OR REFUSE
APPOINTMENT AS ESTATE
TRUSTEE WITH A WILL**
(Form 74.36 under the Rules)

Name, address and telephone number of solicitor, party or person

Brown & Brown
678 Driveway Street
Toronto, Ontario
M3R 2H1

Tel: (416) 111-2222
Fax: (416) 333-4444

Solicitor for the Applicant

Figure 5-3: Order to Accept or Refuse Appointment as Estate Trustee Without a Will (Form 74.37)

Court File No. [insert]

ONTARIO

SUPERIOR COURT OF JUSTICE

IN THE ESTATE OF SAMUEL SMITH, deceased.

ORDER TO ACCEPT OR REFUSE APPOINTMENT
AS ESTATE TRUSTEE WITHOUT A WILL

A motion for this order has been made by JACK SMITH. From an affidavit made by JACK SMITH that has been filed it appears that you may have a prior right to be appointed estate trustee without a will in the deceased's estate.

1. THIS COURT ORDERS THAT you file an application for a certificate of appointment of estate trustee without a will in the court office within [number] days after this order is served on you.

2. THIS COURT ORDERS THAT if you do not do so within that time, you shall be deemed to have renounced your right to be appointed.

_____
Registrar

Address of court office
393 University Avenue
10th Floor
Toronto, Ontario
M5G 1E6

TO: [Name and address of party with prior right

— continued next page

Figure 5-3: ***Order to Accept or Refuse Appointment as Estate Trustee Without a Will (Form 74.37)*** (continued)

Court file no. [INSERT]

ONTARIO
SUPERIOR COURT OF JUSTICE

Proceeding commenced at Toronto
IN THE ESTATE OF

SAMUEL SMITH, deceased

ORDER TO ACCEPT OR REFUSE APPOINTMENT AS ESTATE TRUSTEE WITHOUT A WILL

(Form 74.37 under the Rules)

Name, address and telephone number of solicitor, party or person

Brown & Brown
678 Driveway Street
Toronto, Ontario
M3R 2H1

Tel: (416) 111-2222
Fax: (416) 333-4444

Solicitor for the Applicant

Figure 5-4: Order to Consent or Object to a Proposed Appointment of an Estate Trustee With or Without a Will (Form 74.38)

Court File No. [INSERT]

ONTARIO
SUPERIOR COURT OF JUSTICE

IN THE ESTATE OF SAMUEL SMITH, Deceased.

THE HONOURABLE MISTER/MADAM) [day of the week], the [day] day of [month],
JUSTICE [Name of Justice]) [year]
)

ORDER TO CONSENT OR OBJECT TO A PROPOSED APPOINTMENT OF AN ESTATE TRUSTEE WITH OR WITHOUT A WILL

A motion for this order has been made by JACK SMITH. From an affidavit made by JACK SMITH that has been filed it appears that JACK SMITH is applying for a certificate of appointment as estate trustee with/without a will, that you are a person with a financial interest in the estate and that your consent to the appointment is being sought.

1. THIS COURT ORDERS THAT if you oppose that person's appointment as estate trustee, you must file a notice of objection to appointment of estate trustee, in the form attached as Schedule "A", in the court office within [number] days after this order is served on you.

2. THIS COURT ORDERS THAT if you do not do so within that time, you shall be deemed to have consented to that person's appointment.

_____

Registrar
Address of court office
393 University Avenue
10th Floor
Toronto, Ontario
M5G 1E6

TO:

— continued next page

Figure 5-4: ***Order to Consent or Object to a Proposed Appointment of an Estate Trustee With or Without a Will (Form 74.38)*** (continued)

Court file no. [INSERT]

ONTARIO
SUPERIOR COURT OF JUSTICE

Proceeding commenced at Toronto
IN THE ESTATE OF

SAMUEL SMITH, deceased

ORDER TO CONSENT OR OBJECT TO A PROPOSED APPOINTMENT OF AN ESTATE TRUSTEE WITH OR WITHOUT A WILL
(Form 74.38 under the Rules)

Name, address and telephone number of solicitor, party or person

Brown & Brown
678 Driveway Street
Toronto, Ontario
M3R 2H1

Tel: (416) 111-2222
Fax: (416) 333-4444

Solicitor for the Applicant

Figure 5-5: Order to File a Statement of Assets of the Estate (Form 74.39)

Court File No. [INSERT]

ONTARIO
SUPERIOR COURT OF JUSTICE

IN THE ESTATE OF SAMUEL SMITH, Deceased.

THE HONOURABLE MISTER/MADAM JUSTICE [Name of Justice]	) [day of the week], the [day] day of [month],) [year])

ORDER TO FILE A STATEMENT OF ASSETS OF THE ESTATE

A motion for this order has been made by JACK SMITH. From an affidavit made by JACK SMITH that has been filed it appears that you are an estate trustee of the estate and that you should provide further information about the assets of the estate.

THIS COURT ORDERS THAT you file a statement of the nature of each asset of the estate and its value at the date of death in the court office within [number] days after this order is served on you.

_____
Registrar
Address of court office
393 University Avenue
10th Floor
Toronto, Ontario
M5G 1E6

TO: [estate trustee]

— continued next page

238 THE PRACTICAL GUIDE TO ONTARIO ESTATE ADMINISTRATION

Figure 5-5: *Order to File a Statement of Assets of the Estate (Form 74.39)*
  (continued)

Court file no. [INSERT]

ONTARIO
SUPERIOR COURT OF JUSTICE

Proceeding commenced at Toronto
IN THE ESTATE OF

SAMUEL SMITH, deceased

ORDER TO FILE A STATEMENT OF ASSETS OF THE ESTATE
(Form 74.39 under the Rules)

Name, address and telephone number of solicitor, party or person

Brown & Brown
678 Driveway Street
Toronto, Ontario
M3R 2H1

Tel: (416)111-2222
Fax: (416) 333-4444

Solicitor for the Applicant

Figure 5-6: Order to Beneficiary Witness (Form 74.40)

```
                                                    Court File No. [INSERT]
                            ONTARIO
                    SUPERIOR COURT OF JUSTICE

                IN THE ESTATE OF SAMUEL SMITH, Deceased.

THE HONOURABLE MISTER/MADAM  )  [day of the week], the [day] day of [month],
JUSTICE [Name of Justice]    )  [year]
                             )

                    ORDER TO BENEFICIARY WITNESS
```

A motion for this order has been made by JACK SMITH. From an affidavit made by JACK SMITH, it appears that JOHN SMITH has made an application for a certificate of appointment of estate trustee with a will, that you are a beneficiary under the will or codicil dated June 21, 1973 and that you or your spouse witnessed the will or codicil or signed for the testator.

1. THIS COURT ORDERS THAT if you wish the court to find that neither you nor your spouse exercised any improper or undue influence on the testator, you must make a motion within [number] days after this order is served on you, asking the court to make that finding.

2. THIS COURT ORDERS THAT if you do not make such a motion within that time, the applicant may proceed to obtain a certificate of appointment of estate trustee with a will, bearing a note stating that your benefits under the will are void under section 12 of the *Succession Law Reform Act*.

_____
Registrar
Address of court office
393 University Avenue
10th Floor
Toronto, Ontario
M5G 1E6

TO: [estate trustee]

— continued next page

Figure 5-6: Order to Beneficiary Witness (Form 74.40) (continued)

Court file no. [INSERT]

ONTARIO
SUPERIOR COURT OF JUSTICE

Proceeding commenced at Toronto
IN THE ESTATE OF

SAMUEL SMITH, deceased

ORDER TO BENEFICIARY WITNESS
(Form 74.40 under the Rules)

Name, address and telephone number of solicitor, party or person

Brown & Brown
678 Driveway Street
Toronto, Ontario
M3R 2H1

Tel: (416) 111-2222
Fax: (416) 333-4444

Solicitor for the Applicant

Figure 5-7: Order to Former Spouse (Form 74.41)

Court File No. [INSERT]

ONTARIO
SUPERIOR COURT OF JUSTICE

IN THE ESTATE OF SAMUEL SMITH, Deceased.

THE HONOURABLE MISTER/MADAM) [day of the week], the [day] day of [month],
JUSTICE [Name of Justice]) [year]
)

ORDER TO FORMER SPOUSE

Subsection 17(2) of the *Succession Law Reform Act* provides as follows:

"Except when a contrary intention appears by the will, where, after the testator makes a will, his or her marriage is terminated by a judgment absolute of divorce or is declared a nullity,

(a) a devise or bequest of a beneficial interest in property to his or her former spouse;
(b) an appointment of his or her former spouse as executor or trustee; and
(c) the conferring of a general or special power of appointment on his or her former spouse,

are revoked and the will shall be construed as if the former spouse had predeceased the testator."

A motion for this order has been made by JACK SMITH, who has also made an application for a certificate of appointment of estate trustee with a will. From the application it appears that the will is dated June 2, 1972 (and that the codicil(s) is (are) dated June 2, 1972 (delete if inapplicable), that you are a former spouse of the testator and that your marriage was terminated by a judgment absolute of divorce or declared a nullity after the date of the will or a codicil.

1. THIS COURT ORDERS THAT if you wish to take part in the determination of the question whether the provisions in the will that affect you are revoked under subsection 17(2) of the *Succession Law Reform Act*, you must enter an appearance in the office of the registrar of the court within [number] days after this order is served on you.

2. THIS COURT ORDERS THAT if you do not do so within that time, the question will be determined in your absence and you will be bound by the result.

Registrar
Address of court office
393 University Avenue
10th Floor
Toronto, Ontario
M5G 1E6

TO: [former spouse]

— continued next page

242 THE PRACTICAL GUIDE TO ONTARIO ESTATE ADMINISTRATION

Figure 5-7: *Order to Former Spouse (Form 74.41)* (continued)

Court file no. [INSERT]

ONTARIO
SUPERIOR COURT OF JUSTICE

Proceeding commenced at Toronto
IN THE ESTATE OF

SAMUEL SMITH, deceased

ORDER TO FORMER SPOUSE
(Form 74.41 under the Rules)

Name, address and telephone number of solicitor, party or person

Brown & Brown
678 Driveway Street
Toronto, Ontario
M3R 2H1

Tel: (416)111-2222
Fax: (416)333-4444

Solicitor for the Applicant

Figure 5-8: Order to Pass Accounts (Form 74.42)

Court File No. [INSERT]

ONTARIO
SUPERIOR COURT OF JUSTICE

IN THE ESTATE OF SAMUEL SMITH, Deceased.

THE HONOURABLE MISTER/MADAM) [day of the week], the [day] day of [month],
JUSTICE [Name of Deceased]   ) [year]
)

ORDER TO PASS ACCOUNTS

A motion for this order has been made by JACK SMITH. From an affidavit made by JACK SMITH that has been filed it appears that you are an estate trustee of the estate and that you have made no accounting to the court of your dealings with the estate during the period from June 1, 1978 to June 1, 1995.

THIS COURT ORDERS THAT you file accounts of the estate and an application to pass accounts, in accordance with rules 74.17 and 74.18 of the Rules of Civil Procedure, in the court office within [number] days after this order is served on you.

_____
Registrar
393 University Avenue
10th Floor
Toronto, Ontario
M5G 1E6

TO: [estate trustee]

— continued next page

Figure 5-8: Order to Pass Accounts (Form 74.42) (continued)

Court file no. [INSERT]	***ONTARIO*** **SUPERIOR COURT OF JUSTICE** Proceeding commenced at Toronto IN THE ESTATE OF SAMUEL SMITH, deceased	**ORDER TO PASS ACCOUNTS** *(Form 74.42 under the Rules)*	*Name, address and telephone number of solicitor, party or person* Brown & Brown 678 Driveway Street Toronto, Ontario M3R 2H1

Figure 5-9: Notice of Objection (to Issuing a Certficate of Appointment) (Form 75.1)

Court File No. [INSERT]

**ONTARIO
SUPERIOR COURT OF JUSTICE**

IN THE ESTATE OF SAMUEL SMITH, Deceased.

IN THE MATTER OF an application for a certificate of appointment of estate trustee

NOTICE OF OBJECTION

I, SAMUEL SMITH, object to the issuing of a certificate of appointment of estate trustee to SAMUEL SMITH without notice to me because [indicate reason(s)].

The nature of my interest in the estate is: [set out details].

DATE: [date]

[name, address and phone number of objector or solicitor for objector]

— continued next page

Figure 5-9: Notice of Objection (to Issuing a Certficate of Appointment) (Form 75.1) (continued)

Court file no. [INSERT]

ONTARIO
SUPERIOR COURT OF JUSTICE

Proceeding commenced at Toronto
IN THE ESTATE OF

SAMUEL SMITH, deceased

NOTICE OF OBJECTION
(Form 75.1 under the Rules)

Name, address and telephone number of solicitor, party or person

Brown & Brown
678 Driveway Street
Toronto, Ontario
M3R 2H1

Tel: (416)111-2222
Fax: (416)333-4444

Solicitor for the Applicant

Figure 5-10: Request for Assignment of Mediator (Form 75.1A)

Court File No. [INSERT]

ONTARIO
SUPERIOR COURT OF JUSTICE

IN THE ESTATE OF   , deceased.

late of

occupation

who died on

REQUEST FOR ASSIGNMENT OF MEDIATOR

TO: Mediation co-ordinator for (*county*)

    An order giving directions was made under rule 75.1.05 on (*date of order*). A copy of the order is attached to this request.

    The designated parties have not chosen a mediator under subrule 75.1.06(1). The 30-day period mentioned in subrule 75.1.07(1) has expired.

    This is a request that you assign a mediator from the list for the county.

(*Date*)   (*Name, address, telephone number and fax number, if any, of lawyer of party filing request, or of party*)

— *continued next page*

Figure 5-10: Request for Assignment of Mediator (Form 75.1A) (continued)

Court file no. [INSERT]

**ONTARIO
SUPERIOR COURT OF JUSTICE**

Proceeding commenced at Toronto
IN THE ESTATE OF
SAMUEL SMITH, deceased

REQUEST FOR ASSIGNMENT OF MEDIATOR
(Form 75.1A under the Rules)

Name, address and telephone number of solicitor, party or person

Brown & Brown
678 Driveway Street
Toronto, Ontario
M3R 2H1

Tel: (416)111-2222
Fax: (416)333-4444

Solicitor for the Applicant

Figure 5-11: Notice by Mediator (Form 75.1B)

Court File No. [INSERT]

ONTARIO
SUPERIOR COURT OF JUSTICE

IN THE ESTATE OF _____ , deceased.

late of _____ ,

occupation _____ ,

who died on _____ ,

NOTICE BY MEDIATOR

TO:

AND TO:

I am the mediator whom the mediation co-ordinator has appointed to conduct the mediation session under Rule 75.1. (*Delete this paragraph if mediator was chosen by designated parties under clause 75.1.06(1) (a) or (c).*)

The mediation session will take place on (*date*), from (*time*) to (*time*), at (*place*).

You are required to attend this mediation session. If you have a lawyer representing you in this proceeding, he or she is also required to attend.

You are required to file a statement of issues (Form 75.1C) by (*date*) (seven days before the mediation session). A blank copy of the form is attached.

When you attend the mediation session, you should bring with you any documents that you consider of central importance in the proceeding. You should plan to remain throughout the scheduled time. If you need another person's approval before agreeing to a settlement, you should make arrangements before the mediation session to ensure that you have ready telephone access to that person throughout the session, even outside regular business hours.

YOU MAY BE PENALIZED UNDER RULE 75.1.10 IF YOU FAIL TO FILE A STATEMENT OF ISSUES OR FAIL TO ATTEND THE MEDIATION SESSION.

(*Date*)   (*Name, address, telephone number and fax number, if any, of mediator*)

— continued next page

Figure 5-11: Notice by Mediator (Form 75.1B) (continued)

Court file no. [INSERT]

ONTARIO
SUPERIOR COURT OF JUSTICE

Proceeding commenced at Toronto
IN THE ESTATE OF
SAMUEL SMITH, deceased

NOTICE OF MEDIATOR
(Form 75.1A under the Rules)

Name, address and telephone number of MEDIATOR

Figure 5-12: Statement of Issues (Form 75.1C)

Court File No. [INSERT]

ONTARIO
SUPERIOR COURT OF JUSTICE

IN THE ESTATE OF   , deceased.

late of

occupation   ,

who died on   ,

STATEMENT OF ISSUES

(To be provided to mediator and designated parties at least seven days before the mediation session)

1. Factual and legal issues in dispute

   The undersigned designated party states that the following factual and legal issues are in dispute and remain to be resolved.

   (Issues should be stated briefly and numbered consecutively.)

2. Party's position and interests (what the party hopes to achieve)

   (Brief summary.)

3. Attached documents

   Attached to this form are the following documents that the designated party considers of central importance in the proceeding: *(list)*

(date)   *(party's signature)*

(Name, address, telephone number and fax number, if any, of lawyer of party filing statement of issues, or of party)

NOTE: Rule 75.1.11 provides as follows:

All communications at a mediation session and the mediator's notes and records shall be deemed to be without prejudice settlement discussions.

— *continued next page*

Figure 5-12: Statement of Issues (Form 75.1C) (continued)

Court file no. [INSERT]

**ONTARIO
SUPERIOR COURT OF JUSTICE**

Proceeding commenced at Toronto
IN THE ESTATE OF

SAMUEL SMITH, deceased

STATEMENT OF ISSUES
(Form 75.1C under the Rules)

Name, address and telephone number of solicitor, party or person

Brown & Brown
678 Driveway Street
Toronto, Ontario
M3R 2H1

Tel: (416) 111-2222
Fax: (416) 333-4444

Solicitor for the Applicant

Figure 5-13: Certificate of Non-Compliance (Form 75.1D)

Court File No. [INSERT]

**ONTARIO
SUPERIOR COURT OF JUSTICE**

IN THE ESTATE OF   , deceased.

late of   ,

occupation   ,

who died on   ,

CERTIFICATE OF NON-COMPLIANCE

TO: (*court*)

    I, (*name*), mediator, certify that this certificate of non-compliance is filed because:

☐ (*Identify party(ies)*) failed to provide a copy of a statement of issues to the mediator and the other parties (*or* to the mediator *or* to *party(ies)*),

☐ (*Identify party(ies)*) failed to attend within the first 30 minutes of a scheduled mediation session.

(*Date*)   (*Name, address, telephone number and fax number, if any, of mediator*)

— *continued next page*

Figure 5-13: Certificate of Non-Compliance (Form 75.1D) (continued)

Court file no. [INSERT]

ONTARIO
SUPERIOR COURT OF JUSTICE

Proceeding commenced at Toronto
IN THE ESTATE OF

SAMUEL SMITH, deceased

**CERTIFICATE
OF NON-COMPLIANCE**
(Form 75.1D under the Rules)

Name, address and telephone number of MEDIATOR

Figure 5-14: Notice that Objection Has Been Filed (Form 75.2)

Court File No. [INSERT]

ONTARIO

SUPERIOR COURT OF JUSTICE

IN THE ESTATE OF SAMUEL SMITH, deceased.

IN THE MATTER OF an application for a certificate of appointment of estate trustee

NOTICE THAT OBJECTION HAS BEEN FILED

A notice of objection, a copy of which is attached, has been filed with the court.

No further action regarding issuing a certificate of an appointment to you will be taken until you have complied with subrule 75.03(4) of the Rules of Civil Procedure.

DATE:

_____
Registrar

Address of court office

TO: [applicant or solicitor for applicant]   393 University Avenue
10th Floor
Toronto, ON M5G 1E6

— continued next page

Figure 5-14: *Notice that Objection Has Been Filed (Form 75.2)* (continued)

Court file no. [INSERT]

ONTARIO
SUPERIOR COURT OF JUSTICE

Proceeding commenced at Toronto
IN THE ESTATE OF

SAMUEL SMITH, deceased

NOTICE THAT OBJECTION HAS BEEN FILED
(Form 75.2 under the Rules)

Name, address and telephone number of solicitor, party or person

Brown & Brown
678 Driveway Street
Toronto, Ontario
M3R 2H1

Tel: (416) 111-2222
Fax: (416) 333-4444

Solicitor for the Applicant

Figure 5-15: Notice to Objector (Form 75.3)

Court File No. [INSERT]

ONTARIO
SUPERIOR COURT OF JUSTICE

IN THE ESTATE OF SAMUEL SMITH, Deceased.

IN THE MATTER OF an application for a certificate of appointment of estate trustee

NOTICE TO OBJECTOR

AN APPLICATION for a certificate of appointment of estate trustee in the estate has been made by [name of applicant].

IF YOU WISH TO OPPOSE this application, you or an Ontario lawyer acting for you must within 20 days of service on you of this notice to objector prepare a notice of appearance in Form 75.4 of the Rules of Civil Procedure, serve it on the applicant's lawyer, or where the applicant does not have a lawyer serve it on the applicant, and file it with proof of service in the court office at 393 University Avenue, 10th Floor, Toronto, Ontario, M5G 1E6.

IF YOU FAIL to serve and file a notice of appearance, the application for certificate of appointment of estate trustee shall proceed as if your notice of objection had not been filed.

DATE: [date]

[applicant or solicitor for applicant]

TO: [objector or solicitor for objector]

— continued next page

Figure 5-15: *Notice to Objector (Form 75.3)* (continued)

Court file no. [INSERT]	***ONTARIO*** **SUPERIOR COURT OF JUSTICE** Proceeding commenced at Toronto IN THE ESTATE OF SAMUEL SMITH, deceased	**NOTICE TO OBJECTOR** *(Form 75.3 under the Rules)*	*Name, address and telephone number of solicitor, party or person* Brown & Brown 678 Driveway Street Toronto, ON M3R 2H1 Tel: (416) 111-2222 Fax: (416) 333-4444 Solicitor for the Applicants

Figure 5-16: Notice of Appearance (Form 75.4)

Court File No. [INSERT]

ONTARIO
SUPERIOR COURT OF JUSTICE

IN THE ESTATE OF SAMUEL SMITH, Deceased.

IN THE MATTER OF an application for a certificate of appointment of estate trustee

NOTICE OF APPEARANCE

I desire to oppose the issuing of a certificate of appointment of estate trustee for the reasons set out in the notice of objection filed.

DATE: [date]

[objector or solicitor for objector]

TO: [applicant or solicitor for applicant]

— continued next page

260 THE PRACTICAL GUIDE TO ONTARIO ESTATE ADMINISTRATION

Figure 5-16: Notice of Appearance (Form 75.4) (continued)

Court file no. [INSERT]

ONTARIO
SUPERIOR COURT OF JUSTICE

Proceeding commenced at Toronto
IN THE ESTATE OF

SAMUEL SMITH, deceased

NOTICE OF APPEARANCE

(Form 75.4 under the Rules)

Name, address and telephone number of solicitor, party or person

Brown & Brown
678 Driveway Street
Toronto, Ontario
M3R 2H1

Figure 5-17: Notice of Application for Directions (Form 75.5)

Court File No. [INSERT]

***ONTARIO*
SUPERIOR COURT OF JUSTICE**

IN THE ESTATE OF SAMUEL SMITH, Deceased.

BETWEEN:

[name of applicant(s)]

Applicant(s)

- and -

[name of respondent(s)]

Respondent(s)

NOTICE OF APPLICATION FOR DIRECTIONS

TO THE RESPONDENT

A LEGAL PROCEEDING HAS BEEN COMMENCED by the applicant. The claim made by the applicant appears on the following page.

THIS APPLICATION will come on for a hearing before a judge on June 22, 1996 at 10:00 a.m., at the Court House at 393 University Avenue, 10th Floor, Toronto, Ontario, M5G 1E6.

IF YOU WISH TO OPPOSE THIS APPLICATION, you or an Ontario lawyer acting for you must forthwith prepare a notice of appearance in Form 38A prescribed by the Rules of Civil Procedure, serve it on the applicant's lawyer or, where the applicant does not have a lawyer, serve it on the applicant, and file it, with proof of service, in this court office, and you or your lawyer must appear at the hearing.

IF YOU WISH TO PRESENT AFFIDAVIT OR OTHER DOCUMENTARY EVIDENCE TO THE COURT OR TO EXAMINE OR CROSS-EXAMINE WITNESSES ON THE APPLICATION, you or your lawyer must, in addition to serving your notice of appearance, serve a copy of the evidence on the applicant's lawyer or, where the applicant does not have a lawyer, serve it on the applicant, and file it with proof of service, in the court office where the application is to be heard, as soon as possible, but not later than 2 p.m. on the day before the hearing.

IF YOU FAIL TO APPEAR AT THE HEARING, JUDGMENT MAY BE GIVEN IN YOUR ABSENCE AND WITHOUT FURTHER NOTICE TO YOU.

If you wish to oppose this application but are unable to pay legal fees, legal aid may be available to you by contacting a local Legal Aid office.

DATE:

Issued by: _____

Registrar
Address of court office:
393 University Avenue
10th Floor
Toronto, Ontario
M5G 1E6

— continued next page

Figure 5-17: Notice of Application for Directions (Form 75.5) (continued)

TO: [respondent or solicitor for respondent]

1. The applicant makes application for directions from the court with respect to: [state nature of proceeding].

2. The grounds for the application are rule 75.06 and [statutory provision or Rule].

3. The following documentary evidence will be used at the hearing of the application for directions: [list other documentary evidence].

— continued next page

Figure 5-17: Notice of Application for Directions (Form 75.5) (continued)

Court file no. [INSERT]

ONTARIO
SUPERIOR COURT OF JUSTICE

Proceeding commenced at Toronto
IN THE ESTATE OF

SAMUEL SMITH, deceased

**NOTICE OF APPLICATION
FOR DIRECTIONS**
(Form 75.5 under the Rules)

Name, address and telephone number of solicitor, party or person

Brown & Brown
678 Driveway Street
Toronto, ON M3R 2H1

Tel: (416) 111-2222
Fax: (416) 333-4444

Solicitor for the Applicants

Figure 5-18: Notice of Motion for Directions (Form 75.6)

Court File No. [INSERT]

ONTARIO
SUPERIOR COURT OF JUSTICE

IN THE ESTATE OF SAMUEL SMITH, Deceased.

BETWEEN:

[name of moving party]

Moving Party

- and -

[name of respondent(s)]

Respondent(s)

NOTICE OF MOTION FOR DIRECTIONS

The moving party will make a motion to the court on [date], at [time], or so soon after that time as the motion can be heard at [address of Court House].

The motion is for directions with respect to:

[state nature of proceeding]

The grounds for the motion are rule 75.06 and [specify further grounds or Rule].

The following documentary evidence will be used at the hearing of the motion: [list affidavits or other documentary evidence].

DATE: [date]

[applicant or solicitor for applicant]

TO: [respondent or solicitor for respondent]

— continued next page

Figure 5-18: Notice of Motion for Directions (Form 75.6) (continued)

Court file no. [INSERT]

ONTARIO
SUPERIOR COURT OF JUSTICE

Proceeding commenced at Toronto

IN THE ESTATE OF

SAMUEL SMITH, deceased

**NOTICE OF MOTION
FOR DIRECTIONS**
(Form 75.6 under the Rules)

Name, address and telephone number of solicitor, party or person

Brown & Brown
678 Driveway Street
Toronto, ON M3R 2H1

Tel: (416) 111-2222
Fax: (416) 333-4444

Solicitor for the Applicants

Figure 5-19: Statement of Claim Pursuant to Order Giving Directions (Form 75.7)

Court File No. [INSERT]

**ONTARIO
SUPERIOR COURT OF JUSTICE**

IN THE ESTATE OF SAMUEL SMITH, Deceased.

B E T W E E N :

[name of plaintiff]

Plaintiff

- and -

[name of defendant(s)]

Defendant(s)

- and -

[person(s) submitting rights]

Person(s) Submitting
Rights to the Court

**STATEMENT OF CLAIM
PURSUANT TO ORDER GIVING DIRECTIONS**

TO THE DEFENDANT

A LEGAL PROCEEDING HAS BEEN COMMENCED by the Plaintiff. The claim made is set out in the following pages.

IF YOU WISH TO DEFEND THIS PROCEEDING, you or an Ontario lawyer acting for you must prepare a statement of defence in Form 18A prescribed by the Rules of Civil Procedure, serve it on the plaintiff's lawyer, or, where the plaintiff does not have a lawyer, serve it on the plaintiff, and file it, with proof of service, in the court office, WITHIN 20 DAYS after this statement of claim is served upon you, if you are served in Ontario.

If you are served in another province or territory of Canada or in the United States of America, the period of serving and filing your statement of defence is 40 days. If you are served outside of Canada and the United States of America, the period is 60 days.

Instead of serving and filing a statement of defence, you may serve and file a Statement of Submission of Rights to the Court in Form 75.9 prescribed by the Rules of Civil Procedure.

IF YOU FAIL TO DEFEND THIS PROCEEDING, JUDGMENT MAY BE GIVEN AGAINST YOU IN YOUR ABSENCE AND WITHOUT FURTHER NOTICE TO YOU. IF YOU WISH TO DEFEND THIS PROCEEDING BUT ARE UNABLE TO PAY LEGAL FEES, LEGAL AID MAY BE AVAILABLE TO YOU BY CONTACTING A LOCAL LEGAL AID OFFICE.

DATE:

Registrar
Address of court office:
393 University Avenue
10th Floor
Toronto, Ontario
M5G 1E6

— continued next page

Figure 5-19: Statement of Claim Pursuant to Order Giving Directions (Form 75.7)
   (continued)

> TO: [applicant or solicitor for applicant]
>
> 1. The Plaintiff claims: [facts supporting the claim]
>
> DATE:
>   [plaintiff or solicitor for plaintiff]

— continued next page

Figure 5-19: Statement of Claim Pursuant to Order Giving Directions (Form 75.7)
        (continued)

Court file no. [INSERT]

**ONTARIO
SUPERIOR COURT OF JUSTICE**

Proceeding commenced at Toronto
IN THE ESTATE OF

SAMUEL SMITH, deceased

**STATEMENT OF CLAIM
PURSUANT TO ORDER GIVING
DIRECTIONS**
(Form 75.7 under the Rules)

Name, address and telephone number of solicitor, party or person

Brown & Brown
678 Driveway Street
Toronto, ON M3R 2H1

Tel: (416) 111-2222
Fax: (416) 333-4444

Solicitor for the Applicants

Figure 5-20: Order Giving Directions (Form 75.8) — Whether by Application or Motion

Court File No. [INSERT]

***ONTARIO*
SUPERIOR COURT OF JUSTICE**

THE HONOURABLE MISTER/MADAM) [day of the week], the [day] day of [month],
JUSTICE [Name of Justice]) [year]
)

IN THE ESTATE OF SAMUEL SMITH, Deceased.

B E T W E E N

[name of moving party]

Applicant(s)

- and -

[name of responding party]

Respondent(s)

- and -

[person(s) submitting rights]

Person(s) Submitting Rights to the Court

ORDER GIVING DIRECTIONS

THIS APPLICATION made by [identify applicant] for directions, was heard on [date], at [place], in the presence of counsel for [insert name(s)], and [insert name(s)] appearing in person, and no one appearing for [insert name(s)], although properly served as appears from the affidavit of service, filed.

ON READING the notice of application and on hearing the submissions made,

1. THIS COURT ORDERS that [insert name(s)] shall be plaintiff and [insert name(s)] shall be defendant, and that [insert name(s)] are submitting their rights to the court.

2. THIS COURT ORDERS that the plaintiff(s) shall serve upon the defendant(s) and file with the court a statement of claim in Form 75.7 within [number] days after this order is entered, after which pleadings shall be served and filed under rule 75.07 of the Rules of Civil Procedure.

2.1 THIS COURT ORDERS that (*insert directions relating to mandatory mediation under Rule 75.1*). [Revoked on July 4, 2001]

3. THIS COURT ORDERS that the applicant and respondent shall serve and file affidavits of documents and attend and submit to examinations for discovery in accordance with the Rules of Civil Procedure.

4. THIS COURT ORDERS that on filing the appropriate documents with the court, [insert name] shall be appointed as estate trustee during litigation.

— continued next page

Figure 5-20: Order Giving Directions (Form 75.8) — Whether by Application or Motion (continued)

5. THIS COURT ORDERS that this order giving directions shall be served by an alternative to personal service pursuant to rule 16.03 of the Rules of Civil Procedure, on the following persons: [insert names]

6. THIS COURT ORDERS that the issues be tried by a judge with/without a jury at [place] on a date to be fixed by the registrar.

7. THIS COURT ORDERS that the costs of this application shall be [insert amount].

— continued next page

COURT DISPUTES 271

Figure 5-20: Order Giving Directions (Form 75.8) — Whether by Application or Motion (continued)

Court file no. [INSERT]

ONTARIO
SUPERIOR COURT OF JUSTICE

Proceeding commenced at Toronto
IN THE ESTATE OF

SAMUEL SMITH, deceased

ORDER GIVING DIRECTIONS
(Form 75.8 under the Rules)

Name, address and telephone number of solicitor, party or person

Brown & Brown
678 Driveway Street
Toronto, ON M3R 2H1

Tel: (416) 111-2222
Fax: (416) 333-4444

Solicitor for the Applicants

Figure 5-21: Order Giving Directions (Trial of Issue-Motion) (Form 75.9)

Court File No. [INSERT]

**ONTARIO
SUPERIOR COURT OF JUSTICE**

IN THE ESTATE OF SAMUEL SMITH, Deceased.

THE HONOURABLE MISTER/MADAM) [day of the week], the [day] day of [month],
JUSTICE [Name of Justice]) [year]
)

BETWEEN

[name of moving party]

Applicant(s)

- and -

[name of responding party]

Respondent(s)

- and -

[person(s) submitting rights]

Person(s) Submitting
Rights to the Court

ORDER GIVING DIRECTIONS

THIS APPLICATION (or MOTION) made by [identify applicant] for directions, was heard on [date], at [place], in the presence of counsel for [insert name], and [insert name] appearing in person, and no one appearing for [insert name], although properly served as appears from the affidavit of service, filed.

ON READING the notice of application and on hearing the submissions made,

1. THIS COURT ORDERS that the parties to the proceeding and the issues to be tried be as follows:

    (a) [insert name] affirm and [insert name] denies that [state nature of allegation];
    (b) [list issue specifying who affirm/deny]

2. THIS COURT ORDERS that [insert name] are submitting their rights to the court.

2.1 THIS COURT ORDERS that (*insert directions relating to mandatory mediation under Rule 75.1*). [Revoked on July 4, 2001]

3. THIS COURT ORDERS that the applicant and respondent shall serve and file affidavits of documents and attend and submit to examinations for discovery in accordance with the Rules of Civil Procedure.

4. THIS COURT ORDERS that on filing the appropriate documents with the court, [insert name] shall be appointed as estate trustee during litigation.

5. THIS COURT ORDERS that this order giving directions shall be served by an alternative to personal service pursuant to rule 16.03 of the Rules of Civil Procedure, on the following persons: [insert names]

— *continued next page*

Figure 5-21: Order Giving Directions (Trial of Issue-Motion) (Form 75.9)
      (continued)

6. THIS COURT ORDERS that the issues be tried by a judge with/without a jury at [place] on a date to be fixed by the registrar.

7. THIS COURT ORDERS that the costs of this application shall be [insert amount].

                                                  _____

— continued next page

Figure 5-21: Order Giving Directions (Trial of Issue-Motion) (Form 75.9)
   (continued)

Court file no. [INSERT]

ONTARIO
SUPERIOR COURT OF JUSTICE

Proceeding commenced at Toronto
IN THE ESTATE OF
SAMUEL SMITH, deceased

ORDER GIVING DIRECTIONS
(Form 75.9 under the Rules)

Name, address and telephone number of solicitor, party or person

Brown & Brown
678 Driveway Street
Toronto, ON M3R 2H1

Tel: (416) 111-2222
Fax: (416) 333-4444

Solicitor for the Applicants

Figure 5-22: *Statement of Submission of Rights to the Court (Form 75.10)*

Court File No. [INSERT]

ONTARIO
SUPERIOR COURT OF JUSTICE

IN THE ESTATE OF SAMUEL SMITH, Deceased.

BETWEEN:

[name of applicants]

Applicant(s)

- and -

[name of respondent(s)]

Respondent(s)

STATEMENT OF SUBMISSION OF RIGHTS TO THE COURT

I, [insert name], submit my rights to the court and understand that pursuant to subrule 75.07.1 of the Rules of Civil Procedure, the following consequences apply to me:

(a) I shall not be entitled to receive any costs in the proceeding and shall not be liable to pay the costs of any party to the proceeding, except indirectly to the extent that costs are ordered by the court to be paid out of the estate;

(b) I shall not receive notice of any step taken in the proceeding except the notice of trial and a copy of the judgment disposing of the matter;

(c) If the proceeding is settled by agreement, a judgment on consent will not be given without notice to me.

DATE: [date]

[person or solicitor for person]

TO: [plaintiff or solicitor for plaintiff]

— continued next page

Figure 5-22: Statement of Submission of Rights to the Court (Form 75.10)
   (continued)

Court file no. [INSERT]

ONTARIO
SUPERIOR COURT OF JUSTICE

Proceeding commenced at Toronto
IN THE ESTATE OF

SAMUEL SMITH, deceased

STATEMENT OF SUBMISSION OF RIGHTS TO THE COURT
(Form 75.10 under the Rules)

Name, address and telephone number of solicitor, party or person

Brown & Brown
678 Driveway Street
Toronto, ON M3R 2H1

Tel: (416) 111-2222
Fax: (416) 333-4444

Solicitor for the Applicants

Figure 5-23: Notice of Settlement (Form 75.11)

Court File No. [INSERT]

***ONTARIO**
SUPERIOR COURT OF JUSTICE*

IN THE ESTATE OF SAMUEL SMITH, Deceased.

BETWEEN:

[name of applicant]

Applicant

- and -

[name of respondent(s)]

Respondent(s)

- and -

[person(s) submitting rights]

Person(s) Submitting
Rights to the Court

NOTICE OF SETTLEMENT

Pursuant to rule 75.07 of the Rules of Civil Procedure, attached as Schedule "A" is a copy of the settlement agreement that has been reached among the parties.

A judgment consistent with the settlement agreement will be sought. If you oppose that judgment, you or an Ontario lawyer acting for you must, within 10 days of service on you of this notice of settlement, serve a rejection of settlement in the form attached as Schedule "B" on the solicitor for the party serving this notice, or where the party serving this notice does not have a lawyer, serve it on the party serving this notice, and file it with proof of service in the court office at [place].

If you fail to serve and file a rejection of settlement, the court will consider the request for judgment without further notice to you.

DATE: [date]

[party or solicitor for party]

TO: [persons submitting rights to the court]

— continued next page

Figure 5-23: Notice of Settlement (Form 75.11) (continued)

Court file no. [INSERT]

ONTARIO
SUPERIOR COURT OF JUSTICE

Proceeding commenced at Toronto
IN THE ESTATE OF

SAMUEL SMITH, deceased

NOTICE OF SETTLEMENT
(Form 75.11 under the Rules)

Name, address and telephone number of solicitor, party or person

Brown & Brown
678 Driveway Street
Toronto, ON M3R 2H1

Tel: (416) 111-2222
Fax: (416) 333-4444

Solicitor for the Applicants

Figure 5-24: Rejection of Settlement (Form 75.12)

Court File No. [INSERT]

ONTARIO
SUPERIOR COURT OF JUSTICE

IN THE ESTATE OF SAMUEL SMITH, Deceased.

BETWEEN:

[name of applicant]

Applicant

- and -

[name of respondent(s)]

Respondent(s)

- and -

[person(s) submitting rights]

Person(s) Submitting
Rights to the Court

REJECTION OF SETTLEMENT

I, [insert name], reject the settlement agreement attached to the notice of settlement dated [date], for the following reasons:

[state reasons]

DATE: [date]

[party or solicitor for party]

TO: [party serving notice or solicitor]

— continued next page

Figure 5-24: Rejection of Settlement (Form 75.12) (continued)

Court file no. [INSERT]

**ONTARIO
SUPERIOR COURT OF JUSTICE**

Proceeding commenced at Toronto

IN THE ESTATE OF

SAMUEL SMITH, deceased

REJECTION OF SETTLEMENT
(Form 75.12 under the Rules)

Name, address and telephone number of solicitor, party or person

Brown & Brown
678 Driveway Street
Toronto, ON M3R 2H1

Tel: (416) 111-2222
Fax: (416) 333-4444

Solicitor for the Applicants

Figure 5-25: Notice of Contestation (Form 75.13)

Court File No. [INSERT]

ONTARIO
SUPERIOR COURT OF JUSTICE

IN THE ESTATE OF [name of deceased], Deceased.

BETWEEN:

[name of estate trustee(s)]

Estate Trustee(s)

- and -

[name of claimant]

Claimant

NOTICE OF CONTESTATION

Pursuant to section 44 or 45 of the *Estates Act*, the estate trustee of the estate contests the claim made by you against the estate, on the following grounds:

[state grounds]

You may apply to this court at [address of court office] for an order allowing your claim and determining its amount. If you do not apply within 30 days after receiving this notice, or within 3 months after that date if the judge on application so allows, you shall be deemed to have abandoned your claim and your claim shall be forever barred.

DATE: [date]

[estate trustee or solicitor]

TO: [person submitting claim]

— continued next page

Figure 5-25: *Notice of Contestation (Form 75.13)* (continued)

Court file no. [INSERT]

ONTARIO
SUPERIOR COURT OF JUSTICE

Proceeding commenced at Toronto
IN THE ESTATE OF
SAMUEL SMITH, deceased

NOTICE OF CONTESTATION

(Form 75.13 under the Rules)

Name, address and telephone number of solicitor, party or person

Brown & Brown
678 Driveway Street
Toronto, ON M3R 2H1

Tel: (416) 111-2222
Fax: (416) 333-4444

Solicitor for the Applicants

Figure 5-26: Claim Against Estate (Form 75.14)

Court File No. [INSERT]

ONTARIO
SUPERIOR COURT OF JUSTICE

IN THE ESTATE OF SAMUEL SMITH, Deceased.

B E T W E E N :

[insert name(s)]

Claimant

- and -

[insert name]

Estate Trustee

CLAIM AGAINST ESTATE

1. The claim against the estate is for [amount] for [state grounds for claim]

I, [name of deponent], of the [city, etc.] of [name of city, etc.] in the [name of county], MAKE OATH AND SAY/AFFIRM:

2. The grounds set out in this claim are true.

SWORN BEFORE me at the   of   )
          , in the   this   )
day of   ,   )   _____
) [name of deponent]
)
A Commissioner for Taking Affidavits

— continued next page

Figure 5-26: Claim Against Estate (Form 75.14) (continued)

Court file no. [INSERT]

ONTARIO
SUPERIOR COURT OF JUSTICE

Proceeding commenced at Toronto
IN THE ESTATE OF
SAMUEL SMITH, deceased

CLAIM AGAINST ESTATE

(Form 75.14 under the Rules)

Name, address and telephone number of solicitor, party or person

Brown & Brown
678 Driveway Street
Toronto, ON M3R 2H1

Tel: (416) 111-2222
Fax: (416) 333-4444

Solicitor for the Applicants

Figure 5-27: Election under the Family Law Act, 1986 (Form 210)

ELECTION UNDER THE FAMILY LAW ACT, 1986
CHOIX DU CONJOINT FAIT EN VERTU DE LA
LOI DE 1986 SUR LE DROIT DE LA FAMILLE

Court File No. / Dossier de la cour n°

File No.

This election is filed by (solicitors) / Déposé par (procureurs)

(Name of Law Firm)

Name of deceased / Nom du défunt Surname / Nom de famille

(Last Name of Deceased)

Given name(s) / Prénom(s)

(Given Name(s))

Last address of deceased / Dernière adresse du défunt Street or postal address / Rue et numéro ou adresse postale City, town, etc. / Cité, ville, etc.

Last Address of Deceased

Date of death / Date du décès Day, month, year / Jour, mois, année

Day/Month/Year of Death

Surviving spouse / Conjoint survivant Surname / Nom de famille

(Last Name of Spouse)

Given name(s) / Prénom(s)

(Given Name(s))

Address of spouse / Adresse du conjoint Street or postal address / rue et numéro ou adresse postale City, town, etc. / Cité, ville, etc. Postal Code / Code postal

(Address of Spouse)

I, _____(Print full name of surviving spouse)_____ the surviving spouse elect:
Je soussigné(e) (Please print) / (écrire en caractères d'imprimerie) conjoint survivant, fais le choix suivant:

Check one ☐ to receive the entitlement under section 5 of the Family Law Act, 1986;
Box or   jouir du droit prévu à l'article 5 de la Loi de 1986 sur le droit de la famille;
Another
          OR (check one box only) /
          OU (cocher une seule case)

☐ to receive the entitlement under the will, or under Part II of the Succession Law Reform Act, if there is an intestacy, or both, if there is a partial intestacy. /
bénéficier des dispositions testamentaires; s'il n'y a pas de testament, jouir du droit prévu à la partie II de la Loi portant réforme du droit des successions; s'il s'agit d'une succession en partie testamentaire et en partie sans testament, se prévaloir de ces deux options.

Signature of surviving spouse / Signature du conjoint survivant   Date

NOTE: THIS ELECTION HAS IMPORTANT EFFECTS ON YOUR RIGHTS. YOU SHOULD HAVE LEGAL ADVICE BEFORE SIGNING IT /
REMARQUE: LE PRÉSENT CHOIX ENTRAÎNERA DES EFFETS IMPORTANTS SUR VOS DROITS. VOUS DEVRIEZ OBTENIR DES CONSEILS JURIDIQUES AVANT DE LE SIGNER.

6
PASSING OF ACCOUNTS

Archie J. Rabinowitz

1. Introduction
2. Documents to be Filed with the Court
3. Uncontested Passings
4. Contested Passings
5. Notice of Objection to Accounts
6. Form of Accounts
7. Executor's Compensation and Powers of Investment
    (i) Executor's Compensation
    (ii) Powers of Investment
8. Special Fee
9. Specific Problems which Often Occur in the Preparation of Accounts
    (a) Ex-dividends
    (b) Mortgage Payments
    (c) Accrued Interest to the Date of Death
    (d) Distinguishing Between Capital and Revenue Expenses
10. Costs
11. Unprobated Wills — Jurisdiction of Court to Pass Accounts of Estate Trustees
12. Forms
    Figure 6-1: Order to Pass Accounts (Form 74.42)
    Figure 6-2: Affidavit Verifying Estate Accounts (Form 74.43)
    Figure 6-3: Notice of Application to Pass Accounts (Form 74.44)
    Figure 6-4: Notice of Objection to Accounts (Form 74.45)
    Figure 6-5: Notice of No Objection to Accounts (Form 74.46)
    Figure 6-6: Notice of Non-Participation in Passing of Accounts (Form 74.46.1)
    Figure 6-7: Affidavit in Support of Unopposed Judgment on Passing of Accounts (Form 74.47)
    Figure 6-8: Notice of Withdrawal of Objection (Form 74.48)
    Figure 6-9: Request for Costs (Form 74.49)
    Figure 6-10: Request for Costs (Form 74.49.1)
    Figure 6-11: Request for Increased Costs (Form 74.49.2)
    Figure 6-12: Request for Increased Costs (Form 74.49.3)
    Figure 6-13: Judgment on Passing of Accounts (Unopposed) (Form 74.50)
    Figure 6-14: Judgment on Passing of Accounts (Opposed) (Form 74.51)
    Figure 6-15: Sample Accounts (Form 74.51)

1. INTRODUCTION

A passing of accounts essentially amounts to a court audit of the management by Trustees and/or guardians of assets or money, along with a fixing of compensation, if any, for services rendered. Rule 74.16 clarifies that the procedure and form of accounts to be used for Estate Trustees also applies to other Trustees, including Trustees named in *inter vivos* trusts (as opposed to testamentary trusts), attorneys named in powers of attorney, guardians of property of mentally incapable persons or minors.

Although Estate Trustees are not required by statute to pass their accounts, they are required pursuant to r. 74.17(1) of the Rules of Civil Procedure (the "Rules") to "keep accurate records of the assets and transactions in the estate". Estate Trustees will voluntarily pass their accounts when they wish to claim compensation and there are beneficiaries (residual or contingent) who are minors or mentally incapable persons or where it is not possible to obtain the consent of all beneficiaries. If, in fact, all residual beneficiaries are adults and *sui juris* (*i.e.*, "having capacity to manage one's own affairs; not under legal disability to act for one's self"[1]) and they approve the accounts including any claim for compensation, the Estate Trustee often does not need to formally present the accounts to the court in what is known as a "Passing of Accounts". However, generally the only way the books and records of an estate can be closed for a certain period is to have the accounts formally passed in court. Once the judgment is obtained, the only way the books can be re-opened generally is in the case of mistake or fraud. Accordingly, a passing of accounts benefits or protects both beneficiaries (by way of formal audit of the assets being managed) and the Estate Trustees (by fixing and authorizing compensation and by precluding a subsequent attack or complaint by a beneficiary either as to the method of management of the trust or estate assets, or as to compensation), absent specific circumstances such as fraud or mistake.

Rule 74.15(1)(h) provides that a person having a financial interest in an estate may request an order requiring or citing the Estate Trustees to pass their accounts. The motion may be made without notice to the Estate Trustees. Once served with the order (Form 74.42, see Figure 6-1)* the Estate Trustees are given a certain number of days after the order is served upon them to file their accounts for the period set out in the order, together with an Application to Pass Accounts. If the Estate Trustees are unable to comply with the time limit set by the order, they may move for an order extending the time to file the estate accounts. Should the Estate Trustees ignore the order requesting them to pass their accounts, a beneficiary may seek an order finding the Estate Trustees in contempt and/or removing them as Estate Trustees.

2. DOCUMENTS TO BE FILED WITH THE COURT

1. Draft Notice of Application to Pass Accounts (Form 74.44, see Figure 6-3), in duplicate. Note: The form, Notice of Objection to Accounts (Form 74.45, see Figure 6-4), is attached to the notice.

---

* In this chapter, a *form* number given in parentheses refers to number of the form as stated in the Rules; the *figure* number refers to the order of its representation at the end of this chapter.

1 Black's Law Dictionary, 5th ed., St. Paul, Minn., West Publishing Co. 1979, p. 1286.

2. Affidavit Verifying Estate Accounts (Form 74.43, see Figure 6-2) with the accounts attached as an exhibit thereto.
3. Copy of the certificate appointing the applicants as Estate Trustees.
4. Copy of the latest judgment on previous passing or relating to the passing of accounts, if applicable.
5. Letter to the court with suggested available dates (it may be advisable to call the court in advance to find out about available dates).
6. The applicable court fee, currently $255, payable to the Minister of Finance.

Upon providing the above to the court office, the court will issue the Notice of Application to Pass Accounts.

In order to complete the Notice of Application to Pass Accounts it is necessary to determine the name and address of each person having an interest in the estate, and if a person is under disability, the personal representative of that person is to be indicated. If an address for service cannot be located a Motion for Directions can be brought.

Once the issued Notice of Application is received by the Estate Trustees (or their solicitor) the Notice of Application and a copy of the draft judgment being sought is then served "on each person who has a contingent or vested interest in the estate by regular lettermail" (r. 74.18(3)). If the person resides in Ontario they must be served at least 45 days before the scheduled hearing date and if outside Ontario, the documents must be served at least 60 days before the hearing date.

It is not necessary to provide copies of the accounts to each party being served; however, the Notice of Application does advise the interested parties that a copy of the accounts may be obtained from the Estate Trustees or their solicitor upon their request, or may be inspected at the court office.

When serving the Children's Lawyer and/or the Public Guardian and Trustee's Office, the Estate Trustees must serve the estate accounts verified by affidavit, the certificate of appointment, a copy of the latest judgment, if any, relating to the passing of accounts, the Notice of Application to Pass Accounts and the draft judgment (r. 74.18(3.1)).

3. UNCONTESTED PASSINGS

If no Notices of Objection are received or if they are received and subsequently withdrawn by the objecting beneficiary, a record book containing the following documents will be filed at the court:

1. An affidavit of service;
2. Notices of No Objection received from the Children's Lawyer and the Public Guardian and Trustee, (Form 74.46, see Figure 6-5) if served;
3. An affidavit of the applicants or their solicitor (Form 74.47, see Figure 6-7) confirming that a copy of the accounts was provided to any person served with a Notice of Application who requested a copy, that the time for filing Notices of Objection to accounts has expired and that no Notice of Objection was received or that if a Notice of Objection was received, it was withdrawn, in which case the

Notice of Withdrawal of Objection (Form 74.48, see Figure 6-8) must also be attached to the affidavit;

4. Requests for the costs of the persons served (Form 74.49, see Figure 6-9), if any received;
5. Certificate of the solicitor bringing the application confirming that all documents mentioned above are included in the record;
6. The draft judgment sought (Form 74.50 or 74.51, see Figure 6-13 or 6-14), in duplicate, is also to be provided at this time (albeit not a part of the record book itself).
7. If the Children's Lawyer or the Public Guardian and Trustee was served but did not file a Notice of Objection, a copy of the draft judgment approved by either the Children's Lawyer's Office or the Public Guardian and Trustee's Office should be included, unless a Notice of Non-Participation was served by such office.

The above-mentioned record is to be provided to the court at least ten days before the scheduled hearing date.

The record and draft judgment will then be presented to a judge and either the judgment will be granted (in which case a hearing and attendance before a judge will not be necessary), where the court declines to grant an unopposed judgment, the hearing will proceed on the scheduled date.

It should be noted that under the Rules there will be few surprises at the court date, as an objection cannot be raised at the hearing if it was not raised in a Notice of Objection to Accounts, unless the court orders otherwise (r. 74.18(12). Where the accounts include costs charged by a solicitor employed by the Estate Trustees, the court may assess the costs or refer the bill of costs to an assessment officer. (r. 74.18(13)).

The costs on an uncontested passing are generally granted in accordance with Tariff C to the Rules. However if costs are being sought in excess of the amount allowed in Tariff C, a Request for Increased Costs (Form 74.49.2 or 74.49.3, see Figures 6-11 or 6-12) must be served on all parties and filed together with proof of service (r. 74.18(11)).

4. CONTESTED PASSINGS

Often it is not possible to satisfy all parties' objections within the above-mentioned time limits and therefore it is necessary to attend at the court date. At the hearing the parties make submissions on those items contained in the Notices of Objection and the Court is asked to decide those issues. Even where all beneficiaries agree on the contents of the estate accounts, but the parties do not agree on the compensation being sought by the Estate Trustees, the matter must proceed on a contested basis with a hearing before a judge. (See section 7, Executor's Compensation).

5. NOTICE OF OBJECTION TO ACCOUNTS

A Notice of Objection must be served on the Estate Trustee and filed with proof of service at least 20 days before the hearing date (r. 74.18(7)). In the case of the Children's Lawyer or Public Guardian and Trustee, they also must serve on the Estate Trustee and file with proof of service, at least 20 days before the hearing date, a Notice of Objection to Accounts or a Notice of No Objection to Accounts (Form 74.46, see Figure 6-5). If a beneficiary not represented by the Children's Lawyer or Public Guardian and Trustee fails to deliver a Notice of Objection to Accounts, the beneficiary is deemed to accept the contents of the estate accounts, including the request for compensation and costs. Usually, the Estate Trustees will attempt to respond to the objections before the return date of the hearing of the Passing of Accounts in an effort to resolve the objections. If the objections are satisfied or resolved, the party who has filed the Notice of Objection may file a Notice of Withdrawal of Objection (Form 74.48, see Figure 6-8).

6. FORM OF ACCOUNTS

Rule 74.17 sets out the form of accounts as follows:

74.17 (1) Estate trustees shall keep accurate records of the assets and transactions in the estate and accounts filed with the court shall include,
- (a) on a first passing of accounts, a statement of the assets at the date of death, cross-referenced to entries in the accounts that show the disposition or partial disposition of the assets;
- (b) on any subsequent passing of accounts, a statement of the assets on the date the accounts for the period were opened, cross-referenced to entries in the accounts that show the disposition or partial disposition of the assets, and a statement of the investments, if any, on the date the accounts for the period were opened;
- (c) an account of all money received, but excluding investment transactions recorded under clause (e);
- (d) an account of all money disbursed, including payments for trustee's compensation and payments made under a court order, but excluding investment transactions recorded under clause (e);
- (e) where the estate trustee has made investments, an account setting out,
  - (i) all money paid out to purchase investments,
  - (ii) all money received by way of repayments or realization on the investments in whole or in part, and
  - (iii) the balance of all the investments in the estate at the closing date of the accounts;
- (f) a statement of all the assets in the estate that are unrealized at the closing date of the accounts;
- (g) a statement of all money and investments in the estate at the closing date of the accounts;
- (h) a statement of all the liabilities of the estate, contingent or otherwise, at the closing date of the accounts;
- (i) a statement of the compensation claimed by the estate trustee and, where the statement of compensation includes a management fee based on the value of the assets of the estate, a statement setting out the method of determining the value of the assets; and
- (j) such other statements and information as the court requires.

(2) The accounts required by clauses (1)(c), (d) and (e) shall show the balance forward for each account.

(3) Where a will or trust deals separately with capital and income, the accounts shall be divided to show separately receipts and disbursements in respect of capital and income.

Although they will not form part of the accounts themselves, the Estate Trustee must retain the backup to all items in the accounts which must be produced should they be called upon to do so. This backup, generally referred to as "vouchers", will contain all vouchers and receipts and should be cross-referenced with the accounts themselves. If, for example, there are 17 entries in the Capital Disbursement ("CD") account statement itemed "1-17", the Estate Trustee should maintain a folder with the backup vouchers itemed CD1-CD17. It is the general practice of both the Office of the Children's Lawyer and the Office of the Public Guardian and Trustee to request the voucher material shortly after being served with the notice of the passing.

As stated above, it should be noted that the keeping of accurate records of the assets and transactions, the contents and form of the accounts and the procedure to obtain the Notice of Application to Pass Accounts also applies to Trustees, persons acting under a power of attorney, committees of mentally incompetent persons and of persons who are incapable of managing their affairs, persons acting as guardians of the property of a minor and persons having similar duties who were directed by the court to prepare accounts relating to the management of assets or money pursuant to r. 74.16.

7. EXECUTOR'S COMPENSATION AND POWERS OF INVESTMENT

(i) Executor's Compensation

Although each claim for compensation is looked at on its own merits, it has been determined that there are five factors to be considered by a court when determining compensation as follows:

(1) magnitude of the trust;
(2) care and responsibility and risks assumed by the fiduciary;
(3) time spent by the fiduciary in carrying out its responsibilities;
(4) skill and ability required and displayed by the fiduciary;
(5) results obtained and degree of success associated with the efforts of the fiduciary.

Recent case law suggests a process consisting of three stages in order to determine appropriate compensation, as follows:

(i) apply the tariff which is set out below without regard for a "care management fee";
(ii) compare the result against the five factors set out above in order to assess whether the tariff is "fair and reasonable" having regard to the five factors; and
(iii) consider whether there are special circumstances which would justify an extra allowance for the management of the trust's assets (known as a "special fee"). See Section 8, Special Fee.

The Ontario Court of Appeal has recently approved this three stage process in its decision in *Laing Estate v. Laing Estate*, (sub nom. *Logan v. Laing Estate*) 11 E.T.R. (2d) 268, (sub nom. *Laing Estate, Re*) 89 O.A.C. 321, 1996 CarswellOnt 775 (Ont. Div. Ct.), leave to appeal allowed 1996 CarswellOnt 2019 (Ont. C.A.), affirmed (sub nom. *Laing Estate, Re*) 113 O.A.C. 335, (sub nom. *Laing Estate v. Hines*) 167 D.L.R. (4th) 150, (sub nom. *Laing Estate v. Hines*) 41 O.R. (3d) 571, 25 E.T.R. (2d) 139, 1998 CarswellOnt 4037, [1998] O.J. No. 4169 (Ont. C.A.). See also the recent decision of Haley, J. *Flaska Estate, Re*, 2001 CarswellOnt 2000 (Ont. S.C.J.), for an example of the Court's application of the above-noted principles.

The generally accepted tariff being used today, subject to adjustment on an individual basis is as follows: 2½% of capital receipts, 2½% of capital disbursements, 2½% of revenue receipts, and 2½% of revenue disbursements.

For ongoing estates, where there is no outright distribution, there is an additional fee often allowed called a "care and management fee". This additional fee is calculated as follows: 2/5 of 1% of the average annual value of the estate, which is generally charged 1/3 to revenue and 2/3 to capital.

When charging the compensation to the estate, that portion attributed to capital is usually charged to capital and that portion calculated on the revenue receipts and disbursements is usually charged to the revenue account. (See *Flaska Estate, supra,* for a recent example of how the Court deals with the need to balance the competing interests of capital and income beneficiaries.)

It should be noted that in certain circumstances executor's compensation is subject to G.S.T. This is usually the case for a corporate trustee, or in the case of an Estate Trustee who carries on his duties in the normal course of business.

It is not appropriate for an estate trustee to take compensation without either the prior approval of the Court on a passing of accounts, or by approval of all beneficiaries, in the case where all beneficiaries are adults and *sui juris*. This is referred to as pre-taking and often estate trustees who have pre-taken compensation must reimburse or credit the estate for any lost interest which the estate would have earned but for the pre-taking. Indeed, where a court denies or reduces the compensation being claimed, an estate trustee may even have to reimburse the estate for the actual amounts pre-taken. (See *Flaska Estate, supra,* for a recent example of how the Court deals with the issue of pre-taking).

(ii) Powers of Investment

Effective July 1, 1999, the *Trustee Act* was amended by introducing a "prudent investor" rule in the place of the restricted authorized investments list which had been in place for some time. The effect of this provision allows Trustees to invest in mutual funds and allows Trust companies to invest in common trust funds. Sections 26 to 30, which have replaced old sections 26 to 34 of the *Trustee Act*, provide in part,

> **26.** If a provision of another Act or the regulations under another Act authorizes money or other property to be invested in property in which a trustee is authorized to invest and the provision came into force before section 16 of Schedule B of the *Red Tape Reduction Act, 1998*, the provision shall be deemed to authorize investment in the property in which a trustee could invest immediately before the coming into force of section 16 of Schedule B of the *Red Tape Reduction Act, 1998*.
>
> **27.** (1) In investing trust property, a trustee must exercise the care, skill, diligence and judgment that a prudent investor would exercise in making investments.
>
> (2) A trustee may invest trust property in any form of property in which a prudent investor might invest.
>
> (3) Any rule of law that prohibits a trustee from delegating powers or duties does not prevent the trustee from investing in mutual funds, pooled funds or segregated funds under variable insurance contracts, and sections 27.1 and 27.2 do not apply to the purchase of such funds.
>
> (4) If trust property is held by co-trustees and one of the co-trustees is a trust corporation as defined in the *Loan and Trust Corporations Act*, any rule of law that prohibits a trustee from delegating powers or duties does not prevent the co-trustees from investing in a common trust fund, as defined in that Act, that is maintained by the trust corporation and sections 27.1 and 27.2 do not apply.
>
> . . .

See *Flaska Estate*, *supra*, for an example of how the Court deals with the need to diversify investments and adopt an investment policy.

8. SPECIAL FEE

In certain circumstances it is also possible to claim a special fee over and above the ordinary claim for compensation. However, a detailed claim for this special fee is required which would include time dockets and possibly affidavits detailing the evidence of the special circumstances.

Although the typical judgment on a passing issued by the court deals with compensation, how the compensation is divided among co-estate trustees is not usually determined by the court, unless the Trustees cannot agree. Where an individual shares the duties as Trustee with a corporate trustee, it is common for there to be an agreement between the co-trustees as to how compensation will be split.

9. SPECIFIC PROBLEMS WHICH OFTEN OCCUR IN THE PREPARATION OF ACCOUNTS

When preparing accounts there are certain types of entries that cause confusion. Often there is confusion as to whether entries are capital in nature or whether they represent revenue. If the will of the deceased differentiates between capital and revenue beneficiaries, it is then necessary to keep them separate in the accounts. It should be remembered that the deceased's assets at death are capital in nature and therefore payments made after death to maintain these assets would be capital disbursements (*e.g.* roof repairs to a home or vacation property owned by the deceased). As well, receipt of monies on the realization (*i.e.* sale) of those assets would be considered capital receipts.

(a) Ex-dividends

Ex-dividends are dividends which have been declared at the date of death, but not yet paid. Generally, an ex-dividend would be considered capital in nature and therefore shown in the capital receipt account.

As discussed in more detail in chapter 7, one must remember that these dividends would be treated as income (*i.e.* a receipt of revenue) for income tax purposes although possibly dealt with in a Rights or Things Return, thus providing the estate with additional deductions from income.

(b) Mortgage Payments

Mortgage payments generally consist of a capital and an interest component. If the accounts are being separated as to both capital and revenue accounts, each mortgage payment will also be separated for purposes of preparing the accounts. It is also a good idea to obtain an amortization schedule for each mortgage held by the estate which will provide this breakdown.

At the same time, if an estate holds property which is subject to a mortgage, it would be proper to separate the disbursements (*i.e.* mortgage payments) between both the Capital and Revenue Disbursement Accounts.

(c) Accrued Interest to the Date of Death

Accrued interest to the date of death is actually capital in nature. When valuing the estate as at the date of death, all interest earned up to the date of death would be shown on the Statement of Assets. However, when the first interest payment is received after the date of death, it is necessary to break down the payment between the portion earned up to the date of death (capital) and the portion earned from the date of death to the date of payment (revenue).

(d) Distinguishing Between Capital and Revenue Expenses

Funeral expenses, legal fees for the administration of the estate, accounting fees for preparing income tax returns up to and including the date of death return (or terminal return), and the expenses incurred in disposing of original assets would be considered capital in nature. However, if an asset is income earning (*e.g.* a rental property), or disbursements are incurred in connection with the receipt of income (*e.g.* legal fees for a lease on a rental condominium owned by the deceased), these are shown as a revenue disbursement.

10. COSTS

Unless ordered otherwise, the costs on an unopposed passing of accounts are generally calculated in accordance with Tariff C (see below) to the Rules of Civil Procedure (r. 74.18(10)), although the court can order otherwise.

Tariff C (*REVISED*)

SOLICITORS' COSTS ALLOWED ON PASSING OF ACCOUNTS
WITHOUT A HEARING

(1) *ESTATE TRUSTEE*

Amount of receipts	Amount of costs
Less than $100,000	$ 800
$100,000 or more, but less than $300,000	1,750
$300,000 or more, but less than $500,000	2,000
$500,000 or more, but less than $1,000,000	2,500
$1,000,000 or more, but less than $1,500,000	3,000
$1,500,000 or more, but less than $3,000,000	4,000
$3,000,000 or more	5,000

(2) *PERSON WITH FINANCIAL INTEREST IN ESTATE*

If a person with a financial interest in an estate retains a solicitor to review the accounts, makes no objection to the accounts (or makes an objection and later withdraws it) and serves and files a request for costs, the person is entitled to one-half of the amount payable to the estate trustee.

(3) *CHILDREN'S LAWYER OR PUBLIC GUARDIAN AND TRUSTEE*
If the Children's Lawyer or the Public Guardian and Trustee makes no objection to the accounts (or makes an objection and later withdraws it) and serves and files a request for costs, he or she is entitled to three-quarters of the amount payable to the estate trustee.

Note: If two or more persons are represented by the same solicitor, they are entitled to receive only one person's costs.

Note: A person entitled to costs under this tariff is also entitled to the amount of G.S.T. on those costs.

The above calculation is made by totalling all receipts, both capital and revenue.

In connection with opposed, or contested, passings of accounts pursuant to r. 74.18(13) the court may assess or refer to an assessment officer any bill of costs or charge levied by the solicitor for the Estate Trustee.

11. UNPROBATED WILLS — JURISDICTION OF COURT TO PASS ACCOUNTS OF ESTATE TRUSTEES

Since the decision in *Granovsky Estate v. Ontario*, 156 D.L.R. (4th) 557, 21 E.T.R. (2d) 25, 1998 CarswellOnt 518 (Ont. Gen. Div) the power of the Court to make limited grants of probate and the acceptability of multiple wills as a way of avoiding probate taxes has been confirmed. As such, the administration of estates without first obtaining probate is likely to become a more frequent estate planning technique. The Court in Silver Estate, Re, 31 E.T.R. (2d) 256, 1999 CarswellOnt 4217, [1999] O.J. No. 5026 (Ont. formsS.C.J.) has recently confirmed that the Court has jurisdiction to pass accounts under a will for which a Certificate of Appointment (probate) has not been granted. Obviously, the documents to be filed with the Court under Rule 74 must comply with "necessary modification" given that no Certificate of Appointment can be filed.

Figure 6-1: Order to Pass Accounts (Form 74.42)

ONTARIO

SUPERIOR COURT OF JUSTICE

IN THE ESTATE OF SAMUEL SMITH, deceased.

THE HONOURABLE MISTER/MADAM JUSTICE [Name of Deceased]	)))	[day of the week], the [day] day of [month], [year]

ORDER TO PASS ACCOUNTS

A motion for this order has been made by JACK SMITH. From an affidavit made by JACK SMITH that has been filed it appears that you are an estate trustee of the estate and that you have made no accounting to the court of your dealings with the estate during the period from June 1, 1978 to June 1, 1995.

THIS COURT ORDERS THAT you file accounts of the estate and an application to pass accounts, in accordance with rules 74.17 and 74.18 of the Rules of Civil Procedure, in the court office within [number] days after this order is served on you.

_____

Registrar

Address of court office
393 University Avenue
10th Floor
Toronto, Ontario
M5G 1E6

TO: [estate trustee]

— continued next page

Figure 6-1: Order to Pass Accounts (Form 74.42) (continued)

Court file no. [INSERT]

ONTARIO
SUPERIOR COURT OF JUSTICE

Proceeding commenced at Toronto
IN THE ESTATE OF

SAMUEL SMITH, deceased

ORDER TO PASS ACCOUNTS
(Form 74.42 under the Rules)

Name, address and telephone number of solicitor, party or person

Brown & Brown
678 Driveway Street
Toronto, Ontario
M3R 2H1

Tel: (416)111-2222
Fax: (416)333-4444

Solicitor for the Applicant

Figure 6-2: Affidavit Verifying Estate Accounts (Form 74.43)

***ONTARIO*
SUPERIOR COURT OF JUSTICE**

IN THE ESTATE OF   , deceased.

AFFIDAVIT VERIFYING ESTATE ACCOUNTS

I,   , of the   , MAKE OATH AND SAY/AFFIRM:

1. I am an estate trustee for this estate.
2. The accounts marked as Exhibit "A" to this affidavit are complete and correct.
3. The information contained in the notice of application to pass accounts with respect to this estate is true.
4. All persons having a financial interest in the estate are named as respondents in the notice of application to pass accounts.
5. For any party with a disability, a representative has been identified in the notice of application.

Sworn *or* Affirmed before me at the   )
)
)
)
in the   )
)
on   )
)_____
)
)
)
)
A Commissioner for Taking Affidavits   )

(Fax number of solicitor or person filing this document)
Fax number:

Figure 6-3: Notice of Application to Pass Accounts (Form 74.44)

ONTARIO
SUPERIOR COURT OF JUSTICE

IN THE ESTATE OF   , deceased.

NOTICE OF APPLICATION TO PASS ACCOUNTS

This application to pass accounts will be heard on   , at   , at the court house at ***Court_address***, if any person with a financial interest in the estate objects to the accounts or to the compensation claimed, or if a request for increased costs is served and filed.

The deceased died on

A certificate of appointment of estate trustee was issued to   by this court on   .

The accounts are for the period from   to   .

The compensation claimed by the estate trustee, payable out of the estate, is $

If there is no hearing, the costs of the application claimed by the estate trustee under Tariff C are $.

If there is no hearing, a person with a financial interest in the estate who retains a solicitor to review the accounts and makes no objection to them (or makes an objection and later withdraws it) but serves on the estate trustee and files with the court a request for costs (Form 74.49 under the Rules of Civil Procedure), will be allowed one-half of the costs allowed to the estate trustee. However, where two or more persons are represented by the same solicitor, they are entitled to receive only one person's costs. If the

— continued next page

Figure 6-3: Notice of Application to Pass Accounts (Form 74.44) (continued)

> Children's Lawyer or the Public Guardian and Trustee makes no objection to the accounts (or makes an objection and later withdraws it) but serves on the estate trustee and files with the court a request for costs (Form 74.49.1), he or she will be allowed three-quarters of the costs allowed to the estate trustee.
>
> If the estate trustee or any person with a financial interest in the estate seeks costs of the application greater than the amount allowed in Tariff C, the estate trustee or other person shall serve on every other party and file, with proof of service, a request for increased costs (Form 74.49.2 or 74.49.3 under the Rules of Civil Procedure), at least 10 days before the hearing date specified in this notice of application. In that case, the hearing shall proceed on the date specified.
>
> Any person with a financial interest in the estate who wishes to object shall do so by serving upon the estate trustee, or the solicitor for the estate trustee, a notice of objection to accounts (Form 74.45 under the Rules of Civil Procedure, a copy of which is attached to this notice of application), and by filing a copy of the notice in the court office at least 20 days before the date fixed for the hearing.
>
> At the hearing, the only issues upon which the court adjudicates are those raised in the notices of objection to accounts and requests for increased costs that have been filed, unless the court grants leave to a party to raise other issues.
>
> If no notice of objection to accounts or request for increased costs is served and filed, the estate trustee may, without a hearing, obtain a judgment passing the accounts and allowing the compensation and costs claimed.

— continued next page

Figure 6-3: Notice of Application to Pass Accounts (Form 74.44) (continued)

Any person may contact the estate trustee or the estate trustee's solicitor to find out whether there will be a hearing. A copy of the accounts may be obtained from the estate trustee or the estate trustee's solicitor, or may be inspected in the court office during regular business hours.

DATE:

_____
Registrar

(Name, address, telephone and fax numbers of estate trustee or solicitor for the estate trustee)

Solicitor(s) for the estate trustee

TO:

(Name, address and fax number, of each person having a financial interest in the estate.)
(For a person under disability, also indicate name and address of personal representative)
(Attach blank copy of Form 74.45 (notice of objection to accounts).)

Figure 6-4: Notice of Objection to Accounts (Form 74.45)

SUPERIOR COURT OF JUSTICE

IN THE ESTATE OF

NOTICE OF OBJECTION TO ACCOUNTS

1.   I,

object to the amount of compensation claimed by the estate trustee on the following grounds:

(If applicable, set out each objection in separate consecutively numbered paragraphs. Attach a separate sheet if necessary.)
(a)

2.   I,

object to the accounts of the estate trustee on the following grounds:

(If applicable, set out each objection in separate consecutively numbered paragraphs. Attach a separate sheet if necessary.)
(a)

DATE: *(Name, address, telephone and fax numbers of objecting person or solicitor for objecting person)*

(Name, address and fax number of estate trustee or solicitor for estate trustee)
TO:

— continued next page

304 THE PRACTICAL GUIDE TO ONTARIO ESTATE ADMINISTRATION

Figure 6-4: Notice of Objection to Accounts (Form 74.45) (continued)

Court file no. [INSERT]

ONTARIO
SUPERIOR COURT OF JUSTICE

Proceeding commenced at Toronto

IN THE ESTATE OF

SAMUEL SMITH, deceased

NOTICE OF OBJECTION TO ACCOUNTS
(Form 74.45 under the Rules)

Name, address and telephone number of solicitor, party or person

Brown & Brown
678 Driveway Street
Toronto, Ontario
M3R 2H1

Tel: (416)111-2222
Fax: (416)333-4444

Solicitor for the Applicant

Figure 6-5: Notice of No Objection to Accounts (Form 74.46)

ONTARIO

SUPERIOR COURT OF JUSTICE

IN THE ESTATE OF   , deceased.

NOTICE OF NO OBJECTION TO ACCOUNTS

The Children's Lawyer has no objection to the estate accounts and the claim for compensation by the estate trustee.

DATE: *(Name, address, telephone and fax number of Children's Lawyer or solicitor for Children's Lawyer)*

Solicitor(s) for the
Children's Lawyer

(Name, address and fax number of estate trustee or solicitor for estate trustee)
TO:

Solicitor(s) for the estate trustee

Figure 6-6: Notice of Non-Participation in Passing of Accounts (Form 74.46.1)

ONTARIO

SUPERIOR COURT OF JUSTICE

IN THE ESTATE OF   , deceased.

NOTICE OF NON-PARTICIPATION IN PASSING OF ACCOUNTS

The   does not intend to participate in the passing of accounts.

DATE:

(Name, address, telephone and fax numbers of Children's Lawyer or Public Guardian and Trustee, or solicitor for Children's Lawyer or Public Guardian and Trustee)

Solicitor(s) for
the Children's Lawyer

TO:

Solicitor(s) for the estate trustee
(Name, address and fax number of estate trustee or solicitor for estate trustee)

Figure 6-7: Affidavit in Support of Unopposed Judgement on Passing of Accounts (Form 74.47)

ONTARIO
SUPERIOR COURT OF JUSTICE

IN THE ESTATE OF   , deceased.

**AFFIDAVIT IN SUPPORT OF UNOPPOSED JUDGMENT
ON PASSING OF ACCOUNTS**

I,   , of the   , MAKE OATH AND SAY/AFFIRM:

1. I am the applicant for an unopposed judgment on the passing of accounts in this estate with respect to estate accounts from   to   .

2. A copy of the estate accounts has been provided to each person who was served with the notice of application and who requested a copy of the accounts.

3. The time for filing notices of objection to the estate accounts has expired.

4. No notice of objection has been received from any person served with the notice of application.

OR

4. Any notice of objection that was received has been withdrawn by the filing of a notice of withdrawal of objection.

Sworn *or* Affirmed before me at the   )
)
)
)
in the   )
)
)
)_____
on   )
)
)
A Commissioner for Taking Affidavits   )

(Fax number of solicitor or person filing this document)
Fax number:

Figure 6-8: Notice of Withdrawal of Objection (Form 74.48)

ONTARIO
SUPERIOR COURT OF JUSTICE

IN THE ESTATE OF   , deceased.

NOTICE OF WITHDRAWAL OF OBJECTION

I,   , filed a notice of objection to accounts and hereby withdraw that notice of objection.

DATE: *(Name, address, telephone and fax numbers of person or solicitor for person)*

                                        Solicitor(s) for

(Name, address and fax number of estate trustee or solicitor for estate trustee)
TO:

Solicitor(s) for the estate trustee

Figure 6-9: Request for Costs (Form 74.49)

ONTARIO
SUPERIOR COURT OF JUSTICE

IN THE ESTATE OF   , deceased.

REQUEST FOR COSTS
(PERSON OTHER THAN CHILDREN'S LAWYER OR PUBLIC GUARDIAN AND TRUSTEE)

I,   , have retained   as my solicitor to review the estate accounts. I have no objection to the estate accounts and the claim for compensation by the estate trustee.

I request that I be awarded costs payable out of the estate in the amount of   , representing one-half of the amount payable to the estate solicitor under Tariff C.

DATE: *(Name, address, telephone and fax numbers of party or party's solicitor)*

                                                  Solicitor(s)

TO:
(Name, address and fax number of estate trustee or solicitor for estate trustee)
Solicitor(s) for the estate trustee

310 THE PRACTICAL GUIDE TO ONTARIO ESTATE ADMINISTRATION

Figure 6-10: Request for Costs (Form 74.49.1)

ONTARIO
SUPERIOR COURT OF JUSTICE

IN THE ESTATE OF   , deceased.

REQUEST FOR COSTS
(CHILDREN'S LAWYER OR PUBLIC GUARDIAN AND TRUSTEE)

The   has no objection to the estate accounts and the claim for compensation by the estate trustee.

The   requests that he or she be awarded costs payable out of the estate in the amount of   , representing three-quarters of the amount payable to the estate solicitor under Tariff C.

DATE:

(Name, address, telephone and fax number of Children's Lawyer or Public Guardian and Trustee, or solicitor for Children's Lawyer or Public Guardian and Trustee)

Solicitor(s) for

TO:
(Name address and fax number of estate trustee or solicitor for estate trustee)

Solicitor(s) for the estate trustee

— continued next page

PASSING OF ACCOUNTS 311

Figure 6-10: Request for Costs (Form 74.49.1) (continued)

Court file no. [INSERT]

ONTARIO
SUPERIOR COURT OF JUSTICE

Proceeding commenced at Toronto
IN THE ESTATE OF

SAMUEL SMITH, deceased

**REQUESTS FOR COSTS
(CHILDREN'S LAWYER OR PUBLIC
GUARDIAN AND TRUSTEE)**
(Form 74.49 under the Rules)

Name, address and telephone number of solicitor, party or person

Brown & Brown
678 Driveway Street
Toronto, Ontario
M3R 2H1

Tel: (416)111-2222
Fax: (416)333-4444

Solicitor for the Applicant

Figure 6-11: Request for Increased Costs (Form 74.49.2)

ONTARIO

SUPERIOR COURT OF JUSTICE

IN THE ESTATE OF   , deceased.

REQUEST FOR INCREASED COSTS (ESTATE TRUSTEE)

I request that I be awarded costs payable out of the estate in the amount of

, which is greater than the amount allowed under Tariff C. I understand that this necessitates a hearing on the date specified in the notice of application.

DATE:

(Name, address, telephone and fax numbers of estate trustee or solicitor for estate trustee)

Solicitor(s) for

TO:
(Name and address of each person with a financial interest in the estate)
(For a person under disability, also indicate name and address of personal representative)

— continued next page

Figure 6-11: Request for Increased Costs (Form 74.49.2) (continued)

Court file no. [INSERT]

***ONTARIO*
SUPERIOR COURT OF JUSTICE**

Proceeding commenced at Toronto
IN THE ESTATE OF

SAMUEL SMITH, deceased

**REQUESTS FOR INCREASED COSTS
(ESTATE TRUSTEE)**
(Form 74.49.2 under the Rules)

Name, address and telephone number of solicitor, party or person

Brown & Brown
678 Driveway Street
Toronto, Ontario
M3R 2H1

Tel: (416)111-2222
Fax: (416)333-4444

Solicitor for the Applicant

Figure 6-12: Request for Increased Costs (Form 74.49.3)

ONTARIO
SUPERIOR COURT OF JUSTICE

IN THE ESTATE OF   , deceased.

REQUEST FOR INCREASED COSTS
(PERSON OTHER THAN ESTATE TRUSTEE)

1. I,   , have retained   as my solicitor to review the estate accounts. I have no objection to the estate accounts and the claim for compensation by the estate trustee.

2. I request that I be awarded costs payable out of the estate in the amount of   which is greater than one-half the amount payable to the estate trustee under Tariff C. I understand that this necessitates a hearing on the date specified in the notice of application.

DATE:

(Name, address, telephone and fax numbers of person or person's solicitor)

Solicitor(s) for

TO:
(Name and address of every other person with a financial interest in the estate)
(For a person under disability, also indicate name and address of personal representative)
(Name and address of estate trustee or solicitor for estate trustee)
Solicitor(s) for the estate trustee

— continued next page

Figure 6-12: Request for Increased Costs (Form 74.49.3) (continued)

Court file no. [INSERT]

ONTARIO
SUPERIOR COURT OF JUSTICE

Proceeding commenced at Toronto
IN THE ESTATE OF

SAMUEL SMITH, deceased

REQUESTS FOR INCREASED COSTS (PERSON OTHER THAN ESTATE TRUSTEE)
(Form 74.49.3 under the Rules)

Name, address and telephone number of solicitor, party or person

Brown & Brown
678 Driveway Street
Toronto, Ontario
M3R 2H1

Tel: (416)111-2222
Fax: (416)333-4444

Solicitor for the Applicant

Figure 6-13: Judgment on Passing of Accounts (Unopposed) (Form 74.50)

ONTARIO

Court file no.

SUPERIOR COURT OF JUSTICE

IN THE ESTATE OF   , deceased.

JUDGMENT ON PASSING OF ACCOUNTS

THIS APPLICATION WAS READ   , at   .

ON reading the notice of application to pass accounts, the affidavit of service and the affidavit in support of an unopposed judgment on passing of accounts, as filed, and as there are no objections to the accounts or the claim for compensation by the estate trustee,

1. THIS COURT DECLARES that the estate accounts, as filed by the applicant for the period from   to   , are hereby passed.

2. THIS COURT DECLARES that the capital receipts and capital disbursements of the applicant for the period are as follows:

CAPITAL ACCOUNT

Credit balance forward (*if appli*cable)
Receipts

Debit balance forward (*if applicable*)
Disbursements

Credit (or debit) balance $0.00

— continued next page

Figure 6-13: Judgment on Passing of Accounts (Unopposed) (Form 74.50)
(continued)

3. THIS COURT DECLARES that the revenue receipts and revenue disbursements of the applicant for the period are as follows:

REVENUE ACCOUNT

Credit balance forward (*if applicable*)
Receipts

Debit balance forward (*if applicable*)
Disbursements

Credit (or debit) balance $0.00

4. THIS COURT ORDERS that the estate trustee shall be paid as fair and reasonable compensation for services as estate trustee of the estate and for disbursements expended in administering the affairs of the estate during the period the total amount of (including G.S.T.), of which   shall be paid out of the capital of the estate and shall be paid out of the revenue of the estate.

5. THIS COURT ORDERS that the costs of the passing of the accounts allowed in accordance with Tariff C, and payable out of the capital of the estate, are as follows:

    To the estate trustee   and G.S.T. of   for a total of   .

    To:

6. THIS COURT DECLARES that the accounts show that there remains in the estate trustee's hands the original assets as set out in Schedule "A" attached.

(Signature of judge or registrar)

— *continued next page*

Figure 6-13: Judgment on Passing of Accounts (Unopposed) (Form 74.50)
    (continued)

Schedule "A"

— continued next page

Figure 6-13: Judgment on Passing of Accounts (Unopposed) (Form 74.50)
(continued)

Court file no. [INSERT]

ONTARIO
SUPERIOR COURT OF JUSTICE

Proceeding commenced at Toronto
IN THE ESTATE OF

SAMUEL SMITH, deceased

JUDGMENT ON PASSING OF ACCOUNTS (UNOPPOSED)
(Form 74.50 under the Rules)

Name, address and telephone number of solicitor, party or person

Brown & Brown
678 Driveway Street
Toronto, Ontario
M3R 2H1

Tel: (416)111-2222
Fax: (416)333-4444

Solicitor for the Applicant

— *continued next page*

Figure 6-14: Judgment on Passing of Accounts (Opposed) (Form 74.51)

ONTARIO   Court file no.

SUPERIOR COURT OF JUSTICE

IN THE ESTATE OF   , deceased.

JUDGMENT ON PASSING OF ACCOUNTS

THIS APPLICATION WAS HEARD ON   , at   in the presence of counsel for   ,

ON reading the notice of application to pass accounts and on hearing the submissions made,

1. THIS COURT DECLARES that the estate accounts, as filed by the applicant for the period from   to   , are hereby passed.

2. THIS COURT DECLARES that the capital receipts and capital disbursements of the applicant for the period are as follows:

CAPITAL ACCOUNT

Credit balance forward (*if applicable*)
Receipts

Debit balance forward (*if applicable*)
Disbursements

Credit (or debit) balance

3. THIS COURT DECLARES that the revenue receipts and revenue disbursements of the applicant for the period are as follows:

REVENUE ACCOUNT

Credit balance forward (*if applicable*)
Receipts

Debit balance forward (*if applicable*)
Disbursements

Credit (or debit) balance

— *continued next page*

Figure 6-14: Judgment on Passing of Accounts (Opposed) (Form 74.51) (continued)

4. THIS COURT ORDERS that the estate trustee shall be paid as fair and reasonable compensation for services as estate trustee of the estate and for disbursements expended in administering the affairs of the estate during the period the total amount of   (including G.S.T.), of which   shall be paid out of the capital of the estate and   shall be paid out of the revenue of the estate.

5. THIS COURT ORDERS that the costs of the passing of the accounts allowed in accordance with Tariff C, and payable out of the capital of the estate, are as follows:

   To the estate trustee   and G.S.T. of   for a total of $0.00.
   To:

6. THIS COURT DECLARES that the accounts show that there remains in the estate trustee's hands the original assets as set out in Schedule "A" attached.

_____
(Signature of judge or registrar)

— continued next page

Figure 6-14: Judgment on Passing of Accounts (Opposed) (Form 74.51) (continued)

Schedule "A"

— continued next page

Figure 6-14: Judgment on Passing of Accounts (Opposed) (Form 74.51) (continued)

Court file no. [INSERT]

***ONTARIO*
SUPERIOR COURT OF JUSTICE**

Proceeding commenced at Toronto
IN THE ESTATE OF

SAMUEL SMITH, deceased

JUDGMENT ON PASSING OF ACCOUNTS (OPPOSED)
(Form 74.51 under the Rules)

Name, address and telephone number of solicitor, party or person

Brown & Brown
678 Driveway Street
Toronto, Ontario
M3R 2H1

Tel: (416)111-2222
Fax: (416)333-4444

Solicitor for the Applicant

— *continued next page*

Figure 6-15: Sample Accounts (Form 74.51)

ESTATE OF JOHN SMITH

STATEMENT OF ACCOUNTS

AUGUST 15, 1994 (Date of Death) to MARCH 1, 1997

— continued next page

Figure 6-15: Sample Accounts (Form 74.51) (continued)

ESTATE OF JOHN SMITH

STATEMENT OF ACCOUNTS

AUGUST 15, 1994 (Date of Death) to MARCH 1, 1997

INDEX

	Page
Summary	1
Statement of Original Assets	1
Capital Receipts	2
Capital Disbursements	5
Revenue Receipts	6
Revenue Disbursements	11
Statement of Unrealized Original Assets as at March 1, 1997	13
Statement of Liabilities Outstanding as at March 1, 1997	14
Statements of Investments On Hand as at March 1, 1997	15
Statement of Compensation	16

— continued next page

Figure 6-15: Sample Accounts (Form 74.51) (continued)

ESTATE OF JOHN SMITH

STATEMENT OF ACCOUNTS

AUGUST 15, 1994 (Date of Death) to MARCH 1, 1997

SUMMARY

Capital Receipts	$620,627.30		
Capital Disbursements	<u>60,070.00</u>		$560,557.30
Revenue Receipts	$245,541.92		
Revenue Disbursements	<u>7,860.00</u>		<u>$237,681.92</u>
		Total	$798,239.22

Summary of Assets Remaining:

Bank Account (as at Mar 1/97)	798,239.22
Less:	
Proposed Claim for Compensation	<u>23,352.48</u>
BALANCE	$774,886.74

- 1 -

— continued next page

Figure 6-15: Sample Accounts (Form 74.51) (continued)

ESTATE OF JOHN SMITH

STATEMENT OF ACCOUNTS

AUGUST 15, 1994 (Date of Death) to MARCH 1, 1997

<u>Statement of Original Assets</u>

		How Realized	
Money on Deposit		Page	Item
Toronto Dominion Bank Account 12345-67	$ 76,124.02	3	1
Canada Savings Bonds: Regular Bonds, due November 1, 1998	$100,000.00	4	24
4.5% Interest to date of death being 287 days at $12.328 per diem	$ 3,538.14	3	7
Canadian Imperial Bank of Commerce G.I.C. Certificate:			
6% due on January 1, 1996 #396558	$ 50,000.00	4	22
6% Interest to date of death being 45 days at $8.219 per diem	$ 369.86	3	5
Real Estate:			
Cottage in Simcoe	$140,000.00	4	25
Mortgage Held:			
Factory, John Smith	$242,000.00	3-4	3,4,6, 8-14
		4	15
			21
		5	23
4% Interest to date of death being 14 days at $26.52 per diem	$ 371.38	3	2
	$612,403.30		

- 2 -

— continued next page

Figure 6-15: Sample Accounts (Form 74.51) (continued)

ESTATE OF JOHN SMITH

STATEMENT OF ACCOUNTS

AUGUST 15, 1994 (Date of Death) to MARCH 1, 1997

CAPITAL RECEIPTS

No.	Date	Particulars	Amount
1.	Aug. 15/94	Date of Death Bank Balance in Account 12345-67, Toronto Dominion Bank	$ 76,124.02
2.	Sept. 1/94	John Smith mortgage payment 4% interest to date of death being 14 days at $26.52 per diem	371.28
3.	Sept. 1/94	John Smith mortgage payment principal portion	50.00
4.	Oct. 1/94	John Smith mortgage payment principal portion	50.00
5.	Oct. 1/94	Canadian Imperial Bank of Commerce - G.I.C. Interest to date of death being 45 days at $8.219 per diem	369.86
6.	Nov. 1/94	John Smith mortgage payment principal portion	50.00
7.	Nov. 1/94	Canada Savings Bonds Interest to date of death being 287 days at $12.328 per diem	3,538.14
8.	Dec. 1/94	John Smith mortgage payment principal portion	50.00
9.	Jan. 1/95	John Smith mortgage payment principal portion	50.00
10.	Feb. 1/95	John Smith mortgage payment principal portion	50.00

- 3 -

— continued next page

Figure 6-15: Sample Accounts (Form 74.51) (continued)

11.	Mar. 1/95	John Smith mortgage payment principal portion	50.00
12.	Apr. 1/95	John Smith mortgage payment principal portion	50.00
13.	May 1/95	John Smith mortgage payment principal portion	50.00
14.	June 1/95	John Smith mortgage payment principal portion	50.00
15.	July 1/95	John Smith mortgage payment principal portion	50.00
16.	Aug. 1/95	John Smith mortgage payment principal portion	50.00
17.	Sept. 1/95	John Smith mortgage payment principal portion	50.00
18.	Oct. 1/95	John Smith mortgage payment principal portion	50.00
19.	Nov. 1/95	John Smith mortgage payment principal portion	50.00
20.	Dec. 1/95	John Smith mortgage payment principal portion	50.00
21.	Jan. 1/96	John Smith mortgage payment principal portion	50.00
22.	Jan. 1/96	Canadian Imperial Bank of Commerce - G.I.C. redeemed Principal	50,000.00
23.	Jan. 18/96	John Smith mortgage payment balance of principal	241,150.00
24.	Feb. 1/96	Canada Savings Bonds Cashed	100,000.00
25.	Aug. 1/96	Proceeds of sale of Simcoe Cottage	<u>148,224.00</u>
			$ 620,627.30

- 4 -

— continued next page

Figure 6-15: Sample Accounts (Form 74.51) (continued)

ESTATE OF JOHN SMITH

STATEMENT OF ACCOUNTS

AUGUST 15, 1994 (Date of Death) to MARCH 1, 1997

<u>**CAPITAL DISBURSEMENTS**</u>

<u>No.</u>	<u>Date</u>	<u>Particulars</u>	<u>Amount</u>
1.	Sept. 21/94	Funeral Home Funeral Expenses	$ 6,124.00
2.	Apr. 30/95	Payment to Receiver General re: 1994 Income Tax	7,115.00
3.	May 16/95	Payment to Jane Doe	35,000.00
4.	June 10/95	Payment of legacy to the Hospital for Sick Children	5,000.00
5.	June 21/95	Payment of legal fees and disbursements - Goodman and Carr	1,216.00
6.	Dec. 1/95	Payment of legal fees and disbursements - Goodman and Carr	615.00
7.	Aug. 1/96	Payment of Commission Remax Real Estate	<u>5,000.00</u>
			$ 60,070.00

- 5 -

— continued next page

Figure 6-15: Sample Accounts (Form 74.51) (continued)

ESTATE OF JOHN SMITH

STATEMENT OF ACCOUNTS

AUGUST 15, 1994 (Date of Death) to MARCH 1, 1997

<u>REVENUE RECEIPTS</u>

<u>No.</u>	<u>Date</u>	<u>Particulars</u>	<u>Amount</u>
1.	Sept. 1/94	John Smith mortgage payment interest portion, from Aug.15/94 to Sept.1/94	$ 435.39
2.	Sept. 1/94	Toronto Dominion Bank Interest for Aug./94 at 4.5%	3,425.58
3.	Oct. 1/94	John Smith mortgage payment interest portion at 4% per annum	806.50
3.	Oct. 1/94	Toronto Dominion Bank Interest for Sept./94 at 4.5%	3,579.73
4.	Oct. 1/94	Canadian Imperial Bank of Commerce - G.I.C. Interest from date of death to Oct. 1/94	380.14
5.	Nov. 1/94	John Smith mortgage payment interest portion at 4% per annum	806.33
6.	Nov. 1/94	Toronto Dominion Bank Interest for Oct./94 at 4.5%	3,740.82
7.	Nov. 1/94	Canada Savings Bonds Interest from date of death to Nov.1/94	961.86
8.	Dec. 1/94	John Smith mortgage payment interest portion at 4% per annum	806.00
9.	Dec. 1/94	Toronto Dominion Bank Interest for Nov./94 at 4.5%	3,909.16
10.	Jan. 1/95	John Smith mortgage payment interest portion at 4% per annum	805.83

- 6 -

— *continued next page*

Figure 6-15: Sample Accounts (Form 74.51) (continued)

11.	Jan. 1/95	Toronto Dominion Bank Interest for Dec./94 at 4.5%	4,085.07
12.	Jan. 1/95	Canadian Imperial Bank of Commerce - G.I.C. Interest paid quarterly at 6% per annum	750.00
13.	Feb. 1/95	John Smith mortgage payment interest portion at 4% per annum	805.67
14.	Feb. 1/95	Toronto Dominion Bank Interest for Jan./95 at 4.5%	4,268.90
15.	Mar. 1/95	John Smith mortgage payment interest portion at 4% per annum	805.50
16.	Mar. 1/95	Toronto Dominion Bank Interest for Feb./95 at 4.5%	4,461.00
17.	Apr. 1/95	John Smith mortgage payment interest portion at 4% per annum	805.33
18.	Apr. 1/95	Toronto Dominion Bank Interest for Mar./95 at 4.5%	4,661.74
19.	Apr. 1/95	Canadian Imperial Bank of Commerce - G.I.C. Interest paid quarterly at 6% per annum	750.00
20.	May 1/95	John Smith mortgage payment interest portion at 4% per annum	805.17
21.	May 1/95	Toronto Dominion Bank Interest for Apr./95 at 4.5%	4,871.52
22.	June 1/95	John Smith mortgage payment interest portion at 4% per annum	805.00
23.	June 1/95	Toronto Dominion Bank Interest for May/95 at 4.5%	5,090.74
24.	July 1/95	John Smith mortgage payment interest portion at 4% per annum	804.83
25.	July 1/95	Toronto Dominion Bank Interest for June/95 at 4.5%	5,319.82
26.	July 1/95	Canadian Imperial Bank of Commerce - G.I.C. Interest	

— continued next page

Figure 6-15: Sample Accounts (Form 74.51) (continued)

		paid quarterly at 6% per annum	750.00
27.	Aug. 1/95	John Smith mortgage payment interest portion at 4% per annum	804.67
28.	Aug. 1/95	Toronto Dominion Bank Interest for July/95 at 4.5%	5,559.22
29.	Sept. 1/95	John Smith mortgage payment interest portion at 4% per annum	804.50
30.	Sept. 1/95	Toronto Dominion Bank Interest for Aug./95 at 4.5%	5,809.38
31.	Oct. 1/95	Toronto Dominion Bank Interest for Sept./95 at 4.5%	6,070.80
32.	Oct. 1/95	Canadian Imperial Bank of Commerce - G.I.C. Interest paid quarterly at 6% per annum	750.00
33.	Oct. 1/95	John Smith mortgage payment interest portion at 4% per annum	804.33
34.	Nov. 1/95	Toronto Dominion Bank Interest for Oct./95 at 4.5%	6,343.99
35.	Nov. 1/95	John Smith mortgage payment interest portion at 4% per annum	804.17
36.	Nov. 1/95	Canada Savings Bonds Interest Nov. 1/94 - Nov. 1/95	4,500.00
37.	Dec. 1/95	Toronto Dominion Bank Interest for Nov./95 at 4.5%	6,629.47
38.	Dec. 1/95	John Smith mortgage payment interest portion at 4% per annum	804.00
39.	Jan. 1/96	Toronto Dominion Bank Interest for Dec./95 at 4.5%	6,927.79
40.	Jan. 1/96	John Smith mortgage payment interest portion at 4% per annum	803.83
41.	Jan. 18/96	John Smith mortgage payment of interest portion being 17 days at $26.43 per diem	449.31
42.	Feb. 1/96	Toronto Dominion Bank	

- 8 -

— continued next page

Figure 6-15: Sample Accounts (Form 74.51) (continued)

		Interest for Jan./96 at 4.5%	7,239.54
43.	Feb. 1/96	Canada Savings Bonds cashed Interest for 3 months at $375.00 per month	1,125.00
44.	Mar. 1/96	Toronto Dominion Bank Interest for Feb./96 at 4.5%	7,565.32
45.	Apr. 1/96	Toronto Dominion Bank Interest for Mar./96 at 4.5%	7,905.76
46.	May 1/96	Toronto Dominion Bank Interest for Apr./96 at 4.5%	8,261.52
47.	June 1/96	Toronto Dominion Bank Interest for May/96 at 4.5%	8,633.29
48.	July 1/96	Toronto Dominion Bank Interest for June/96 at 4.5%	9,021.79
49.	Aug. 1/96	Toronto Dominion Bank Interest for July/96 at 4.5%	9,427.77
50.	Sept. 1/96	Toronto Dominion Bank Interest for Aug./96 at 4.5%	9,852.02
51.	Oct. 1/96	Toronto Dominion Bank Interest for Sept./96 at 4.5%	10,295.36
52.	Nov. 1/96	Toronto Dominion Bank Interest for Oct./96 at 4.5%	10,758.65
53.	Dec. 1/96	Toronto Dominion Bank Interest for Nov./96 at 4.5%	11,242.79
54.	Jan. 1/97	Toronto Dominion Bank Interest for Dec./96 at 4.5%	11,748.72
55.	Feb. 1/97	Toronto Dominion Bank Interest for Jan./97 at 4.5%	12,271.41
56.	Mar. 1/97	Toronto Dominion Bank Interest for Feb./97 at 4.5%	<u>12,829.89</u>
			$ 245,541.92

— *continued next page*

Figure 6-15: Sample Accounts (Form 74.51) (continued)

ESTATE OF JOHN SMITH

STATEMENT OF ACCOUNTS

AUGUST 15, 1994 (Date of Death) to MARCH 1, 1997

REVENUE DISBURSEMENTS

No.	Date	Particulars	Amount
1.	Dec. 1/94	Payment to Ontario Hydro re: hydro for Simcoe Cottage	$420.00
2.	Feb. 1/94	Payment to Ontario Hydro re: hydro for Simcoe Cottage	240.00
3.	Apr. 1/94	Payment to Ontario Hydro re: hydro for Simcoe Cottage	240.00
4.	June 1/94	Payment to Ontario Hydro re: hydro for Simcoe Cottage	240.00
5.	Aug. 1/94	Payment to Ontario Hydro re: hydro for Simcoe Cottage	240.00
6.	Oct. 1/94	Payment to Ontario Hydro re: hydro for Simcoe Cottage	240.00
7.	Dec. 1/94	Payment to Ontario Hydro re: hydro for Simcoe Cottage	240.00
8.	Jan. 1/95	Payment to Town of Collingwood re: taxes on Simcoe Cottage	450.00
9.	Feb. 1/95	Payment to Ontario Hydro re: hydro for Simcoe Cottage	240.00
10.	Feb. 1/95	Payment to Town of Collingwood re: taxes on Simcoe Cottage	450.00
11.	Apr. 1/95	Payment to Ontario Hydro re: hydro for Simcoe Cottage	240.00
12.	June 1/95	Payment to Ontario Hydro	

- 11 -

— continued next page

Figure 6-15: Sample Accounts (Form 74.51) (continued)

		re: hydro for Simcoe Cottage	240.00
13.	June 1/95	Payment to Town of Collingwood re: taxes on Simcoe Cottage	450.00
14.	July 1/95	Payment to Town of Collingwood re: taxes on Simcoe Cottage	450.00
15.	Aug. 1/95	Payment to Ontario Hydro re: hydro for Simcoe Cottage	240.00
16.	Oct. 1/95	Payment to Ontario Hydro re: hydro for Simcoe Cottage	240.00
17.	Dec. 1/95	Payment to Ontario Hydro re: hydro for Simcoe Cottage	240.00
18.	Jan. 1/96	Payment to Town of Collingwood re: taxes on Simcoe Cottage	450.00
19.	Feb. 1/96	Payment to Ontario Hydro re: hydro for Simcoe Cottage	240.00
20.	Feb. 1/96	Payment to Town of Collingwood re: taxes on Simcoe Cottage	450.00
21.	Apr. 1/96	Payment to Ontario Hydro re: hydro for Simcoe Cottage	240.00
22.	June 1/96	Payment to Ontario Hydro re: hydro for Simcoe Cottage	240.00
23.	June 1/96	Payment to Town of Collingwood re: taxes on Simcoe Cottage	450.00
24.	July 1/96	Payment to Town of Collingwood re: taxes on Simcoe Cottage	450.00
25.	Aug. 1/96	Payment to Ontario Hydro re: hydro for Simcoe Cottage	240.00

$ 7,860.00

— *continued next page*

Figure 6-15: Sample Accounts (Form 74.51) (continued)

ESTATE OF JOHN SMITH

STATEMENT OF ACCOUNTS

AUGUST 15, 1994 (Date of Death) to MARCH 1, 1997

STATEMENT OF UNREALIZED ORIGINAL ASSETS

NIL

- 13 -

— continued next page

Figure 6-15: Sample Accounts (Form 74.51) (continued)

ESTATE OF JOHN SMITH

STATEMENT OF ACCOUNTS

AUGUST 15, 1994 (Date of Death) to MARCH 1, 1997

STATEMENT OF OUTSTANDING LIABILITIES

NIL

— continued next page

Figure 6-15: Sample Accounts (Form 74.51) (continued)

ESTATE OF JOHN SMITH

STATEMENT OF ACCOUNTS

AUGUST 15, 1994 (Date of Death) to MARCH 1, 1997

STATEMENT OF INVESTMENTS

NIL

— continued next page

Figure 6-15: Sample Accounts (Form 74.51) (continued)

ESTATE OF JOHN SMITH

STATEMENT OF ACCOUNTS

AUGUST 15, 1994 (Date of Death) to MARCH 1, 1997

STATEMENT OF COMPENSATION

Capital Receipts

$620,627.30 x 2½% $15,515.68

Capital Disbursements

$60,070.00 x 2½% $ 1,501.75

Revenue Receipts

$245,541.92 x 2½% $ 6,138.55

Revenue Disbursements

$7,860.00 x 2½% $ 196.50

Total: $23,352.48

CARE AND MANAGEMENTS

As this estate is an outright distribution there will be no charge for care and management.

7

TAXATION ON DEATH

Angelique L. Hamilton

1. Preparation of Tax Returns for the Terminal Year
2. Calculating Income in the Terminal Year
    (a) General Principles
        (i) Residence
        (ii) Sourcing of Income
        (iii) Cash versus Accrual Basis of Accounting
    (b) Sources of Income in the Terminal Year
        (i) Income Received Prior to Death
        (ii) Periodic Payments
        (iii) Rights or Things
        (iv) Proprietorship or Partnership Income
            Death Terminates the Partnership
            Death does not Terminate the Partnership
        (v) Income from a Testamentary Trust
        (vi) Capital Property
            Non-Depreciable Capital Property
            Depreciable Capital Property
            Capital Gains Exemption
            Principal Residence Exemption
        (vii) Eligible Capital Property
        (viii) Resource Properties and Land Inventories
        (ix) Registered Retirement Savings Plan Income
            Unmatured Registered Retirement Savings Plan
            Matured RRSP
            RRSP Contribution in the Terminal Year
        (x) RRIF Income
        (xi) Registered Pension Plan Income
        (xii) Deferred Profit Sharing Plan Income
        (xiii) Life Insurance Proceeds
        (xiv) Reserves
        (xv) Employee Stock Options
3. Miscellaneous Special Rules Regarding Death
    (a) Tax Credits in the Year of Death
        (i) Medical Expenses
        (ii) Charitable Donations
        (iii) Foreign Tax Credits

    (b) Capital Losses
    (c) Death Benefits
    (d) Forgiveness of Debt
    (e) Alternative Minimum Tax
    (f) Tax Instalments
    (g) Avoiding Double Tax on Shares of a Private Corporation
4. Interpretation Bulletins Dealing with Taxation on Death
5. Schedule A
    (a) Tax Treatment of Partnership Income
6. Glossary of Terms

1. PREPARATION OF TAX RETURNS FOR THE TERMINAL YEAR*

The personal representatives often delegate the preparation of tax returns to tax accountants or law firms. The preparation of tax returns for the deceased and for the estate can be extremely complex. It is strongly suggested that, in at least the following situations, the returns should be prepared by a tax accountant:

(1) where the deceased carried on a business as a sole proprietor;
(2) where the deceased carried on business in partnership with others; or
(3) where the deceased invested in tax shelters (for example, limited partnerships).

While Chapters 7 and 8 are intended to provide guidance with respect to the preparation of simple tax returns, they deal with the above situations in sparse detail.

The taxation year of a deceased person begins on January 1 of the year of death and ends on the date of death. This period is referred to as the terminal year. It is the responsibility of the personal representatives of the deceased to prepare and file the income tax return for the terminal year (called the "terminal return" or "T1") as well as any income tax returns for prior years which have not been filed.

The terminal return must be filed by the later of:

(1) April 30 of the calendar year following the year of death; and
(2) six months after the date of death.

In other words, the terminal return for a taxpayer who dies between January 1 and October 31 will be due by the following April 30th. If the taxpayer dies between November 1 and December 31, the terminal return will be due six months after the date of death.

Where property of the deceased passes to a *tainted spouse or common-law partner trust* pursuant to s. 70(7) of the *Income Tax Act*, R.S.C. 1985, c. 1 (5th Supp.)[1] (the "*ITA*"), the terminal return may be filed within 18 months of death.

The terminal return must be filed on Form T1 and must be signed by the personal representatives. It is similar to the annual tax return which would have been filed if the taxpayer had survived. However, the death of a taxpayer results in the application of special rules in the preparation of the terminal return.

---

* A Glossary of Terms is presented at the end of this chapter. Definitions of italicized words and phrases in this chapter may be found in the Glossary.
1 As amended. All section references in this chapter are to the *Income Tax Act*, unless otherwise stated.

The *ITA* allows the personal representatives to elect to file a separate return ("elective returns") for each of three sources of income:

(1) rights or things;
(2) income from a proprietorship (that is, an unincorporated business) or a partnership; and
(3) income from a testamentary trust.

These sources of income will be discussed later in this chapter. The separate "rights and things" return must be filed by the later of:

(1) one year after death; and
(2) 90 days after the mailing of the notice of assessment for the terminal year.

The other two separate returns are due at the same time as the terminal return.

It is generally advantageous to file a separate return for these sources of income where possible because it allows for income splitting. Tax will be paid in each separate return at the marginal rates, as if the income from that source were the only income of the deceased taxpayer. In addition, in each elective return the deceased taxpayer will be able to claim the usual tax deductions and tax credits, except that the total deductions under s. 110 and the total credits under s. 118(3), and ss. 118.1 to 118.7 and s. 118.9 cannot exceed the total which would have been claimed if only the terminal return had been filed.[2]

2. CALCULATING INCOME IN THE TERMINAL YEAR

(a) General Principles

(i) Residence

Canada taxes individuals who are residents of Canada on worldwide income. Section 250(3) provides that a resident of Canada includes a person who is, at the relevant time, ordinarily resident in Canada. Residence is not defined in the *ITA*. Therefore, one must look to the case law to determine which factors are relevant in assessing the residency of an individual.[3] IT-221R2, "Determination of an Individual's Residence Status", provides a good summary in that regard.

An individual may be deemed to be a resident of Canada under s. 250(1). For example, a person is deemed to be a resident under para. 250(1)(a) if the person sojourned in Canada in the year for 183 days or more.

---

2 Sections 114.2 and 118.93. See also *Interpretation Bulletin* ("IT") - 326R3, "Return of Deceased Person as Another Person". Interpretation Bulletins are publications released by the Canada Customs and Revenue Agency setting out their interpretation of various sections of the *ITA*.
3 See *Thomson v. Minister of National Revenue* (1945), [1946] S.C.R. 209, 2 D.T.C. 812, [1946] 1 D.L.R. 689, [1946] C.T.C. 51, 1945 CarswellNat 23 (S.C.C.).

The *ITA* also provides special rules for individuals who are either immigrating to or emigrating from Canada. A part-time resident will be taxed on worldwide income earned during that portion of the year during which he/she was a resident.[4]

An individual must be a resident of at least one country, and may be a resident of two or more countries at the same time. In this latter situation one must look to rules set out in Canada's international tax conventions (or "treaties"), which often provide tie-breaking rules so that one individual will be a resident of only one country and double taxation will be avoided.

A non-resident will only be subject to tax in Canada if the non-resident was employed in Canada, carried on business in Canada, or disposed of *taxable Canadian property*. In this case, the non-resident will only be subject to tax in Canada on taxable income earned in Canada (as opposed to worldwide income.)[5] A non-resident who dies (just like a resident who dies) will be deemed to have disposed of all capital properties at fair market value ("FMV") under s. 70(5). This will give rise to a tax liability with respect to *taxable Canadian property* of the non-resident which has appreciated. A Canadian tax return (a T1 General for Non-Residents) must be filed reporting the disposition and paying any resulting tax. The *rollover* provisions in s. 70(6) will not apply even if the property is bequeathed to the surviving spouse because the *rollover* is only available to residents of Canada. However, a U.S. resident and his or her surviving spouse will be deemed to be residents of Canada under Paragraph 5 of Article XXIXB of the Canada-U.S. Income Tax Convention.

Unless stated otherwise, it will be assumed in Chapters 7 and 8 that the deceased taxpayer was a resident of Canada in the year of death.

(ii) Sourcing of Income

As in taxation years prior to death, the deceased must include in income all income from sources inside and outside Canada. Section 3 sets out the primary sources of income, being income from an office, employment, business or property. The deceased must also include in income *taxable capital gains* net of *allowable capital losses*. For greater certainty, s. 56 sets out other sources of income which must be included in calculating income under s. 3, such as alimony payments, annuity payments, pension benefits and *death benefits*.

(iii) Cash versus Accrual Basis of Accounting

Although an individual usually pays tax based on income received and expenses paid in the year (the cash basis of accounting), in the year of death the deceased taxpayer must pay tax based on income and *capital gains* accrued to the date of death (the accrual basis of accounting). This is achieved mainly through ss. 70(1), 70(2) and 70(5) of the *ITA*, dealing with periodic payments accrued to the date of death, other amounts receivable

---

4 Section 114.
5 Sections 2(3) and 115.

but not received by the date of death, and unrealized *capital gains* at the date of death, respectively. These provisions are discussed in greater detail, below.

(b) Sources of Income in the Terminal Year

(i) Income Received Prior to Death

Income actually received by the deceased taxpayer from January 1 to the date of death must be included in the terminal return; for example, income received from an office, employment, business, property or other source. Also, *taxable capital gains* realized on the sale of *capital property* prior to death must be included in income.

(ii) Periodic Payments[6]

A deceased taxpayer must include in income the amount of all periodic payments accrued to, and unpaid at, the date of death. Section 70(1) provides that interest, rents, royalties, certain annuities, remuneration from an office or employment, or other amounts payable periodically shall be deemed to have accrued in equal daily amounts over the period during which the amount was payable. The amount so deemed to have accrued to the date of death must be included in income in the terminal return.

(iii) Rights or Things[7]

Section 70(1) does not apply to amounts which were due or payable before death. Amounts which were due or payable before the taxpayer's death are known as "rights or things" and their tax treatment is governed by the rules in ss. 70(2) and (3). The main feature which distinguishes rights or things from amounts which fall within s. 70(1) is that rights or things could have been demanded by the deceased during his or her lifetime.[8]

For example, assume a taxpayer dies June 15 and is paid at the end of each month. His/her salary was not paid for May. The May salary will be considered a right or thing while the June salary will be subject to a mandatory inclusion pursuant to s. 70(1).

If an amount could be considered to be a periodic payment under s. 70(1) or a right or thing under s. 70(2), the *CCRA*'s policy is to resolve the matter in favour of the taxpayer.[9]

There are two types of rights or things: cash amounts and inventories. Some common examples of rights or things include:

- uncashed matured bond coupons;
- accounts receivable;

---

[6] See IT-210R2, "Income of Deceased Persons — Periodic Payments and Investment Tax Credit".
[7] See IT-212R3, "Income of Deceased Persons — Rights or Things".
[8] See paragraph 1 of IT-210R2, "Income of Deceased Persons — Periodic Payments and Investment Tax Credit".
[9] See paragraph 4 of IT-210R2, "Income of Deceased Persons — Periodic Payments and Investment Tax Credit".

- dividends which are declared but unpaid;
- salaries and wages which are owing but unpaid for a pay period ending prior to death, and retroactive salary or wage adjustments including accrued vacation pay;
- commissions earned and payable but not paid before the date of death;
- unharvested farm crops; and
- the right of a deceased partner to share in the profits of the partnership.

The rights or things classification is significant because the tax treatment of rights or things allows for tax planning which is unavailable for periodic payments falling within s. 70(1). The personal representatives will have three options regarding how rights or things will be taxed:

(a) The value of the rights or things may be included in the terminal return. This tax treatment is automatic and does not require an election.
(b) An election may be made to file a separate rights or things return by virtue of s. 70(2).
(c) The value of the rights or things may be transferred or distributed to a beneficiary or beneficiaries under s. 70(3). Amounts so transferred will be taxed in the hands of the beneficiary or beneficiaries as long as the rights or things are transferred before the time for making an election under s. 70(2) has expired.

Although it would appear from the wording of s. 70(3) that options (a) and (b) above are not available if a right or thing has been transferred to a beneficiary within the time for filing a rights or things return, the *CCRA*'s administrative practice is to allow options (a) and (b), above, in these circumstances.

In determining whether to opt for (a), (b) or (c) the personal representatives should determine which alternative will minimize the amount of tax payable overall. They will need to consider whether the beneficiaries pay tax at the lowest or highest marginal tax rates. In addition, they should consider that when a right or thing is transferred to a beneficiary under s. 70(3), there may be a deferral of tax as the beneficiary will only have to bring the right or thing into income when it has been realized or when there has been a disposition of it. The best alternative may be to distribute particular rights and things to low income beneficiaries and elect to file a separate rights and things return with respect to the balance of the rights and things.

It is important to note that where a s. 70(2) election is made, *all* of the rights or things must be included in the separate return rather than the terminal return. In other words, one cannot report some rights or things in the terminal return and the remaining rights or things in the rights or things return. By contrast, a particular right or thing may be included in the income of a beneficiary under s. 70(3) even though the rest of the rights or things are taxable in the terminal return or in the separate rights and things return.

(iv) Proprietorship or Partnership Income[10]

Death Terminates the Partnership

Where a partner dies and the death causes the fiscal period of the partnership to end, the tax consequences vary depending on whether or not the date of death is in the same calendar year as the preceding fiscal year end of the partnership. If so, then s. 150(4)[11] allows the personal representatives of the deceased's estate to elect to file a separate return to report the deceased's income from the partnership from the end of the preceding fiscal year of the partnership to the date of death (the "stub period"). If an election is not filed, the stub period income should be included in the deceased's terminal return pursuant to ss. 12(1)(l) and 96(1)(f).[12]

For example, if the year end of the partnership is January 31 and the deceased died on June 30th, 1997, the personal representatives could elect to report the deceased's income from the partnership from February 1, 1997 to June 30, 1997 in a separate return under s. 150(4).

On the other hand, if the year end of the partnership is June 30th and the deceased died on January 31, 1997, s. 150(4) will have no application because the deceased did not die in the same calendar year as the preceding fiscal year. In this case the stub period income will be included in the deceased's terminal return pursuant to ss. 12(1)(l) and 96(1)(f).[13]

Death does not Terminate the Partnership

Where the partner's death does not cause the fiscal period of the partnership to end, s. 150(4) does not apply and any income during the stub period should be included in income as a right or thing and a separate rights or things return may be filed.[14]

Schedule A, *infra*, illustrates the tax treatment of partnership income for the stub period set out above.

(v) Income from a Testamentary Trust

Where the deceased is an income beneficiary of a testamentary trust, s. 104(23)(d) allows the personal representatives to elect to file a separate return to report the deceased's share of the trust's income from the end of the preceding fiscal year of the trust to the date of death (the "stub period") provided that the date of death is in the same calendar year as the preceding fiscal year end of the trust.

---

10 See IT-278R2, "Death of a Partner or of a Retired Partner", and IT-353R2, "Partnership Interests — Some Adjustments to Cost Base".
11 This section also applies to a sole proprietorship where the date of death is in the same calendar year as the preceding fiscal year end of the proprietorship.
12 See paragraph 1 of IT-278R2, "Death of a Partner or of a Retired Partner".
13 *Ibid.*
14 See paragraph 2 of IT-278R2, "Death of a Partner or of a Retired Partner" and paragraph 3 of IT-353R2, "Partnership Interests — Some Adjustments to Cost Base".

(vi) Capital Property

Taxable capital gains realized on the actual sale of *capital property* prior to death will be included in income in the terminal return.

In addition, there will be a *deemed disposition* immediately before death of all capital properties beneficially owned by the deceased at FMV under s. 70(5)(a). The estate will be deemed to have acquired these capital properties at the FMV immediately before death under s. 70(5)(b).

If *capital property* is transferred to the deceased's spouse or *common-law partner* or to a *spouse or common-law partner trust*, there will be an automatic *rollover* of the property to the spouse or *common-law partner* or trust. This defers the tax which would otherwise be payable until the death of the surviving spouse or until there is a disposition of the property by the spouse, *common-law partner* or trust. This *rollover* (the "spousal *rollover*") will be discussed in greater detail in Chapter 8.

Rollovers also exist for farm property,[15] shares in a family farm corporation[16] or an interest in a family farm partnership[17] transferred to the deceased's child or parent. These *rollovers* are discussed in greater detail in Chapter 8.

Non-Depreciable Capital Property

With respect to non-depreciable *capital property*, a *capital gain* will be realized to the extent that the FMV exceeds the *adjusted cost base* ("ACB"). A capital loss will be realized to the extent that the ACB exceeds the FMV.

Special rules exist for *personal use property*. The minimum FMV and ACB for a *personal use property* will be deemed to be $1,000.[18] As a result, if the actual FMV is less than $1,000, a gain or loss will not be realized. A capital loss arising from the *deemed disposition* of a *personal use property*, other than *listed personal property*, will be deemed to be nil.[19] *Listed personal property* losses can only be used to offset *listed personal property* gains.[20]

Depreciable Capital Property

With respect to depreciable *capital property*, the *deemed disposition* may result in a recapture (and, in some cases, a *capital gain*) or a *terminal loss*. The determination is made at the class level, rather than with respect to each property in the class.

There will be a recapture where the FMV of the property in the class exceeds the undepreciated capital cost (the "UCC") of the class. The full amount of the recapture is included in ordinary income. However, the amount of recapture cannot exceed the difference between the *capital cost* of the property in the class and the UCC of the class.

---

15 Described in s. 70(9).
16 Defined in s. 70(10).
17 Defined in s. 70(10).
18 Section 46(1).
19 Section 40(2)(g)(iii).
20 Section 3(b)(ii) and s. 41(2).

A *capital gain* will be realized to the extent that the FMV exceeds the *capital cost* of the property in the class.

There will be a *terminal loss* to the extent that the UCC of the class exceeds the FMV of the property in the class. The full amount of the *terminal loss* will be deductible from ordinary income.

To illustrate, assume the UCC of the class is $50, and the *capital cost* of the property in the class is $80. If the FMV is $40, there will be a $10 *terminal loss*, deductible from ordinary income. If the FMV is $65, there will be a $15 recapture included in ordinary income. If the FMV is $100, there will be a $30 recapture included in ordinary income, and a $20 *capital gain* (or a $10 *taxable capital gain*).

It should be noted that the *capital cost allowance* (the "CCA") cannot be taken in the year of death.

Capital Gains Exemption

The general $100,000 *capital gains exemption* (the "CGE") can no longer be used to exempt a *capital gain* from tax arising on the disposition or *deemed disposition* of property. This CGE is called the general CGE because it could exempt a *capital gain* arising on the disposition of any *capital property*.

If the deceased owned qualified small business corporation shares[21] or qualified farm property[22] on the date of death and if the deceased had not previously utilized all of the $500,000 CGE available on gains arising on these types of properties, the personal representatives should determine if the deceased's unused portion of the $500,000 CGE may be utilized. Cumulative net investment losses ("CNIL") or allowable business investment losses ("ABIL") of the deceased could affect access to the CGE. However, alternative minimum tax ("AMT"), which is often a factor to consider regarding the use of the CGE, is irrelevant as AMT does not apply in the year of death.[23]

Principal Residence Exemption

Since a *principal residence* is a *capital property*, there will be a *deemed disposition* on death unless the property is left to a spouse, *common-law partner* or a *spouse or common-law partner trust*. Before 1982, it was possible for each spouse to designate a different *principal residence* where a couple had two or more residences. For taxation years after 1981, a family may only designate one residence each year as a *principal residence* for purposes of the *principal residence* exemption. As a result, the decision as to which residence to designate as a *principal residence* cannot be looked at in isolation; the choice of designation must consider not only which residence has the largest *capital gain* but also whether the spouse has already made a designation. Additionally, in the calculation of any *capital gain* it is necessary to determine if the $100,000 CGE has been used to increase the ACB of the residences.

---

21 Defined in s. 110.6(1).
22 Defined in s. 110.6(1).
23 Section 127.55.

Where a *principal residence* designation is made, the *capital gain* will be totally exempt from tax if the home is designated as the *principal residence* of the taxpayer for the entire period during which it was owned by the taxpayer and the taxpayer was a Canadian resident throughout that period.

A *principal residence* is a personal-use property. Accordingly, any loss will be deemed to be nil.[24]

(vii) Eligible Capital Property[25]

Where, *as a consequence of death, eligible capital property* of the deceased is transferred to anyone (other than a spouse, *common-law partner* or a corporation that was controlled by the deceased before death), the *eligible capital property* will be transferred on a *rollover* basis.[26] If the *eligible capital property* is transferred to a spouse, *common-law partner* or controlled corporation, the transfer will also be on a *rollover* basis.[27] In both cases the deceased will not have to include an amount in income. However, a deduction from income may not be claimed under s. 20(1)(b) in the terminal return.

If the *eligible capital property* is not transferred to anyone, then the cumulative eligible capital (which is three quarters of the *eligible capital property* less any depreciation previously claimed under s. 20(1)(b)) may be deducted in calculating income in the terminal return.[28]

(viii) Resource Properties and Land Inventories

There will be a *deemed disposition* immediately before death of any Canadian resource properties, foreign resource properties and land inventories owned by the deceased at FMV at that time.[29] With respect to land inventory, the amount by which the FMV exceeds the cost must be included in income (it is not a *capital gain*). The tax consequences with respect to resource properties are beyond the scope of this chapter.[30] If resource or land inventory properties have vested indefeasibly within 36 months of death in a spouse, *common-law partner* or *spouse or common-law partner trust as a consequence of death*, the transfer will automatically occur on a *rollover* basis with respect to land inventories,[31] and may occur on a *rollover* basis with respect to resource properties.[32] In this case, no amount will have to be included in the deceased's income for the terminal year.

---

24 Section 40(2)(g)(iii).
25 See IT-313R2 "Eligible Capital Property — Rules Where a Taxpayer has Ceased Carrying on a Business or Has Died".
26 Section 70(5.1).
27 Section 24(2).
28 Section 24(1).
29 Sections 70(5.2)(a) and 70(5.2)(c).
30 See IT-125R4, "Dispositions of Resource Properties" and *Canadian Estate Planning Guide*, (North York: CCH Canadian Limited, 1995) at para.13,250.
31 Section 70(5.2)(d).
32 Section 70(5.2)(b).

(ix) Registered Retirement Savings Plan Income

Unmatured Registered Retirement Savings Plan

Where the annuitant of an unmatured Registered Retirement Savings Plan ("RRSP") dies, the general rule is that the FMV of the assets in the RRSP must be brought into income in the terminal return.[33] However, if the deceased designated a spouse, *common-law partner* or a financially dependant child or grandchild to receive the proceeds of the RRSP, then such proceeds will be a *refund of premiums* and there will be a corresponding deduction in calculating income in the terminal return.[34] As a result, no tax will be payable by the deceased.

A *refund of premiums* must be included in the income of the recipient (the spouse, *common-law partner* or dependant child or grandchild).[35] If the spouse or *common-law partner* contributes the *refund of premiums* into his or her own RRSP or RRIF, or uses the proceeds to buy a life annuity, within 60 days of the year end in which the *refund of premiums* is received, there will be a corresponding deduction in calculating income and no tax will be payable by the spouse or *common-law partner*.[36] In other words, the deceased's RRSP will have been transferred to the RRSP, Registered Retirement Income Fund ("RRIF") or life annuity of the spouse or *common-law partner* on a *rollover* basis and no tax will have been paid. Similarly, a dependant child or grandchild will have a corresponding deduction from income if the *refund of premiums* is used to purchase an annuity for that person which is payable until the age of 18 years.[37] Further, if the child or grandchild is financially dependant because of physical or mental infirmity, a deduction will be available if the proceeds are used to purchase a life annuity, RRSP or RRIF.[38] If a child or grandchild is over 17 years of age and financially dependant, but not because of mental or physical infirmity, there will be no deduction and the RRSP proceeds will be taxable in that person's hands.

Where the deceased has not made a beneficiary designation, the RRSP proceeds will be payable to the deceased's personal representatives. In these circumstances, if there is a surviving spouse or *common-law partner*, or if there is a financially dependent child or grandchild, the personal representatives and the beneficiary should consider filing a joint election which will have the effect of treating the proceeds as a *refund of premiums* in the beneficiary's hands, with the ensuing tax advantages.[39] Without the election the RRSP proceeds would not be a *refund of premiums* because the proceeds were paid to the personal representatives rather than directly to the spouse or *common-law partner*, child or grandchild, as the case may be. It should be noted that the joint election can only be filed where the spouse or *common-law partner*, child, or grandchild, as the case may

---

33 Section 146(8.8).
34 Sections 146(8.8) and 146(8.9).
35 Section 146(8).
36 Section 60(1).
37 *Ibid.*
38 *Ibid.*
39 Section 146(8.1).

Matured RRSP

Where the annuitant of a matured RRSP dies, the general rule, once again, is that the FMV of the assets in the RRSP must be brought into income in the terminal return. However, if the surviving spouse or *common-law partner* is designated as the beneficiary of the plan, the deceased will not have to include the FMV of the assets in the RRSP in income.[40] In this case, the surviving spouse or *common-law partner* will have to pay tax on any payments received. The payments received by the surviving spouse or *common-law partner* will not be a *refund of premiums,* and therefore cannot be rolled into the RRSP, RRIF or life annuity of the surviving spouse or *common-law partner*.

If a financially dependant child or grandchild is designated as a beneficiary, the RRSP proceeds will be a *refund of premiums* and, therefore, will not be taxed in the terminal return.[41] The same *rollovers* discussed above with respect to unmatured RRSP's will exist for the financially dependant child or grandchild.

Where the deceased has not made a beneficiary designation, the RRSP proceeds will be paid to the personal representatives. There is an election available for the personal representatives and a surviving spouse or *common-law partner* if, *as a consequence of death,* the spouse or *common-law partner* is entitled to receive the RRSP payments.[42] Where an election is filed, the deceased will not have to include the FMV of the RRSP in income in the terminal year and the surviving spouse or *common-law partner* will have to include any RRSP payments in income when received.

Similarly, if there is no beneficiary designation, the personal representatives and a financially dependant child or grandchild may file a joint election to treat any RRSP payments as a *refund of premiums* with all the ensuing tax advantages.[43]

The portion of an annuity payment under a matured RRSP accruing to the date of death must be included in the deceased's income in the terminal year.[44]

RRSP Contribution in the Terminal Year

The personal representatives cannot make a contribution to the deceased's RRSP in the terminal year, but may (on behalf of the deceased) make a contribution to the RRSP of the surviving spouse or *common-law partner* which can be deducted from income in the terminal return.[45]

---

40   Section 146(8.8).
41   Sections 146(8.8) and 146(8.9).
42   Section 146(8.91).
43   Section 146(8.1).
44   Section 70(1).
45   Section 146(5.1).

TAXATION ON DEATH   353

(x) RRIF Income

The tax consequences on the death of an annuitant of a RRIF are essentially the same as on the death of an annuitant of an RRSP.

If the surviving spouse or *common-law partner* becomes the annuitant under the RRIF on the death of the deceased, no amount has to be included in the income of the deceased in preparing the terminal return.[46] The surviving spouse will be taxed on payments received from the RRIF.[47] The payments will not be designated benefits which qualify for a deduction if contributed to an RRSP, RRIF or life annuity.[48]

The FMV of the RRIF property must be included in income only if the deceased is the last annuitant under the RRIF.[49] If the deceased is the last annuitant and the RRIF proceeds are paid directly to the surviving spouse or *common-law partner*, or a financially dependant child or grandchild there will be a corresponding deduction from income in the terminal return.[50] The recipient spouse, *common-law partner*, child or grandchild will have to include the RRIF proceeds received (called a "designated benefit", which is similar to a *"refund of premiums"* in the RRSP context) in income.[51] However, a corresponding deduction exists in the same circumstances where there would be a deduction of a *refund of premiums* in the RRSP context.[52]

If RRIF proceeds are paid directly to the deceased's personal representatives because there is no beneficiary designation, a joint designation can be filed by the personal representatives and the surviving spouse, *common-law partner* or a financially dependent child or grandchild which would allow the RRIF proceeds to be designated benefits with all the ensuing tax advantages.[53]

(xi) Registered Pension Plan Income

Unlike RRSPs and RRIFs, the deceased will not have to include in income any amount with respect to any Registered Pension Plans ("RPPs") held by the deceased at death. Amounts received prior to death from an RPP must be included in income under s. 56(1). Since the 1997 Federal Budget, the amount of a death benefit under the Canada Pension Plan or similar provincial plan is included in the income of the estate rather than the terminal return.[54]

The beneficiary who receives payments from the RPP must include these payments in income.[55] However, if the benefit is paid as a lump sum directly from the RPP into an RRSP, RRIF or RPP for the surviving spouse or *common-law partner* a *rollover* exists.[56]

---

46 Section 146.3(6).
47 Section 146.3(5).
48 See the definition of designated benefit in s. 146.3(1).
49 Section 146.3(6).
50 Section 146.3(6.2).
51 Section 146.3(5).
52 Section 60(l).
53 See the definition of "designated benefit" in s. 146.3(1) and Form T1090.
54 Section 56(1)(a.1).
55 Section 56(1)(a).
56 Sections 147.3(7) and 147.3(9).

In this case, the amount of the benefit is not included in the income of the surviving spouse or *common-law partner*.

If a child or grandchild is entitled to a lump sum benefit from an RPP, the amount must be included in income but can be deducted to the extent it is used to purchase an annuity to age 18 for such child or grandchild.[57]

(xii) Deferred Profit Sharing Plan Income[58]

A Deferred Profit Sharing Plan ("DPSP") must provide that all amounts vested in an employee will become payable not later than the earlier of the end of the year in which the employee turns 69 and 90 days after the earliest of

(a) the date of death of the employee,
(b) the day the employee ceases to be an employee of the employer (unless another employer of the employee participates in the DPSP) and
(c) the termination of the DPSP.[59]

The amount payable must be paid in a lump sum unless the employee elects either (i) to receive the amount in equal instalments payable at least annually over a period not exceeding ten years from the date on which the amount became payable or (ii) to purchase an annuity which must commence by the end of the year in which the employee turns 69.[60] If the employee makes the election, the payments may continue after the employee's death to his estate or a designated beneficiary.

The recipient (the employee, estate or designated beneficiary, as the case may be) is taxed on amounts received from the DPSP.[61] There is, however, an exception if, *as a consequence of death*, the employee's spouse or *common-law partner* is entitled to a lump sum payment and the payment is made directly from the DPSP to a RPP, RRSP or certain DPSPs for the benefit of the surviving spouse or *common-law partner*.[62] A *rollover* is also available if

(a) the recipient is a Canadian resident,
(b) the recipient receives shares of the employer (or a corporation which deals with the employer on a non-arm's length basis), and
(c) the recipient files an election in Form T2078 within the prescribed time.[63]

---

57 Section 60(1).
58 See IT-363R2, "Deferred Profit Sharing Plans — Deductibility of Employer Contributions and Taxation of Amounts Received by a Beneficiary", and IT-281R2, "Elections on Single Payments from a Deferred Profit — Sharing Plan".
59 Section 147(2)(k).
60 Sections 147(2)(k)(v) and (vi).
61 Section 147(10). A deduction is available under s. 147(12) if the employee made contributions to the DPSP.
62 Sections 147(19) and 147(20).
63 Section 147(10.1).

(xiii) Life Insurance Proceeds

Life insurance proceeds are generally not taxed on death. Where the insurance policy has been acquired after December 1, 1982 and is not an exempt policy, tax may be payable on a portion of the insurance proceeds.[64] The definition of an exempt policy is found in Regulation 306 to the *ITA*, and it is complex.

If the policy is a post-1982 non-exempt policy, there is a *deemed disposition* of the policyholder's interest in the policy immediately before death.[65] The amount by which the proceeds of disposition exceed the adjusted cost basis of the policyholder's interest in the policy must be included in the income of the policyholder.[66]

The determination of whether the policy is exempt and, if not, the amount to be included in the income of the policyholder should be made by the insurance company which issued the policy.

(xiv) Reserves

If a taxpayer sells a property during the year but receives payment of the purchase price over several years, a reserve may be claimed so that the taxpayer pays tax only on the portion of the gain or profit actually received in the year.[67] The amount of the reserve claimed must be brought into income in the following year.[68] However, a further reserve may then be claimed with respect to the portion which will not be received until a later year.

For example, assume the taxpayer sells a property and realizes a $90 taxable gain or profit and the purchase price is payable over three years in equal instalments. The taxpayer would include $30 in income in the first year ($90 – $60), $30 in income in the second year ($60 – $30) and $30 in income in the third year.

A taxpayer cannot claim these reserves in the year of death[69] unless the right to receive the unpaid portion of the purchase price is, *as a consequence of death,* transferred to the deceased's spouse or *common-law partner,* or to a *spouse or common-law partner trust* and a joint election is filed in Form T2069.[70]

In the above example, if the taxpayer died in the second year, $60 would have to be included in income in the terminal return. If the spouse, *common-law partner,* or a *spouse or common-law partner trust* receives the right to the unpaid purchase price, the reserve can be claimed in the terminal return and only $30 would have to be included in income. The spouse, *common-law partner,* or *spouse or common-law partner trust* then steps into the deceased's shoes and must include the remaining $30 in income in the third year.

---

64 See paragraph (j) of the definition of "disposition" in s. 148(9).
65 Section 148(2)(b).
66 Section 148(1).
67 The reserve for capital property is found at ss. 40(1)(a)(iii) and 44(1)(e)(iii) and discussed in IT-236R4. "Reserves — Dispositions of Capital Property". The reserve for property sold in the course of business is found at s. 20(1)(n).
68 Section 12(1)(e) with respect to a s. 20(1)(n) reserve and s. 40(1)(a)(ii) with respect to a s. 40(1)(a)(iii) reserve.
69 Section 72(1).
70 Section 72(2).

If the deceased earned commissions, the reserve for commissions under s. 32(1) cannot be claimed in the year of death unless the right to receive the commissions is transferred to the surviving spouse, *common-law partner*, or a *spouse or common-law partner trust*.[71]

Other reserves (for example, the reserve for goods or services to be delivered or the reserve for doubtful debts) are not affected and may be claimed in the year of death.

(xv) Employee Stock Options

If the deceased owned unexercised stock options at the time of death, the amount by which the value of the options immediately after death exceeds the amount paid by the deceased to acquire the options must be included in employment income in the terminal return.[72]

3. MISCELLANEOUS SPECIAL RULES REGARDING DEATH

(a) Tax Credits in the Year of Death[73]

Where an elective return is being filed in addition to the terminal return, personal tax credits (being the basic personal tax credit, the married tax credit, the married equivalent tax credit, the dependant tax credit and the age tax credit) may be claimed not only in the terminal return but also in each elective return. Deductions under s. 110 and tax credits under s. 118(3) and ss. 118.1 to 118.7 and s. 118.9 (for example, credits for medical expenses and charitable donations) can be claimed on any of the terminal return or the elective returns but the total claimed must not exceed the amount that would have been claimed if only the terminal return had been filed.[74]

There are special rules which apply in the year of death with respect to medical expenses and charitable donations.

(i) Medical Expenses[75]

Medical expenses which are paid within any 24-month period which includes the date of death may be claimed in calculating the medical expense credit in the year of death.[76] This allows the personal representatives to claim expenses actually paid by the personal representatives after the deceased's death. Medical expenses are defined in s. 118.2(2).

---

71 Sections 72(1) and 72(2).
72 Section 7(1)(e).
73 See IT-326R3, "Returns of Deceased Persons as Another Person".
74 Sections 114.2 and 118.93.
75 See IT-519R2, "Medical Expense and Disability Tax Credits and Attendant Care Expense Deduction".
76 Section 118.2(1).

(ii) Charitable Donations

Section 118.1 allows a tax credit for charitable donations. This credit is calculated at top marginal rates for gifts in excess of $200.

The tax credit cannot exceed 75% of income, plus 25% of taxable capital gains (excluding gains on which the CGE is claimed) and recaptured depreciation arising from gifts to certain donees. However, there are two exceptions to this rule.[77] First, there is no limit for ecological or cultural gifts. Secondly, in the year of death and the preceding taxation year this limitation is increased to 100% of the donor's income.

Charitable donations in the year of death include not only actual donations made by the deceased prior to death, but also charitable donations made in the deceased's Will[78] and charitable donations made by the deceased designating a charity as the beneficiary of the deceased's RRSP, RRIF or insurance proceeds.[79] Where the amount of the donations exceeds 100% of income, the excess may be carried back and claimed as a tax credit in the prior year's return.[80] The estate is a different taxpayer than the deceased. Therefore, the estate cannot use the five year carry forward which would normally be available for donations in excess of the limit.

(iii) Foreign Tax Credits

Generally, a foreign tax credit can only be claimed with respect to foreign income taxes (as opposed to estate or inheritance taxes) payable by the deceased in the year of death. However, since the ratification of the Third Protocol to the Canada-United States Income Tax Convention, residents of Canada can now claim a tax credit for United States estate tax payable by their estates. This will be discussed in greater detail in Chapter 8.

(b) Capital Losses

Generally, where a taxpayer's *allowable capital losses* for a taxation year exceed the taxpayer's *taxable capital gains* for that taxation year there is a net capital loss. This loss can be carried back three years and forward indefinitely, but generally can only be used to reduce *taxable capital gains* (as opposed to ordinary income).

However, a net capital loss in the year of death or in the preceding year may be used to reduce ordinary income. In addition, net capital losses carried forward to the year of death, or the preceding year, may also be used to reduce ordinary income.[81]

---

77 To prevent abuses in non-arms length situations, deductions for gifts of non-qualifying securities (shares and debt of private companies) will be disallowed unless the donee disposes of those securities within five years of the gift. See sections 118.1(13), (18) and (19).
78 Section 118.1(5).
79 Sections 118.1(5.1), (5.2) and (5.3).
80 Section 118.1(4).
81 Section 111(2). This section is quite complex. The losses must be claimed in a particular order and may be reduced if the deceased utilized the CGE.

(c) Death Benefits[82]

Death benefits are usually paid by a private company in which the deceased owned shares. The deceased's beneficiaries, collectively, may receive up to $10,000 as *death benefits* free of tax.[83] This $10,000 is allocated first to the surviving spouse or *common-law partner*. If the surviving spouse or *common-law partner* receives less than $10,000 then the balance can be received tax free by the other beneficiaries who are entitled to it on a *pro rata* basis.

For example, assume the surviving spouse and the deceased's two children each receive a *death benefit* of $5,000. The spouse's benefit will not be taxable. The children will each have to pay tax on $2,500 (being $5,000 x ($5,000/$10,000)).

(d) Forgiveness of Debt

There are usually adverse income tax consequences to a debtor under s. 80 when the debtor's debt is forgiven. However, there is an exception made for debts which are forgiven on death or debts which are extinguished on death by operation of law because the debts are bequeathed to, or inherited by, the debtor.[84]

(e) Alternative Minimum Tax

Alternative minimum tax ("AMT") does not apply in respect of the terminal return or any elective returns.[85]

(f) Tax Instalments

The personal representatives can elect (Form T2075) to pay the tax arising as a result of the *deemed disposition* of capital properties under s. 70(5), or land inventories or resource properties under s. 70(5.2), or as a result of rights and things under s. 70(2), to pay that tax over a period of up to ten years.[86] Security must be posted with the Minister of National Revenue. Interest must be paid at the prescribed rate at the time of the election.[87]

It should also be noted that if the deceased was required to make instalment payments prior to death and these instalment payments are not in arrears at the time of death, the personal representatives do not have to make instalment payments for the year of death. Further, an estate is exempt from the requirements to make quarterly instalments pursuant to s. 104(23)(e).

---

82 See IT-508R, "Death Benefits".
83 See the definition of "death benefit" in s. 248(1).
84 Section 80(2)(a) and IT-382, "Debts Bequeathed or Forgiven on Death".
85 See s. 127.55.
86 Section 159(5).
87 Section 159(7).

(g) Avoiding Double Tax on Shares of a Private Corporation

Where a taxpayer dies owning shares of a private corporation there is a potential for double tax. This can usually be avoided if the corporation is wound up within the first taxation year of the estate.[88] A detailed discussion of this issue is beyond the scope of this book. If the estate assets include shares of a private corporation, a tax accountant or tax lawyer should be consulted.

4. INTERPRETATION BULLETINS DEALING WITH TAXATION ON DEATH

IT-99R5	Legal and Accounting Fees
IT-118R3	Alimony and Maintenance
IT-120R5	Principal Residence
IT-125R4	Dispositions of Resource Properties
IT-139R	Capital Property Owned on December 31, 1971 — Fair Market Value
IT-150R2	Acquisition from a Non-Resident of Certain Property on Death or Mortgage Foreclosure or by Virtue of a Deemed Disposition
IT-172R	Capital Cost Allowance — Taxation Year of Individual
IT-179R	Change of Fiscal Period
IT-210R2	Income of Deceased Persons — Periodic Payments and Investment Tax Credit
IT-212R3	Income of Deceased Persons — Rights or Things
IT-221R2	Determination of an Individual's Residence Status
IT-232R3	Losses — Their Deductibility in the Loss Year or in Other Years
IT-234	Income of Deceased Persons — Farm Crops
IT-236R4	Reserves — Disposition of Capital Property
IT-242R	Retired Partners
IT-278R2	Death of a Partner or of a Retired Partner
IT-281R2	Elections on Single Payments from a Deferred Profit-Sharing Plan
IT-286R2	Trusts — Amount Payable
IT-288R2	Gifts of Capital Properties to a Charity and Others
IT-305R4	Testamentary Spouse Trusts
IT-307R3	Spousal Registered Retirement Savings Plans
IT-313R2	Eligible Capital Property — Rules Where a Taxpayer Has Ceased Carrying on a Business or Has Died
IT-325R2	Property Transfers After Divorce and Annulment
IT-326R3	Returns of Deceased Persons as Another Person
IT-337R3	Retiring Allowances

---

88 Section 164(6).

IT-349R3	Intergenerational Transfers of Farm Property on Death
IT-353R2	Partnership Interests — Some Adjustments to Cost Base
IT-363R2	Deferred Profit Sharing Plans — Deductibility of Employer Contributions and Taxation of Amounts Received by a Beneficiary
IT-381R3	Trusts — Capital Gains and Losses and the Flow-Through of Taxable Capital Gains to Beneficiaries
IT-382	Debts Bequeathed or Forgiven on Death
IT-394R2	Preferred Beneficiary Election
IT-410R	Debt Obligations — Accrued Interest on Transfer
IT-416R3	Valuation of Shares of a Corporation Receiving Life Insurance Proceeds on Death of a Shareholder
IT-420R3	Non-residents — Income Earned in Canada
IT-427R	Livestock of Farmers
IT-430R3	Life Insurance Proceeds Received by a Private Corporation or a Partnership as a Consequence of Death
IT-447	Residence of a Trust or Estate
IT-449R	Meaning of "Vested Indefeasibly'
IT-457R	Election by Professionals to Exclude Work in Progress From Income
IT-465R	Non-Resident Beneficiaries of Trusts
IT-484R2	Business Investment Losses
IT-499R	Superannuation or Pension Benefits
IT-500R	Registered Retirement Savings Plans — Death of an Annuitant
IT-508R	Death Benefits
IT-513	Personal Tax Credits
IT-517R	Pension Tax Credit
IT-519R2	Medical Expense and Disability Tax Credits and Attendant Care Expense Deduction
IT-524	Trusts — Flow-Through of Taxable Dividends to a Beneficiary — After 1987

5. SCHEDULE A

(a) Tax Treatment of Partnership Income

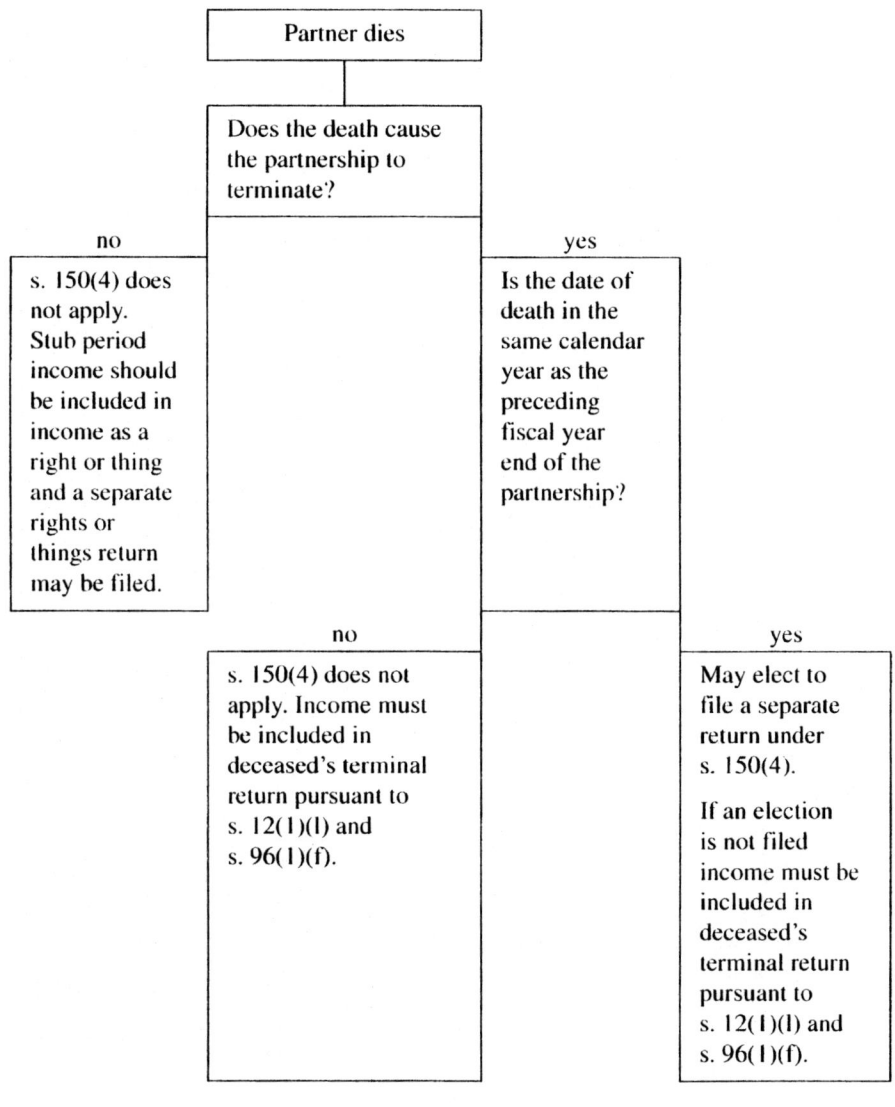

6. GLOSSARY OF TERMS

In this chapter and Chapter 8, italicized words have the meanings set out below:

adjusted cost base ("ACB"):[89] the *capital cost* of depreciable property and, with respect to non-depreciable capital property, the cost of such property as adjusted under s. 53.

allowable capital loss: one-half of a capital loss; since the *Income Tax Act* (the "*ITA*") only taxes one-half of a *capital gain*, only one-half of a capital loss can be deducted from taxable *capital gains* in computing the net taxable capital gain or net capital loss.

as a consequence of death: various rollover provisions in the *ITA* arising on death require that property be transferred "as a consequence of death". Section 248(8) provides that a transfer of property to someone because of the laws of intestacy, or because another beneficiary has disclaimed, released or surrendered his or her right to a property, will be deemed to be a transfer "as a consequence of death".

CCRA: the Canada Customs and Revenue Agency (previously Revenue Canada).

capital cost: the cost of acquiring depreciable capital property.

capital cost allowance ("CCA"): a deduction (representing depreciation) in calculating income for tax purposes. Properties are divided into classes and CCA is taken at a percentage rate, which can be found in the regulations to the *ITA*. A taxpayer can only claim CCA if the taxpayer owns the property at the end of the taxation year. Since a taxpayer is deemed to have disposed of all capital properties immediately before death, the taxpayer cannot claim CCA in the year of death.

capital gain: the amount by which the proceeds of disposition exceed the aggregate of the ACB and the expenses of disposition.[90]

capital gains exemption ("CGE"): an exemption which can exempt *capital gains* of up to $500,000 in the aggregate on qualified small business corporation shares[91] and qualified farm properties.[92]

capital property:[93] property which can be depreciated under the CCA rules (depreciable capital property) and property the disposition of which would give rise to a *capital gain* or capital loss (non-depreciable capital property) such as shares or land which are not inventory.

---

[89] Defined in s. 54 of the ITA.
[90] Section 40(1)(a)(i).
[91] Defined in s. 110.6(1).
[92] Defined in s. 110.6(1).
[93] Defined in s. 54.

clearance certificate: a form, issued by the *CCRA* by application, absolving personal representatives from personal liability which would otherwise arise if property were to be distributed to beneficiaries and the remaining assets in the estate or trust are insufficient to pay the outstanding tax liabilities of the estate or trust.

common-law partner: a person who cohabits at that time in a conjugal relationship with the taxpayer and:

(a) has so cohabited for a continuous period of at least one year, or

(b) is the parent of a child of whom the taxpayer is a parent.

Accordingly, same-sex partners are included in the definition of common-law partner.

death benefit: amounts received by any person in a taxation year upon or after the death of an employee in recognition of that employee's service in an office or employment.[94]

deemed disposition: although there has not been an actual disposition of property, the *ITA* in certain circumstances will deem a person to have disposed of certain types of property at fair market value ("FMV") with all ensuing tax consequences; for example, the deemed disposition immediately before death under s. 70(5), or the deemed disposition of an estate or trust, other than a spousal trust, every 21 years under s. 104(4).

depreciable property: property on which the taxpayer may claim CCA deductions.[95]

eligible capital property: intangible personal property used in a business which can be depreciated under s. 20(1)(b); generally it is goodwill or franchise or concession rights which do not have a fixed term.

ex-dividend: a share on which a dividend has been declared but not paid.

FMV: fair market value.

Information Circular ("IC"): a publication released by the *CCRA* setting out their administrative and procedural practice with respect to the *ITA*.

Interpretation Bulletin ("IT"): a publication released by the *CCRA* setting out their interpretation of various sections of the *ITA*.

listed personal property: personal use property that is a print, etching, drawing, painting, sculpture, or similar work of art, jewellery, rare folio, manuscript or book, a stamp or coin.[96]

median rule: the cost for determining the ACB of certain *capital property* owned on December 31, 1971 is the median (middle) value of (a) its actual cost, (b) its FMV on the Valuation Day, and (c) its proceeds of disposition (or deemed proceeds of disposition).[97] Since the *ITA* did not tax *capital gains* prior to 1972, this ensures the gain accruing to 1972 (the "tax-free zone") will not be taxed.

---

94 Defined in s. 248(1).
95 Section 13(21).
96 Section 54.
97 Defined in s. 26(3) of the Income Tax Application Rules, 1971 ("ITAR").

personal use property: property owned by the taxpayer and used primarily for the personal use or enjoyment of the taxpayer or a related person.[98]

preferred beneficiary: a resident beneficiary of an estate who meets the qualifications for a disability tax credit under ss. 118.3(1)(a) to (b) (or who is at least 18, dependent on another because of mental or physical impairment, and whose income is less than the basic personal credit (currently $7,412)) and who is the spouse or *common-law partner* or former spouse or former *common-law partner* of the deceased, or a child, grandchild or great grandchild of the deceased or a spouse or *common-law partner* of such child, grandchild or great grandchild.[99]

preferred beneficiary election: an election jointly filed in the prescribed manner and within the prescribed time by the estate and a preferred beneficiary which will allow accumulating income of the trust (that is, income which is neither paid nor payable to any beneficiary) to be taxed in the hands of the preferred beneficiary.[100] Without such an election the accumulating income would be taxed in the estate.

principal residence: a housing unit which is owned either alone or jointly by the taxpayer and ordinarily inhabited in the year by the taxpayer, the taxpayer's spouse or *common-law partner* or former spouse or former *common-law partner* or a child of the taxpayer.[101] After 1981 a family cannot designate more than one principal residence per year.

recaptured depreciation (or recapture): the amount included in calculating income for tax purposes when assets in a class have been over-depreciated for tax purposes relative to their FMV. There will be recapture on death when the FMV of all assets in the class exceeds the UCC of the class.

refund of premiums: (a) an amount (other than a tax-paid amount) paid out of the deceased's unmatured Registered Retirement Savings Plan ("RRSP") to the deceased's spouse or *common-law partner as a consequence of death*; or (b) an amount (other than a tax-paid amount) paid out of the deceased's RRSP (whether matured or unmatured) to the deceased's dependant child or dependant grandchild.[102]

rollover: a transfer of property from one person to another or from a deceased to the deceased's estate which takes place at the ACB of the property with respect to non-depreciable *capital property* and at the UCC of the property for depreciable *capital property*, so that a tax liability will not arise on the transfer even though the FMV of the property exceeds the ACB or UCC, as the case may be.

---

98   Section 54.
99   Defined in s. 108(1).
100 Sections 104(14) and 104(15) and Regulation 2800 to the *ITA*.
101 Section 54.
102 Defined in s. 146(1).

spouse or common-law partner trust: a trust which qualifies for the *rollover* under s. 70(6). A trust will qualify for the *rollover* where:

(a) the trust is resident in Canada;
(b) property is transferred to the trust *as a consequence of death*;
(c) the trust is created by the deceased's Will;[103]
(d) the deceased's spouse or *common-law partner* is entitled to receive all of the income of the trust that arises before his or her death;
(e) no person except the spouse or *common-law partner* may, before the death of the spouse or *common-law partner*, receive or otherwise obtain the use of any of the income or capital of the trust; and
(f) the property has become indefeasibly vested in the trust within 36 months after death.

tainted spouse or common-law partner trust: a trust created under a Will in favour of the deceased's spouse or *common-law partner* that does not qualify for the *rollover* under s. 70(6).

taxable Canadian property: as currently defined in s. 248(1) includes:

(a) real property situated in Canada;
(b) *capital property* used in carrying on business in Canada;
(c) shares of a private corporation resident in Canada;
(d) shares of a public corporation in certain circumstances;
(e) an interest in a partnership in which at least 50% of the FMV of assets consists of Canadian resource properties, timber resource properties, income interests in trusts resident in Canada or any other taxable Canadian properties;
(f) units of certain unit trusts resident in Canada; and
(g) capital interests in trusts (other than unit trusts) resident in Canada.[104]

The actual definition is complex and broader than the enumerated property referred to above.

taxable capital gain: one-half of a *capital gain*; the remaining one-half is exempt from tax and does not have to be included in income.[105]

terminal loss: the amount deductible in calculating income for tax purposes when assets in a class have been under-depreciated for tax purposes relative to their FMV. There will

---

103 Section 248(9.1) provides that a trust will be deemed to be created by the deceased's will where it is created by an order of the court made under provincial laws relating to dependant's relief or support.
104 See paragraphs 16 and 17 of IT-420R3, "Non-residents — Income Earned in Canada".
105 There are two exceptions. The taxable capital gain is reduced to one-quarter of the capital gain arising on a gift of shares listed on a prescribed stock exchange, and a gift of shares or units of a mutual fund, if such gifts are made to a qualified donee (other than a private foundation). See subsection 38(a.1). It is also reduced to one-quarter of the capital gain arising from an ecological gift made to a qualified donee (other than a private corporation). See subsection 38(a.2).

undepreciated capital cost ("UCC"):[106] this represents the portion of the *capital cost* of *depreciable property* on which CCA has not yet been claimed. In other words, it is the amount by which the *capital cost* exceeds the CCA claimed. This is a simplified definition because UCC is determined for a prescribed class rather than for each asset in the class.

valuation day: December 22, 1971, with respect to a publicly traded share or security, and December 31, 1971 with respect to all other property.[107] The *ITA* did not tax *capital gains* prior to 1972. Certain *capital property* acquired prior to 1972 should be valued as at December 31, 1971 as the gain accruing to December 31, 1971 (the "tax-free zone") is not taxable.

vest indefeasibly: The *CCRA* defines it as the unassailable right to ownership of a particular property that, in consequence of death of the owner, has been transferred or distributed either to a spouse, a spouse trust or a child of the deceased. In the *CCRA*'s view a property vests indefeasibly in a person when such person obtains a right to absolute ownership of that property in such a manner that such right cannot be defeated by any future event, even though that person may not be entitled to the immediate enjoyment of all the benefits arising from that right.[108] Section 248(9.2) provides that property is deemed not to vest indefeasibly in a *spouse or common-law partner trust* if the spouse or *common-law partner* dies before the property is indefeasibly vested in the trust and, in the case of an individual, unless the property is vested indefeasibly before the individual's death.[109]

---

106 Defined in s. 13(21).
107 Defined in s. 24 of the ITAR.
108 See paragragh 1 of IT-449R, "Meaning of Vested Indefeasibly".
109 See also, Vern Krishna, "Testamentary Transfers of Capital Property Between Spouses: When Does Property "Vest Indefeasibly'?" (1984-86) 1 Can. Current Tax C1.

8
ROLLOVERS AND ESTATE TAXATION

Angelique L. Hamilton*

1. Rollovers
    (a) Property Left to Spouse, Common-Law Partner or Trust
    (b) Property Left to Children
        (i) Farm Property
        (ii) RRSP and RRIF Proceeds
2. Estate Taxation
    (a) Introduction
        (i) Residence of Estate
        (ii) Testamentary versus *Inter-vivos* Trusts
        (iii) Filing Requirements
        (iv) Multiple Trusts
    (b) Estate Income and Distribution
        (i) Income Paid or Payable to a Beneficiary
        (ii) Benefits to Beneficiaries
        (iii) Preferred Beneficiary Elections
        (iv) Flow-Through (or Sourcing) of Trust Income
        (v) Non-Resident Beneficiaries
        (vi) Cashing Out an Income Interest
    (c) Distributions of Estate Capital
        (i) Distributions
        (ii) Clearance Certificates
        (iii) 21-Year Deemed Disposition Rule
        (iv) Land Transfer Tax
    (d) Notice of Objection
    (e) Goods and Services Tax
        (i) Application of Part IX of the *ETA*
        (ii) Supply (Distribution) of Business Assets
        (iii) Supply (Distribution) of Other Assets
        (iv) Clearance Certificate
        (v) Executor's Fees
    (f) U.S. Estate Tax
        (i) U.S. Situs Assets

---

* The author acknowledges the kind assistance of David Glicksman, a partner at Stikeman and Elliott, who prepared the section of this chapter dealing with the Goods and Services Tax, and the kind assistance of Nick Mantas, in connection with the preparation of this chapter.

       (ii) Taxable Estate
       (iii) U.S. Estate Tax Rates
       (iv) Exemptions and Credits in Calculating U.S. Estate Tax
       (v) Foreign Tax Credit
       (vi) Filing Requirements
3. Schedule A
   (a) U.S. Estate Tax Rates in U.S. Dollars

1. ROLLOVERS†

(a) Property Left to Spouse, Common-Law Partner or Trust

The *deemed disposition* rules discussed in Chapter 7 may result in an onerous tax liability in the terminal year. It is possible for taxes payable to be greater than the liquid assets of the estate necessitating an actual disposition of assets or the borrowing of money in order to satisfy the taxes owing. There is, however, one important exception to the *deemed disposition* rules.

Section 70(6) of the *Income Tax Act*, R.S.C. 1985, c. 1 (5th Supp.) (the "*ITA*"),[1] provides that the *deemed disposition* of *capital property* rules in s. 70(5) do not apply where the transfer of property is to a spouse, *common-law partner* or a *spouse or common-law partner trust*. This *rollover* is the keystone to tax planning in most wills as it allows a *capital gain* which would otherwise be realized and subject to tax to be deferred. Where s. 70(6) applies, tax will be payable on the earlier of the death of the surviving spouse or *common-law partner* or the actual disposition of the property by the spouse, *common-law partner* or the *spouse or common-law partner trust*, as the case may be.

The following criteria must be satisfied in order for s. 70(6) to apply:

(1) the deceased must have been a Canadian resident immediately before death;
(2) if the property is gifted outright to the spouse or *common-law partner*, the spouse or *common-law partner* must also have been a resident of Canada immediately before the deceased's death;
(3) the property of the deceased must pass to the spouse, *common-law partner* or *spouse or common-law partner trust* as a consequence of death; and
(4) the property of the deceased must *vest indefeasibly* in the spouse, *common-law partner* or *spouse or common-law partner trust* within 36 months after the death of the deceased (or such longer period of time as is permitted by the Minister of National Revenue on application).

In addition to these requirements, where the transfer is to a *spouse or common-law partner trust*, para. 70(6)(b) provides that:

(1) the trust must be created by the deceased's Will;
(2) the deceased's spouse or *common-law partner* must be entitled to receive all of the trust's income that arises before his or her death; and

---

† Italicized words and phrases in this chapter are defined in the Glossary of Terms at the end of the preceding chapter.
1 As amended. All section references are to the *Income Tax Act*, unless otherwise stated.

(3) no one other than the deceased's spouse or *common-law partner* may receive or otherwise obtain the use of any of the trust's income or capital while the deceased's spouse or *common-law partner* is alive.

A trust will be deemed to be created by the deceased's Will where it is created by an order of the court made under provincial laws for dependant's relief or support.

A trust which provides that income may be accumulated during the lifetime of the spouse or *common-law partner* will not satisfy the requirement that the deceased's spouse or *common-law partner* must be entitled to receive all of the trust's income during his or her lifetime.

Where the deceased's spouse or *common-law partner* is a beneficiary and one or more of these criteria are not met, the trust is known as a "tainted" *spouse or common-law partner trust*. For example, if the trustee has the power to encroach on capital for someone other than the spouse or *common-law partner* during his or her lifetime, or if the Will provides that the right to income of the spouse or *common-law partner* terminates on remarriage, the trust will be tainted and any inherent gain will be taxable.

A trust which provides for the payment of debts out of the trust may not meet the requirements of s. 70(6). Section 70(7) sets out rules for the "untainting" of this type of trust.

If all of the requirements of s. 70(6) are satisfied, the *rollover* is automatic, that is, an election does not have to be filed. Non-depreciable *capital property* is deemed to have been disposed of immediately before the taxpayer's death and immediately reacquired by the surviving spouse, *common-law partner* or *spouse or common-law partner trust* for proceeds of disposition equal to the deceased's *adjusted cost base* ("ACB"). *Depreciable property* is deemed to have been disposed of immediately before the taxpayer's death and immediately reacquired by the surviving spouse, *common-law partner* or *spouse or common-law partner trust* at the undepreciated capital cost (the "UCC") of the property.

The *rollover* of Registered Retirement Savings Plan (RRSP) and Registered Retirement Income Fund (RRIF) proceeds to a surviving spouse or *common-law partner* are discussed in Chapter 7.

In some circumstances, the personal representatives may want to create a *capital gain* (or recapture) in the terminal return. For example, the deceased may have capital losses in the terminal return or capital loss carry-forwards from previous years which could be used to offset the *capital gain* from the *deemed disposition*. The deceased may have died owning property which qualifies for the Capital Gains Exemption (the "CGE"). Section 70(6.2) allows the personal representatives to elect out of the automatic *rollover* in s. 70(6) in order to utilize these losses or the CGE. The surviving spouse, *common-law partner* or the *spouse or common-law partner trust* would benefit because the ACB of the property would be higher, thereby reducing any gain on a subsequent disposition (or *deemed disposition*) of the property.

(b) Property Left to Children

While the most common *rollover* on death is the *rollover* of property to a spouse, *common-law partner* or *spouse or common-law partner trust*, there are additional *rollovers* available on the transfer of certain types of assets to children.

(i) Farm Property[2]

A *rollover* exists for property transferred to a child[3] if the property consists of land in Canada or *depreciable property* in Canada which was used (immediately before the deceased's death) principally in the business of farming in which the deceased, the deceased's spouse or *common-law partner* or a child of the deceased was actively engaged on a regular and continuous basis.[4] Another *rollover* is available for shares of a family farm corporation[5] or an interest in a family farm partnership[6] which is transferred to a child on death.[7]

The other requirements for either *rollover* to apply are as follows:

(1) the child must be a resident of Canada immediately before the deceased's death;
(2) the property must be transferred to the child *as a consequence of death*; and
(3) the property must *vest indefeasibly* in the child within 36 months after the deceased's death (or such longer period of time as is permitted by the Minister of National Revenue on application).

Although the personal representative cannot elect out of these automatic *rollover* provisions, they can elect for the proceeds of disposition and cost of acquisition of the property to be any value between the tax cost of the property and its fair market value ("FMV"). In other words, the personal representatives can elect to realize a gain if desired. This would be desirable if the property qualified for the CGE or if the deceased had losses which could shelter the gain and increase the cost of the property to the child for tax purposes.

A share of a family farm corporation or an interest in a family farm partnership which is transferred to a *spouse or common-law partner trust* may qualify for a further *rollover* on the death of the spouse or *common-law partner* if such property is transferred to a child of the deceased.[8] Furthermore, land or *depreciable property* in Canada which is transferred to a *spouse or common-law partner trust* may also be entitled to a further *rollover* if such property is used in the business of farming at the time of death of the

---

2 See IT-349R3, "Inter-generational Transfers of Farm Property on Death".
3 For all purposes of this section dealing with the rollover of farm property to children, a child includes an adopted child (in law or in fact), a step-child, a grandchild, a great-grandchild, and a spouse or *common-law partner* of a child (daughter-in-law or son-in-law) (see ss. 70(10) and 252(1)).
4 Section 70(9).
5 Defined in s. 70(10).
6 Defined in s. 70(10).
7 Section 70(9.2).
8 Section 70(9.3).

surviving spouse or *common-law partner* and such property is transferred to a child of the deceased.[9] There are additional requirements which must be met for either of these two *rollover* provisions to apply.

Where property is transferred from a parent to a child by virtue of ss. 70(9), 70(9.1), 70(9.2) or 70(9.3) or during the parent's lifetime pursuant to ss. 73(3) or 73(4), the *ITA* provides for a rollback to a parent on the child's death if the transfer occurs *as a consequence of death*.[10]

(ii) RRSP and RRIF Proceeds

Tax may be deferred on RRSP and RRIF proceeds payable to the deceased's financially dependant child or grandchild as discussed in Chapter 7.

2. ESTATE TAXATION

(a) Introduction

Upon the death of a taxpayer, a new taxpayer comes into existence, namely, the estate of the deceased.

(i) Residence of Estate

The estate will have a residence for tax purposes. Generally, an estate is resident where a majority of the executors and trustees are resident, although other factors are relevant as well.[11] It is assumed in this chapter that the estate is resident in Canada. If a majority of the executors and trustees appointed in a Will are non-residents, consideration should be given to having one or more non-residents renounce as executor and trustee to ensure the estate remains resident in Canada.

(ii) Testamentary versus *Inter-vivos* Trusts

The estate will be a testamentary trust for tax purposes. A testamentary trust is a trust which arises on, and as a consequence of, the death of an individual, as long as the testator is the only person who has contributed to the trust.[12] An *inter-vivos* trust[13] is a trust which is not a testamentary trust. There are two important distinctions in the taxation of testamentary and *inter-vivos* trusts.

First, a testamentary trust is taxed at the progressive tax rates found in s. 117(2). An *inter-vivos* trust is taxed at the top marginal tax rate pursuant to s. 122(1).

---

9   Section 70(9.1).
10 Section 70(9.6).
11 See IT-447, "Residence of a Trust or Estate".
12 Section 108(1).
13 Section 108(1).

Secondly, *inter-vivos* trusts must have a taxation year which corresponds with the calendar year. In other words, all *inter-vivos* trusts have a year-end of December 31 for tax purposes. However, a testamentary trust may choose a fiscal and taxation year-end on any day up to 12 months from the date of death. The chosen year-end cannot be changed thereafter without the consent of the Minister of National Revenue.[14]

(iii) Filing Requirements

The personal representatives must file an estate income tax return (known as a T3 Income Tax and Information Return, or a "T3") within 90 days of the estate's year-end.[15] Returns must be filed thereafter for each 12 month period until the year in which the assets are completely distributed to the beneficiaries. In that year a return is filed for the period up to the distribution date. This return, and any taxes payable, must be filed within 90 days of the distribution date.

In certain circumstances, the *CCRA* will allow an estate not to file a T3. Those circumstances in which filing is not required are set out in the T3 Guide which accompanies the T3 form.

(iv) Multiple Trusts

A Will can create more than one trust. Where the beneficiaries of the trusts are not identical, the *CCRA* allows each trust to file a tax return as a separate taxpayer. This can be advantageous because it allows income to be taxed at the progressive rates in each trust. Where a Will creates separate trusts for various beneficiaries, each trust must file a T3 for each year of the trust until all of the assets of that trust have been distributed to the beneficiaries.

For the sake of simplicity, the balance of this chapter will assume that there are no trusts established in the deceased's Will, and that the administration of the estate will require several years.

(b) Estate Income and Distribution

An estate, being a testamentary trust, is taxed as an individual.[16] Although the estate is taxed as an individual, the estate may not claim personal tax credits.[17]

The general rule is that the income of the estate is taxed in the estate. However, there are currently three exceptions.

(i) Income Paid or Payable to a Beneficiary

Where the income of an estate is paid or payable to a beneficiary in the year, the personal representatives *may* deduct that income in calculating the income of the estate

---

14 Paragraph 104(23)(a).
15 Paragraph 150(1)(c).
16 Section 104(2).
17 Section 122(1.1).

for the year.[18] If the personal representatives decide to deduct such an amount from the income of the trust, the beneficiary is required to include that amount in his or her income for tax purposes.[19] This ensures that tax is not avoided on the income.

An amount is paid or payable if it is paid to the beneficiary in the year or if the beneficiary is entitled to enforce the payment of it in the year.[20]

Even though an amount is paid or payable in the year, the personal representatives may choose to tax that amount in the trust. In this case, a designation must be filed pursuant to ss. 104(13.1) or 104(13.2) to ensure that the amount is not taxed in the hands of the beneficiary. It may be preferable to tax an amount in the estate if there are unutilized losses in the estate. It may also be preferable where the beneficiary pays tax at the top marginal rate and the amount would be taxed at progressive rates in the estate.

However, one cannot artificially prolong the existence of the estate just to obtain the tax advantages of splitting income with the estate. The personal representatives cannot be compelled to transfer estate assets to the beneficiaries during the first 12 months of the estate, known as the "executor's year".[21] This is a common law concept which allows the personal representatives a period of time in which to administer the estate. Complex estates can reasonably take several years to administer, particularly if there is litigation. It is important to ensure that once all issues have been resolved, taxes paid and *clearance certificates* obtained, the estate is distributed to the beneficiaries forthwith.

(ii) Benefits to Beneficiaries

If an amount is paid out of the income of the estate for the upkeep, maintenance or taxes of a property that the estate is required to maintain for the use of a beneficiary, such amount must be included in the income of that beneficiary.[22] However, a designation can be filed pursuant to s. 104(13.1) if the personal representative would prefer to tax such amount in the estate.

Beneficiaries must also include in income any benefits received from the estate in the year to the extent that the benefits are not otherwise required to be included in their income.[23]

It is currently the *CCRA*'s administrative position not to assess a benefit for the rent-free use of a *personal-use property* by a beneficiary of the estate. Further, where the beneficiary is a child, a parent of the child will not be assessed a benefit for the rent-free use of the property either. However, payments for upkeep discussed above will be a benefit and taxable under s. 105(2).[24]

---

18 Section 104(6).
19 Section 104(13).
20 Section 104(24). See also paragraph 2 of IT-286R2, "Trusts Amount Payable".
21 *Perrin, Re* (1925), 28 O.W.N. 173 (Ont. H.C.), affirmed (1925), 28 O.W.N. 289 (Ont. C.A.).
22 Section 105(2).
23 Section 105(1).
24 See Technical News, Issue 11, published by the *CCRA*.

(iii) Preferred Beneficiary Elections[25]

The *ITA* allows an estate and a *preferred beneficiary* to file a joint election with respect to such part of the accumulating income of the estate (that is, the income which is not paid or payable to a beneficiary) as is designated in the election provided such designation does not exceed the *preferred beneficiary's* share of the accumulating income. Such amount as is designated is deducted from the income of the estate and taxed in the hands of the beneficiary.[26]

Prior to the 1995 Federal Budget there was no requirement that a beneficiary be entitled to the disability tax credit in order to qualify as a preferred beneficiary. Accordingly, these elections had a much broader application and were used quite frequently because they allow income of the estate to be taxed in the hands of the beneficiaries (who may be in lower tax brackets) even where the income remains in the estate and is added to capital.

A *preferred beneficiary's* share of the accumulating income will be either all or none of such income.[27]

The election must be filed within 90 days from the end of the estate's taxation year and must contain the documents set out in Regulation 2800(1)(a) and (b) to the *ITA*.

Accumulating income of the trust which is taxed in the trust or in the hands of a *preferred beneficiary* is added to the capital of the estate and can be distributed to beneficiaries in later taxation years without tax. It should be noted that the filing of a *preferred beneficiary election* does not mean that the *preferred beneficiary* is entitled in the future to the income which is the subject of the election.

(iv) Flow-Through (or Sourcing) of Trust Income

The general rule is that the income of a trust which is taxed in the hands of a beneficiary (whether because it is paid or payable or because a *preferred beneficiary election* has been filed) is taxed as income from property and does not maintain its source.[28]

However, there are a number of exceptions. These exceptions are generally advantageous to the beneficiary in that often when income maintains its source it is subject to a more favourable tax treatment.

Dividends received from taxable Canadian corporations may flow through the estate, allowing the beneficiary to claim a dividend tax credit for the year.[29] Similarly, net taxable *capital gains* realized by the estate can flow through to the beneficiary.[30] If the *capital gain* is realized on qualified small business corporation shares or on qualified farm property, s. 104(21.2) allows the beneficiary to utilize the CGE.

---

25 See IT-394R2, "Preferred Beneficiary Election".
26 Sections 104(12) and 104(14).
27 See s. 104(15).
28 Section 108(5).
29 Section 104(19). See also IT-524, "Trusts — Flow-Through of Taxable Dividends to a Beneficiary — After 1987".
30 Section 104(21). See also IT-381R3, "Trusts — Capital Gains and Losses and the Flow-Through of Taxable Capital Gains to Beneficiaries".

The personal representatives may also make designations to allow foreign source income[31] (for purposes of the foreign tax credit), pension benefits,[32] Deferred Profit Sharing Plan ("DPSP") benefits[33] and *death benefits*[34] retain their source in the hands of the beneficiaries. In other words, for tax purposes it is as if the trust did not exist and the beneficiaries earned the income directly.

(v) Non-Resident Beneficiaries[35]

Income of an estate which is paid or payable to a non-resident beneficiary is subject to a 25% Canadian withholding tax.[36] This includes capital dividends which are paid or payable to the beneficiaries. The rate of withholding may be reduced by treaty.[37] For example, the Canada - U.S. Treaty reduces the rate of withholding to 15%. The *ITA* also contains a few exceptions to the imposition of withholding tax on estate income.

Although the tax is imposed on the non-resident beneficiary, the personal representatives are required to deduct, withhold and remit the tax, and are liable if they do not.[38] The income of the non-resident beneficiary is deemed to have been paid or credited by the personal representatives on the earlier of:

(1) the day on which it was paid or credited; and
(2) 90 days after the end of the estate's taxation year.[39]

The *CCRA*, takes the position that the information return and the withholding tax must be remitted by the 15th of the month following the month in which the amount is deemed to have been paid or credited as set out above.[40]

(vi) Cashing Out an Income Interest[41]

Occasionally, an income beneficiary will receive estate property in satisfaction of his or her income interest in the estate. In this situation there will be a *deemed disposition* of the distributed property by the estate and a deemed acquisition of such property by the beneficiary at FMV.

---

31   Section 104(22).
32   Section 104(27).
33   Section 104(27.1).
34   Section 104(28).
35   See IT-465R, "Non-Resident Beneficiaries of Trusts" and paragraphs 34-37 of IC-77-16R4, "Non-Resident Income Tax".
36   Paragraph 212(1)(c).
37   See IC-76-12R4, "Applicable Rate of Part XIII Tax on Amounts Paid or Credited to Persons in Treaty Countries".
38   Sections 215(1) and 215(6).
39   Paragraph 214(3)(f).
40   See paragraph 54 of IC-77-16R4, "Non-Resident Income Tax".
41   Section 106 and IT-385R2, "Disposition of an Income Interest in a Trust".

(c) Distributions of Estate Capital

(i) Distributions

As a general rule, capital distributions can be made out of an estate to beneficiaries in satisfaction of their capital interests in the estate on a *rollover* basis. The estate is deemed to have disposed of the property and the beneficiary is deemed to have acquired the property at its ACB (for non-depreciable *capital property*) or its UCC (for depreciable *capital property*).[42] There are two exceptions.

A *rollover* is not available where capital is distributed to a beneficiary who is not the spouse or *common-law partner* or a *spouse or common-law partner trust* while the spouse or *common-law partner* is still alive.[43] A *rollover* is also not available where certain property is distributed to a non-resident beneficiary.[44] However, distributions of capital to non-resident beneficiaries are not subject to Canadian withholding tax.

In these two circumstances there will be a *deemed disposition* by the estate and a deemed acquisition by the beneficiary at FMV.

Although there is no tax on the distribution of property to resident beneficiaries out of a *spouse or common-law partner trust* after the death of the surviving spouse or *common-law partner*, there is a *deemed disposition* in the *spouse or common-law partner trust* at FMV of capital properties, land inventories and foreign and Canadian resource properties on the death of the surviving spouse or *common-law partner*.[45] Accordingly, tax must be paid by the *spouse or common-law partner trust* on the death of the surviving spouse or *common-law partner*.

(ii) Clearance Certificates

The personal representatives are required to obtain a *clearance certificate* from the Minister of National Revenue prior to distributing any estate assets to the beneficiaries.[46] A *clearance certificate* certifies that all income taxes, penalties, interest, Canada Pension Plan contributions and Employment Insurance premiums owing by the deceased or the estate have been paid or that adequate security therefor has been provided. If a certificate is not obtained, the personal representatives are *personally* liable for any amounts owing up to the value of the estate assets which have been distributed to the beneficiaries.[47] It is important to note that while a *clearance certificate* absolves the personal representatives from any personal liability, it does not prevent the *CCRA* from reassessing the estate.[48]

---

42 Section 107(2).
43 Section 107(4).
44 Section 107(5).
45 Paragraph 104(4)(a) and ss. 104(5) and 104(5.2).
46 Section 159(2).
47 Section 159(3).
48 See *Boger Estate v. Minister of National Revenue* (1988), [1989] 1 C.T.C. 2110, 89 D.T.C. 15, 1988 CarswellNat 516 (T.C.C.), reversed (sub nom. *Boger Estate v. R.*) 91 D.T.C. 5506, [1991] 2 C.T.C. 168, (sub nom. *Boger Estate v. Canada*) [1992] 1 F.C. 152, 43 E.T.R. 27, 46 F.T.R. 241, 1991 CarswellNat 501, 1991 CarswellNat 798 (Fed. T.D.), affirmed (sub nom. *R. v. Boger Estate*) 93 D.T.C. 5276, 155 N.R. 303, 50 E.T.R. 1, [1993] 2 C.T.C. 81, 65 F.T.R. 160 (note), 1993 CarswellNat 930 (Fed. C.A.).

Where the personal representatives and the beneficiaries of the estate are the same people, *clearance certificates* are not always obtained because the personal representatives will be liable for unpaid taxes in any event as beneficiaries of the estate.

IC-82-6R2, "Clearance Certificates" sets out the steps which must be taken and the information which must be provided to obtain *clearance certificates*. The *CCRA* used to issue three different types of certificates. Form TX21 was the final certificate which was obtained on the final distribution of all of the assets out of the estate. Form TX21B covered the period between the date of death and the date on which a partial distribution of assets was made. Form TX21A covered the deceased's terminal return and prior returns. Forms TX21A and B did not have to be obtained prior to obtaining a Form TX21. The *CCRA* now only issues a Form TX21. However, it can be obtained to the date of death or for a partial distribution; it is not issued solely on a final distribution.

In applying for a clearance certificate, there is no box on Form TX19 to check off what type of clearance (date of death/partial/final) is being requested. This should be typed in on the form or set out in a cover letter.

To obtain Form TX21 on a final distribution of assets to the beneficiaries, the personal representatives should prepare a scheme of distribution as of a particular date which is prior to the date on which they request a *clearance certificate*. A final T3 should be prepared covering the period to the chosen date and tax paid as if the distribution had occurred on that date. If everything is in order, the *CCRA* will issue the *clearance certificate*. The personal representatives must distribute the assets forthwith upon obtaining the certificate. The *CCRA* will then treat the chosen date as the actual date of distribution for tax purposes.

(iii) 21-Year Deemed Disposition Rule

In order to ensure that the realization of gains accruing on property cannot be deferred indefinitely, every 21 years a trust (except a *spouse or common-law partner trust*) will be deemed to have disposed of certain types of property.[49] The types of property subject to a *deemed disposition* are the same as the types of property which are subject to a *deemed disposition* on death. A *spouse or common-law partner trust* will be subject to a *deemed disposition* on the death of the surviving spouse or *commpon-law partner*.[50]

The 21-year rule will obviously not be relevant for estates which provide for an outright distribution of assets. It will only be relevant where trusts are established for beneficiaries.

(iv) Land Transfer Tax

Under the *Land Transfer Tax Act*, R.S.O. 1990, c. L.6, land transfer tax is generally not imposed on the distribution of real estate out of an estate to a beneficiary pursuant

---

49 Section 104(4).
50 Paragraph 104(4)(a).

to the terms of the deceased's will, or under the laws of intestacy. The Ontario Ministry of Finance has orally confirmed that this is the case even if the real estate being distributed is subject to a mortgage.

However, it is currently the position of the Ontario Ministry of Finance that land transfer tax is payable where the residuary beneficiaries are not each getting an undivided equal share of each real estate property forming part of the residue.

For example, assume that the deceased's Will provides that the residue is to be divided equally among the children. There are three children and nine condominiums of equal value forming part of the residue. If each condominium is distributed to the children as equal tenants-in-common, there will be no land transfer tax.

However, if three units are distributed to each of the three children, the Ontario Ministry of Finance believes land transfer tax is payable on two-thirds of the FMV of each unit because each child is legally entitled to one-third of each asset in the residue. It is not clear whether this position is correct in law.

(d) Notice of Objection

If the personal representatives disagree with the *CCRA*'s assessment or reassessment of the terminal return or any T3 returns, they may file a notice of objection (Form T400A) with the *CCRA*.[51] If the personal representatives disagree with the amount of a loss as ascertained by the *CCRA*, they may request a determination.[52] If the personal representatives disagree with the notice of determination, they may then file a notice of objection.

A notice of objection must be filed on the later of:

(1) one year after the balance-due day of the deceased or the estate, as the case may be, for the year; and
(2) 90 days after the day on which the notice of assessment (or determination) is mailed.[53]

The date on which a notice of objection must be filed may be extended by the Minister of National Revenue in certain circumstances.[54]

(e) Goods and Services Tax

There are provisions in Part IX of the *Excise Tax Act*, R.S.C. 1985, c. E-15 (the "*ETA*"), which deal specifically with the application of the Goods and Services Tax (the "GST") to the estate of a deceased person.

---

51 Section 165(1).
52 Section 152(1.1).
53 Section 152(1.2).
54 Section 166.1(1) and 166.1(7).

(i) Application of Part IX of the *ETA*

Section 267 of the *ETA* provides that, in general, Part IX of the *ETA* will apply to the estate of the individual as though the individual had not died.

Paragraphs 267(a) and (b) provide that the reporting period of the individual ends on the date of death and the first reporting period of the estate begins on the day after the individual's death and ends on the day the individual's reporting period would have ended had the individual not died.

(ii) Supply (Distribution) of Business Assets

Where immediately before death an individual holds property for consumption, use or supply in the course of a business, no tax will be payable in respect of the supply of that property by the executor to an individual who is a beneficiary of the estate and is a registrant under the *ETA*, provided that the property is received for consumption, use or supply in the course of commercial activities of the beneficiary and the executor and beneficiary jointly elect pursuant to s. 167(2) of the *ETA*.

(iii) Supply (Distribution) of Other Assets

Section 269 of the *ETA* provides that a distribution of property to beneficiaries or other persons (*e.g.* an assignee of a beneficiary's interest in the estate) shall be deemed to be a supply of property for consideration equal to the amount determined under the *ITA* to be the proceeds of disposition of the property.

In many cases, no GST will be payable in respect of the supply. For example, a distribution of stocks and bonds will be characterized as an exempt supply. Further, as discussed above, a distribution of business assets to a beneficiary may also be made without payment of GST.

(iv) Clearance Certificate

Before distributing any property to beneficiaries, s. 270 of the *ETA* provides that an executor of a deceased who was a registrant under the *ETA* is required to obtain a *clearance certificate* certifying that all amounts that are payable or remittable or that may reasonably be expected to become payable or remittable have been paid or that security for such amounts has been posted. An executor who fails to obtain a *clearance certificate* will be personally liable for the payment or remittance of those amounts to the extent of the value of the property distributed.

Where the estate controls a corporation and the executor is also a director of the corporation, a failure by the corporation to remit an amount of net tax (in general, GST collected and collectible less GST paid and payable) could result in an assessment of the director for payment of such tax under s. 323 of the *ETA*. It should be noted that a *clearance certificate* obtained under s. 270 of the *ETA* prior to the distribution of the shares of the corporation to the beneficiaries will not protect the executor, in his role as director, from liability under section 323 of the *ETA*.

(v) Executor's Fees

GST may be payable on executor's fees, depending upon the circumstances. Where executor's fees are earned in the course of a business (for example, where a trust company acts as an executor) GST will be payable. Further, a lawyer who acts as an executor as part of his professional practice will be required to charge GST on executor's fees. However, executor's fees earned on a more casual basis will not be subject to GST. A lawyer who acts as an executor otherwise than in the course of his professional practice (for example, as a favour to a friend or family member) will not be required to charge GST.

(f) U.S. Estate Tax

If the deceased was either a resident or a citizen of the U.S. at the time of death, the deceased will be subject to U.S. estate tax based on the FMV of his or her worldwide assets. Worldwide assets before deductions are known as the "gross estate".

However, even where the deceased was neither a U.S. citizen nor a U.S. resident (called a "non-resident alien" in the U.S. Internal Revenue Code) the deceased will be subject to U.S. estate tax on the FMV of the deceased's U.S. "situs" assets (meaning those assets which are situated in the U.S.).

(i) U.S. Situs Assets

Generally, U.S. situs assets are:

(1) real estate situated in the United States;
(2) shares of U.S. corporations;
(3) debts owed by U.S. residents, citizens, corporations or governments;
(4) U.S. bank accounts used in connection with a U.S. trade or business; and
(5) tangible personal property situated in the United States (for example, furnishings or works of art in a Florida condominium).

(ii) Taxable Estate

The "taxable estate" is the amount which is subject to U.S. estate tax. In calculating the taxable estate various deductions are allowed. There is a deduction for a portion of the estate expenses and debts that the FMV of the U.S. situs assets is of the FMV of the gross estate. For example, if one-tenth of the assets in the estate are U.S. situs assets, then one-tenth of the overall debts and expenses of the estate may be deducted from the FMV of the U.S. situs assets. Marital and charitable deductions may also be available.

(iii) U.S. Estate Tax Rates

Schedule A at end of this chapter sets out the current rates of U.S. estate tax, which vary from 18% to 60% of the taxable estate.

(iv) Exemptions and Credits in Calculating U.S. Estate Tax

There has always been a basic exemption for non-resident aliens of $60,000 (U.S.).[55] In other words, if the taxable estate was less than $60,000, no U.S. estate tax was payable.

On November 9, 1995 the Third Protocol to the Canada - U.S Income Tax Convention (the "Protocol") was ratified and came into force. As a result, additional relief from U.S. estate tax is available in the following circumstances:

(1) The basic credit for 2001 exempts $675,000 of assets.[56] The value of assets that is exempt from U.S. estate tax in a given year is hereinafter referred to as the "Exempt Amount". However, for non-resident aliens this credit must be pro-rated based on the percentage of the worldwide estate that is represented by the U.S. situs assets. For example, if the total tax is $100,000 and the basic credit is $200,000 and the proportion of the worldwide estate that is represented by U.S. situs assets is 30%, the tax payable after the basic credit would be $40,000 (being $100,000 – (30% x 200,000)).

(2) If the FMV of the gross estate does not exceed the Exempt Amount, no U.S. estate tax will be payable.

(3) If the taxable estate is less than $60,000 no U.S. estate tax will be payable.

(4) If the FMV of the gross estate exceeds the Exempt Amount, but does not exceed $1,200,000, U.S. estate tax will only apply to the FMV of U.S. real estate and personal property forming part of the business property of a U.S. permanent establishment or fixed base. For example, if the only U.S. situs property is U.S. stocks, U.S. estate tax would not be payable.

(5) If U.S. situs property is left to the deceased's spouse, an additional credit is available and some part or all of the U.S. estate tax may be deferred until the death of the surviving spouse. The calculation of the credit can be complex.

---

55 Dollar amounts from here to end of the chapter are in U.S. funds.
56 Under amendments to the U.S. laws, the basic credit will increase exempt to the following value of assets:
    2002 $1,000,000
    2004 $1,500,000
    2006 $2,000,000
    2009 $3,500,000
    2010   U.S. estate tax repealed for this year
    2011 $1,000,000 (reverts to 2002 amount)

(v) Foreign Tax Credit

The Protocol also provides, for the first time, that Canadian residents will get a foreign tax credit to reduce Canadian taxes owing on U.S. source income, including the *deemed disposition* of U.S. situs property.

This credit is only significant if the deceased had U.S. source income, for example, if the U.S. situs property had an inherent gain. If the deceased died owning a Florida condominium with a FMV and ACB of $500,000, the U.S. estate tax will be substantial but no credit will be available because there is no U.S. source income.

(vi) Filing Requirements

If no U.S. estate tax is payable, a U.S. estate tax return does not have to be filed as a general rule. However, if the deceased's estate is claiming the *pro-rata* unified credit, a return must be filed showing the calculation of the credit and providing all information necessary to verify and compute the credit. If tax is payable, the return is due and tax is payable within nine months of the date of death.

3. SCHEDULE A

(a) U.S Estate Tax Rates in U.S. Dollars

Taxable Estate	Tax Rate on Excess	
Up to 10,000		18%
10,000-20,000	1,800 plus	20%
20,000-40,000	3,800 plus	22%
40,000-60,000	8,200 plus	24%
60,000-80,000	13,000 plus	26%
80,000-100,000	18,200 plus	28%
100,000-150,000	23,800 plus	30%
150,000-250,000	38,800 plus	32%
250,000-500,000	70,800 plus	34%
500,000-750,000	155,800 plus	37%
750,000-1,000,000	248,300 plus	39%
1,000,000-1,250,000	345,800 plus	41%
1,250,000-1,500,000	448,300 plus	43%
1,500,000-2,000,000	555,800 plus	45%
2,000,000-2,500,000	780,800 plus	49%[57]
2,500,000-3,000,000	1,025,800 plus	53%[57]
3,000,000-10,000,000	1,290,800 plus	55%[57]
10,000,000-21,040,000	5,140,800 plus	60%[57]
21,040,000-	11,764,800 plus	55%[57]

---

[57] Under amendments to the U.S. laws, the maximum rate will be reduced to 50% in 2002, and will be reduced by 1% per year until the maximum rate reaches 45% in the year 2007. However, in 2011 the maximum rates will revert to those set out in Schedule A.

INDEX

ABATEMENT OF LEGACY, 21

ADEMPTION OF LEGACY, 21

ADMINISTERING ESTATE *See also* ASSETS OF ESTATE
assets, locating and dealing with
  bank account, opening estate, 170 *See also* money on deposit
    letter instructing bank to issue cheque for probate fees (Figure 4-11), 170, 198
  bonds and shares
    with certificate, 176
      procedures required, 176
    without certificate, 175-176
      procedures required, 175
    valuing bonds, 175
    valuing public shares, 175
  Canada Pension Plan benefits
    death benefit, 178-179
      documents required, 178-179
    generally, 178-180
    orphan's benefit, 179-180
      documents required (Figure 4-8), 179-180, 195
    survivor's benefit, 179
      documents required (Figure 4-8), 179, 195
  Canada Savings Bonds or other Government of Canada securities
    with court certificate, 174
      forms required (Figure 4-14), 174, 201
    without court certificate, 174
      forms required (Figure 4-14), 174, 201
  generally, 174
  life insurance
    estate as beneficiary, 177
      documents required (Figure 4-3), 177, 190
    generally (Figure 4-2), 176-177, 189
    named beneficiary, where there is, 176-177
      documents required (Figure 4-3), 177, 190

ADMINISTERING ESTATE – *continued*
assets, locating and dealing with – *continued*
  money on deposit (Figure 2-4), 46, 54, 171
  motor vehicles, 180
  other assets, 180
  pension plans, 178
  real estate
    difficulties, possible, 173-174
    Land Titles Act, under
      joint property, 173
      with court certificate, 173
      without court certificate, 173
    land transfer tax, 377-378
    Registry Act, under
      Affidavit of Execution on title, whether required, 173
      joint property, 172
      with court certificate, 173
      without court certificate, 173
  Registered Retirement Savings Plans and spouses
    estate is beneficiary or no beneficiary named, 178
    named beneficiary, 177-178
    tax rollover, 177-178
  safety deposit box, 170-171
    authorization re listing contents (Figure 4-20), 171, 207
  term deposits and guaranteed investment certificates, 172
    declaration of transmission (Figure 4-22), 172, 209
    letter to institution or bank (Figures 4-13, 4-14), 172
    power of attorney to transfer bonds - shares (Figure 4-21), 172, 208
  without court certificate, 171
    letter to bank without certificate (Figure 4-12), 171, 199
distributions, 184-185
executor's year, 184

384 INDEX

ADMINISTERING ESTATE – *continued*
finalizing estate
  distributions, 184-185
  documents to be filed, 183-184
  generally, 183-187
  ongoing estates, 185
  payment of money into court, 185-186
  security, arranging for return of, 184
  status certificates, obtaining, 187
  succession duties, 187
  tickler system, keeping, 186-187
  valuing estate with court, 183
liabilities, locating and dealing with
  advertising for creditors, 182, 187
    notice to creditors and others (Figure 4-6), 182, 193
  debts, payment of, 182
  Family Law Act election
    consent to distribution (Figure 4-25), 181, 212
    election form (Figure 4-24), 181, 211
    equalization entitlement, 4, 181
    life insurance, effect of, 181
    priority of, 181
  insolvent estates, 182
powers of investment, 293-294
proof of death, 170
  letter to Registrar General requesting death certificate (Figure 4-1), 170, 188
security, arranging return of, 184
  application for release of bond, 184

ADMINISTRATION BOND *See also* APPLICATIONS FOR ESTATE TRUSTEE
dispensing with
  affidavit in support of request for order (Figure 3-49), 66, 69, 71, 72, 73, 74, 152
  order to dispense with bond (Figure 3-50), 66, 69, 71, 72, 73, 74, 153-154
forms
  insurance or guarantee company (Figure 3-45), 66, 69, 144-145
  personal sureties (Figure 3-46), 66, 69, 146-147
release of bond
  application to court, 184
resealing of appointment of estate trustee with or without will, confirmation by, (Figures 3-40, 3-41), 72-73

ADVERTISING FOR CREDITORS
generally, 182
notice to creditors and others (Figure 4-6), 193

ANCILLARY APPOINTMENT OF ESTATE TRUSTEE WITH WILL, 73-74 *See also* APPLICATIONS FOR ESTATE TRUSTEE

APPLICATIONS FOR ESTATE TRUSTEE *See also* ADMINISTRATION BOND *and* CONTENTIOUS PROCEEDINGS
addresses of court offices, 161-166
ancillary appointment of estate trustee with will, certificate of
  documents to be filed with court, 74
    letter to court (Figure 3-6), 74, 81
    other documents that may be required, 74
  generally, 73-74
application for certificate of appointment as succeeding estate trustee with will
  documents to be filed with court, 70
    letter to court (Figure 3-3), 70, 79
    other documents that may be required, 70-71
  generally, 70
application for certificate of appointment as succeeding estate trustee without will
  documents to be filed with court, 71
    letter to court (Figure 3-4), 71, 80
    other documents that may be required, 72
  generally, 71
application for certificate of appointment of estate trustee with a will limited to assets referred to in the will
  documents to be filed with court, 67
    affidavit of execution of will or codicil (Figure 3-16), 67, 99
    affidavit of service of notice of application with a will limited to assets referred to in the will (Figure 3-14), 67, 94-95
    affidavit re multiple wills (Figure 3-53), 67, 157-158
    certificate of appointment of estate trustee with a will limited to the assets referred to in the will (Figure 3-22), 67, 106-107
    notice of (Figure 3-15), 67, 96-98
    order (Figure 3-54), 67, 159-160
  generally, 67
  other documents that may be required, 67
application for certificate of appointment of estate trustee with will
  documents to be filed with court, 65-66
    letter to court (Figure 3-1), 66, 77
    other documents that may be required, 66
  generally, 64-65
application for certificate of appointment of estate trustee without will
  documents to be filed with court, 69

INDEX 385

APPLICATIONS FOR ESTATE TRUSTEE – *continued*
application for certificate of appointment of estate trustee without will – *continued*
  letter to court (Figure 3-2), 69, 78
  other documents that may be required, 69
  generally, 67-69
application for certificate of appointment of foreign estate trustee's nominee as estate trustee without will
  documents to be filed with court, 75
    application (Figure 3-30), 75, 119-120
    certificate (Figure 3-32), 75, 122
    nomination of applicant (Figure 3-31), 75, 121
  generally, 74-75
calculating court fees, 61-62
  final review and additional payment or refund, 183
    advising court of decrease in assets (Figure 4-18), 183, 205
    advising court of increase in assets (Figure 4-17), 183, 204
    affidavit re decrease in probate value (Figure 4-27), 183, 214
    affidavit re increase in probate value (Figure 4-26), 183, 213
  payment from deceased's bank account, 170
  undertaking (Figure 3-52), 66, 69, 71, 72, 73, 74, 76, 156
during litigation, certificate of estate trustee
  documents to be filed with court, 76
    letter to court (Figure 3-7), 76, 83
    other documents that may be required, 76
  generally, 75-76
jurisdiction to file grant, 61
notice of application
  form
    notice with will (Figure 3-15), 64, 65, 96-98
    notice without will (Figure 3-26), 68, 69, 113-114
  generally, 63-64
  proof of service
    affidavit of service with will (Figure 3-14), 65, 94-95
    affidavit of service without will (Figure 3-25), 68, 69, 112
resealing of appointment of estate trustee with or without a will, confirmation by
  documents to be filed with court, 73
    letter to court (Figure 3-5), 73, 81
    other documents that may be required, 73
  generally, 72
succeeding estate trustee *See* application for appointment as succeeding estate trustee with/without will
will depository, role of court as, 62-63
  notice of deposit to estate trustee (Figure 3-8), 84

APPLICATIONS FOR ESTATE TRUSTEE – *continued*
will depository – *continued*
  notice of withdrawal to estate trustee (Figure 3-9), 85
  registrar's notice of application with will (Figure 3-47), 150

ASSETS OF ESTATE *See also* ADMINISTERING ESTATE
calculating court fees
  final review and additional payment or refund, 183
  generally, 61-62
  undertaking (Figure 3-52), 66, 69, 71, 72, 73, 74, 76, 156
Canada Savings Bonds, 47
  letter to Bank of Canada re (Figure 2-3), 53
generally, 43
money on deposit, 46
  letter to bank, general (Figure 2-2), 52
  letter to bank where deceased held assets (Figure 2-4), 54
other, 47
real estate
  Estates Administration Act, effect of, 45
  registered under Land Titles System, 45
  registered under Registry System, 44-45
safety deposit box, 46-47
shareholdings
  letter to transfer agent requesting waiver of requirement of court certificate (Figure 2-5), 55
  private corporations, 46
  public corporations, 46
statement of assets
  final review, 183
  generally, 169
  order to file, 217
  sample of information required for (Figure 2-7), 57-58
valuing, 47

BEQUESTS *See* LEGACIES

BOND *See* ADMINISTRATION BOND

BONDS AND SHARES (Figure 2-5), 45-46, 47, 55, 174, 175-176

CANADA PENSION PLAN BENEFITS *See* ADMINISTERING ESTATE

CANADA SAVINGS BONDS (Figure 2-3), 47, 53, 174

CAPITAL GAINS EXEMPTION *See* TAXATION ON DEATH

386 INDEX

CHILDREN'S LAW REFORM ACT, 5

CLAIMS AGAINST ESTATE
form (Figure 5-26), 227, 283-284
generally, 227
notice of contestation (Figure 5-25), 227, 281-282

COMMON-LAW PARTNER
defined, 363

COMMON-LAW PARTNER TRUST *See* ROLLOVERS

CONSENT TO APPLICANT'S APPOINTMENT AS ESTATE TRUSTEE
application for certificate of appointment as succeeding estate trustee with will (Figure 3-34), 70, 125
application for certificate of appointment as succeeding estate trustee without will (Figure 3-37), 71, 72, 130
application for certificate of appointment of estate trustee with will (Figure 3-20), 64, 66, 103
application for certificate of appointment of estate trustee without will (Figure 3-28), 68, 69, 116

CONTENTIOUS PROCEEDINGS *See also* APPLICATIONS FOR ESTATE TRUSTEE *and* ORDERS FOR ASSISTANCE
application or motion for directions, 226
  notice of application for directions (Figure 5-17), 226, 261-263
  notice of motion for directions (Figure 5-18), 226, 264-265
    order giving directions (Figures 5-20, 5-21), 226
    statement of claim (Figure 5-19), 226, 266-268
    statement of submission of rights to court (Figure 5-22), 226-227, 275-276
case management, 224
Estates List, metro Toronto Region
  case management and, 224
  court name change and, 224
  proceedings to be heard on notice to profession, 219-220
generally, 219-227
mediation, mandatory
  additional session, consent order for, 224
  attendance at mediation session, 222-223
    authority to settle, 223
    failure to attend, 223
    who must attend, 222
  confidentiality, 223
  definitions, 221
  directions for conduct, 221-222
    directions, 221-222

CONTENTIOUS PROCEEDINGS – *continued*
mediation, mandatory – *continued*
  directions for conduct – *continued*
    motion for directions, 221
    non-compliance, 222
  exemption from, 221
  forms
    certificate of non-compliance (Figure 5-13), 253-254
    notice by mediator (Figure 5-11), 249-250
    request for assignment of mediator (Figure 5-10), 247-248
    statement of issues (Figure 5-12), 251-252
  mediators, 222
    choice of, 222
    report, 223
  non-compliance, remedy for, 223
  outcome of, 223
    agreement, 223
      failure to comply with signed, 223
    mediator's report, 223
    no agreement, 223
  procedure before mediation session, 222
    non-compliance, 222
    statement of issues, 222
  scope of rule, 221
objection to issuing certificate of appointment, 224-225
  notice of objection (Figure 5-9), 224, 245-246
  notice to objector (Figure 5-15), 225, 257-258
    notice of appearance (Figure 5-16), 225, 259-260
request for notice of commencement of proceedings (Figure 5-1), 216, 230
return of certificate, 225
revocation of certificate of appointment, 225
settlement
  notice of settlement (Figure 5-23), 227, 277-278
  rejection of settlement (Figure 5-24), 227, 279-280

CORPORATIONS
bonds, 175
private, 46, 175-176, 359
public, 46, 175-176
waiver of requirement of court certificate (Figure 2-5), 55

COURT GRANT OR NOT, 44-47

DEPENDANT'S RELIEF CLAIMS
generally, 28-29, 227-228
procedure, 28-29, 227-228
who may bring application, 28-29, 227-228

INDEX 387

ESTATE ADMINISTRATION TAX ACT, 1998, 62, 184

ESTATE PLANNING *See* TRUSTS IN ESTATE PLANNING

ESTATE TAXATION
administration tax, 6, 62-63
  multiple wills, as means of avoidance, 9, 296
assessment or reassessment
  notice of objection, 378
distributions of estate capital
  clearance certificates, 376-377
    final distribution, 377
  distributions, 376
    rollover basis, 376
  land transfer tax, 377-378
  21-year deemed disposition rule, 377
estate income and distribution
  benefits to beneficiaries, 373
  cashing out an income interest, 375
  flow-through of trust income, 374-375
    capital gains and exemptions, 374-375
    dividends and dividend tax credit, 374
  income paid or payable to beneficiary, 372-373
  non-resident beneficiaries, 375
    withholding tax, 375
  preferred beneficiary elections, 374
estate income tax return, 372
general principles, 371-372
  filing requirements, 372
  multiple trusts, 372
  residence of estate, 371
  testamentary versus inter-vivos trusts, 371-372
Goods and Services Tax, 378-380
  application of Part IX of the Excise Tax Act, 379
  clearance certificate, 379-380
  executor's fees, 380
  supply (distribution) of business assets, 379
  supply (distribution) of other assets, 379
multiple wills, as means of avoidance, 9, 296
tax clearance certificates
  generally, 376-377
  Goods and Services Tax, 378-380
  letter requesting (Figure 4-7), 185, 194
U.S. estate tax
  generally, 380-382
  estate tax rates, 381, 382
  exemptions and credits in calculating, 381
  filing requirements, 382
  foreign tax credit, 382
  taxable estate, 380
  U.S. situs assets, 380

EXECUTOR'S COMPENSATION, 292-293
Goods and Services Tax, 380
special fee, 294

EXECUTOR'S YEAR, 184

FAMILY LAW ACT
solicitor's responsibility, 41
spousal equalization entitlement, 4, 27-28, 181, 228-229
  consent to early distribution, 229
  deductibility of life insurance proceeds, 176-177, 181, 229
  distributions, 184-185, 228-229
  election form (Figures 4-24, 5-27), 27-28, 181, 229
    letter to court filing election (Figure 4-16), 27-28, 203
  priority of, 181, 229
  testamentary dispositions, effect on, 27-28
will exclusion, 6, 27-28

FARM PROPERTY
capital gains exemption, 349, 374-375
tax rollovers, 370-371

FOREIGN ESTATE TRUSTEE *See* APPLICATIONS FOR ESTATE TRUSTEE

GOODS AND SERVICES TAX, 378-380

INCOME TAX ACT *See* ESTATE TAXATION, ROLLOVERS, *and* TAXATION ON DEATH

INTESTACY
distribution on, 3-4, 48
generally, 3-4, 47-50
posting security, 49-50
preferential share, 3, 48, 50
who is entitled to apply as estate trustee, 49

INVESTMENTS
trustee's powers to make, 293-294

LEGACIES
abatement, 21
ademption, 21
demonstrative, 20, 21
devise, defined, 21
general, 20, 21
lapse, 21-22
  anti-lapse provision, 22
memoranda, 22
  legal, 22

LEGACIES – *continued*
memoranda – *continued*
  precatory, 22
  specific, 20, 21

LETTERS TESTAMENTARY *See*
  APPLICATIONS FOR ESTATE TRUSTEE

LIFE INSURANCE, 20, 176-177, 181, 229

LIMITED GRANTS OF PROBATE *See*
  UNPROBATED WILLS

MEDIATION, MANDATORY
additional session, consent order for, 224
attendance at mediation session, 222-223
  authority to settle, 223
  failure to attend, 223
  who must attend, 222
confidentiality, 223
definitions, 221
directions for conduct, 221-222
  directions, 221-222
  motion for directions, 221
  non-compliance, 222
exemption from, 221
forms
  certificate of non-compliance (Figure 5-13), 253-254
  notice by mediator (Figure 5-11), 249-250
  request for assignment of mediator (Figure 5-10), 247-248
  statement of issues (Figure 5-12), 251-252
mediators, 222
  choice of, 222
  report, 223
non-compliance, remedy for, 223
outcome of, 223
  agreement, 223
    failure to comply with signed, 223
    mediator's report, 223
    no agreement, 223
procedure before mediation session, 222
  non-compliance, 222
  statement of issues, 222
scope of rule, 221

MEMORANDA
legal, 22
precatory, 22

MONEY ON DEPOSIT (Figure 2-4), 46, 54, 171

MOTION FOR DIRECTIONS *See*
  CONTENTIOUS PROCEEDINGS

MOTOR VEHICLES, 180

NOTICE OF COMMENCEMENT OF
  PROCEEDINGS, 216

ORDERS FOR ASSISTANCE *See also*
  CONTENTIOUS PROCEEDINGS
generally, 216-219
order for further details, 218
order for other matters, 219
order to accept or refuse appointment (Figures 5-2, 5-3), 217
order to beneficiary witness (Figure 5-6), 218, 239-240
order to consent or object to proposed appointment (Figure 5-4), 217, 235-236
order to file statement of assets of estate (Figure 5-5), 217, 237-238
order to former spouse (Figure 5-7), 218, 241-242
order to pass accounts (Figure 5-8), 218, 243-244

PASSING OF ACCOUNTS *See also*
  PREPARATION OF ACCOUNTS
Children's Lawyer, 289, 289, 290, 290-291, 292
costs, 290
  requests for costs (Figures 6-9, 6-10), 290
  requests for increased costs (Figures 6-11, 6-12), 290
documents to be filed with court
  contested passing, 288-289
    affidavit verifying estate accounts (Figure 6-2), 289, 299
    notice of application to pass accounts (Figure 6-3), 288, 300-302
    notice of objection to accounts (Figure 6-4), 288, 303-304
  notice of non-participation in passing of accounts (Figure 6-6), 306
  uncontested passing, 289-290
    affidavit in support of unopposed judgment (Figure 6-7), 289, 307
    judgment on unopposed passing (Figure 6-13, 6-14), 290, 316-323
    notice of no objections to accounts (Figure 6-5), 289, 291, 305
    notice of withdrawal of objection (Figure 6-8), 290, 308
    request for costs (Figures 6-9, 6-10), 290
      Children's Lawyer and Public Guardian and Trustee (Figure 6-10), 290, 310-311
      Person other than (Figure 6-9), 290, 309
    request for increased costs
      estate trustee (Figure 6-11), 290, 312-313

INDEX 389

PASSING OF ACCOUNTS – *continued*
documents to be filed with court – *continued*
uncontested passing – *continued*
request for costs – *continued*
person other than (Figure 6-12), 290, 314-315
sample accounts (Figure 6-15), 324-340
solicitor's costs, 295-296
executor's compensation, 292-293
special fee, 294
form of accounts, 291-292
capital disbursement, 291, 294-295
revenue disbursement, 294-295
generally, 288
order to pass accounts (Figures 5-8, 6-1), 218
powers of investment, 293-294
Public Guardian and Trustee, 289, 289, 290, 290-291, 292
solicitor's costs, 295-296
special fee, 294
Tariff C, 295-296
unprobated wills, 296

PERSONAL REPRESENTATIVE, ROLE OF
differing from role of solicitor, 39-42
generally, 17-20
requirements, 18
responsibilities
locating assets, 43, 169-180 *See also* ADMINISTERING ESTATE
letter to bank, general (Figure 2-2), 52
letter to Bank of Canada (Figure 2-3), 53
letter to bank where deceased held assets (Figure 2-4), 54
locating liabilities, 43-44
location of will, 42-43
letter to solicitor and authorization to deliver (Figure 2-1), 51
notarial certificate (Figure 2-6), 56

PREFERRED BENEFICIARY ELECTIONS, 374

PREPARATION OF ACCOUNTS *See also* PASSING OF ACCOUNTS
specific problems, 294-295
capital, general, 294-295
ex-dividends, 294
interest 295
mortgage payments, 294-295

PROBATE FEES *See* ESTATE ADMINISTRATION TAX ACT

REAL ESTATE, 44-45, 172-174, 380
Land Titles system, 45, 173
Registry system, 44-45, 172-173

REGISTERED RETIREMENT INCOME FUND (RRIF) *See* ROLLOVERS *and* TAXATION ON DEATH

REGISTERED RETIREMENT SAVINGS PLAN (RRSP) *See* ADMINISTERING ESTATE, ROLLOVERS *and* TAXATION ON DEATH

RENUNCIATION OF RIGHT TO CERTIFICATE OF APPOINTMENT
application for certificate of appointment as succeeding estate trustee with will (Figure 3-19), 70, 102
application for certificate of appointment of estate trustee with will (Figure 3-19), 64, 66, 102
application for certificate of appointment of estate trustee without will (Figure 3-27), 68, 69, 115

RESEALING OF APPOINTMENT OF ESTATE TRUSTEE *See* APPLICATIONS FOR ESTATE TRUSTEE

ROLLOVERS
children, property left to, 370-371
farm, 370-371
RRSP and RRIF proceeds, 371
Deferred Profit Sharing Plan proceeds
to surviving spouse or common law partner, 354
Registered Retirement Income Fund (RRIF) proceeds
to surviving spouse, common-law partner, or dependent children, 353, 371
Registered Retirement Savings Plan (RRSP) proceeds
to surviving spouse, common-law partner, or dependent children, 177-178, 351-352, 371
spouse, common-law partner, spousal or common-law partner trust; property left to
capital distributions, 348-350, 376
deemed disposition not apply, 368-369
statutory requirements, 368-369
farm property, 370-371
land transfer tax, 377-378
"tainted" spousal or common-law partner trust, 342, 369
21-year deemed disposition rule not applying, 377

SAFETY DEPOSIT BOX, 46-47

SMALL BUSINESS CORPORATION SHARES, QUALIFIED, 349, 374

SOLICITOR, ROLE OF
duties
  assessing testamentary capacity, 10
  gathering information, 14-17
  taking instruction, 17-26
generally, 41-42

SPOUSAL TRUST *See* ROLLOVERS

SUBSTITUTE DECISIONS ACT, 65, 68

SUCCEEDING ESTATE TRUSTEE *See* APPLICATIONS FOR ESTATE TRUSTEE

SUCCESSION DUTIES, 174, 187

SUCCESSION LAW REFORM ACT
alterations to wills and codicils
  after execution, 13
  before execution, 13
  codicils, 13
dependants' relief
  generally, 28-29, 227-228
  procedure, 28-29, 227-228
  who may bring application, 28-29, 227-228
formal requirements for valid will, 6-9
  foreign wills, 8
  formal or attested wills, 6-7
  holograph wills, 7
  international wills, 8, 8
  members of forces or active service, wills by, 8
  multiple wills, 9
former spouse as estate trustee, 218
intestacy
  distribution on, 3-4, 48
  generally, 3-4, 47-50
  posting security, 49-50
  who is entitled to apply as estate trustee, 49, 68-69
lapse of legacy, 21-22
preferential share, 47
revival of will, 14
revocation of will
  destruction, 12
  divorce, effect of, 13
  marriage, 12
  subsequent will, 12
  written declaration, 12
who may make wills
  age requirement, generally, 9
witness, beneficiary as, 7, 218

TAXATION ON DEATH *See also* ROLLOVERS *and* ESTATE TAXATION
calculating income in terminal year
  general principles
    cash versus accrual basis of accounting, 344-345
    residence
      non-resident of Canada, 344
      resident of Canada, 343-344
    sourcing of income, 344
  sources of income in terminal year
    capital property, 294-295, 348-350
      capital gains exemption
        generally, 348-350, 374-375
        principal residence, 349-350
        qualified farm property, 349, 374
        qualified small business corporation shares, 349, 374
      depreciable, 348-349
        recapture, 348-349
      eligible, 350
      ex-dividends, 294
      rollovers
        regarding family farm, 349
        to spouse or spousal trust, 348
      taxable capital gains
        allowable capital losses, 357
        deemed disposition, 348-349
        generally, 348-349
    Deferred Profit Sharing Plan income, 354
      amount payable, 354
      rollover, 354
      when payable, 354
    employee stock options, 356
    life insurance proceeds, 355
    periodic payments, 345
    prior to death, income received, 345
    proprietorship or partnership income, 347, 361
      death not terminating partnership, 347, 361
      death terminates partnership, 347, 361
    Registered Pension Plan income, 353-354
    Registered Retirement Income Fund (RRIF) income
      generally, 353
      "refund of premiums", 353
    Registered Retirement Savings Plan (RRSP)
      income, 351-352, 353, 354
      contributions in terminal year, 352
      matured plan, 352
        "refund of premiums", 352
          rollovers for spouse or common-law partner, and dependent children, 352
      unmatured plan, 351-352
        "refund of premiums", 351-352

INDEX 391

TAXATION ON DEATH – *continued*
calculating income in terminal year – *continued*
    rollovers for spouse or common-law partner, and dependent children, 351-352
  reserves, 355-356
    right to receive transferred to spouse, common-law partner, spousal or common-law partner trust, 355-356
  resource properties and land inventories, 350
  "rights or things", 345-346
    three options regarding tax treatment, 346
    types of, 345-346
  testamentary trust, 347
glossary of terms, 362-366
interpretation bulletins, 359-360
special rules regarding death
  alternative minimum tax, 358
  capital losses, 357
  death benefits, 358
  forgiveness of debt, 358
  shares of private corporation, avoiding double tax on, 359
  tax credits in year of death
    charitable donations, 357
    foreign tax credits, 357
    generally, 356-357
    medical expenses, 356
  tax instalments, 358
tax returns for terminal year, preparation of, 342-343
  elective returns, 343
    income splitting, 343
    "rights or things" return, 294, 343
  terminal return, 342
trust information tax return, 185-186

TAX CLEARANCE CERTIFICATES
generally, 376-377
Goods and Services Tax, 378-380
letter requesting (Figure 4-7), 185, 194

TRUSTS IN ESTATE PLANNING, 17-20

UNDERTAKING (Figure 3-52), 66, 69, 71, 72, 73, 74, 76, 156

UNPROBATED WILLS
court's jurisdiction, 296
generally, 296

U.S. ESTATE TAX *See* ESTATE TAXATION

VALUING ESTATE, 47

WILLS
advantages
  appoint guardians, ability to, 5
  avoid rules of intestacy, 3-4
  choose beneficiaries, ability to, 4-5
  choose executors, ability to, 4
  effective immediately, 4
  Family Law Act protection, 6
  minor beneficiaries, property provision for, 5-6,
  tax and probate planning, 6
alterations to wills and codicils, 13
  affidavit of condition of will or codicil (Figure 3-18), 64, 66, 101
  after execution, 13
  before execution, 13
  codicils, 13
defined, 2-3
deposit with court, 43, 62-63
drafting
  example (Figure 1-1), 31-38
  gathering information, 14-17
    personal information
      assets and liabilities, 16
      location of assets, 17
      plans and policies, 17
      type of ownership, 16
      children, 15
      citizenship, 14-15
      generally, 14-17
      marital status, 15
  limitations on freedom to dispose of property
    contractual obligations, 29
      marriage contract, 27-28, 29
    dependants' relief, 28-29
    Family Law Act entitlement, 4, 27-28
    jointly-owned property with right of survivorship, 27
    other restrictions, 30
  taking instructions, 17-26
    executors and trustees, generally, 17-20
      alternative, 19
      compensation, 20
      death of, 19
      delegation of powers, 19-20
      minor as, 18
      multiple, 18
      powers, scope of, 19
      removal, 19
      special, 18
    effect of Trustee Act, 19-20
    funeral arrangements, 20
    gifts
      charity, 23
      individuals, 23
    insurance policies, 20

WILLS – *continued*
drafting – *continued*
  taking instructions – *continued*
    gifts – *continued*
      legacies, 20-23
        abatement, 21
        ademption, 21
        demonstrative, 20, 21
        general, 20, 21
        lapse, 21-22
        anti-lapse provision, 22
        memoranda, 22
        legal memoranda, 22
        precatory memoranda, 22
        specific, 20, 21
      organ donation, 20
      residue
        common accident, 26
        outright, or in trust, 23-25
        per capita distribution, 24
        per stirpes distribution, 24
        spouse or "spousal trust", dispositions to, 25
        survivorship clause, 25-26
      RRSPs, 20
  execution of
    generally, 64-66
    proof
      affidavit as to evidence of signature (Figure 3-51), 66, 155
  affidavit attesting to handwriting and signature of holograph will or codicil (Figure 3-17), 64, 66, 100
    affidavit of execution of will or codicil (Figure 3-16), 64, 66, 99
  formal requirements for executing valid will
    foreign wills, 8
    formal or attested wills, 6-7
    holograph wills, 7
    international wills, 8, 8
    members of forces or active service, wills by, 8
    multiple wills, 9
  generally, 2-3
  invalidating will, grounds for
    fraud or forgery, 11-12
    improper execution, 11
    lack of testamentary capacity, 10-11
    suspicious circumstances, 11
    undue influence, 11, 218
  locating will, 40, 42-43
  revival of will, 14
  revocation of will
    destruction, 12
    divorce, effect of, 13
    marriage, 12
    subsequent will, 12

WILLS – *continued*
revocation of will – *continued*
  written declaration, 12
sample will (Figure 1-1), 31-38
who may make wills
  age requirement, generally, 9
  testamentary capacity, 10
witness, beneficiary as, 7, 218